WORSHIP AND ETHICS

Worship and Ethics

A Study in Rabbinic Judaism

Max Kadushin

BLOCH PUBLISHING COMPANY
NEW YORK

Copyright © 1963 by Max Kadushin
Library of Congress Catalog Card Number: 63-10586
SNB 0-8197-0011-8
Printed in the United States of America

To

P.K. and C.G.K.

Preface

In rabbinic Judaism worship and ethics are cultural phenomena. Each individual has his own personal experiences in both spheres, but what make the experiences possible are the values of society. Theories depicting the individual as the creative rebel who overcomes the bonds of routine and inertia with which the tribe would enslave him certainly do not apply to rabbinic Judaism, and in essence probably to no religion. Such theories willy-nilly must use terms like worship, repentance, or love, terms and ideas provided by the tribe, by society.

Worship and ethics are closely associated in rabbinic Judaism. The creative agency which developed both spheres is Halakah, the rabbinic law, and their close association is likewise largely due to Halakah. The aim of this book is to describe how Halakah, working with the value concepts of the folk as a whole, enables the individual to achieve religious experience.

What are rabbinic value concepts? They are rabbinic terms such as Torah, miẓwah (a religious commandment), charity, holiness, repentance, man. Such terms are noun forms, but they have a different character than other types of terms or concepts. These terms are connotative only, and hence are not amenable to formal definition. Again, they refer to matters which are not objects, qualities, or relations in sensory experience. Their function is to endow situations or events with significance. These value concepts are related to each other not logically but organismically. This means that the value concepts are not deduced from one another and that they cannot be placed in a logical order. Instead, the coherence or relatedness of the value concepts is such that they interweave dynamically. This entire theory will be further discussed and illustrated here when the ethical concepts are taken up.

I wish to acknowledge my profound indebtedness to the late

Professor Louis Ginzberg and יבלח"א to Professor Saul Lieberman. For the elucidation of many of the rabbinic texts bearing on this study, I have used Dr. Ginzberg's *A Commentary on the Palestinian Talmud*,[1] and Dr. Lieberman's edition of the Tosefta, his commentary there,[2] and his *Tosefta Ki-Fshuṭah, A Comprehensive Commentary on the Tosefta.*[3] These works are invaluable and they represent what is undoubtedly the greatest modern contribution to the critical study of rabbinic sources.

Contents

WORSHIP AND ETHICS

CHAPTER I

Introduction

A. Rabbinic Worship and Halakah

Rabbinic worship is personal experience and yet it is governed by Halakah, law. Were Halakah merely a set of rules, procedures intended to win divine favor, rabbinic worship would be at most an external art, not a personal experience. But the personal experience of an individual is never raw experience. On the one hand, it is unique and always something newly achieved; on the other hand, to be intelligible at all, what has been achieved must have a form of some kind, a form supplied to the individual by the society of which he is a member. Forms of that kind, which are flexible enough to allow full scope to the individual's temperament and originality and yet which are shared by all other individuals of his society, are value concepts. Even the simplest experience of worship is impossible unless it is literally informed by a value concept. The halakic rules make the experience of worship possible by calling into play the various value concepts which can be associated with worship.

The rabbinic designation for the sacrificial worship in the Temple is 'abodah—literally "work," "service." The same word is also used by the rabbis as a common designation for berakot (benedictions), the 'Amidah or the Eighteen Berakot said daily in the morning, afternoon and evening, the Ḳeri'at Shema' (the recitation of the Shema'), and *talmud Torah* (study of Torah). Since all these are things to be said by the individual wherever he may be, to designate them as 'abodah is to say that they are acts of nonsacrificial worship. All these acts have a certain character in common. Every one of them represents an experience wherein there is felt to be a manifestation of God in one manner or another. Furthermore, in all of them that manifestation of God is conveyed by a value concept.

Halakah calls into play the various value concepts which can be associated with worship and does so in a number of ways. For one thing, it designates the occasions for worship, many of which would otherwise have been stimuli to worship only for especially sensitive individuals. Among those occasions, for example, is the morsel of bread we are about to eat or the water we are about to drink—commonplace, ordinary things which Halakah points to as manifestations of God's love, *middat raḥamim*, and hence to be acknowledged as such in a berakah. Again, in a more complex experience, the experience of holiness, Halakah brings into play not only the concept of *middat raḥamim* but also those of *ḳedushah* (holiness) and miẓwot (commandments). Once more, it is Halakah which enables Ḳeri'at Shema' to evoke the concepts of *malkut Shamayim* (kingship of God) and *talmud Torah* (study of Torah). Several of these concepts convey what are felt to be manifestations of God. At the same time, however, other concepts are also given expression in the experience of worship. How can that be?

A value concept is represented by a conceptual term. But the conceptual term in itself is merely connotative, suggestive. Value concepts take on content only when they are combined in a statement or a situation. We may illustrate this point with the example of the concept of *malkut Shamayim*. "As it combines with other concepts, *Malkut Shamayim*, we learned, signifies that God's dominion is everywhere, that God will ultimately be recognized as King by the whole world, that it negates basically the dominion of the Nations of the World over Israel, that it is acknowledged after experiencing God's love or mercy, that it immediately implies the observance of the *Miẓwot*. Had we found it necessary to cite more passages, we should have drawn forth more ideas implicit in the concept of *Malkut Shamayim*."[1] The content of any particular rabbinic value concept is, therefore, a function of the entire complex of concepts as a whole. If every rabbinic concept depends for its meaning upon all the rest, then all the concepts together constitute an organismic whole.

A prime characteristic of the organismic complex is the potential simultaneity of the value concepts. "It is as if the whole complex were constantly at trigger-point, ready to pour forth *all* its concepts on any occasion or situation. In saying this we are saying no more than that the complex is organic, of one piece. Each situation has focused upon it the whole organic complex, and the concepts that are concretized in that situation represent the maximum possible concretization of the whole organic complex."[2] What always limits the actualization of the whole complex are the particular conditions imposed by a specific situation, and here Halakah displays another role. It ensures that within the limits imposed by the specific situation the maximum number of value concepts will be actualized—in other words, that the value complex will, so to speak, exploit to the full all the possibilities of a situation. For example, when ten men are present, a *ẓibbur*, the delegate of the *ẓibbur* says certain berakot, known as Birkot 'Abelim, in a house of mourners. One of the berakot addresses itself to the mourners with moving words of comfort, words more moving certainly than those generally at the command of men on these occasions, although it is also incumbent upon individuals, during the days of mourning, to comfort the mourners as best they can. Halakah has taken such cognizance of this situation that a berakah, an act of worship, is also an act of *gemilut ḥasadim* (lovingkindness). An ethical concept has been given expression in an experience of worship.

The organismic coherence of the value concepts makes ethical concepts *possible* elements of an experience of worship. What makes them *actual* elements of the experience of worship is Halakah.

B. Ethical Concomitants and Motifs in Worship

There is no rabbinic definition of worship. To identify the various forms of nonsacrificial worship, it is necessary simply to ascertain those things to which the rabbis applied the concept of 'abodah. True, all the forms of rabbinic worship have a common character, all of them being experiences wherein there is felt to be a manifestation of God, but 'abodah can also refer to pagan worship, worship that for the rabbis does not have this character.

Similarly, to designate what today we call the ethical sphere, the rabbis employ the concept of *derek ereẓ* (literally, "the way of the world") without defining that term. Possessing a number of aspects or phases, *derek ereẓ* is broad enough to include an extremely wide range of human acts and attitudes, but these very phases prevent *derek ereẓ* from being an amorphous concept. In fact, one of the phases consists of concepts which further differentiate among human acts or attitudes, concepts which the rabbis recognized as being common to mankind in general—*raḥamim* (love or compassion), *din* (justice), *ẓedaḳah* (charity), *gemilut ḥasadim* (acts of lovingkindness), *shalom* (peace), *'emet* (truth) and the like. These are among the concepts in which great emphatic trends of the value complex rise to expression—the emphasis on love, the emphasis on the individual, and the emphasis on universality.

Rabbinic worship has ethical concomitants and is filled with ethical motifs. An instance of an ethical concomitant in worship is the berakah mentioned above, in which the mourners are addressed with words of comfort, a berakah characterized as *gemilut ḥasadim.* Another berakah which is *gemilut ḥasadim*, one in a parallel series of berakot, the Birkot Ḥatanim, is recited at a wedding. In that berakah the delegate of the assembled *ẓibbur* recites a prayer for the bride and groom, beginning with, "O make these beloved companions greatly rejoice." Here are acts of worship where the whole act is also characterized as *gemilut ḥasadim*, an act engaged in for the benefit of others. In these instances the ethical concomitant is really more than a concomitant. What is said is both an act of worship and an ethical act.

In the Birkat ha-Miẓwot the ethical concomitant is an element in the act of worship. This berakah, which is said before fulfilling a miẓwah and which points to the significance of such an act, embodies a number of concepts, one of them being *ḳedushah.* The concept of *ḳedushah* connotes the imitation of God in acts of *ẓedaḳah* (charity) and *gemilut ḥasadim* and the abstention from cardinal sins; hence, when the individual says the berakah and fulfills the miẓwah he also dedicates himself to this ethical imitation of God. The ethical concomitant now is only an element in an entire experience, for the experience of *ḳedushah* is also informed with the concepts of miẓwot, *middat raḥamim* and berakah; nevertheless, since the ethical concomitant is a constituent element of a unitary experience, it makes the entire experience one that is character building, a source of moral energy. An experience in which a person dedicates himself to the imitation of God in deeds of *ẓedaḳah* and *gemilut ḥasadim* and to refraining from cardinal sins is an experience charged with ethical motive power.

Rabbinic worship endows the individual with a larger self. When the individual is bidden today to identify himself with humanity, there is an implicit assumption that ordinarily he does not feel himself to be so identified. In rabbinic worship, it is not a matter of the individual being *identified* with humanity but of his being *associated* with humanity. Self-identity is never lost—it is a primary factor of the rabbinic experience of worship—but the individual feels himself to be associated with unspecified others. This happens when one of the concepts embodied in a berakah, especially in the closing formula, is the concept of man, a value concept which has a connotation of both universality and love. The term itself is mentioned in the Fourth Berakah of the daily 'Amidah, a berakah acknowledging God's love in granting man knowledge and discernment. The concept of man is embodied, however, in a number of acts of worship—for example, in other berakot of the 'Amidah, in the First Berakah of the grace after meals, in the berakot on the various kinds of food, in the berakah on the light of the day. When saying these berakot, the individual feels himself to be a representative of man. More technically and more accurately, by being expressed through the concept of man the individual's self-awareness is now conceptualized, with the result that the individual retains awareness of his self-identity while feeling himself to be associated with unspecified others. Similarly, in other acts of worship, the individual's self-awareness is conceptualized through the concept of Israel. It is in acts of worship, then, that the ethical implications of man and of Israel are apprehended in living, experiential contexts. Indeed, what is here an ethical concomitant of worship is probably seldom a matter of actual experience outside of worship, even when an individual does wish to identify himself with humanity.

It is hardly necessary to point out that the emphatic trends mentioned earlier are expressed in the ethical concomitants of worship. But an emphatic trend, the emphasis on love, is also present as an ethical motif in most berakot, namely, when the emphasis on love is given expression in the concept of *middat raḥamim*, God's love. *Middat raḥamim* is obviously not a concept of *derek ereẓ*, human morality, but it is most certainly an ethical concept. Primarily a concept which conveys a felt manifestation of God, its embodiment in berakot also has an effect on the ethical life of man, since it is an ethical concept and one which strengthens the emphatic trend on love.

Our purpose has been to call attention to specific ethical concomitants and motifs in worship. We have therefore not included here the commitment in Ḳeri'at Shema', which is a commitment to the miẓwot in general. A knowledge of Torah is a knowledge as well of the ethical life in all its details, and the study of Torah, accordingly, has its specific ethical concomitants.[3]

The great fault with modern representations of rabbinic ethics is the assumption that the true approach to ethics is the philosopher's approach. Rabbinic ethics has been forced into the framework of Kantian ethics, even by some who find fault with others on that score. In line with the philosophers' view that ethics must exhibit an ultimate criterion, it is customary to represent this or that rabbinic statement as consisting of an ultimate ethical criterion. It is no wonder, therefore, that the crucial role of the ethical concepts has been all but overlooked. Thus, to give an extreme example, works dealing with rabbinic ethics fail to consider the concept of *derek ereẓ* at all. Eminent scholars even go so far as to claim there is no such thing as rabbinic ethics. The rabbis, they say, do not discriminate between ethical acts and other miẓwot; and one writer declares—mark the philosophic approach!—that the rabbis "had no notion of a rationalistic ethics, still less of an intuitive ethics."

In view of all this, there is need for a more authentic representation of rabbinic ethics. Our first task, it seems to us, ought to be an endeavor to meet that need. We regard ethics not as a system thought out by a philosopher but as a pattern of concepts developed by society.

C. Interrelation of Halakah and Haggadah

"Haggadah and Halakah are so closely related because both are concretizations of the value-concepts—Haggadah in speech, Halakah in law and action."[4] This close relationship does not, of course, obliterate the fact that Haggadah and Halakah do constitute two different categories.* Each haggadic interpretation is a unit in itself, a complete entity. Only through certain forms of composition, art-forms, are these essentially independent statements brought together and made into larger wholes.[5] In contrast, a halakah is not an independent entity. There is an implicit nexus between the halakot, a nexus which becomes more and more explicit as the result of logical procedures—classification and discursive reasoning; classification in the Mishnah and discursive reasoning in the Talmud.[6] A haggadic idea is grasped not step by step but as a unitary whole; it is an expression of organismic thought. On the other hand, a halakah, although embodying a value concept, to a certain extent requires the step-by-step procedures of logical thought for its formulation.

Because Halakah and Haggadah embody the same value complex, the two categories are not mutually exclusive but interrelated. Halakah is reflected in the Haggadah, numerous haggadot taking for granted specific halakot. According to the Haggadah, to cite a single illustration, Joseph not only acted according to the fifth, sixth, seventh, and eighth commandments but also observed certain regulations regarding the slaughtering of animals.[7] Occasionally, too, a halakah involves a haggadah. For example, the Mishnah[8] requires that a warning must be given to witnesses in capital cases, and that warning includes an interpretation of Genesis 4: 10 which is also found elsewhere as an independent haggadic statement.[9] Ginzberg has called attention to this interrelation of Haggadah and Halakah. He pointed out that the halakic difference between two versions of an opinion held by R. Joḥanan b. Zakkai is indicated by the respective haggadot employed in those versions.[10]

Halakah governs rabbinic worship. It determines not only the occasions and the forms of the various acts of worship but the content of the acts as well. Like other halakot, acts of worship, too, are taken for granted in the Haggadah, as in the well-known haggadah which associates the 'Amidah† with the patriarchs. But rabbinic worship has an especial affinity with the Haggadah. An idea in a berakah may also be a teaching in a haggadah—for example, the

* Haggadah consists of religious and ethical teaching and is nonjuristic in character.

† A unit of nineteen benedictions (originally eighteen), recited in the morning, afternoon, and evening, and said standing.

idea in the First Berakah of the grace after meals that God feeds the whole world, or the idea in the Birkat ha-Miẓwot that Israel is sanctified through the miẓwot. A haggadah may even reflect an experience of worship. One instance is the haggadah alluding to Ḳeri'at Shema' as being a call and a response, a call to which Israel responds by "testifying" for God; another is the haggadic teaching that to be holy Israel must imitate God in acts of *ẓedaḳah* and *gemilut ḥasadim*, a teaching that reflects the experience of *ḳedushah* initiated by the Birkat ha-Miẓwot. Besides, the concepts which in rabbinic worship convey or interpret manifestations of God—such as God's love and *malkut Shamayim*—were made all the more vivid by being frequently embodied in the Haggadah, and hence were all the more warmly apprehended in acts of worship.

Haggadah made vivid the value concepts as a whole, nurtured and cultivated them; Halakah put those concepts into practice, concretized them in daily living. Haggadah and Halakah are interrelated, but that interrelation is especially marked in two spheres. One is the sphere of rabbinic worship; the other is a sphere associated with rabbinic worship, that of rabbinic ethics.[11]

D. Organismic Thought in Halakah

Haggadah is organismic thought par excellence. Each haggadic statement is an independent entity, so that Haggadah has to employ forms of literary composition in order to make larger entities out of what are essentially discrete statements. Moreover, each haggadic statement is not only an independent entity; it is an organismic entity as well. A haggadah usually embodies not one but several value concepts in combination, concepts interlacing in a single idea.[12] The haggadah on the imitation of God, for example, embodies in a single idea the concepts of God's love, *ḳedushah*, *ẓedaḳah*, *gemilut ḥasadim*, and Israel. No less characteristic of organismic thought is the point of departure for a haggadic idea. Such an idea, being a discrete entity and not a link in a logical chain of ideas, needs a stimulus, a point of departure, and that stimulus is usually a biblical text. Even this characteristic of Haggadah is completely consonant with organismic thought. A biblical text is a nondetermining stimulus, for it can set off any number of haggadic interpretations.[13]

The nexus in Halakah means that the halakot are not independent entities. The implicit nature of that nexus, however, is never completely overcome. Logical procedures, although making the nexus more and more explicit, do not succeed in achieving for Halakah a completely rigid, logical structure. The fact is that Halakah, despite the nexus, also possesses some of the characteristics of organismic thought. Thus, just as in the case of a haggadic idea, an act governed by Halakah, too, concretizes a number of value concepts in combination, a characteristic of Halakah particularly evident in acts of worship. Even the simplest form of an act of worship, for example, a form typified by the berakah on bread, embodies at least two concepts; the concept of God's love and that of berakah. But an act governed by Halakah does not, by reason of embodying a number of concepts, convey its meaning in stages; rather, by very reason of the value concepts embodied, the act is an organismic whole, a unitary entity, again just as in the case of a haggadic idea. This is perhaps most apparent in such instances as those of the Birkot Ḥatanim and Birkot 'Abelim. Here an act as a whole is interpreted by two concepts at once, that of berakah and that of *gemilut ḥasadim*; the meaning of the act is conveyed not by these concepts severally but by both together.

A feature of organismic thought is the role played by emphasis. Emphasis is not achieved in any one manner. It may consist of stressing one concept over against another, both in Haggadah and in Halakah. In one haggadic statement, for example, the plea is made that Israel survive lest Torah disappear; in another statement, as an answer to a direct question, Israel is given precedence over Torah.[14] An emphatic trend, however, represents not this type of emphasis but one that is due to repetition, the emphasis now being the result of a repeated effect produced by a number of different value concepts. In any particular haggadah or halakah several types of emphasis may be present simultaneously and so re-enforce each other.

The stressing of one concept rather than another is still another type of emphasis. Ḳeri'at Shema' is an act of worship whereby a person accepts upon himself the kingship of God, but the Ḳeri'at Shema' is also study of Torah. This dual character of the Ḳeri'at Shema' allows the time for reciting the Shema' to be associated with *talmud Torah* in one halakic statement, and in another with the acceptance of *malkut Shamayim*. In the one statement the stress is on the concept of *talmud Torah*, whereas in the other it is on the concept of *malkut Shamayim*. An instance in which one concept is stressed over against another has to do with the 'Amidah, an act of worship which is characterized both as 'abodah and as tefillah, prayer. Here, on a certain issue, R. Joḥanan stressed the concept of tefillah as against that of 'abodah.

Emphasis is a valuational mode which does not rule out what is not emphasized. This is especially true in Halakah. The emphasis on love does not mean that there are not other occasions when the several concepts of justice are concretized. Even when one concept is stressed over against another, the concept not stressed remains relevant: R. Joḥanan's rule (see p. 128, below) stresses the concept of tefillah as against that of 'abodah, yet this does not affect the idea that, even in this case, the 'Amidah is a reminder of the daily communal sacrifice in the Temple, i.e., of 'abodah. Of all the types of emphasis, however, the stressing of one concept rather than another is least exclusive of the concept not stressed: Ḳeri'at Shema' is both the acceptance of *malkut Shamayim* and study of Torah no matter whether, in regard to the time for the recital, one concept is stressed rather than the other.

It is this type of emphasis which allows the rabbis to regard ethical acts as miẓwot and yet to discriminate them from other miẓwot, to be sensitive in the fullest degree to the particular ethical quality informing such an act. We must first of all recognize that an ethical act is interpreted or grasped by two concepts at once, by the concept of miẓwot and by an ethical concept. A striking example is an act of *ẓedaḳah* (charity), an act which is often referred to by the term miẓwah. Now all acts which are miẓwot are to be preceded, according to a rule in the Tosefta and the Yerushalmi,* by the Birkat ha-Miẓwot; nevertheless, this rule is not applied when it comes to ethical acts. Omitting the Birkat ha-Miẓwot does not, of course, change their character and make them acts which are not miẓwot, but it does result in stressing the ethical concept embodied

* The Tosefta is a collection of laws parallel to the Mishnah. The Jerusalem Talmud was developed in Palestine and compiled about 400 C.E., in contradistinction to the Babylonian Talmud, which was developed in Babylon and compiled about 500 C.E. These will be referred to throughout as "Yerushalmi" and "Babli," respectively.

in each particular act rather than the concept of miẓwot. Attention is focused on the special circumstances of the particular act, on the human relationships involved in the act, in a word, on the particular ethical implication of the act. We are saying no more than that they who possess the concepts of *ẓedaḳah* and *gemilut ḥasadim*, concepts which are drives, are obviously motivated by these concepts to perform acts of *ẓedaḳah* and *gemilut ḥasadim*, and that, since these are ethical concepts, they are fully aware of the ethical character of such particular acts.

Discrimination of ethical acts from other miẓwot comes to the fore when there is a conflict of miẓwot. For example, the rule is that a high priest must avoid all contact with a corpse since that would make him "unclean"; yet, because of *kebod ha-beriyyot*, the honor of mankind, he is required to attend to the burial of a *met miẓwah*, the corpse of one whose relatives are not known. There is an emphasis here on an ethical concept by making the act embodying it an overriding miẓwah. An ethical concept has been stressed, but not against the concept of miẓwot.

One characteristic of organismic thought in Halakah is only partly similar to organismic thought in Haggadah. The point of departure for a haggadic idea, as we have said, is a nondetermining stimulus. An act governed by Halakah, too, must have a point of departure: the stimulus for the berakah on bread is the bread about to be eaten, and the stimulus for an act of *ẓedaḳah* is the physical need of another person. But an act governed by Halakah, although an organismic entity, is not an idependent entity, and this is reflected in the stimulus. An independent entity is something which is not predictable, and its stimulus accords with this feature. On the other hand, an organismic act governed by Halakah *is* predictable, else there is no Halakah. Its stimulus, therefore, can only be a determining stimulus.[15]

E. Normal Mysticism and the Common Man

There is an experience of God in an act of rabbinic worship. To the individual who says a berakah, God seems so near that he addresses God with the pronoun "Thou," just as he would address a person facing him. "Thou" is the only word which can express the sense of God's nearness, yet the feeling of God's nearness is obviously different from anything the individual may feel when he addresses a fellow human being with the same pronoun. When God is addressed with the word "Thou," the content of the experience remains unrevealed. The fact is that, so far as nonsacrificial worship is concerned, there is no rabbinic concept which connotes the content of the experience of God's nearness, no way of communicating that experience even by suggestion. It is a wholly private experience and hence a form of mysticism. At the same time, the pronoun "Thou" gives some indication of the kind of mysticism this is. The word does enable the individual to address God, so that this entirely private experience, while not communicable, is not altogether inexpressible. Certainly at one point, therefore, this kind of mysticism is not completely outside the realm of normal experience.

In prayer, too, there is the experience of God's nearness, for in a prayer, as in a berakah, God is likewise addressed with the pronoun "Thou." A prayer, however, though thus related to worship, is not in itself worship; it differs from worship because it is solely a petition, a *baḳḳashah*, not a berakah. A prayer usually consists of a petition for a specific manifestation of God's love not yet experienced but only hoped for. A berakah is usually an acknowledgment of such a manifestation, of something which has just taken place or else which is felt as still taking place. In a prayer we have the only valuational experience wherein not all the concepts involved are concretized. The concept of *baḳḳashah* is concretized, and that enables the individual to experience God's nearness, but the hoped-for manifestation of God's love has not yet been experienced; a prayer, a *baḳḳashah*, is thus an experience, but an incomplete experience. On the other hand, a berakah is an element in a complete, unitary experience. The other element in this unitary experience is the stimulus for the berakah, and that stimulus most often consists in an event or a situation which is interpreted as a manifestation of God's love, *middat raḥamim*. For example, the stimulus for the berakah on bread, as we pointed out at the end of the previous section, is the bread about to be eaten.

Related to the experience of God are not only the concepts of berakah and *baḳḳashah* (or tefillah) but also a large number of other concepts in the value complex: *middat raḥamim*, *middat ha-din* (God's justice), *malkut Shamayim*, Torah, miẓwot, *ḳedushah*, *ḳiddush ha-Shem* (sanctification of the Name), *teshubah* (repentance), *biṭṭaḥon* (trust in God), *'emunah* (trust especially in God's promise). These concepts have to do, each in its own way, with the experience of God and this means that the experience of God is to a degree communicable. Furthermore, these concepts are elements of the organismic complex, enmeshed with all the other concepts in the complex; notice, for example, that ethical acts are also miẓwot. A number of concepts which have a factor in common represent an emphatic trend, and the experience or awareness of God is therefore an emphatic trend of the organismic complex. In other words, the experience of God is an aspect of the normal valuational life, just as the other emphatic trends are aspects of the normal valuational life. The concepts relating to the experience of God are accordingly neither philosophical ideas nor philosophically inspired—nor have they any philosophical implications unless we force them into a framework that adds nothing, pragmatically, to the experience of God itself. When we spoke of the ethical concepts we were obliged similarly to indicate they are not ideas in a philosophical system.

Partly communicable and partly noncommunicable, this dual character of the experience of God is especially evident, once again, in acts of worship. A berakah interprets an event or situation as a manifestation of *middat raḥamim*, yet while saying the berakah the individual has a consciousness of God's nearness which is not communicable. When reciting the Ḳeri'at Shema', the individual accepts "the yoke of *malkut Shamayim*" through a meditative act whereby he makes God "King above and below and in the four directions of the world." To the degree to which this experience is communicable it is expressed in the term *malkut Shamayim* and in the figure of "above and below and in the four directions," but the experience as a whole wherein God is made king is private, noncommunicable. That experience requires *kawwanah* on the part of the individual, a state of mind completely personal. It is devotion of the heart and concentration on the ideas involved in the Shema'. The rabbinic experience of God presents a paradox, the kind of paradox which, as has often been said, is a feature of the spiritual life. Rabbinic experience of God is personal, mystical experience which is nevertheless mediated by concepts that are elements of the normal valuational life. We have, therefore, called the rabbinic experience of God normal mysticism.

Normal mysticism is not infrequently accompanied by changes, for the time being, in the psychological constitution of the individual. We have observed how in some acts of worship the individual achieves a larger self. More striking is the change that occurs, during the recitation of several berakot, in the individual's consciousness of time, the past and the future coalescing with the present. Certain events ordinarily conceived as having taken place in the past or as bound to take place in the future become events that are felt to be experienced in the present.

An act of rabbinic worship is filled with an experience of God. The occasion, the form, even the verbal expression of an act of worship, are governed by Halakah and therefore represent the product of the rabbis. On the other hand, the concepts informing the experience and the normal mysticism which the concepts mediate are not the product of the rabbis but are inherent in the culture of the folk. The concepts relating to the experience of God are an aspect of the normal valuational life, that is to say, of the valuational life of the people as a whole. These value concepts are folk concepts. They offer irrefutable evidence that normal mysticism was the experience of the common man, not only of the rabbis.

The capacity for normal mystical experience on the part of the common man was a basic characteristic of rabbinic Judaism. It made possible, in the sphere of worship, a remarkable interaction between the rabbis, who were the spiritual and intellectual leaders, and the folk. True, without the forms developed by the rabbis the life of worship would no doubt have been very limited. The rabbis tell of a brief berakah on bread recited by Benjamin, the shepherd; and other berakot equally simple must have been evoked spontaneously by the folk. But it is unlikely that the meditative acts of worship would have arisen, and still less likely that acts of worship would have had ethical concomitants without the Halakah on these matters developed by the rabbis. At the same time, these more subtle acts of worship would not have been possible had the folk at large lacked the capacity for normal mysticism.*

* In a later chapter we shall find that the same interaction between the rabbis and the folk also took place in the sphere so closely associated with that of worship, the ethical sphere.

Men differed, of course, in their capacity for normal mysticism. Some of the rabbis themselves, on their own admission, could not achieve *kawwanah* at certain times. This was doubtless true of many common men as well. Nevertheless, the fact remains, as evidenced in the numerous value concepts relating to the experience of God, that normal mysticism was a steady factor in the valuational life of the people as a whole.

CHAPTER II

Rabbinic Ethics

A. The Problem of Morality

Philosophers have oversimplified and, paradoxically, overtheorized the problem of morality and ethics. They oversimplify the problem when they attempt to find a single, universal criterion for morality, whether it be Aristotle's ultimate of well-being, or Kant's categorical imperative, or Bentham's hedonic calculus. Each of such criteria is a test to determine whether an action is truly ethical or moral, and a test only. The individual is left to struggle by himself with what is really the major task, or rather an endless series of tasks. He alone must analyze every situation confronting him—often an urgent, immediate situation—and he alone must find his way to a solution conforming to the ultimate criterion. As a tool to be used in the resolution of human problems, with all their variety and complexity, the ultimate criterion itself is of little help. It has oversimplified those problems.

The fact is, of course, that men do not and cannot make the moral life one long and dreary process of intellectual analysis of situations and problems. Were a man to ponder over every situation, he would have neither time nor will to act at all. There would be only moral stagnation. Moral acts have an emotional, not only a mental aspect, are propelled by inner drives. In directing men to what is primarily an intellectual process, the ultimate criterion oversimplifies the problem of morality and is rendered quite futile as well.

At the same time the universal criterion has overtheorized the problem of morality and ethics. A universal criterion acts as a test in the resolution of moral situations, as we have said. But it also acts as a definition of morality or ethics. Deeds in accord with the criterion are ethical; deeds not in accord are not ethical. Was there no genuinely moral life before any of these definitions was formulated? But if moral life obtained—as obviously it did—men must have been able to distinguish a moral from an immoral act without these definitions to guide them. Apparently, then, the moral life is altogether possible without definitions of morality. In that case, can we not perhaps assume that men act "intuitively" in accord with a definition of morality? Yet if men are not automatons, they must be aware of these intuitions and aware that they are ethical intuitions. Men, in other words, can be aware of the sphere of morality without benefit of definitions of morality. The universal criterion not only oversimplifies morality; it overtheorizes it by attempting to give an abstract definition of morality.

The problem of morality emerges from the foregoing discussion as a threefold one. The first part is concerned with the variety and complexity of the moral life. Since men do not employ an intellectual criterion as a guide, how do they cope with its variety and subtlety? Second, what is the character of the emotional drives that propel men to moral acts? Third, how is it possible for men to have an awareness of morality without having a definition of morality?

A consideration of rabbinic ethics will supply the answers to these and kindred questions. Rabbinic ethics is not the product of philosophic reflection but of a historically evolved tradition. It has to do with the moral life of a people to whom that tradition has given character and continuity over many centuries. It is concerned with day-to-day issues, takes account of social, economic, and political factors, and affects the relations of individual to individual. This is true, of course, of other historically evolved traditions as well; thus we shall be able occasionally to cull from studies of other groups such illustrative material as may suit our purpose.[1]

B. Ethical Value Concepts

The variety of the moral life is spelled out in rabbinic literature in terms of a moral vocabulary. It is a large vocabulary, containing not only terms for matters recognized as ethical or moral, but also for things recognized as immoral. In the one category are such terms as *'emet*[2] (truth), *shalom*[3] (peace), *ẓedaḳah*[4] (charity), *'anawah*[5] (humility); in the other, such terms as *shefikut damim*[6] (murder), *zenut*[7] (unchastity), *gezel*[8] (robbery), *sheḳer*[9] (falsehood). Most of the terms given here are used in the Bible as well as by the rabbis.[10]

When we go on to distinguish between the meanings of related terms in the ethical vocabulary, we get a further impression of complexity, of subtlety. *Ẓedaḳah* (charity) and *gemilut ḥasadim* (deeds of lovingkindness), for example, are terms closely allied in meaning. They can be interchanged,[11] for both have the connotation of love.[12] Nevertheless, the rabbis do discriminate between *gemilut ḥasadim* and *ẓedaḳah* on the basis of actual practice. *Ẓedaḳah* involves an expenditure of money, *gemilut ḥasadim*, of money or personal service; the former has for its object the poor; the latter, both the poor and the rich: the former can have reference only to the living, the latter, both to the living and the dead.[13] Similarly, *'alub* (submissive, lowly, humbled) and *'anaw* (meek, kind, forgiving) are also kindred words and may be used interchangeably,[14] yet each has its own distinctive connotation.[15]

An ethical or moral term refers to a complete act, a complete event, or a situation as a whole. A robbery, for instance, involves a number of things: a definite thing taken, definite circumstances when the event took place, definite individuals. The event may be described in minute detail, so far as all these matters are concerned, and yet, unless the idea of "robbery" is conveyed, the event as a whole will not be communicated. We may say, then, that a moral term unifies a situation or an act. Because a moral term or idea has this unifying function, the moral idea is integral to the event, is an essential element in the situation.

But how does the moral idea act as the integrating agent? Without the moral idea, what do the details lack? What makes each of them merely a disparate element even if we name them all? What is missing is the meaning of the act. When a moral idea unifies an act or situation it gives significance to it. The significance conveyed is to be found in the moral term itself; that is to say, the moral term is a value term. Every moral or immoral act is a value act, the valuation being none other than the moral idea integrating the act and thus conveyed by the act. The moral life is a succession of value acts; it is a life of valuation, full of significance, or rather, in view of the large number of moral terms or ideas, a life full of significances.

The moral life is varied and subtle because the significances of its value ideas are varied and subtle.

We can now see why there is no need for an ultimate criterion as a test for every human act. The ultimate criterion would invest a human act with meaning; it would make us aware of the bearing of an act. But that is exactly what the value ideas do, and without the necessity of continually weighing and pondering, and so hampering all action. Every act charged with a moral idea is filled with significance, and what is more, with a particular significance. If awareness of the implication of our acts is a *desideratum*, we have it here in the awareness of the particular significance of any given act; and we are aware of the particular significance because it is conveyed by a particular term or moral idea.

The value idea gives significance to the act as a whole. It is not something isolated in any detail of the act, but it is something conveyed by the whole act. The same value idea is conveyed, however, by any number of acts or situations. There are, happily, many acts of charity, many instances of lovingkindness, and, unhappily, also many exhibitions of arrogance and many acts of robbery. A moral term like *ẓedaḳah* or *gezel* is a generalization standing for one act or for any number of acts; yet can we say that when we are confronted by an instance of charity or robbery, we stop to analyze and thus draw forth the general idea from the concrete act? Obviously not, for the act would not be an integrated value act, its significance would not register at all without the general idea or the concept to start with. What, then, is the relation of the general idea in all these instances to the concrete act? The general idea, the concept, or as we now can say, the value concept, was there to start with. The act is a concretization of the value concept. If the value concept does not refer to any one specific detail of the act, that does not mean that it has no concrete application. On the contrary, the act as a whole embodies the value concept, so to speak. The act as a whole, carrying its particular significance, possesses that significance because it embodies, concretizes a value concept. Nor would the value concept exist without any concrete applications.

This does not mean that the value concept does not exist apart from its concretizations. What we wish to emphasize is that the value concept functions through its concretizations. There is the value term itself, and the conceptual term is of paramount and absolute importance. The term stands for the concept, and without the term there would be no concept. Here we encounter what is no doubt one of the chief characteristics of the value concept—the paramount importance of the value term, the conceptual term itself. The value concept does not stand for any concrete object or relationship that is conveyed to us through our senses. The word "tree," for example, stands for certain objects in our sensory experience. We could, conceivably, substitute a new word for the term "tree" and have the new word stand for the same objects. Definite, concrete objects have the effect of rendering the conceptual term for them of secondary importance, so long as we do have *a* conceptual term. We demonstrate the validity of all this when we say "car" instead of "automobile," or "fiddle" instead of "violin." Again, an abstract concept that is defined also has a certain definite character: it has a definition; and here, too, the particular term used is a secondary matter, for it is the definition that is of prime importance. We could use any other word in place of "gravity" and still convey the same idea—so long as we continued to imply by it our present definition, or rather equation for gravity. The abstract value concept, however, is in rabbinic literature never given a definition. Even when a distinction is drawn between *gemilut ḥasadim* and *ẓedaḳah*, there is no formal definition of either concept, no general statement or formula defining either concept. The value concept depends for its life, one may say, on the term itself. Here the conceptual term is of primary importance.

A term that is not made explicit, either through sensory experience or through a definition, can be only connotative, suggestive. The abstract value concept is therefore merely connotative or suggestive. Nevertheless, it is a potent concept for it seldom remains abstract. The value concept is embodied most often in an act and we are then conscious of a concretization of the concept; we get an impression of definiteness, of concreteness, fully as strong as that of any sense experience. Indeed, the value concept has unified the details of sense experience into an act or situation.

What is the relation between the abstract value concept and the concrete act? The abstract value concept in itself, we have said, is connotative or suggestive. Upon closer view, we see that the value concept is indeterminate and that it becomes determinate in an act or situation or event. Were a value concept to remain indeterminate for long, it would die, for connotation alone is too indefinite, too fragile in its content to persist. A value concept lives in its concretizations, each concretization being a fresh and unique expression of the concept.

The value concept is kept vital through its concretizations; but what induces the concretization of the concept? The answer is that a value concept has its own drive toward concretization. The value concept is a dynamic concept that is least dynamic when it merely interprets an event or situation, and yet here, too, the indeterminate concept is made determinate in a situation. When we see one man helping another, that situation spells out to us *gemilut ḥasadim*; we interpret the situation and thus concretize the concept merely by having witnessed the event. Now, despite the idea element in it, this interpretation is not an intellectual act. The valuation here is warm and emotional, and this implies a degree of involvement, of participation on the part of the witness to the act.

It is no wonder, therefore, that the value concept can—and so often does—really involve us in action, that it has the force of a genuine emotional drive. To keep to our illustration, we shall cite a halakic concretization of the concept of *gemilut ḥasadim* or of *ẓedaḳah*. A rabbinic ordinance,[16] in consonance, no doubt, with the practice of the rabbis, sets the desirable amount[17] to be given to the poor as a fifth of one's property or profits;[18] on the other hand, it also sets up that amount as the maximum,[19] for otherwise a person might himself become an object of charity.[20] One version of this ordinance stresses its restraining character,[21] and hence there must have been a need for making the restraining feature as forceful as possible. It would almost seem as if the propensity the law sought to curb had the drive of a natural impulse, certainly in a group large enough to warrant legislation, and we would not be altogether wrong if we so regarded the drive possessed by the concept of charity in that society. Indeed, an instance is given in this connection of a Tanna* who had actually divided all his property among the poor,[22] or who had been prevented from doing so.[23]

* An authority quoted in the Mishnah or in the Baraitot, the Baraitot being traditions and opinions related to the Mishnah but not embodied there.

The drive toward concretization is a property only of the positive value concepts. There are negative value concepts, too, concepts that connote a negative valuation, and which thus stigmatize immoral acts. Such concepts have a drive away from concretization. Again our examples are taken from the Halakah, for if it is the practice of the folk we look for, we shall find it reflected in one way or another in the Halakah. *'Azzut panim* (brazenness) is, of course, a negative value concept. According to Rabbah, a debtor will surely not brazen it out before his creditor, and will therefore not deny his indebtedness completely.[24] An important detail of legal procedure, taking an oath, rests on this observation, an observation that is manifestly the fruit of long experience. *'Azzut panim*, then, possessed a negative drive strong enough to affect a man's actions in business affairs, even to his own detriment. The strongest negative drives of the folk were those associated with *shefikut damim* (murder), *gilluy 'arayot* (incest), and *'abodah zarah* (idolatry). A famous halakah declares that, in order to save his life, a man may yield on other matters but never on these three, under any circumstances;[25] and this ordinance, enacted during a most critical period,[26] can only represent a crystallization in law of the profoundest feelings of the people as a whole.*

If the value concepts represent drives, positive or negative, then they constitute a vital aspect of a man's personality. They are not merely motives, for these may be short ranged. They are dynamic elements of personality, focal points in a continuous process of valuation, primary factors in the experience of significance. A rich personality has many and varied experiences of significance, or more technically, a valuational life governed by a large number of value concepts. A moral act, therefore, involves other concepts besides

* The negative concepts, and in fact the value concepts in general, do not all have the same force or drive. Some are weaker than others. Furthermore, opinions on the strength or weakness of a drive may differ widely, doubtless as the result of differences in observation or experience. Thus, in *Giṭṭin* 81b, a mishnah is interpreted as meaning that Bet Hillel regards it as a presumption that a man does not want to make his intercourse with a woman one of prostitution, and that Bet Shammai's presumption is that he does want to. (Of the two early tannaitic schools of interpretation, Bet Shammai tends to be the more rigorous.) Reflected here are divergent judgments on the strength of the negative drive associated with the concept of *zenut* (unchastity, prostitution) (see, however, Maimonides' view in Hilkot *Gerushin* X.19).

those embodied in it. Although a moral act is the direct concretization of a particular value concept, it constitutes, in fact, the projection of a personality informed by many value concepts. Thus it is not a single emotional drive that propels a man to a moral act, but his entire personality. Any particular valuational drive, any value concept, is but a constituent of an individual's personality, and hence the other value concepts also contribute to the concretization of a concept, even if indirectly.

The value concepts are concretized in acts, situations, or events by the individual who is moved to act or who interprets situations and events. But where does the individual take them from? The value concepts are terms in the common vocabulary of groups, and the individual acquires the value terms just as he acquires his general vocabulary, that is, from childhood on. Society supplies the indeterminate value concepts, and the individual makes them determinate in acts or situations. Were society and the individual two separate and distinct entities, it would still be impossible to assign a specific concretization of a value concept either wholly to the one or wholly to the other; but the fact is that society and the individual cannot even be set up one against the other.[27] "The individual is formative of the society, the society is formative of the individual."[28] These considerations ought to make us aware once more of how abstract ethical theories oversimplify the moral life. Since society and the individual both share in any concretization of a value concept, the division between autonomous and heteronomous acts[29] is hardly a valid one. In fact, this division is an oversimplification, a logical dichotomy that ignores socio-psychological facts.

C. The Role of Emphasis

One of the problems of the moral life is its complexity, and this complexity is due to the variety and sheer number of the value concepts. An ultimate criterion would, in theory, simplify the moral life, to be sure, but it would do so by ignoring the role of the value concepts; it would thus oversimplify. How do men in daily life and practice cope with the complexity of the moral life?

The moral life is characterized by great emphatic trends. In rabbinic ethics there can be distinguished an emphasis on love, an emphasis on the individual, and an emphasis on universality. We shall, first, endeavor to establish the presence of these trends; second, we shall try to indicate how the emphatic trends simplify the moral life without thereby eliminating any of the value concepts.

Although an emphatic trend is not something that the rabbis have actually named for us in so many words, it is nonetheless something easily discernible. It is, indeed, more than discernible, for a genuine emphatic trend practically forces itself on our attention. It is a repeated effect produced by a number of distinct but related value concepts. Thus, in the concepts of *ẓedaḳah*, *gemilut ḥasadim*, *'ahabah* (love),[30] and *raḥamim* (compassion),[31] we recognize an emphasis on love, for each of them connotes love in one way or another. Among these concepts, *gemilut ḥasadim* stands primarily for acts of love and personal service to individuals,[32] but there are also other concepts that emphasize the individual, as we shall soon see. Another group of value concepts—man, the world, *bereshit* (that which was made during the first six days of creation)—have in common a connotation of universalism.[33]

In no case is a conceptual term mentioned here merely synonymous with another conceptual term. As we have shown elsewhere, a rabbinic value term always represents a concept having a distinctive character of its own, and differing in some respects from any other rabbinic value concept.[34] What we have, then, is a repeated effect produced by a number of related but different value concepts, all exhibiting a common general quality or trend; in other words, an emphatic trend has risen to expression in those concepts.

Deeper examination of the value concepts reveals further evidence of the presence of these emphatic trends. Rabbinic laws are based in great measure on biblical laws, and haggadic statements are usually interpretations of biblical texts.[35] This is to say that the foundation of both Halakah and Haggadah is the Bible. We might, therefore, expect a conceptual term of the Bible to retain its meaning or connotation when used by the rabbis as well. Instead, rabbinic usage is different from biblical in regard to many biblical terms, and the new meanings are clearly influenced by the rabbinic emphatic trends. A striking illustration is the term *ẓedaḳah*. Words formed from the root *ẓdḳ*, as found in the Bible, have a common ground in the idea of "right," but *ẓedaḳah* in rabbinic usage, as we have observed, refers to acts of charity and has the wider connotation of love. Even when the word occurs in a biblical verse, it is very often interpreted by the rabbis as referring to charity or love.[36]

Further instances of the difference between rabbinic and biblical usage reflect the presence of the other emphatic trends. The word "Israel" in the Bible is a collective noun; in rabbinic literature it also designates the members of the people individually.[37] In the Bible, the word *goy* means "nation," is a collective noun, and is applied both to Israel and to other nations, whereas in rabbinic usage it refers to the individual non-Jew.[38] *'Olam* in the Bible refers to "time"; in rabbinic literature it means "world."[39] The *ger* in the Bible is a resident alien, but the *ger* in rabbinic literature is a convert.[40] When the change in usage makes room for, or designates, the individual, as is the case with Israel and *goy*, there is obviously an emphasis on the individual; and when the change spells a wider, more universalistic idea, as is the case with *'olam* and *ger*, it clearly reflects a trend toward universality. Again, even when these words occur in biblical verses, the rabbis often interpret them in accordance with their new usage.[41]

We must recognize one thing more. The emphatic trends are not mutually exclusive. A concept expressive of love may also emphasize the individual, as we noticed in the example of *gemilut ḥasadim*. *Ger* reflects the trend toward universality, but it also stresses the individual; and that is likewise true of the concept of man. In the moral life the presence of one emphatic trend does not eliminate the others. This is the same as saying, of course, that the *concepts* expressive of the trends are not eliminated.

The emphatic trends simplify the moral life, yet without damage to its richness or variety. Simplification is achieved by stressing a common element in various concepts, not by eliminating those concepts. Nor does one emphatic trend imply the exclusion of the others, but rather the contrary. A concept belonging to the orbit of one emphatic trend may also belong to the orbit of another, and hence be a factor in the coalescence of the trends. The emphatic trends, in fine, are dependent on the value concepts.

Frequently we are made aware of an emphatic trend through an arresting statement or a law. "There are times," says Resh Laḳish, "when the neglect of Torah is its establishing."[42] Rashi rightly takes

Torah here to refer to the study of Torah and the general statement to mean that there are times when one ought to interrupt one's study, namely, in order to take part in a funeral escort or in a wedding procession (acts of *gemilut ḥasadim*).[43] A paradoxical statement, it calls attention to the importance of acts of lovingkindness, and it makes us aware of an emphasis on love. Emphasis on kindness and compassion made also for breadth of compassion. Kindness is not to be confined to human beings: "It is forbidden a man to eat before he has given food to his animal."[44]

We become aware of the emphasis on the individual too, through a striking statement or law. "The individual prays and God hears his prayer," and hence "a man ought not to say, 'I am not worthy to pray for the Temple and for the land of Israel' "[45]—that is, even though he feels himself not qualified to pray for these things, implying as they do the redemption of all Israel.[46] The emphasis on the individual is no less striking in ethical relationships. A group is not permitted to save itself by handing over any individual to be dishonored or killed. If Gentiles threaten to violate an entire group of women unless the women themselves deliver up one from among them to be violated, the law in the Mishnah states: Let them all be violated, "but let them not deliver up a single soul of Israel."[47] Again, if Gentiles threaten to kill an entire group of men unless the men themselves deliver up one from among them to be killed, the law in the Tosefta states: Let them all be killed, "but let them not deliver up a single soul of Israel."[48] The "Gentiles" here are marauders or soldiers, and both passages apparently reflect a period of disorder and strife.

A statement in the Sifra declares that "even a Gentile who studies the Torah [or who practices the Torah][49] is like the high priest," the proof-text being, "Which, if a *man* do, he shall live by them" (Lev. 18:5).[50] To emphasize this teaching, the statement further interprets other biblical verses to the effect that in each case the verse refers not to "priests, Levites and Israelites," but either to mankind, the righteous Gentile, or to the righteous in general. For example, II Samuel 7:19 is rendered to mean, "This is the Torah of mankind," and Isaiah 26:2 as, "Open ye the gates that a righteous Gentile keeping faithfulness may enter in."[51] The same statement is found in the Talmud,[52] however, without the corroborative interpretation of verses that makes it so emphatic, and the discussions there tend to limit or even nullify what is left of it. In other words, the trend toward universalism encountered some resistance, probably because of frequent persecution of the Jews.

We have presented here an instance of how the trend toward universalism is expressed in a statement, and of the resistance encountered by that trend; our illustration reflects both. But the prevalence of universalism as an emphatic trend is not to be determined by ascertaining whether there are more passages on one side or on the other, for the basic elements of the ethical life, propulsive yet subtle, are the value concepts. A genuine emphatic trend is primarily a repeated effect produced by a group of value concepts, and the emphatic trend toward universalism is just such a repeated effect. Indeed, as we have shown elsewhere, the very structure of the value concepts reflects the trend toward universalism: ". . . the very structure of the rabbinic value-concepts necessitates the concept of 'the righteous of the Nations of the World.' "[53] A statement, if it is a striking one, does call attention to an emphatic trend, but the trend is established by a group of value concepts, not by a number of statements.

The trend toward universalism manifests itself, among other ways, in the recognition of non-Jewish legal institutions. As given in the Mishnah, a law declares valid writs or documents signed by Gentile witnesses and confirmed by Gentile officials.[54] One authority extends this law even to bills of divorcement and writs of manumission,[55] despite the religious implications of these documents,[56] and there is a report that this is the opinion, not only of R. 'Aḳiba, but of the *Ḥakamim* (scholars) as well.[57] Such recognition of Gentile institutions, Alon says,[58] was entirely voluntary. There is thus a whole class of cases in which the rabbis voluntarily made Gentile institutions competent under Jewish law. Embodied in this law is the concept of *din*, a concept with universalistic connotations, as we shall see later.[59]

All these statements and laws are expressions of emphatic trends. But they are primarily concretizations of value concepts, and in every instance the value concept involved itself belongs to the orbit of an emphatic trend. An emphatic trend rises to expression in a particular value concept, and when the value concept, charged in that manner, is made concrete in statements or laws, the statements or laws, too, will often reflect the same trend. Conversely, no matter how emphatic a statement may be, it can only be an expression of a particular emphatic trend, and no more. It will be a concretization of a value concept belonging to the orbit of an emphatic trend.

If we have established the presence of emphatic trends, have we not also apparently established the presence of intuitive morality? An emphatic trend, as we have said, is not something that the rabbis have actually indicated for us in so many words. Nevertheless, men do feel in accordance with it and act in accordance with it. Are they not moved, therefore, by a kind of intuition? Let us remember that every act, every statement, informed by an emphatic trend is a concretization of a value concept. At the basis of every action is not an intuition but a concept, a connotative idea, not mere feeling alone. A value concept is not submerged when it is part of an emphatic trend that includes other concepts as well. On the contrary, its effect is heightened. An emphatic trend, in fine, has primarily to do with the functioning of the value concepts concerned, and is not something that displaces them.

D. Devices for Emphasis

Our contention is that rabbinic literature does not contain all-inclusive, general ethical principles, nor was there any attempt to formulate such principles. Some modern scholars, it is true, do claim that a number of rabbinic statements are general ethical rules. Their conclusion is, we believe, the result of a tendency to look for an ultimate criterion and is not warranted by the rabbinic statements themselves. A passage in the Sifra reads as follows: " 'And thou shalt love thy neighbor as thyself' [Lev. 19:18]—R. 'Akiba says: This is a comprehensive rule in the Torah [*kelal gadol ha-Torah*]. Ben 'Azzai says: 'This is the book of the generations of man; (in the day that God created man, in the likeness of God made He him)' [Gen. 5:1]—this is a more comprehensive rule [*kelal gadol mi-zeh*]."[60] *Kelal gadol* is a halakic term, and it does not mean that a principle so designated is the most important or the most inclusive or the most comprehensive; it apparently means, rather, that a rule so designated is *more* inclusive than another rule.[61] Our passage is no exception.

As used by R. ʻAḳiba here, the term means that the rule, "Thou shalt love thy neighbor as thyself," is more inclusive or more comprehensive than some other rules also stated in the Torah, the very rules, perhaps, that are given in the first half of the verse (vs. 18) and in the verse immediately preceding (vs. 17). We can now understand more readily Ben ʻAzzai's dictum—a dictum, be it noticed, in which the comparative, "more comprehensive," is used, and not the superlative. Ben ʻAzzai sees implied in Genesis 5:1 a more comprehensive rule than the one explicitly stated in Leviticus 19:18.[62]

Neither of these rules, then, is an ultimate criterion. Each is an emphatic statement, to be sure, and not only an emphatic but also an arresting statement. We have just studied other striking or arresting statements, however, and found them to be expressions of emphatic trends. We shall find that this is true of R. ʻAḳiba's and Ben ʻAzzai's statements as well. Both statements, we must add, are to be taken as representing rabbinic rather than biblical thought, despite the fact that the rules quoted are biblical verses. When a verse is given a certain character by the rabbis, even if it be only a matter of emphasis, the new character is, in effect, a rabbinic interpretation.

A statement expressive of an emphatic trend has the following characteristics: the statement is a concretization of a value concept; the concept involved belongs to the orbit of an emphatic trend—that is to say, the concept belongs to a group of concepts which have an element in common and hence produce a repeated effect; the statement is striking enough to make us aware of the emphatic trend. All of these characteristics are exemplified by R. ʻAḳiba's statement: "ʻAnd thou shalt love thy neighbor as thyself' [Lev. 19:18]—this is a comprehensive rule in the Torah." That statement is a concretization of the value concept of *'ahabah*, love, and *'ahabah* is a conceptual term not only in the Bible but in rabbinic usage as well.[63] Again, as we saw above, *'ahabah* is one of a number of concepts, each of which has its own particular connotation, but also connotes love; it is thus a concept belonging to the orbit of an emphatic trend. Finally, the words, "this is a comprehensive rule in the Torah," focus attention on our verse as against other verses or rules, and they make us acutely aware of the sentiment the verse contains, the sentiment of love.

Ben 'Azzai wishes to make his statement even more emphatic: " 'This is the book of the generations of man; (in the day that God created man, in the likeness of God made He him)' [Gen. 5:1]—this is a more comprehensive rule." The concept involved here is "man," a biblical term, but as used by the rabbis it is one of a group of concepts that emphasize universalism. We have noticed before, however, that the emphatic trends are not mutually exclusive, so that, for example, a concept reflecting the trend toward universalism may also stress the individual. Indeed, in a version of Ben 'Azzai's statement, it is the individual that is stressed, the following being added: "For thou shalt not say, 'Since I have been despised let my neighbor be despised with me.' R. Tanḥuma said: 'If thou actest so, know Whom thou dost despise—in the likeness of God made He him.' "[64] The concept involved in this additional statement, too, is none other than man—only now the emphasis is on the individual rather than on universalism. Moreover, the verse here is not necessarily associated with the individual: elsewhere the verse, "For in the image of God made He man" (Gen. 9:6) is made to refer, apparently, to mankind.[65]

What do these statements of R. 'Aḳiba and Ben 'Azzai convey? Modern scholars have attempted to draw certain implications from the statements, to formulate principles of ethics and conduct ostensibly inherent in them, to distinguish between a principle inherent in the one statement as against that of the other;[66] in a word, to make these statements explicit and precise. If the scholars differ in their interpretations,[67] however, it is because the rabbinic statements do not lend themselves to such treatment. In fact, Ben 'Azzai's original statement is, strictly speaking, not anything as definite as a rule at all, but a suggestive verse, a verse made more suggestive by Ben 'Azzai's emphasizing it as more important than Leviticus 19:18.

The two rabbinic statements were not put forth either as new or as definitive statements. So far as the elements of the statements are concerned, they represented nothing new to the people of the time. The biblical verses pointed out were familiar to those people. Nor were these biblical verses made the criteria for a new post-biblical ethic informing personal conduct and law. The people already possessed a new pattern of ethical value concepts, concepts rooted in the Bible, dynamic concepts that acted as drives in personal conduct and in the formulation of laws. Among them were the very concepts embodied in the two statements—*'ahabah* (R. 'Aḳiba) and man (Ben 'Azzai). Not even the emphatic trends expressed in the two statements were new to the people. The statements simply express, as we have noticed, already existing emphatic trends.

Just because the elements of the two statements were all familiar to the people, the statements themselves could be meaningful and effective. Being expressions of emphatic trends, they acted primarily as reminders of those emphatic trends and strengthened them. That is why it does not matter so much if a statement is not pointed, if it is not actually stated as a rule. R. 'Aḳiba's statement is a rule whereas Ben 'Azzai's statement is not; yet the latter is no less effective or moving. Indeed, even R. 'Akiba's statement, although a rule in form, is not a halakic rule; it does not point to any specific act. We are not dealing, then, with specific or concrete rules, but simply with reminders of emphatic trends.

Kelal gadol (comprehensive rule), the term used by both R. 'Aḳiba and Ben 'Azzai, turns the biblical verses they selected into emphatic statements. The term is admirably suited for this purpose. It is a halakic term for indicating greater scope or inclusiveness, yet here it does not refer to halakic matters. *Kelal gadol* is thus used here as a device for calling attention to the verse selected, for stressing that verse.

There is another device for calling attention to an ethical idea or statement. Sometimes an idea is emphasized by making the claim, in one way or another, that it amounts to the entire Torah. The claim is, of course, a trope, a hyperbole, for there are obviously other things, too, to be found in the Torah. The claim is a device, and an effective one, whereby a statement so characterized becomes an emphatic statement.

The Torah, says R. Simla'i, begins and ends with *gemilut ḥasadim* (deeds of lovingkindness); and as proof he cites Genesis 3:21 (which tells of how God clothes the naked) and Deuteronomy 34:6 (which tells that He buried the dead).[68] This statement is, in effect, a lesson concerning *gemilut ḥasadim*, and it implies that the entire burden of the Torah consists in that lesson. A later version strengthens this implicit claim by adding the idea that the middle of the Torah, too, teaches that lesson.[69] Why has there been no outright claim?

Because the purpose of the hyperbole has already been achieved, attention has been drawn to *gemilut ḥasadim*, and the statement as a whole is already an emphatic statement. What is recalled in the statement is the emphasis on love, for *gemilut ḥasadim* is one of a group of concepts that have love as a common connotation.[70]

An outright claim is made in Hillel's famous statement. To the Gentile who asked to be taught the entire Torah while he stood on one foot, Hillel said: "What is hateful to yourself, do not do to your fellow. That is the entire Torah; the rest is explanation. Go and learn."[71] The words, "What is hateful to yourself, do not do to your fellow" are in the vernacular Aramaic,[72] and they stand out, therefore, against the rest of the passage, which is in Hebrew; this is also the case in the other version of the story where R. 'Aḳiba is the authority instead of Hillel.[73] What we have here is a characteristically terse maxim of the folk, and it is to be found elsewhere in cognate literatures.[74] As to the claim itself—"That is the entire Torah"—it is a teaching device, a hyperbole no different from the one we have just examined. Leaving altogether out of account prayers and even ethical matters such as punishment for crimes, at best this statement can refer only, as Rashi says, "to most of the mizwot."[75]

Hillel's maxim is a negative form of the teaching in Leviticus 19:18, "And thou shalt love thy neighbor as thyself." Later Jewish authorities regarded it as equivalent to that verse;[76] indeed, it is incorporated in the Targum Jonathan on that verse. Furthermore, the value concept embodied in the maxim is none other than *'ahabah* (love), the concept embodied in the biblical verse. By means of the claim or hyperbole attention is called to the maxim, and the statement as a whole thus becomes an emphatic statement. It is an emphatic statement serving as a reminder of the already existing emphasis on love.[77]

An emphatic trend which we spoke of in Chapter I is the emphasis on the experience of God. This emphatic trend, too, is reflected in emphatic statements, and again it is the hyperbole or claim that makes the statements emphatic. In fact, the same form is used, a particular biblical verse being characterized as central to, or a summary of the Torah as a whole. Bar Ḳappara makes such a claim for the following verse: "In all thy ways acknowledge [literally, know] Him, and He will direct thy paths" (Prov. 3:6). He speaks of this verse as "the small section on which all essentials of the Torah depend";[78] but he makes no attempt to relate "the essentials of the Torah" to the verse, nor does he tell us what these essentials are. His characterization of the verse can, therefore, be only a hyperbole which draws our attention to the verse, and which thus emphasizes the experience of God that the verse reflects. A more elaborate statement of the same kind has as its author R. Simla'i who, we may remember, is also the author of another "hyperbole-claim" statement cited earlier in this section. R. Simla'i taught: Six hundred and thirteen miẓwot were given to Moses; David reduced them to eleven (Ps. 15), Isaiah to six (Isa. 33:15), Micah to three (Micah 6:8), Isaiah again to two (Isa. 56:1), Amos to one—"Seek Me and live" (Amos 5:4).[79] R. Naḥman declared that it was Habakkuk who reduced them to one—"But the righteous man shall live by his faith" (Hab. 2:4).[80] Here, again, there is no attempt to demonstrate that Amos 5:4 or Habakkuk 2:4 is either basic or equivalent to all the miẓwot. The elaborately formulated claim only emphasizes the verses chosen, especially the ultimate one, the verse reflecting the experience of God. In the statements of both Bar Ḳappara and R. Simla'i, the same emphatic trend has been recalled and strengthened.

All of the statements given here have a distinctive feature in common. That distinctive feature is their form. In every instance, an idea or biblical verse is presented and the claim is made, in one fashion or another, that it is the epitome of the entire Torah, or else that it is a comprehensive rule in the Torah. In no instance, however, is there any attempt whatsoever to substantiate the claim; the claim remains, in fact, but a teaching device. As a teaching device, it calls attention to the idea or verse presented.

Does each of these statements, taken individually, perhaps represent an attempt at presenting a single ethical criterion, a single basis for ethics? Surely not, for the verse or idea pointed to is only suggestive, and not a definite rule. Moreover, the verse or idea was already familiar to the people, and the concept embodied in the verse was already a dynamic factor in their daily lives. If the verse or idea is merely suggestive and if it was not in any sense new to the people, pointing to it can only mean stressing it, making it emphatic. That is exactly what we have tried to demonstrate in the case of each statement presented here. Each individual statement in this section is an emphatic statement, not an ultimate criterion.

The emphatic statements are not to be taken simply as isolated ideas or rules struck off by a few great men. On the contrary, the emphatic statements issue out of the entire background of rabbinic thought and the direction taken by them was not essentially new. The emphatic statements expressed already existing emphatic trends —the emphasis on love, on universality, on the individual, on the experience of God. The emphatic statements, each in its own way, recalled and strengthened and reinforced the emphatic trends; and that is why they were so suggestive and effective. They were charged, so to speak, with the energy of the emphatic trends. Although a similar effect was also achieved by emphatic statements lacking this form, as we saw in the preceding section, the form made the emphasis much stronger.

CHAPTER III

The Sphere of Ethics and Morality

A. The Phases of *Derek Ereẓ*

The rabbis, as we have just observed, establish no ultimate criterion for morality. This is tantamount to saying that the rabbis have no definition of morality and ethics.[1] How can the rabbis have an awareness of morality and ethics, then, if they lack such a definition? We are faced here with a problem presented by all ethical traditions that are nonphilosophical. So far as the rabbinic tradition is concerned, that problem is resolved by a study of the various phases of the rabbinic concept of *derek ereẓ*.[2]

In one of its phases, *derek ereẓ* refers to phenomena or modes of behavior common to all of mankind. Normal sex behavior is *derek ereẓ*.[3] "Man's purposeful direction of his daily activities toward practical and useful ends is also *derek ereẓ*"—his work or business activity, his effort to make a livelihood for himself.[4] To recognize that these are universal human traits or activities does not require any wide experience of the world; they are matters of common observation. On the other hand, sometimes what is characterized as *derek ereẓ* is the shrewd conclusion of a man versed in the ways of the world. Such observations as the following, for example, are called *derek ereẓ*: "When a man gets angry in his house, he fixes his eyes upon the person of least importance";[5] when a man is young he is given to singing songs, when he is older he is given to telling proverbs, when he is old he is given to saying, "All is vanity."[6]

On the basis of these examples, how can we classify *derek ereẓ*? What kind of concept is it? Common observation teaches that certain forms of behavior are characteristic of and may be expected of mankind. Labor is *derek ereẓ*; but it is also *derek ereẓ* to expect that when a man builds a house, he does so in order to store fruit, furniture, and other things in it, and not to destroy it by fire; or when he plants a vineyard he does so in order to have grapes and wine, and not just to fill it with weeds.[7] Our concept thus implies both observation and predictability, and these implications are perhaps contained in the literal meaning of the conceptual term—"the way of the world" (or, "of the land"). Are we not, then, dealing with a concept akin to a scientific concept, since the latter, too, directs observation and makes for predictability? Furthermore, it is not only to obvious instances that our concept directs observation. Those shrewd conclusions as to a man when he is angry, or as to the three stages of a man's life, bespeak not only wide experience but close observation. We are not suggesting, of course, that *derek ereẓ* is a scientific concept. In order to be definite and exact a scientific concept depends upon a formal definition, whereas *derek ereẓ* is an undefined concept. We can say, nevertheless, that *derek ereẓ*, with respect to the phase we have discussed here, is a popular, quasi-scientific concept.[8]

Another phase of the concept refers to matters of practical wisdom. The following statements are introduced with the phrase, "the Torah taught you *derek ereẓ*": A man should not put all his property in one corner;[9] if a man wishes to build a ship that will stand in the harbor (i.e., remain afloat), let him make its width one-sixth its length, and its height one-tenth its length;[10] if a field has brought forth thorns, it is well to sow it with wheat, and if it has brought forth sour grapes, it is well to sow it with barley.[11] Predictability is a factor in this phase of *derek ereẓ*, too, for it is assumed that these teachings, with the authority of the Torah behind them, are sound. Again, although now no longer directed to new instances, observation is a factor as well, since the teachings call for confirmation from experience. This phase of *derek ereẓ*, therefore, may likewise be regarded as quasi-scientific.

Yet in this phase something has been added—a note of obligation. If a matter of *derek ereẓ* is also a teaching of the Torah, it is expected that a person will heed that teaching. When you go on a journey, arrive and leave in the daytime, says the Mekilta, giving instances of how "the patriarchs and the prophets conducted themselves in accordance with [this principle of] *derek ereẓ*;" and concluding with the admonition that if the patriarchs and the prophets did so, "who went to do the will of Him Who spake and the world came to be," all the more ought "the rest of mankind."[12] The phase of *derek ereẓ* containing practical wisdom thus also contains moral overtones, overtones ranging from sound advice to straight admonition.[13]

We have depicted two phases of the concept of *derek ereẓ*. Each phase has an area of its own, the first covering traits or modes of behavior common to all of mankind, whereas the second is limited to definite matters of practical wisdom. With regard to terminology, however, these conceptual phases are not distinguished from each other. Neither conceptual phase has a name of its own, and the term *derek ereẓ* stands for either phase. Nevertheless, the second phase does have a feature not possessed by the first phase. Statements belonging to it are introduced with the words, "the Torah taught you *derek ereẓ*," and hence the second phase is not only an aspect of *derek ereẓ* but also of Torah.

This second conceptual phase thus is not altogether nameless; it is called *derek ereẓ*. Since it is an aspect of Torah, and since it is also symbolized by a term or name, we may speak of it as a subconcept of Torah. A subconcept is an aspect of a concept, but it is also identified by its own name. In this case, definite matters of practical wisdom are identified as *derek ereẓ*; they are also identified as Torah; this phase of *derek ereẓ*, therefore, is a subconcept of Torah.[14]

Still another phase of the concept of *derek ereẓ* refers to good manners. Such teachings, too, are frequently inferred from biblical texts and introduced by the formula, "the Torah taught *derek ereẓ*." " 'And Moses reported the words of the people unto the Lord' [Exod. 19:18]: was there any need for Moses to report? The Torah, however, taught *derek ereẓ*: Moses came and reported back to Him that sent him."[15] " 'And the Lord called unto Moses and spoke to him' [Lev. 1:1]: why did calling precede speaking? The Torah taught *derek ereẓ* [namely], that one should not say anything to his fellow without having first called him."[16] "['Where is Sarah, thy wife?']—the Torah taught *derek ereẓ* [namely], that one must inquire after the health of his hostess."[17]

Rules of good manners are not limited to those deduced from biblical texts, nor are they always specifically designated as *derek ereẓ* in their rabbinic sources. There are, for example, post-talmudic collections of rabbinic statements and anecdotes to which the name "*Derek Ereẓ*" has been given;[18] and much of the material there presented belongs to the sphere of good manners, as Higger has shown.[19] Similarly, statements belonging to other phases of *derek ereẓ*, as well, are often not specifically designated as *derek ereẓ* by the rabbis. Yet, as Friedmann has pointed out—and correctly—the many rabbinic prescriptions on the ways to maintain bodily health, and kindred matters do, in fact, belong to Hilkot *Derek Ereẓ*;[20] or, according to our scheme here, to the phase referring to practical wisdom.

Like *derek ereẓ* as practical wisdom, *derek ereẓ* as good manners is a subconcept of Torah—"the Torah taught *derek ereẓ*." Now, however, it is no longer a matter of sound advice at all but purely of admonition. By the same token, the term *derek ereẓ* in this third phase does not refer to anything quasi-scientific. Here the factors of observation and predictability play no role whatsoever; a person is enjoined to act in a certain way not because it will lead to success or ward off a danger, but simply because it is the proper way to act. The term *derek ereẓ* now means, apparently, that acts of this kind are incumbent upon all of mankind, that they ought to be "the way of the world."

There is a fourth phase to the concept of *derek ereẓ*. In this phase are the matters which, the rabbis say, are essential to the existence of mankind, matters that have, thus, a crucial character.

Ẓedaḳah (charity) and *gemilut ḥasadim* (deeds of lovingkindness) are called *derek ereẓ*. The people of Israel who lived in the days of the First Temple, though often idol-worshippers, nevertheless had *derek ereẓ* in them. "And what was that *derek ereẓ* that was in them? *Ẓedaḳah* and *gemilut ḥasadim*."[21] Furthering peace among men and refraining from talebearing are characterized as *derek ereẓ*;[22] and so, too, is refraining from taking anything illegitimately, "fleeing from the *gezel*."[23] The principle that testimony is to be accepted only from an actual eyewitness to an event, and not from him who merely heard of it from even a trustworthy person, is also referred to as *derek ereẓ*;[24] in this case, *derek ereẓ* has to do with law and justice, with *din*,[25] and also, of course, with truth.[26]

The concepts here designated as *derek ereẓ* are grouped together, as we shall now see, in various rabbinic statements. What the rabbis say about these concepts as a group constitutes the nature of these concepts. Some of the rabbinic statements, it is true, depict other concepts—not specifically designated as *derek ereẓ*—as also having the same character. But this only means that the concepts which are designated as *derek ereẓ* do not exhaust what we have called the fourth phase of *derek ereẓ*; all the concepts mentioned that are thus grouped together and given the same character belong to that fourth phase. We noticed above that matters belonging to other phases of *derek ereẓ*, as well, are often not specifically designated as *derek ereẓ*.[27]

"The world [*ha-'olam*] endures [קים] because of three things," says R. Simeon ben Gamaliel, "because of truth, because of justice [law], and because of peace."[28] A later source speaks of four things whereby civilization is established—charity, justice (law), truth, and peace.[29] Are these things modes of behavior common to all of mankind, just as the traits in the first phase of *derek ereẓ* are common to all of mankind? They are, indeed, common to mankind in the round, but the idea is also present that were they lacking, society or civilization would not exist. Furthermore, the rabbis speak of human traits, some of them hardly uncommon, because of which "the world is destroyed." "Because of eight things is the world destroyed: injustice in the courts [על הדינין], idolatry, incest, murder, *ḥillul ha-Shem* [the profanation of God's Name], because of foul things a person utters, arrogance, and the evil tongue [scandal-mongering], and some say also because of covetousness."[30] These things, too, are modes of human behavior, but behavior that a person should refrain from. The modes of behavior given here, then, are in a different category from those in the first phase. Whereas the first phase is descriptive only, here the rabbis insist on the necessary character of the "four things," and on the dangerous character of the "eight things."

In the Sifra, an early source, and in several parallels, there occurs the following passage: " 'Mine ordinances [*mishpaṭai*] shall ye do' [Lev. 18:4]. Those are the things that are written in the Torah, which, had they not been written, it stands to reason that they should have been written [בדין היה לכתבן]; for example, [ordinances in respect to] theft and incest and idolatry and blasphemy and murder. Had they not been written, it stands to reason that they should have been written."[31] A whole class of laws is here apparently depicted as being affirmed by man's reason. Moreover, man could have learned certain moral qualities from the animals. Had the Torah not been given, says R. Joḥanan, we might have learned decency (*ẓeni'ut*) from the cat, refraining from theft (*gezel*) from the ant, chastity from the dove, sexual manners from the rooster.[32]

By using the phrase, "it stands to reason," or by saying that proper behavior might have been "learned" from the animals, the rabbis are not pointing to social utility as a basis for ethics. That idea is found in medieval Jewish philosophy and it is applied there at least to a segment of the moral life, but the idea is not rabbinic. Yehudah Ha-Levi speaks of "rational laws" and of "social laws" as being indispensable in the conduct of every human society;[33] "even a band of robbers must have justice among themselves, for if not, their association could not last."[34] On the basis of our passage in the Sifra, Maimonides says that *mishpaṭim* (ordinances) are commandments the utilitarian purpose of which (תועלתם) is clear to everyone.[35] Albo says that to prevent quarrels, every society must administer justice; that it must maintain order so as to give protection against murder, theft, robbery, and the like; and that this order "the wise men call natural law."[36] All such theories of social utility more or less imply that justice, truth, and so on are fruits of reason, that they are products of "practical wisdom."[37] "Practical wisdom" always posits a utilitarian end. The end may be social utility, or it may apply only to an individual in a specific situation, as is true of our second phase of *derek ereẓ*. The rabbis, however, posit no end whatever, specific or otherwise. Phrases like "it stands to reason" must not lead us to *supply* the "reason."

What the rabbis have in mind becomes evident when we examine the second part of the passage in the Sifra. There are other matters in the Torah, besides those things that "stand to reason." There are laws in the Torah (designated in Lev. 18:4 as *ḥukkotai*) against which the evil *yeẓer* and the nations of the world raise objections (משיבין עליהם)—the laws against eating pork and against wearing garments of linsey-woolsey, the law of *ḥaliẓah* (see Deut. 25:5–14), the law of the cleansing of the leper, the law of the scapegoat.[38] The objections raised against these laws are not stated, nor need they be, so far as the contrast between these laws and the laws that "stand to reason" is concerned. On the one hand are laws "written in the

Torah, which, had they not been written, it stands to reason that they should have been written"; on the other, are laws against which the evil *yeẓer* and the nations of the world raise objections. Obviously the contrast is between the laws which the nations of the world and Israel possess in common and those that Israel alone possesses. The former, then, are universal laws—"for example, [laws about] theft and incest," etc. "It stands to reason" simply refers to the fact that those things are universal. They are characteristic of man as man. Further, there are things so universal as to be found distributed even among various animals, and although not all of them are found together in any one animal, man might have learned them, in order to be man, from the different animals.

It has been assumed that the contrast drawn by the passage in the Sifra is between ethics and ritual.[39] But do the nations raise objections against the ritual laws as such? If so, why do they not object to rites that are really typical and frequent, to sacrifices and festivals? Sacrifices and festivals, however, are the kind of rites practiced by the nations as well; they are universal institutions. What the nations and the evil *yeẓer* question are rites that appear peculiar because they are found only in Israel. The contrast, then, is not between ethics and ritual, but between laws that are universal and laws possessed by Israel alone.

Yet the nations practiced idolatry. How, then, could the rabbis have seemed to imply that the nations negated idolatry?[40]

The idea of social utility is not contained in the other rabbinic statements either. When the rabbis tell of three things because of which the world endures, or of four things whereby civilization is established, they are not ascribing to these things any social utility. When we assign to ethics a utilitarian role, we tend to reduce ethics to something neutral, to a means to an end, to mechanics, as it were. In our rabbinic statements, on the contrary, the object is, patently, to extol justice, truth, peace, and charity. These are virtues not because they have social utility; they are virtues in their own right. Moreover, they are virtues of such importance that without them mankind would not be civilized, nor be fit to endure.[41] Nor need we only surmise that it is the intention of the rabbis to extol the "four things" as virtues. The same passage also says that "because of eight things is the world destroyed," and it enumerates the wicked men who, because they engaged in these things, "were uprooted from the world." If the passage condemns the "eight things" as vices, it must also extol the "four things" as virtues.

All of the concepts grouped together in these various statements have a common character. Not only do the groupings overlap, but the statements grouping the concepts all contain the same idea. All of the statements declare, in one way or another, that the concepts are common to mankind and that without them, man cannot be; in one case, the concepts are "things" man must refrain from doing, else he cannot be. In other words, the rubric *derek ereẓ*, the way of the world, applies here as well,[42] but with a somewhat different connotation. What we have here is the fourth phase of *derek ereẓ*. It connotes that there are certain positive matters, common to all mankind, that man must do, and that there are negative matters he must refrain from doing. Between this fourth phase of *derek ereẓ* and the third phase, good manners, there is kinship, but in this fourth phase the mandatory element is far, far stronger.

In one important respect the fourth phase differs from all the other phases of *derek ereẓ*. We described the first three phases of the concept on the basis of rabbinic usage, but that was the only guide we had. The rabbis themselves do not specifically classify them. Here, however, the phase—to use our terminology—has been made by the rabbis; it is they who group the concepts, and they group them by means of statements which underscore the character of those concepts. The character of this phase is literally the character ascribed by the rabbis to the concepts of the phase.

Another distinction, with even greater implications, must likewise be evident by now. The rabbis group "three things," "four things," "eight things," "things" which "stand to reason." What are these "things"? They are, in each case, concepts—justice, peace, charity, truth, theft, and so on. They are generalizations, abstract ideas that give meaning to concrete situations and events. In contrast to these lists of concepts, the first three phases of *derek ereẓ* are concerned, by and large, with specific acts or situations, and the generalizing term there is *derek ereẓ* alone. Now, if the rabbis use such terms as "justice" or "charity" in describing events or acts, they obviously have an awareness of justice or charity as such. Further, they are also aware of the character of justice and charity. These things, these concepts, they say, are characteristic of man as man; without them there would be no society or civilization. In short, the concepts of justice and charity and theft give meaning to *specific events*; and the concept of *derek ereẓ*, in turn, gives character to the other concepts, to the concepts of justice, charity, and the like.

Justice and charity and the other universal concepts give meaning to specific events; as value concepts, they also constitute emotional drives, and are concretized in laws. The concept of *derek ereẓ* is, therefore, almost displaced in this phase by the universal concepts. There are many passages, however, in which the rabbis definitely associate the universal concepts with the concept of *derek ereẓ*. Those passages indicate that the universal concepts are classifications of *derek ereẓ*, or subconcepts of *derek ereẓ*.[43]

In ascribing a certain character to concepts like justice and charity, are not the rabbis establishing a definition of ethics and morality? A definition enables one to recognize new instances that conform to the definition and deliberately to seek out such new instances.[44] Had the rabbis ascribed social utility to such concepts as justice and charity, they would, indeed, have posited a definition, vague though it would have been; we should then have been directed, at least, to look for further instances of social utility. But the rabbis do no more than extol the positive ethical concepts and warn against the negative ones. The character which the rabbis ascribe to the ethical concepts does not constitute, then, a definition of ethics and morality.[45]

Nevertheless, had the rabbis given a definite list of the ethical concepts, such a list might have served as a definition. But there is no definite list. When the rabbis speak of "things" which "stand to reason," how do they introduce them? By the phrase, "for example." When they do group the concepts by means of numbers, one group consists of "three things" and another of "four things." The lists of ethical concepts, then, also do not constitute a definition of ethics and morality.

Finally, there is still another phase of the concept of *derek ereẓ*. It consists entirely of ethical rules and concepts, although a number of these rules may also have to do with good manners. We should, therefore, place this phase between the third phase, good manners, and the fourth phase, that which refers to universal ethical concepts.

This final phase of *derek ereẓ*, like all the other phases except the first, is a subconcept of Torah as well.[46] "The Torah taught you *derek ereẓ*—[namely] that the bridegroom does not enter the bridal chamber until the bride has given him permission."[47] "The Torah taught you *derek ereẓ*"—namely, that a man travelling in a land not his own, instead of eating of the sustenance he brings with him, must put that aside and buy from the local storekeeper to the latter's profit.[48] In these instances, what is enjoined is not courtesy alone, but ethical behavior. Again, in the following statement, what is given is not only a rule of hospitality but what amounts to a law of *ẓedaḳah*. "The Torah taught you *derek ereẓ*"—a man must take care of his relative for a month.[49]

There is no real line of demarcation between manners and morals. A collection of rabbinic statements and anecdotes to which the name "*Derek Ereẓ*" has been given, and which has been referred to above,[50] tells a story that may serve as an illustration. R. Simeon, the son of Eleazar, was once riding leisurely on an ass along the lake shore when he came upon a man there who was exceedingly ugly. " 'Wretch!' R. Simeon called to him, 'How ugly are thy deeds! How ugly are the children of our father Abraham!' 'What can I do?' the man answered, 'Go and tell this to the Artisan who made me!' " The story goes on to relate that R. Simeon thereupon pleaded with the man to forgive him, and the man did forgive, but only after the townspeople also pleaded, and only on condition that R. Simeon would "not act in this manner again."[51]

The same tractate, avowedly teaching *derek ereẓ*, presents rules that are solely ethical halakot and that are definitely beyond the sphere of manners. Often such halakot are not only rules of *derek ereẓ* but concretizations of other value concepts as well. According to our text, for example, a person is forbidden to say to a seller in the market place, " 'How much do you charge for this article?' when he does not intend to buy," and the reason given here is that he thereby raises false hopes in the seller.[52] Precisely the same prohibition is found in the Mishnah—"He must not say, 'How much do you charge for this article?' when he does not intend to buy";[53] and now the question of the pretended buyer is cited as an instance of *'ona'ah* by means of words—*'ona'at debarim*, a wrong or injury done by means of words.[54] Our text and the Mishnah give the selfsame reason for the halakah; our text merely indicates what *'ona'ah* consists in, specifically in this case. The halakah here is thus a concretization of both *derek ereẓ* and *'ona'ah*. Indeed, if concepts like *gemilut ḥasadim* and others of the same sort represent classifications of *derek ereẓ*—that is, are subconcepts of *derek ereẓ*—then *'ona'ah*, too, is a subconcept of *derek ereẓ*.

Similarly, other matters prohibited by our text are not only violations of *derek ereẓ*, but are stigmatized as acts with a taint of robbery, "a manner of *gezel*."[55] A person must not give his friend new wine to drink, telling him that it is old wine, "for this is a manner of *gezel*."[56] Again, a person selling wine to ass-drivers—that is, to a caravan—should not say (to his helpers), " 'Remove this wine and give that wine,' for this is a manner of *gezel*."[57] Apparently, in this instance also, it is not a case of perpetrating an actual fraud, for that would definitely be *gezel*, not "a manner of *gezel*."

With regard to the concepts of the fourth phase, the rabbis say that not only are they common to all mankind, but that without them civilization would not exist. No such claim is made with regard to the rules included in the final phase. Enjoined or else prohibited in the final phase are acts on which, so to say, the fate of the world does not depend, and yet which do fall within the sphere of ethics. The final phase is thus sufficiently distinguishable from the fourth phase to have some individuality of its own. Nevertheless, the fourth phase does have a tendency to absorb the final phase. Certain acts are stigmatized as "a manner of *gezel*," and *gezel* itself is in the fourth phase; the rule which enjoins proper sexual behavior on the part of the bridegroom is not only a rule of good manners but of universal moral behavior;[58] a rule of hospitality toward a poor relation amounts to a law of *ẓedaḳah*. But it is thus also evident that the fourth phase has a relationship with the third phase, the phase of good manners, as well.

We can now, at last, address ourselves to the question posed at the beginning of this section: Do the rabbis have an awareness of ethics and morality as such, despite having no definition or ultimate criterion for ethics or morality? The answer is that not only do they have this awareness, but they also outline the *sphere* of ethics and morality. The concept of *derek ereẓ* expresses their awareness of morality and ethics, and the phases of *derek ereẓ* adumbrate the sphere of morality and ethics.

In all the phases of the concept except the first, the connotation of *derek ereẓ* is morality and ethics. No one can question the fact that the fourth phase deals with morality and ethics. The fourth phase refers to the concepts which, according to the rabbis, are common to all mankind, and without which, the rabbis also say, civilization would not exist. But is the sphere of morality limited to this crucial kind of morality? Are there not other areas as well? We find that this fourth phase tends to absorb another phase without, however, actually being identical with it; the "absorbed" phase apparently thus refers to ethical acts which are not crucial. We find, again, that the fourth phase, crucial morality, is also related to good manners. Moreover, these three phases are all subconcepts of Torah —"the Torah teaches *derek ereẓ*." If the three phases are all *derek ereẓ*, and furthermore, are all subconcepts of Torah, then if *derek ereẓ* connotes morality in the one phase, it must do so in the other phases as well, and especially so if these three phases are related to one another. On the other hand, we find that the phase of practical wisdom is not related to these three, and that it is nonetheless a subconcept of Torah. *Derek ereẓ* here, too, connotes morality, but of a more indirect kind, and the note of admonition or obligation is stronger in some cases than in others.

The term *derek ereẓ* does not necessarily point to any one phase of *derek ereẓ*. One source declares that *derek ereẓ* preceded Torah by twenty-six generations,[59] meaning that the world practiced *derek ereẓ* in the twenty-six generations before the Torah was given on Sinai. Another source has God saying that He gave the Torah in order that men might study it and "learn from it *derek ereẓ*."[60] *Derek ereẓ* is used in these passages in a general sense, and refers patently to moral behavior.

Do the phases represent a hierarchy of ethical behavior? Are they gradations of the moral life in which one phase contains higher or more urgent moral demands than another phase? To the extent that there is a hierarchy in the moral life, it is the Halakah that establishes such a hierarchy, and not the phases of *derek ereẓ*. A phase of *derek ereẓ* is not a unit, so far as the moral implications or consequences of the act it refers to are concerned. The phase of practical wisdom, for example, contains sound advice as to investments, but it also contains urgent admonitions and rules concerning personal safety and the proper rearing of children. The phase which refers to universal human concepts places among them not only theft but also murder. Further, the phases themselves are not altogether separable: there is no real demarcation between manners and morals, and the fourth phase tends to absorb the final phase. The phases are the result of the effort to concretize the concept of *derek ereẓ* in as many ways as possible, rather than an attempt to establish an ethical hierarchy.

Like all value concepts, *derek ereẓ* is a dynamic concept and has a drive toward concretization. The phases are the means whereby the sphere of the concept is continually being extended. Even the proper way to rehabilitate a field has a moral implication of some kind—"the Torah taught you *derek ereẓ*." To be sure, here (and in similar instances) the note of obligation contained in the teaching is a faint one, whereas in other teachings belonging to the same phase, the phase of practical wisdom, the admonitory tone is emphatic.[61] Faint or emphatic, the note of obligation is there. The teaching with the fainter note of obligation or admonition is no less a concretization of *derek ereẓ* than the teaching with the emphatic note.

We have thus far left out of consideration the first phase of *derek ereẓ*, the phase referring to phenomena or modes of behavior common to all of mankind. This is the only phase of *derek ereẓ* which is not a subconcept of Torah—there is hardly room for admonition with respect to matters set down as sheer human phenomena. The first phase is thus merely descriptive and not admonitory. What has this descriptive phase to do with the other phases, all of which are admonitory?

The first phase is purely descriptive, certainly, and yet it contains a number of traits that are not morally neutral. Modes of behavior are included in this phase which are always either moral or immoral. Normal sexual behavior, for example, is a basic form of human behavior; but it is always either moral, as when there is no incest[62] and the proprieties are observed, or else immoral, as in the case of incest. The same thing is true of another mode of human behavior—work or business activity. It is immoral even if it is but tainted with *gezel*; otherwise it is moral.[63] These modes of behavior, then, have immediate moral implications, positive or negative, and it is only when moral implications are put aside that the traits wear a neutral aspect. Further, there are traits which are not moral but even so are characteristic of man. Among these is that of the angered head of the family "fixing his eyes upon the person of least importance." We, too, tend to speak of such a trait as "all too human."[64]

Since this phase of *derek ereẓ* refers to general human phenomena, it is natural that it should also include phenomena that have no moral implications. Rapid success (literally, ascent) and rapid decline (literally, descent) are not according to *derek ereẓ*;[65] the opposite, therefore, is according to *derek ereẓ*. Attending to natural functions is *derek ereẓ*.[66] Using a synecdoche—"an ox" for "oxen," "an ass" for "asses" (Gen. 32:6)—is *derek ereẓ*, for it is the way men speak.[67] These and other morally neutral phenomena can be included in the first phase because that phase is merely descriptive and not admonitory. Yet even in the phase which is purely descriptive, many of the human phenomena there included are not, in fact, morally neutral. The first phase is, therefore, not incompatible with the other phases of *derek ereẓ*: it represents, on the contrary, an extension of the concept.

The first phase of *derek ereẓ* includes only general human phenomena. General physical or natural phenomena are represented by another concept; *sidre bereshit*, "orders of *bereshit*," for which there is also an alternate term, *sidre 'olam*, "orders of the world." That concept, as we have pointed out elsewhere, is a quasi-scientific concept.[68] In that respect, it is like both the first and second phases of *derek ereẓ*.[69]

The quasi-scientific character of the first and second phases of *derek ereẓ* limits, to some degree, its effectiveness as a value concept. To function freely, a value concept must be free from admixture with any other type of concept, must be a pure *value* concept.[70] Being simply descriptive, the first phase designates as *derek ereẓ* phenomena that have no moral implications whatever; moreover, being nonadmonitory, it naturally ignores the moral implications of matters that are not morally neutral; and again, since this phase is concerned with observations concerning human nature, it can include, as well, traits that are not moral at all. At the very least, therefore, the concept must have been at times ambiguous.[71]

Similarly, the second phase, too, sometimes weakened *derek ereẓ* as a value concept. Practical wisdom may lead to sound advice rather than to outright admonition. There were occasions, as we have just seen, when the note of obligation was only faint, and this despite the formula, "the Torah taught you *derek ereẓ*." The effectiveness of the formula was bound to be weakened when the admonitory tone was not emphatic.

Flaws notwithstanding, *derek ereẓ* remains an effective value concept on the whole. The weak first phase is, after all, only an extension of the concept, and usually the second phase is quite emphatic in its admonitions. All the other phases are purely valuational, not quasi-scientific. Furthermore, what we have called subconcepts of *derek ereẓ*, concepts such as *din*, *ẓedaḳah*, or *'ona'ah*, are also value concepts in their own right and hence are not affected by the limitations of *derek ereẓ*.

The limitations of the concept of *derek ereẓ* are another indication that the term *derek ereẓ* does not define the universal ethical concepts. *Din*, *ẓedaḳah*, and the other ethical concepts have a common ground in *derek ereẓ*, are subconcepts of *derek ereẓ*. Nevertheless, the concept of *derek ereẓ*, by pointing to these subconcepts as matters characteristic of man, does not define them, for *derek ereẓ* has, in addition, a quasi-scientific, morally neutral phase and that phase, too, refers to matters characteristic of man.

The concept of *derek ereẓ* does two things at the same time. It expresses awareness of morality and ethics, and through its phases, it also limns the sphere of morality and ethics. In thus exercising a dual function *derek ereẓ* is by no means unique. As depicted here, *derek ereẓ* is not more complex than other rabbinic concepts. There are other rabbinic concepts which are similarly constituted, and they, too, exercise a dual function—that is to say, every concept which possesses conceptual phases not only expresses a valuational idea, but it also indicates, through its phases, the range of that idea.[72] *Derek ereẓ* is actually no more complex than any other concept having conceptual phases. What gives the impression of complexity is simply the fact that *derek ereẓ* has an unusually large number of conceptual phases.[73]

The concept of *derek ereẓ* gives to morality and ethics a much wider scope than that ordinarily envisaged by modern man.

Charity and justice and love and truth and all the rest of the virtues are *derek ereẓ*, but so are other matters which we usually do not think of as within the scope of morality. If those other matters are called to our attention, however, do we not recognize that they have moral implications? To lose the savings of a lifetime through a rash investment in a single venture is no small matter, and hence warning against it does have a moral implication. Manners imply, at the very least, considerateness. The moral sphere expands as we begin to reflect upon it.

Modern scholars have failed to recognize how wide indeed is the scope of rabbinic morality and ethics; as a result, they find it difficult to convey the meaning of *derek ereẓ*. Thus Bacher says that *derek ereẓ* has to do "not with matters of religion, and also not with matters of morality, but refers to the wide circle beyond them, to the habits of men, to social manners, to day-to-day life."[74] But the province of morality is precisely day-to-day life, and that includes the manners and customs of society. One of the great achievements of the rabbis is so to enlarge the sphere of morality, by means of the concept of *derek ereẓ*, as to include within that sphere acts that are undramatic and commonplace, the very acts that form the texture of daily living.

Most of the examples of *derek ereẓ* cited by Bacher himself[75] afford just so many instances of everyday morality. Some of them are rules of practical wisdom: a person ought not to accustom himself to meat—that is, not develop a need for expensive food;[76] those who are about to start on a journey ought to be alert (that is, not tarry or dally);[77] a person who is ill ought to cease working and seek a cure.[78] There are also rules of good manners: Moses reported back to Him Who sent him (a rule to be followed by all agents);[79] if a person wishes to speak to one of two men who happen to be together, he must not tell the other man to go away, but rather draw the former off and speak with him.[80] Prayer, too, must not be devoid of good manners: petitions to God ought always to be preceded by words of supplication.[81]

The scope of morality cannot be delimited or defined. Like all value concepts,[82] *derek ereẓ* is never defined; nor do the various phases, taken together, constitute a definition of *derek ereẓ*. In the first place, except for the fourth phase, the phases have not been designated as such by the rabbis; they are our own constructs, based on rabbinic usage, and are intended only as helpful guides. Second, the phases themselves are not closed and static, but remain open and dynamic. When the rabbis list concepts of the fourth phase, those concepts are given as "examples," and hence the list is not definitive. The other phases are even less definitive. They consist of rules and laws called forth by the circumstances of daily life, and not only of those already crystallized in the tradition. Can there be a point, therefore, at which a phase may be regarded as closed? Can there be a fixed limit to the phase, let us say, of practical wisdom, to the rules having to do with long-range moral effects? The concept of *derek ereẓ* is a dynamic concept, as we have said, and this means that, in rabbinic experience, there are no set boundaries to the moral life. The moral life is not, for the rabbis, contained in any definitive rule or in any formula.

The scope of the moral life, we repeat, cannot be described by a formula, not even by the formula "between a man and his fellow man." That phrase, or its equivalent, is used by the rabbis in one context and in one context only, and it is not a general designation for ethics or morality. However the statements in which the phrase occurs may differ in expression, the context in those statements is always the same, namely, the sins forgiven and the sins not forgiven by God. "For sins that are between a man and God, the Day of Atonement brings forgiveness; for sins that are between a man and his fellow man, the Day of Atonement brings no forgiveness until he has conciliated his fellow man."[83] " 'He will show thee favor' [Num. 6:26]—in matters that are between you and Him; 'He will not show favor' [Deut. 10:17]—in matters that are between you and your fellow man."[84] " 'And acquitting' [Exod. 34:7, *we-naḳḳeh*]—in matters that are between you and Him; 'He will not acquit' [*ibid., lo'yenaḳḳeh*]—in matters that are between you and your fellow man."[85] We may say, indeed, that not only the context but the idea in these statements remains the same. A phrase limited to a specific context and to a particular idea cannot be regarded as a general classification.

In point of fact, the scope of morality includes much else besides "matters between a man and his fellow man." There are moral rules and admonitions with regard to the safety and welfare of one's own person, such as the rule that when going on a journey a person must arrive and leave in the daytime, or the admonition to a person who is ill to cease working and seek a cure. A man's general outlook, his affirmative or negative attitude toward life, is a moral matter. The rabbis condemn the man who wearies of life, of "the good life in this world," and after adding a parable in which a subject wished to leave in the midst of a feast given him by the king, stigmatize such behavior as not being *derek ereẓ*.[86]

Within the scope of the concept of *raḥamim* (compassion), the rabbis include not only human beings but also animals. On the basis of Leviticus 22:27–28, for example, they say that just as God has compassion on mankind, so has He compassion on the animals, and Deuteronomy 22:6 enables them to conclude that "just as the Holy One blessed be He bestowed His compassion [*raḥamim*] on beasts," so also has He compassion on fowl.[87] Again, according to rabbinic legend, Moses' tenderness toward Jethro's flock which he was herding demonstrated his fitness to lead Israel, so that God said: "Thou takest compassion [*raḥamim*] on a flock belonging to a man of flesh and blood! As thou livest, thou shalt pasture Israel, My flock."[88] These instances prove that the term *raḥamim* refers to compassion for animals as well as for human beings. Most often, however, there is no need to mention the abstract value-term; the concept is embodied in a concretization, whether the latter be a midrashic interpretation or a halakah.[89] Numerous halakot are thus concretizations of the concept *raḥamim*, as it applies to animals, even though these halakot do not contain the conceptual term itself.[90]

In still another and more striking respect, the scope of rabbinic morality cannot be limited to relations "between a man and his fellow man." Idolatry and blasphemy are patently "sins between a man and God." Nevertheless, the rabbis group idolatry and blasphemy together with theft, incest, and murder.[91] We found that these negative concepts, negative because they represent things men must refrain from doing, are among a group of concepts, some positive and some negative, which the rabbis regard as characteristic of man in general, and which constitute what we have called the fourth phase of *derek ereẓ*.

By placing the negative concept of idolatry among the concepts characteristic of mankind in general, the rabbis certainly suggest that non-Jews, too, rejected idolatry. Where did the rabbis see non-Jews who rejected idolatry and accepted the other moral laws as well? They had in mind, undoubtedly, the "fearers of Heaven," the many non-Jews who rejected idolatry, and who also practiced the other moral laws, but who were not actually proselytes.[92] Among such non-Jews, very likely, were those "who raised objections" to the laws against eating pig and against wearing garments of linsey-woolsey, and to several other laws, the objectors being, apparently, of various nationalities and representatives, so to speak, of the nations of the world.[93] We ought to add that the rabbis were also well aware of the genuine virtues to be found in Gentile society itself, and that they took occasion to extol these virtues.[94]

Rejection of idolatry by non-Jews in rabbinic times was, then, far from uncommon, and this affected the scope of rabbinic ethics. It permitted the rabbis to name idolatry, and blasphemy too, as negative concepts characteristic of man in general, alongside such other negative concepts as theft and murder, and thus to include idolatry and blasphemy in the scope of *derek ereẓ*, "the way of the world."

A proper evaluation of the rejection of idolatry cannot be made at this time. In later discussions we hope to show that the relationship to God is at the very center of the moral life, and that this relationship is expressed through concepts which have vast moral implications. Rejection of idolatry was thus an indispensable condition of the moral life. The morality and practice of the "fearers of Heaven" constituted a confirmation of the rabbis' own moral experience. Rejection of idolatry and the practice of morality proved to be bound up with each other. But is not rejection of idolatry a matter "between man and God"? How can we say, then, that either this formula or the formula "between a man and his fellow man" is a hard and fast category?[95]

B. The Interaction of the Rabbis and the Folk

The development of rabbinic morality and ethics is a social phenomenon. Rabbinic morality developed as a result of the interaction between the rabbis as an intellectual class and the folk in general; and that interaction was possible because the rabbis, although trained in the academies, were bound up with the life of the people as a whole and did not constitute a separate professional class.[96] The concept of *derek ereẓ*, and its subconcepts as well, were elements of the culture of the folk in general, for they were terms in the common vocabulary.[97] What, then, was the contribution of the rabbis?

Can we say that it was the task of the rabbis, through their teachings and halakot, to make it possible for the people to concretize the concepts of morality? Unmodified, this statement is unjust to the common people. An abstract value concept does not exist for long apart from its concretizations,[98] nor are abstract ideas the métier of the common people. There certainly were occasions when the common people concretized a moral concept without any guidance from the rabbis: on the other hand, it is hard to imagine what the moral pattern might have been without the rabbis, even assuming the existence of the valuational terms, a very doubtful assumption. Social interaction is always intricate and subtle, and the interaction of the rabbis with the folk was no exception.

The role of the folk predominates in the first phase of *derek ereẓ*, doubtless for the very reason that this phase is only an extension of the concept. Everybody can recognize that normal sexual behavior, engaging in work or business, and attending to natural functions are universal human modes of behavior; such observations are clearly those of the folk. An observation such as the one on the use of a synecdoche, however, is an academic observation.

When it comes to the other phases of *derek ereẓ*, the ethical phases proper, the role of the rabbis grows increasingly larger, although the role of the folk is still to be discerned. In the second phase, there are rules of practical wisdom which are patently common-sense rules of the folk, but which the rabbis reinforce by declaring them also to be teachings of Torah[99]—rules like not putting all your property in one corner, and that you must arrive and leave in the daytime. Where practical wisdom has to do with long-range effects, as in the warning against accustoming a child to expensive food,[100] the rules apparently originate with the rabbis. The phase of good manners, too, has unquestionably a folk background, but again, the delicacy and refinement so characteristic of many of its rules bespeak a tutored and cultivated class; rules like those telling a bridegroom not to enter until the bride has given permission, or a traveler to buy from the local storekeeper, or what to do when a person wishes to speak to one of two men who happen to be together.

The fourth phase, as we may remember, is the only one given a distinctive feature by the rabbis themselves, the other phases being distinguished from each other only through rabbinic usage. What we have called the fourth phase consists of concepts which the rabbis regard as universal, since the rabbis relate them, in one way or another, to mankind as a whole—positive concepts such as truth, justice, peace, and charity, and negative concepts such as theft, murder, incest, and idolatry. These concepts are, by and large, emotional drives, matters of the heart, and that is one reason, no doubt, why the rabbis regard them as universal. At a first glance, therefore, the fourth phase may appear as one in which the role of the folk predominates. But it is precisely here, in the realm of positive and negative moral drives, that a society depends on its most gifted members. Justice and laws, for example, have always been the concern of some of the best minds of every people; peace became a vivid ideal when envisioned by prophets and poets; charity was not left to the whim of the individual but was embodied in institutions; there is no need to add examples of how the intellect has canalized the emotional drives. It is no wonder, then, that so much of the Halakah, and even a larger portion of the Haggadah, is concentrated on the fourth phase of *derek ereẓ*. Of course, had the emotions of the folk not been engaged, the work of the rabbis would have been futile. Without the training, guidance, and laws of the rabbis, however, what could the folk have done?

The universal concepts are always mediated by a particular culture. We recognize today that every culture imparts to a universal concept a special quality, overtones of significance that the concept does not have elsewhere. "Patience," for instance, has overtones for the Siamese it does not have for us, according to Kroeber. " 'Patience' . . . involves calm circumspection and acting with worldly wisdom; it gives peace as well as success. Patience is really self-control over disturbing emotion, and leads to a species of self-reliance."[101] Kroeber calls attention earlier to differences in form even among kindred cultures. "There is an Italian, a French, a British pattern or form of European civilization."[102]

The rabbis refined and enriched the universal ethical concepts, especially the concept of love. Instead of having a single concept, "love," they have a number of conceptual terms—among them being *'ahabah*, *raḥamim*, *ẓedakah*, and *gemilut ḥasadim*. Each of these terms has its own connotations; and since the terms are not defined, their connotations can be expressed verbally only in teachings or laws. Rabbinic law did not stifle love, as some have asserted. On the contrary, rabbinic law sensitized a man to occasions for expressing love through action. Formal modes of concretization, laws, enabled a person to recognize occasions for concretizing the concept of deeds of lovingkindness,[103] for example. The many laws and the multiplicity of moral concepts went together; the laws were the concretizations of the concepts. To deny that the multiplicity of moral cencepts gave morality a wide range and made for moral depth and sensitivity is to deny the potency of any value concept.

In the fifth phase, the phase associated with universal morality but not identified with it, the role of the rabbis predominates. Only the spiritual leaders could take it upon themselves to stigmatize as "a manner of *gezel*" acts that are not *gezel* in themselves. The concept of *'ona'ah*, like all value concepts, was doubtless a folk concept, but it was the rabbis who, so to say, built up that concept. Rabbinic law decided what constitutes *'ona'at mamon*, a fraudulent business transaction, both in regard to objects which have ordinary market value and in regard to objects that do not.[104] *'Ona'at mamon* is one aspect of the concept. The other is *'ona'at debarim*, an instance of which was given above,[105] but which connotes any injury done by means of words, such as reminding anyone of his past misdeeds, shaming anyone in public, or causing a woman to shed tears.[106] Only men of sensitivity and insight could have depicted the occasions of *'ona'at debarim*.

The interaction between the folk and the rabbis was an extraordinary phenomenon. It was a continuous interaction between a society and its ethical leaders, a process in which the ordinary man was often raised to the level of the gifted man.[107]

The universal concepts are concretized in laws, and many tractates of the Mishnah are devoted to these laws. These laws were taught in the academies, as were the other laws of the Mishnah. But besides the Mishnah, there were also nonofficial collections of rules and laws, among them collections known as Hilkot *Derek Ereẓ*.[108] Such collections of Hilkot *Derek Ereẓ* were not part of the official and regular studies of the academies.[109] The term *derek ereẓ* thus seems to apply only to the rules in Hilkot *Derek Ereẓ*, and not to the universal concepts concretized in laws of the Mishnah.

It remains true, nevertheless, that the universal concepts are a phase of *derek ereẓ*. They are classifications of matters that are also *derek ereẓ*. In an extra-mishnaic collection of rules and laws called *Tosefta Derek Ereẓ*, an entire chapter consists of laws of *'arayot* (incest, forbidden marriages), laws that are also found in the official texts.[110] *'Arayot*, a universal concept, hence constitutes a classification of matters designated also as *derek ereẓ*. We have called attention earlier to other passages in which the rabbis indicate that universal concepts are classifications under, or subconcepts of, *derek ereẓ*.

A law in the Mishnah or Talmud which is a concretization of a universal concept is also a concretization of *derek ereẓ*, but it is a halakah and not merely a guiding rule. Indeed, the Mishnah contains other halakot of *derek ereẓ*, as well. For example, a law with respect to *'ona'at debarim*, a concept of the fifth phase of *derek ereẓ*, is a mishnaic law, as we noticed above. We therefore must conclude again that there is no dichotomy between the laws of the Mishnah on the one hand, and concretizations of *derek ereẓ*, on the other. Many laws of the Mishnah are concretizations of *derek ereẓ*, and among such mishnaic laws are the concretizations of the universal concepts.

Is it possible to have awareness of morality and ethics without having an ultimate criterion for morality? Is it possible, in other words, to have an awareness of morality without recourse to a formal definition of morality? In this chapter we have shown that the rabbis had a most profound awareness of what is moral or ethical, that they even adumbrated the sphere of morality, and that all this was achieved without recourse to a formal definition or an ultimate criterion. It was achieved through a concept, that of *derek ereẓ*.

The concept of *derek ereẓ* gives to morality a scope and a range larger than that of any system of philosophic ethics. Included in that scope are not only the concepts of "crucial morality" but commonplace acts, and every possible occasion of moral significance.

Not contained in any formula, nor governed by any definition, the scope of rabbinic ethics and morality cannot be delimited.

Rabbinic morality is not simply a folk product. It is the product of the interaction between a society and its best minds, the product of the continuous interaction between the folk and the rabbis.

CHAPTER IV

The Experience of Worship

A. Berakah—An Act of Worship

At every turn, the rabbis saw manifestations of *middat raḥamim*,[1] God's love, and of *middat ha-din*,[2] God's justice. By means of these concepts and their subconcepts,[3] the rabbis interpreted the national catastrophes and calamities of their own times,[4] and events in the lives of individuals as well.[5] More illuminating, however, are the instances of God's love or of His justice to be found in rabbinic interpretations of the narratives of the Bible. There the rabbis not only add details, but often supply entire incidents or stories in order to make these concepts more vivid,[6] and—be it noted—also to emphasize God's love.[7] Through such interpretations of Scripture, the rabbis taught the folk at large to see manifestations of God's love and justice everywhere.

The concepts of God's love and justice are usually embedded in the interpretations. That is to say, when the rabbis interpret an event as a manifestation of God's love or of His justice, they seldom employ the conceptual term itself; rather, the concept is embodied in the interpretation. Various passages, for example, depict disasters that befell Israel as punishments of God: the first Exile, the scattering of the Ten Tribes, the destruction of the Temple, the degrading servitude to Rome.[8] In none of these passages does the conceptual term itself, *middat ha-din*, occur. Instead, the concept has been, so to speak, embedded in the interpretation.

What we have just described is a prime characteristic of a value concept. It is only a value concept that is usually embodied in an interpretation of an event, as we have observed in Chapter II. The value concept, since it is embodied in an event, is integral to the event; indeed, it integrates all the definite, concrete details of that event into a single, unitary entity. But the event, we must remember, has been interpreted by the value concept. When this takes place, the concept not only integrates the details of the event but gives them meaning, as well. An event embodying a value concept is a unitary entity fraught with significance.[9]

We can now classify the concepts of God's love and God's justice. They are value concepts, integrating happenings into unitary entities and endowing the integrated events with significance. When they interpret events they act very much in the same way as do the concepts of human morality, the subconcepts of *derek ereẓ*.

But the subconcepts of *derek ereẓ*, such as *gemilut ḥasadim* or *ẓedaḳah*, not only interpret events; they also possess a drive toward concretization of the concepts impelling a person to act.[10] This can hardly be the case, of course, with the concepts of God's love and justice. All that a person can do, apparently, is to interpret in their light events that have happened. The concepts of human morality seem to have, so far as human action is concerned, more vitality than do the concepts of God's love and of His justice.

A consideration of the main features of Jewish worship, however, tells another story. The concepts of God's love and God's justice utilize drives toward concretization, but in their own manner.

The simplest form of Jewish worship is a "short berakah"[11]—that is, any berakah in which reference is made to only a single matter.[12] "Blessed [or praised] art Thou, O Lord our God, King of the world, Who bringest forth bread from the earth"[13] is an example of a short berakah. Simple in form, it contains only the formula "Blessed art Thou, O Lord our God, King of the world" and an appositive clause in which reference is made to a single matter, bread. The berakot on other foods have the same pattern.[14]

A berakah by itself is merely a literary form. To be a genuine religious expression, to be worship, it must be stimulated by an occasion in the life of the individual. A berakah not called forth by an occasion, "an unnecessary berakah," is so far from being worship as to be stigmatized as the taking of God's name in vain.[15] Thus, if no bread is eaten, saying the berakah on the eating of bread is obviously uttering "an unnecessary berakah." On the other hand, when that berakah precedes the actual eating of a morsel of bread, its recitation constitutes true worship.[16] So intimately related is the occasion to the berakah that the specific character of the berakah most often corresponds to the occasion.

The recitation of the berakah and its occasion form a unitary entity, a total event or situation. When the berakah corresponds to the occasion, the berakah interprets the occasion; in that case, any irrelevant interruption by word or deed breaks the association between the interpretation and the occasion[17] and destroys the unitary entity. The halakah here guards against destroying what is not merely a unitary entity, but a value experience, for there are value concepts embedded in a berakah. Holding to our example, the bread assumes significance when we are conscious that it is a concretization of God's love—"Who bringest forth bread from the earth"—and this consciousness is deep enough to move us to an expression of gratitude to God, an expression that is a berakah, worship. The concepts of God's love and berakah have, so to speak, cut a unitary event out of the flow of daily life, an event which includes not only the reciting of the berakah but also ordinary acts, the breaking of bread,[18] the eating of the first morsel.[19] A commonplace thing and ordinary acts in daily life have now become a unitary entity full of significance.

Any valuational experience, as we have said, must be a unitary entity. Every berakah, of whatever type, must be an element in that entity. The berakah we have just discussed, and all the berakot of that type, are joined to commonplace things, to daily foods and to ordinary daily acts. Normal occurences, happenings of the now and the everyday, become occasions for worship.

A unitary entity charged with significance always bears the imprint of personality. (We came to this conclusion in an earlier work when we discussed the kinship between Haggadah and poetry.[20] A poem expresses an aesthetic insight of an individual, while a haggadic statement expresses a valuational insight of an individual; in both cases there is an expression of individuality, of personality.)[21] Now, we have just seen that when a berakah is recited, that berakah is an element in a unitary entity charged with significance. Here we have a unitary entity which not only "bears the imprint of personality," as in a haggadic statement, but which almost palpably molds and enlarges the individual.

Again we illustrate with the berakah on bread. To the individual who is about to recite that berakah, the bread represents a manifestation of God's love both for mankind in general and for himself in particular. Having naturally his own need in mind, he regards himself as a recipient of God's bounty and an object of God's love; nevertheless, he thanks God for His bounty to all mankind—"Who bringest forth bread from the earth." When the individual recites the berakah, therefore, he does so as a member of society. This is the view taken by R. Levi in a reason he gives for reciting a berakah of this type. Upon reciting the berakah, says R. Levi, the individual is permitted to have, as a member of society, what up to that moment had belonged solely to God. Before the berakah, "the earth is the Lord's and the fullness thereof" (Ps. 24:1), but after the berakah, "the earth hath He given to *the children of men*" (Ps. 115:16).[22]

As in all value experiences, the recitation of the berakah engages the personality of the individual, varying in depth of significance as individuals vary in depth of personality, and in accordance, too, with circumstances; now, however, the sheerly personal experience is enlarged by an awareness on the part of the individual that he is a member of society, and the personal experience thus becomes one with vast social import. Without minimizing the character of the occasion as a personal experience, the recitation of the berakah has the effect of bringing to consciousness society at large.

Everything associated with a berakah, as well as the berakah itself, is in the sphere of Halakah,[23] and the unitary entity characterized by the berakah on bread is an example of the creative power of that sphere. The berakah embodies the concept of God's love, of His universal love, in the appositive clause, "Who bringest forth bread from the earth," an idea reaffirmed in general terms in the First Berakah after the meal by the words, "Who feedest the whole world."[24] Now, the Haggadah as well teaches that "the Holy One Blessed be He feeds the whole world,"[25] and the appositive clause of the berakah on bread is thus but a more specific form of a haggadic teaching. Halakah, therefore—not only Haggadah—embodies value concepts and has to do with teachings and ideas. But Halakah does more than teach. Out of a commonplace event it makes an occasion for a personal experience of God's love, attaches to that experience social import, and provides expression for that experience in worship.

As a rule, berakot embody the concept of God's love, being expressions of gratitude for manifestations of that love. A berakah is also said, however, at the loss of a near relative (e.g., one's father),[26] at evil tidings,[27] at serious damage to one's property;[28] and this berakah, praising "the true Judge,"[29] embodies the concept of God's justice. A man who has so often seen manifestations of God's love must now see, in his personal tragedy and loss, a manifestation of God's justice; nor is that enough, but he must also thank and praise Him. "A man is duty bound to give thanks for the evil just as he gives thanks for the good. . . . Whatever be the measure He metes out to thee, be thou exceedingly thankful to Him."[30] This is a statement in the Mishnah. Another tannaitic source, after repeating the statement and enlarging upon it with an exhortation to be "beautiful in *pur'anut* (punishment)," adds that a man ought to rejoice in *yissurim* (chastisements) more than in "the good," for *yissurim* cause his sins to be forgiven.[31] The evil that befalls a man, it would seem, may be interpreted not only as *pur'anut*, punishment or retribution, but also as *yissurim*, chastisements sent by God out of love.[32]

The concepts of God's love and God's justice connote experience of God, and are thereby distinguished from the concepts of human love and human justice. Further, both the concept of God's love and that of His justice possess aspects which human love and human justice do not have. *Yissurim*, for example, may be regarded as aspects of God's love,[33] and vicarious atonement is one of the aspects, or subconcepts, of God's justice.[34]

At the same time, it is also true that there is little to distinguish the conceptual terms for God's justice and love from the conceptual terms for human justice and love. Literally, *middat ha-din* simply means "the quality of justice," and *middat raḥamim* "the quality of love," and it is only in usage that these terms are primarily associated with God's justice and with God's love;[35] indeed, occasionally the terms are used with respect to human justice[36] and to human love.[37] Even the faint linguistic distinction between the two sets of concepts is sometimes lacking, the single word *din* standing both for God's justice[38] and for human justice, and the single word *raḥamim* both for God's love and human love. *Din* and *raḥamim*, therefore, are not wholly to be distinguished from *middat ha-din* and *middat raḥamim.* But *din* and *raḥamim* are concepts which belong to the fourth phase of *derek ereẓ*, the phase of universal human morality, as we saw in the preceding chapter; if these concepts connote morality then so do *middat ha-din* and *middat raḥamim.*

The ways in which the rabbis depict God's love also indicate that for them it was a moral experience. They depict God's love as *ẓedaḳah* (charity, love) and *gemilut ḥasadim* (deeds of lovingkindness), and these concepts, again, belong to the fourth phase of *derek ereẓ*, the phase of universal human morality. According to a passage in the Talmud, God "did *ẓedaḳah*" to Israel in scattering them among the nations, for, being now scattered, they could not all be destroyed by any one nation;[39] whilst a passage in the Midrash has it that one-third of the day God "does *ẓedaḳah* and feeds and sustains and provides for the whole world,"[40] a statement more than reminiscent of the First Berakah after the meal. Similarly, acts of God told of in Genesis 3:21 and in Deuteronomy 34:6 are designated by the rabbis as *gemilut ḥasadim*, and in several berakot God is praised as *Gomel Ḥasadim*, or "he who does deeds of lovingkindness."[41] The rabbis regard *ẓedaḳah* and *gemilut ḥasadim*, we know, as elements of universal human morality; if they also employ these concepts in telling of God's love, it can be only because an event experienced as a manifestation of God's love was, for them, a moral experience.[42]

In a unitary entity characterized by a berakah, at least two concepts usually are concretized, namely, berakah and either the concept of God's love or, far less frequently, the concept of God's justice. Here the concepts are concretized in Halakah, and such concretizations are markedly different from concretizations in Haggadah. A happening may or may not prove to be a stimulus for a concretization of a concept in Haggadah; in Halakah, the stimulus (bread, for example) is a steadily repeated occasion for the concretization of the concepts of berakah and God's love. An interpretation in Haggadah does not call for an action; in the Halakah, the interpretation of the occasion, the berakah, often does call for an act, such as the eating of bread. In Haggadah, the statement embodying the concepts is itself the unitary entity, a literary entity; in Halakah, the statement embodying the concepts, the berakah, is itself only an element in the situation as a whole, and the unitary entity is not a literary but an experiential entity.

Of the two concepts embedded in an experiential entity characterized by a berakah, the concept of berakah alone possesses a genuine drive toward concretization. With respect to the concepts of God's love and His justice, a man can act only as an interpreter, designating an event or occasion as a manifestation either of God's love or else of His justice. Here, however, we have a unitary entity, and the berakah, the interpretation, is not separable from the occasion. When there is an occasion, the value concept of berakah impels a man to recite a berakah, just as on certain occasions the value concept of *ẓedaḳah* impels a man to an act of *ẓedaḳah*. But a berakah interprets an occasion to be a manifestation of God's love or of His justice. The drive toward concretization of the concept of berakah results, therefore, in steadily repeated interpretations of the concepts of God's love or justice—in what almost amounts to their steady concretizations.

Jewish worship, in its simplest form, is an element in a unitary entity consisting of a berakah and the occasion for reciting it. It is praise of God at the same time that there is an experience of God's love or, sometimes, of His justice—an experience which is akin to that of human love or justice and hence a moral experience. In that experience there is an awareness of the self as an object of God's love, but an awareness of the self that includes society as well.

B. The Role of Form in Worship—Birkat ha-Mazon

The Birkat ha-Mazon, grace after meals, consists of four berakot. "The order of the Birkat ha-Mazon is as follows: The First Berakah is Birkat ha-Zan ['Who feedest']; the Second is Birkat ha-'Areẓ ['the Land']; the Third is '[Who] buildest Jerusalem'; the Fourth is 'Who art good and doeth good.' "[43] Although cited in rabbinic literature, as in this baraita and elsewhere,[44] these berakot are not given there in full.[45] In the course of our discussion, therefore, we shall present or quote from these four berakot as they are given in *Siddur R. Saadia Gaon*,[46] "the oldest prayer book available to us."[47]

Akin to the berakah on the eating of bread which interprets a specific, concrete occasion, the First Berakah similarly interprets a specific occasion, a meal. "Blessed [or praised] art Thou, O Lord our God, King of the world, Who feedest [us and] the whole world with goodness, with grace, with lovingkindness and with mercy. Blessed [or praised] art Thou, O Lord, Who feedest all."[48] In this berakah, the food which has been eaten is taken to be a manifestation of God's lovingkindness, and once more a commonplace event has thus been invested with significance. But the berakah is, of course, more than just an interpretation of the meal: reciting the First Berakah after eating a meal is an act of worship; the meal has been the occasion and the stimulus for worship, and this is reflected in the interpretation of the meal as a manifestation of God's love. To put it differently, when the First Berakah is recited after eating, the meal and the recitation of the berakah constitute a unitary entity in time, and the meal, as the occasion for the berakah, is then an element in an integrated religious experience. By the same token, the recitation of the First Berakah is an expression, through worship, of the experience of God's love represented by the meal.

In this instance, too, it is the Halakah itself which indicates that we have to do with a unitary entity. The association between the meal and the Birkat ha-Mazon must not be broken. The Birkat ha-Mazon ought to be said at the place where one has eaten the meal.[49] A man who is about to leave the place where he has eaten in order to speak to a friend (even if it be no further than to the door), ought first to say the Birkat ha-Mazon.[50]

Primarily, the association is not between the meal and the entire Birkat ha-Mazon but, as we have just indicated, between the meal and the First Berakah. It is the First Berakah alone that actually corresponds to the occasion. Indeed, since the unitary entity of meal and berakah is an experiential entity, the meal stimulating a man to say a berakah in gratitude for it, the meal and any berakah called forth by it constitute a unitary entity. A shepherd by the name of Benjamin, before a scant meal of a piece of bread "wrapped around" (with some herbs possibly), said in vernacular Aramaic, "Blessed is the Master of this bread,"[51] and the Talmud declares that brief berakah to be an equivalent also of the First Berakah if said after the meal.[52] Benjamin's berakah is equivalent to the First Berakah because the one as well as the other is called forth by the meal and interprets it to be a manifestation of God's love.[53] Of course, there is also a marked difference between the two berakot. An individual reciting the First Berakah has in mind not himself alone but "the whole world,"[54] whereas there is no such enlargement of the self when he recites the shepherd's berakah.

Worship of the kind we have been describing is not possible without an occasion or stimulus. Such worship consists of two elements—a thing or an event experienced as a manifestation of God's love (or justice) and the expression of that experience in a berakah praising and thanking God. The berakah interprets the occasion, but it is not, so to say, an explanation; the recitation of the berakah is itself an element in the situation, giving it character. Here is an experiential, unitary entity, not two successive states of experience, and so the recitation of the berakah enhances and heightens the original apprehension of God's love touched off by the occasion. At the same time, through the recitation of the berakah, the very apprehension of the self is enlarged, and the individual has a sense of kinship with society, with the whole world. Worship is thus a moral experience not only because it is an experience of God's love or of His justice, but also because it engenders an awareness of, and a sense of kinship with, the whole world.[55]

The experiential entity characterized by the First Berakah is partly phenomenal and partly literary: the occasion is a phenomenon while the berakah is a literary form. Another literary form, often employed elsewhere in the liturgy, enables this original experience of worship to become an impetus in its own right to a further act of worship, the Second Berakah, and the religious experience represented in the latter, an impetus for still a third act of worship, the Third Berakah. An actual concrete experience of God's love, a phenomenal experience, here initiates the chain of religious experiences; it is now possible for the first act of worship to be an impetus to a second and, in turn, for the second, a nonphenomenal experience, to be an impetus to still another act of worship. Again, when a religious experience gives rise to another religious experience, we have a conceptual continuum. Since the initial experience was a concretization of God's love, the successive experiences in the chain must also be concretizations of God's love. An integral factor in an act of worship, this more inclusive form in addition helps to create successive acts of worship.

A prime characteristic of this more inclusive form is "the berakah which is joined to the immediately preceding berakah."[56] The

Second Berakah of the Birkat ha-Mazon is of that kind.[57] "We thank Thee, O Lord our God, because Thou didst give as a heritage unto us a desirable, good and ample Land [of Israel], a covenant and Torah, life and food; and for all these we thank Thee and bless [or, praise] Thy Name forever. Blessed art Thou, O Lord, for the Land and for the food."[58] No opening formula—"Blessed art Thou," etc.—marks this berakah, but only a closing formula, and that is the distinguishing feature of "a berakah which is joined to the immediately preceding berakah."[59] Some say that the closing formula of the "immediately preceding berakah" serves also "as a sort" of opening formula for the berakah which follows;[60] accordingly, "Blessed art Thou, O Lord, Who feedest all," the closing formula of the First Berakah, serves also as a sort of opening formula for the Second Berakah. These and other halakic details reflect an experience of worship more subtle than those we have already studied.

No concrete phenomenon or other vivid occasion touches off the Second Berakah; that is why it does not have an opening formula. Instead, it begins with a meditation. A meditation by itself, however, is hardly equivalent to a phenomenal stimulus. In order to become an experience of worship, the meditation must start with an impetus toward worship, and that impetus is supplied by the First Berakah. Concretized there are the concepts of God's love and berakah, and these concepts proceed to inform the meditation which follows. Nor do we have here a departure from other types of valuational experience. Every value experience is strongly affected by the one preceding it.[61] We can now see why the Second Berakah is "a berakah that is joined to the immediately preceding berakah," and how it is that the closing formula of the immediately preceding berakah can be regarded as a sort of opening formula for the Second Berakah.

A meditative experience of worship requires more of a person than a phenomenal experience of worship. A phenomenal experience of worship can be achieved even by a man untutored in Halakah—witness the brief berakah in the vernacular uttered by Benjamin the shepherd. When it comes to a meditative experience of worship, however, the guidance of the Halakah is indispensable, and so the rabbis have formulated a number of rules with respect to the Second Berakah. The Halakah indicates the subject of the meditation, namely, the land. Thanksgiving (הודאה) is to be said both at the beginning and at the end of the meditation,[62] obviously to ensure direction to the meditation. In this "berakah of the Land," a person ought to say the words "a desirable, good and ample Land,"[63] a phrase conveying the biblical delight in the land.[64] One authority teaches that the covenant (of Abraham) should be mentioned (for the covenant is linked with God's promise of the land);[65] another declares that Torah should be mentioned (for the Bible speaks of the land as reward for Torah).[66] In this wise does the Halakah endeavor to build up an apprehension of God's love as manifested in the heritage of the land.[67]

A general rule requires that the idea mentioned immediately preceding the closing formula be also contained in the formula itself;[68] in our case, and in most berakot, this rule simply requires that the closing formula refer to the subject of the meditation.[69] "Blessed art Thou, O Lord, for the Land and for the food."[70] The closing berakah thus both expresses and enhances the particular expression of God's love built up in the meditation. Meditation and berakah constitute a unitary entity, an experience achieved by the individual now in his role as one of the people of Israel.

Both the phenomenal and the meditative experiences of worship demand of the individual a deliberate focusing of the mind. But there were other factors, we must not forget, that encouraged and made possible this focusing of the mind. The rabbis and the people they taught were always eager to find fresh manifestations of God's love and God's justice. The concept of berakah had the effect of sensitizing the individual to such manifestations in his own life and so to see in them occasions for worship. In a phenomenal experience, to focus the mind, therefore, was simply to be aware of the occasion. In a meditative experience such as the Second Berakah, what corresponds to the occasion had to be built up, and hence required a greater mental effort; but here, too, the initial impetus had been supplied, after all, by the First Berakah.

The Third Berakah is likewise a meditative experience developed in accordance with the Halakah. A person must not fail to include the phrase "the kingship of the house of David."[71] On the opening and closing phrases, there are various opinions. R. Sheshet says, "If he begins with 'Have mercy upon Israel, Thy people,' he closes with '[Who] savest Israel,' and if he begins with 'Have mercy upon Jerusalem,' he closes with '[Who] buildest Jerusalem' "; while R. Naḥman says, "Even if he begins with 'Have mercy upon Israel,' he closes with '[Who] buildest Jerusalem.' "[72] As support, R. Naḥman cites and interprets Psalm 147:2; [when] "the Lord doth build up Jerusalem, He gathereth together the dispersed of Israel."[73] The Palestinian version began with "O comfort us," and closed with "[Who] comfortest His people in the building of Jerusalem."[74] The full text of the Third Berakah in Saadia's *Siddur* reads: "Have mercy, O Lord our God, upon us, upon Israel, Thy people, and upon Jerusalem, Thy city, and upon Thy Temple, and upon Thy dwelling place, and upon Zion, the abiding place of Thy glory, and upon the great and holy house that was called by Thine own Name; and mayest Thou restore the kingship of the house of David to its place in our days, and build Jerusalem speedily. Blessed art Thou, O Lord, [Who] buildest Jerusalem. Amen."[75]

Does not this entire berakah seem to contradict what we know about the basic character of a berakah? We have recognized that a berakah is an expression of gratitude for a manifestation of God's love. Indeed, the meditation in the Second Berakah explicitly begins with thanksgiving for a specific manifestation of God's love. In contrast, the meditation in the Third Berakah seems hardly to be a meditation at all. It begins with such phrases as "have mercy," or "O comfort us"; that is to say, it begins with a supplication or petition, *baḳḳashah.*[76] Surely a supplication is not equivalent to a meditation of thanksgiving. But there are also other peculiarities. The closing formula, the berakah itself, is always an affirmation, and so it is here. But how can a petition lead directly to an affirmation? Further, the affirmation here is in the present tense, and this is true of every version—"[Who] buildest Jerusalem," "[Who] savest Israel," "[Who] comfortest." How can a petition, necessarily referring to the future, close with a berakah referring to the present?

What appear to be peculiarities in this berakah, however, are really the characteristics of a special type of berakah, other examples of which are found in the 'Amidah. The supplication has for its theme the days of the Messiah, the future era when "the kingship of the house of David" will be restored, when Jerusalem and the Temple will be rebuilt, when "the dispersed of Israel will be gathered together." It is this theme that marks off this berakah as belonging to a special type. As we have concluded elsewhere, the concept of the days of the Messiah and the other concepts of the hereafter associated with it are not pure value concepts but rabbinic dogmas.[77] They possess a degree of specificity which the value concepts, being indeterminate, do not have: A value concept is only suggestive or connotative, whereas the rabbinic dogmas point to specific events:[78] in the case of the days of the Messiah, to the restoration of the house of David, to the ingathering of the Diaspora, and to the building of Jerusalem. The petition in the Third Berakah, then, has to do with a rabbinic dogma. It is a petition concerning an event believed to be a future certainty and a supplication that this event take place "in our days."

But the petition is also informed by a value concept, the concept of *'emunah*. "*'Emunah* has the connotation of general faith or trust in God, general in the sense that it does not necessarily imply reliance on God for security or personal welfare."[79] Often such trust in God is related to faith in His promise or word.[80] Now the theme of the petition is a preordained event, a promise of God; hence dwelling upon that event evokes *'emunah*, complete, unbounded trust in God, a trust so unaffected by present circumstances as to create a sense of the promise being fulfilled "in our days." The situation has thus a meditative aspect; that is why it closes with "Who builds Jerusalem" in the present tense, a phrase affirming and enhancing something quite like a meditative experience, an "as if" experience.

The rabbis link *'emunah* with berakot of this type, including one which is practically identical with the Third Berakah of the Birkat ha-Mazon in a comment on Psalm 31:24.[81] They extol Israel by applying to them the text, "the Lord preserveth the faithful (*'emunim*)." For they (i.e., the people of Israel) say, "Blessed [art Thou, O Lord] Who quickenest the dead," though the resurrection of the dead has not yet come; they say, "Redeemer of Israel," though they are not yet redeemed; they say, "Blessed [art Thou, O Lord,] Who buildest Jerusalem," though Jerusalem is not yet built. The Holy One Blessed be He says, "Israel was redeemed for only a little while and then went back into servitude, and [yet] they have faith [*ma'aminim*] in Me that I shall redeem them in a time to come!"

The Third Berakah is an experiential entity which embodies a number of concepts. It owes its impetus to the Second Berakah,[82] and hence, like that berakah, it embodies the concept of God's love. Unlike the Second Berakah, however, the specific manifestation of God's love is something petitioned for rather than something which has occurred, and the petition consists in a plea for the restoration of the house of David and for the building of Jerusalem, specific events summed up in the concept of the days of the Messiah. Since those events are matters of dogma and hence felt to be preordained events, the thought of them evokes trust in God, *'emunah*, an unbounded trust that finally gives the individual the assurance that the events are indeed taking place in the present. At the end, when gratitude is uttered in the closing berakah for the building of Jerusalem, the entire berakah, petition and all, has the vividness of a meditative experience; once more we see that the meditation or the occasion and their expression in a berakah are not successive states but constitute a unitary entity. Of course, being a unitary entity, the experience both affects and is affected by the personality of the individual, although now it is an experience of the individual in his role as a member or representative of the people of Israel.

In the form characterized by "the berakah which is joined to the immediately preceding berakah," we have a dynamic form which makes it possible for an impetus to be given toward a new meditation, that is, toward a new experiential entity. It is an elastic form. Since it is a form that consists of a series of unitary entities, any one of which, once achieved, is complete in itself, the series may close with any new entity, and yet there need be no given limit to the successive experiences. Traditions may well differ, therefore, as to the closing of a series of this kind, and there are indeed two such differing traditions regarding the closing of the Birkat ha-Mazon. At one time, undoubtedly, the Birkat ha-Mazon closed with the Third Berakah, for early tannaitic sources speak of three berakot after a meal.[83] Other tannaitic statements tell also of a Fourth Berakah[84] which, apparently beginning with a meditation[85] and closing with "Who hath bestowed upon us all good,"[86] was thus a berakah that was "joined to the immediately preceding berakah."[87] Since the closing formula embodied the concept of God's love, this berakah, as we should expect, held to the conceptual continuum.

The Halakah did establish a Fourth Berakah, not one "which is joined to the immediately preceding berakah," but one which has an opening formula: "Blessed art Thou, O Lord our God, King of the world, O God, our Father, our King, our Creator, our Redeemer, O King Who art good and doeth good, Who many a time, day by day, doeth good unto us, and Who wilt ever bestow upon us grace and lovingkindness and relief and mercy and all good."[88] A berakah with an opening formula is usually related to an occasion of some kind and, according to both the Jerusalem and the Babylonian Talmud, this berakah was established when "the slain of Bettar," after the disastrous revolt of Bar Kokeba, were permitted to be buried.[89] The berakah as established, Albeck points out, is similar to the one on hearing good tidings;[90] it also contains, however, phrases from the original version of the Fourth Berakah ("wilt bestow") and from the First Berakah ("grace, lovingkindness, mercy"). In any case, however the berakah arose, it is an acknowledgment of God's love solely in general terms.[91]

We can discern now another feature of the form we have been studying. Under special circumstances it permits deviations or departures from the pattern. Unlike the Second and Third Berakot, the Fourth Berakah, as established by the Halakah, has no meditation, and yet the experiential character of the pattern as a whole is not impaired. Each an embodiment of the concept of God's love, the first three berakot have a cumulative effect, an effect which, in this instance, enables the Fourth Berakah to be the culmination of the preceding berakot. The impact of the first three berakot takes the place of a meditation, as it were, and the Fourth Berakah, as finally established, is the response to that impact. The Fourth Berakah is truly the climax of the Birkat ha-Mazon, an experience of worship achieved as the result of preceding acts of worship, a profound acknowledgment of God's love and mercy in themselves rather than as manifested in any specific thing or manner.[92]

Characterized by the rabbis as "the berakah which is joined to the immediately preceding berakah," the form exemplified by the Birkat ha-Mazon allows the individual to achieve successive experiences of worship. The series begins with a berakah called forth by a specific manifestation of God's love, a phenomenal experience which the berakah both interprets and enhances, the occasion for the berakah and the berakah itself being a unitary experiential entity. This experience of worship imparts an impetus toward a new experiential entity; a nonphenomenal, meditative experience of God's love, built up in accordance with Halakah and having its own response of gratitude in a berakah. In the Birkat ha-Mazon, the Second Berakah, in its turn, imparts an impetus toward another meditative experience of worship, and there are still longer chains of successive meditative experiences of this kind in the liturgy. Since every experience in the series, once achieved, is complete in itself, the series may close with any new entity; in other words, the form as such sets no limit to the series. On the other hand, although each experiential entity is a unit in itself, the successive berakot do have a cumulative effect, so that when a berakah, under special circumstances, deviates from the form, the cumulative effect of the preceding berakot overcomes the deviation and maintains unimpaired the experiential character of the pattern as a whole. An example is the manner in which the cumulative effect of the preceding berakot overcomes the deviation of the Fourth Berakah of the Birkat ha-Mazon.[93]

C. The Shema'—Worship, Commitment, and Study

We have thus far discussed berakot, the initial occasions for which are phenomenal experiences. However, the occasion for a berakah may also be a more complex experience. Further, there is a liturgical act which is at once worship, self-commitment, and study. These features of worship and liturgy are to be found in the Ḳeri'at Shema' and its berakot.

Although the Shema' is composed of two separate passages from Deuteronomy (6:4–9 and 11:13–21) and, following them, a third from Numbers (15:37–41), the proper recitation of the Shema', Ḳeri'at Shema', makes of those three passages a unitary entity. When the Shema' is recited, the several passages in their prescribed order convey certain logically related commitments and so the passages constitute, in that respect, a logical unit. Doubtless because the Shema' was taken to be a logical unit, a person reciting it was not permitted to reverse the order of the passages, according to the Tosefta.[94] But the Shema' is a unitary entity not alone by virtue of possessing an internal unity. Preceded and followed by berakot, it is nevertheless, authorities say, independent of these berakot.[95] Despite its position in the liturgy, the Shema' is thus held to be a complete entity in its own right.

The first section of the Shema' (Deut. 6:4–9) has to do with the acceptance upon oneself of the kingship of God, and the second section (Deut. 11:13–21) with commitment to the mizwot. In the sequence of these passages as recited in the Ḳeri'at Shema', R. Joshua b. Ḳorḥah sees a logical relationship: "so that a person shall first accept upon himself the yoke of the kingship of Heaven [God], and after that accept upon himself the yoke of mizwot."[96] Acceptance of the kingship of God takes place when reciting the first verse of the first section: "Hear, O Israel, the Lord our God, the Lord is One," a verse which implies also the negation or exclusion of idolatry (*'abodah zarah*);[97] acceptance of "the yoke of mizwot" takes place when reciting the first verse of the second section: "And it shall come to pass if ye shall hearken diligently unto My commandments which I command you this day."[98] Commitment to God's commandments necessarily must follow, and not precede, acceptance of God's sovereignty. In the opinion of R. Simeon b. Yoḥai, the sequence of the passages in the Shema' is due to another series of commitments, again of a necessarily successive character, namely, commitments to learn Torah, to teach it, and to practice it.[99] According to the Talmud, R. Simeon agrees with R. Joshua but merely offers an additional reason for the sequence.[100] The recitation of the Shema' hence consists of accepting commitments which logically follow upon each other, the logical coherence of the commitments making of the recitation a single act, a unitary entity.

Ḳeri'at Shema' is a liturgical act in which the acceptance of God's kingship is followed by the commitment to the mizwot. The rabbis stress this conjunction between the two commitments not only with respect to Ḳeri'at Shema', however, but when interpreting several other biblical passages. Thus, in an interpretation of the Ten Commandments, they emphasize the successive character of the two commitments by a parable telling of a king of flesh and blood who, upon entering a province, was advised by his attendants to issue decrees to the people but who refused to do so until the people should accept his kingship. " 'For if they will not accept my kingship they will not accept my decrees'. Likewise, God said to Israel: 'I am the Lord thy God, Who brought thee out of the land of Egypt. . . . Thou shalt have no other gods' [Exod. 20:2–3]. He said to them, 'I am He Whose kingship you accepted upon yourselves in Egypt'; [and when] they said, 'Yes,' He continued, 'Now just as you accepted My kingship upon yourselves, accept [now] My decrees'— 'Thou shalt have no other gods before Me' [*ibid.*]."[101] Following upon this interpretation is a similar one by R. Simeon b. Yoḥai on a different passage: " 'I am the Lord your God,' which is said further on [Lev. 18:2] means: 'I am He Whose kingship you accepted upon yourselves at Sinai'; [and when] they said, 'Yes, yes,' He continued, 'You have accepted My kingship, accept [now] My decrees—'After the doings of the land of Egypt', etc. [*ibid.*, v.3]."[102] R. Simeon's teaching here, incidentally, is patently at one with R. Joshua's teaching on the Shema'.

Both *malkut Shamayim*, the kingship of God, and miẓwot, commandments of God, since they convey significance, are value concepts. Now, value concepts have an organismic and not a logical coherence; a value concept depends for its meaning upon the integrated value complex as a whole, and its idea content expands and grows as it interweaves with the other value concepts. Concepts that are logically related are defined concepts, whereas abstract value concepts are indeterminate and merely connotative.[103] To all this *malkut Shamayim* and miẓwot prove to be no real exception, notwithstanding the logical coherence of the passages of the Shema', for the two concepts are not permanently interlocked. Each of them combines and interweaves with the other value concepts so vividly, indeed, as to illustrate the very process of organismic integration.[104] True, there are occasions which exhibit a logical relation between value concepts, but important as these occasions are, they are too few to imperil the general organismic process.[105]

To accept the kingship of God is to achieve a meditative experience of God. A meditative religious experience, one that does not arise out of an actual phenomenal occasion is, we recognized, achieved by most men only with the aid of halakic rules or guides. Thus, after the first verse of the Shema' a response is inserted, an early practice surely, since in both the Mishnah and the Tosefta it appears as the established rule.[106] Evidently consisting originally of the phrase "Blessed is His glorious Name forever" (after Ps. 72:19), Finkelstein has pointed out, the response was changed to "Blessed is the Name of His glorious Kingship forever" in order, as Finkelstein says, "to emphasize the Kingship of God."[107] There are also instructions regarding the utterance of the first verse of the Shema', the declaration or affirmation of God's kingship. The last word in the affirmation, *'ehad* (אחד), is to be lengthened[108] so as to permit the utterance to be a meditative experience,[109] and a rule given by R. Ḥiyya bar 'Abba indicates the character of that experience. When R. Ḥiyya noticed that R. Jeremiah greatly prolonged the word, he said, "When you have made Him King above and below and in the four winds [i.e., directions] of heaven, you need do no more."[110] In the Yerushalmi, the same incident is reported with R. Ze'ira in place of R. Ḥiyya, and the rule there says that it is sufficient "to make Him King in heaven and on earth and in the four winds of the world."[111]

Acceptance of *malkut Shamayim*, the kingship of God, is the end, the rules being but helpful guides in achieving this experience. It was the custom of the men of Jericho to omit the response after saying the first verse of the Shema', according to R. Judah, and the rabbis did not prohibit their doing so.[112] Had the acceptance of *malkut Shamayim* depended on the insertion of the response, it is inconceivable that the rabbis would have permitted them to omit it. Apparently the men of Jericho had been accustomed to accept God's kingship in Ḳeri'at Shema', doubtless from early times, without inserting the response, and the rabbis were aware of that. Similarly, R. Jeremiah obviously had an approach of his own with respect to the meditative experience different from that of R. Ḥiyya.[113]

Experience of God is never raw experience but an experience mediated by a concept. In the case of a berakah, the mediating concept is usually *middat raḥamim*, God's love. Here the concept is *malkut Shamayim*, and its scope is larger than that of *middat raḥamim*. Whereas the concept of God's love is solely interpretive, endowing an event or occasion with significance, the significance achieved in accepting *malkut Shamayim* goes beyond interpretation of this or that event to an interpretation of the world as a whole. Acceptance of *malkut Shamayim* usually consists in making "Him King in heaven and on earth and in the four directions of the world." The individual who accepts God's kingship thus interprets the world itself to be a manifestation of that kingship. This interpretive act is also a commitment. The individual commits himself to loyalty and obedience, loyalty implying a negation of idolatry[114] and obedience implying a readiness to observe the miẓwot or commandments.[115] In this entire experience, the individual acts both on his own private behalf and, at the same time, as a representative of the world.

Acceptance of miẓwot in this commitment is but implied. That is why the rabbis teach that another commitment ought to follow in which there is explicit acceptance of "the yoke of miẓwot." In the priests' service in the Temple, the commitments were made still more explicit. Preceding the recitation of the three sections of the Shema' was the recitation of the Ten Commandments, says a mishnah formulated toward the close of the Temple era;[116] and the Ten Commandments, in addition to representing the miẓwot in their own right, also represent, in the tannaitic tradition, Israel's acceptance at that cataclysmic moment in their history of the same commitments as those contained in the Shema'.[117] It was felt, indeed, that the reading of the Ten Commandments together with the Shema' ought to be the daily practice of the people at large,[118] and in fact there were several attempts to establish such a practice[119] during the amoraic period in Babylon, one being as late as in the generation of R. 'Ashi. The desire not to seem to give support to sectarians prevailed, however, for it was the ardent contention of sectarians that the Ten Commandments alone were given to Moses on Sinai;[120] later, this precedent prevailed, too, against all the Babylonian attempts to attach the Ten Commandments to the Shema'.[121] But the tradition that the Ten Commandments made explicit what was implicit in the Shema' was maintained, nevertheless. R. Ba' declares in a halakic context that the Ten Commandments are integral to the Shema',[122] containing the same theme;[123] and R. Levi, interpreting the sections of the Shema' haggadically, shows how they contain (or hint at) every one of the Ten Commandments.[124]

Complete devotion of the mind and heart, unwavering focusing of attention, are required if the commitments of the Shema' in all the richness of their connotations are to be matters of genuine experience. Some authorities insist that the whole Shema' be recited with this kind of sustained concentration, else it must be repeated. "He that reads the Shema' must direct his heart—שיכוין את לבו."[125] On the other hand, R. Me'ir, obviously reckoning with the powers of the ordinary man, declares that only the first verse of the Shema' need be recited with "direction of the heart—כוונת הלב," and this rule became the final halakah.[126] Naturally, the rest of the Shema', too, even according to the least demanding view, must not be read mechanically.[127]

We have tried to suggest by words like "attention," "devotion," and "concentration" something of what the rabbis mean in this connection by the term *kawwanah*, a word just quoted both in verbal and nominal forms.[128] In the context here, *kawwanah* refers to the great commitments and inward experience in Ḳeri'at Shema', and elsewhere it similarly refers to profound inward experiences. But it also occurs in other discussions by the rabbis on the Shema', and there it is used in a more limited sense, namely, in the sense of one's being aware during the recital of the Shema' that he is observing a miẓwah.[129] The concept of *kawwanah* thus possesses at least two phases.[130] We shall accord it fuller consideration in due course.

The inward experience in Ḳeri'at Shema' is an experience of God. As in manifestations of *middat raḥamim* and *middat ha-din*, the experience of God here, too, is brought to man through the medium of a concept, the concept of *malkut Shamayim*. The concept does not intervene between God and man; it merely canalizes the experience of God, enabling that experience now to have the whole wide world for its setting and making the individual himself conscious of a cosmic status and of a high, indeed the highest duty. In other words, here the experience of God is at once man's experience of God's kingship, his awareness of God's kingdom, and his apperception of his own role in that kingdom. All these things are accomplished when a man "directs his heart" in reciting the Shema'.

Ḳeri'at Shema', like a berakah, is worship; in fact, when the rabbis characterize Ḳeri'at Shema' as worship, they do so by employing the same verse (Exod. 23:25)[131] by which they characterize a berakah as worship.[132] In the case of a berakah we found that an experience of worship is a unitary entity in which there is experience of God. These are also the characteristics of Ḳeri'at Shema'. Acceptance of *malkut Shamayim* is an experience of God, and this experience is achieved in the recital of discrete passages of the Bible that in the Shema' are felt to be logically related and sensed as elements of a unitary entity.[133]

Besides being a liturgical act, Ḳeri'at Shema' is study of Torah, and this function of Ḳeri'at Shema' is stressed no less than its liturgical function. The term Ḳeri'at Shema' itself indicates that the recital of the Shema' is the study or reading of Scripture, for the root קרא refers specifically to scriptural study.[134] By reciting the Shema' a man fulfills the minimum that is required by the duty to study Torah.[135] A man who does no more than recite Ḳeri'at Shema' morning and evening, says R. Joḥanan in the name of R. Simeon b. Yoḥai, already fulfills the charge, "This Book of the Torah shall not depart out of thy mouth, but thou shalt meditate therein day and night" (Josh. 1:8).[136] Because the study of Torah and Ḳeri'at Shema' are thus of a piece—"one matter," as Ginzberg puts it—the rabbis interpret "and ye shall teach them [to] your children" to refer to Ḳeri'at Shema'.[137] Again, in another discussion, Ḳeri'at Shema' is not only identified as study of Torah but both are put on the same plane, these ideas being needed to account for R. Simeon b. Yoḥai's practice of not interrupting his study even for Ḳeri'at Shema'.[138] This was a divergence from the general rule, but that rule itself emphasizes Ḳeri'at Shema' as study of Torah. When the rabbis say that it is an obligation upon each individual to recite the Shema' "with his own mouth," the basis of that obligation is study of Torah.[139]

The dual function of Ḳeri'at Shema' is an instance of organismic thought in the Halakah. As a liturgical act, Ḳeri'at Shema' embodies the concept of *malkut Shamayim*, whereas as recital of Scripture it embodies the concept of *talmud Torah*. Neither function is an alternative function; that is why the berakah preceding and anticipating the Shema' refers to both functions of the Shema' and embodies both concepts.[140] Actually, Ḳeri'at Shema' itself embodies not only these concepts but others, among them the concept of miẓwot, and is thus a halakic example of how a number of value concepts may be combined in a single act. Elsewhere we saw that this feature of organismic thought is typical of the Haggadah,[141] and earlier in this chapter we found it also to be a characteristic of all berakot (p. 68).[142]

In organismic thought, the same situation may be interpreted in various ways and this occurs when a situation is interpreted by different value concepts.[143] Further, a situation embodying several value concepts may give rise to various interpretations, the interpretation now depending upon the emphasis placed on one rather than on another of these concepts.[144] This characteristic of organismic thought is not confined to Haggadah but is to be found in Halakah as well. It is exhibited by halakic discussions or statements bearing on mishnaic rules with respect to the Shema', rules telling when the period for recital begins in the evening[145] and when in the morning.[146] In one such discussion, it is assumed that the Shema' is recited because it is study of Torah. "Why are these two passages recited every day?" asks the Yerushalmi.[147] Although referring to the Shema', the Yerushalmi poses the problem of "these two passages" as if they were discrete passages and quite as if other passages might not be recited instead;[148] the concept implicit here, therefore, is not acceptance of *malkut Shamayim* but study of Torah. R. Simon's reply, "Because they [the two passages] contain [speak of] 'lying down' and 'rising up,' "[149] likewise relates to study of Torah. The verses to which he points, Deuteronomy 6:7 and 11:19, enjoin study of Torah, to be engaged in "when thou liest down and when thou risest up," that is, at night and at dawn,[150] every day. The time for reciting the Shema' is, then, in this statement directly associated with study of Torah. Other authorities, however, associate the time for reciting the Shema' in the morning with the acceptance of *malkut Shamayim*. By saying the 'Amidah after Ḳeri'at Shema', they teach, a man thus first accepts God's kingship and then stands in prayer, and thus also, since the Shema' is to be recited at dawn, the 'Amidah will be said after dawn, which is proper.[151]

Emphasis on one concept rather than on another may, in Halakah, make for divergence in practice. R. Simeon b. Yoḥai's practice, already mentioned, is a case in point. When he was engaged in study, he did not interrupt it even for Ḳeri'at Shema' because, the explanation is, Ḳeri'at Shema', too, is study of Torah.[152] The emphasis on Ḳeri'at Shema' as study of Torah made, in this instance, for a divergence from the general practice.

Ḳeri'at Shema' has, then, a dual character, being both an act of worship and study of Torah. It could not have this dual character were the proper study of Torah in general solely an intellectual activity.

"Just as the 'Abodah of the altar is called 'abodah, so is Study [of Torah] called 'abodah."[153] By characterizing study of Torah as 'abodah, worship,[154] the rabbis are saying that the proper study of Torah is a mystical experience, an experience wherein there is felt to be a manifestation of God in some manner. What this experience ought to be is made explicit in a comment on the words, "*This day* they came into the wilderness of Sinai [Exod. 19:1]" (emphasis supplied). "When you study Torah, do not regard them [the words of the Torah] as old but as though [the] Torah were given you this day."[155] Similarly: " 'All the statutes and the ordinances which I set before you *this day*' [Deut. 11:32]—let them be as beloved of you as though you received them from Mount Sinai this day, be as conversant with them as though you heard them this day."[156] These statements are not just exhortations. If study of Torah is indeed 'abodah, then the person who is studying the laws of the Torah has an experience akin to that of hearing them from God here and now, an experience as though he is receiving those laws "this very day." The phrase "this day" in Deuteronomy 6:6 again conveys to the rabbis the same message. That verse—"and these words which I command thee this day"—is interpreted to mean that they ("these words") must not be regarded as an old edict which no one minds, but as a new one which everyone is eager to read.[157] Since each edict or law is a unitary entity, the study of Torah as an act of worship may consist of the study of one law or of many.

In study of Torah as worship, a dogma practically loses its character as dogma and becomes, instead, a personal experience. The dogma is *mattan Torah*,[158] now so transformed that it can be referred to only by phrases like "as though you received" or "as though you heard." We called attention to such transformations of dogma when we discussed the Birkat ha-Mazon, and we shall take note of further instances in subsequent discussions.

Ḳeri'at Shema' is a call and a response whereby Israel can testify that God alone is King.[159] That is how ענה בי in Micah 6:3 is interpreted in a midrash at the beginning of a passage found in a number of sources. " 'O My people, what have I done unto thee? And wherein have I wearied thee? Testify for Me [ענה בי]'—said R. 'Aḥa': Testify for Me and receive reward, but if you will not testify you will be punished."[160] Further on in the same passage is another, closely related midrash on the same verse, Micah 6:3, in which Ḳeri'at Shema' is designated as God's edict. " 'And wherein have I wearied thee?'—[It may be compared] to a king who sent his edict [פרוסדוגמא] to a province. What did the people of the province do? They stood on their feet and uncovered their heads, and read it with awe and with fear, with trembling and with agitation. [But] thus did the Holy One blessed be He say to Israel: This Ḳeri'at' Shema' is My edict [פרוסדיגמא]; I did not cause you to be wearied, and I did not tell you to read it standing on your feet and with uncovered heads, but 'when thou sittest in thy house, and when thou walkest in the way' [Deut. 6:7]."[161] This midrash is quoted in *Seder R. Amram Gaon*, and the Gaon prefaced it with the statement, "Every time a man recites the Shema' he ought to regard it as a new edict —כפרוזדגמא חדתא."[162] But in what sense can Ḳeri'at Shema' be characterized as an edict? Furthermore, what are the words in Micah 6:3 which can be taken to mean that the verse refers to Ḳeri'at Shema'? We need only continue with the verse being interpreted, however, to recognize that the edict is "testify for Me" and that it refers to the call in Ḳeri'at Shema' to testify to God's kingship. By the same token, the words "testify for Me" are taken to mean that the verse refers to Ḳeri'at Shema'.

Study of Torah is itself an act of worship. Only if this is recognized can the Ḳeri'at Shema' as an act of worship be accounted for. Only because the Ḳeri'at Shema' is really a special instance of the study of Torah can the particular act of worship take place which constitutes compliance with the edict contained in the Shema'.[163]

Several rabbinic sources indicate, it seems to us, that acceptance of *malkut Shamayim* through study of Torah was not limited to Ḳeri'at Shema'. A tannaitic source teaches that the words of the Torah as a whole can lead the individual to accept upon himself the kingship of Heaven, if they are studied and reflected upon. Commenting on Deuteronomy 32:29, the Sifre says: "Had Israel reflected upon [נסתכלו] the words of the Torah that was given them, no nation or kingdom would have had dominion over them. And what did it say to them? Accept upon yourselves the yoke of the kingship of Heaven, and exceed [הכריעו] one another in fear of Heaven, and act toward one another with deeds of lovingkindness."[164]

All of the charges here are directed to the individual, as is evident specifically in the last two; all of them must represent ideals and reflect practices of the rabbis' own day. Now, how does the Torah admonish the individual to be God-fearing and to engage in deeds of lovingkindness? Obviously through the medium of its texts, which the individual is bidden to reflect upon, that he may draw forth from them their full implication. This must also be the way, therefore, in which the individual is to carry out the behest to accept upon himself the yoke of the kingship of Heaven. He is to do so as he recites a text which teaches or implies upon reflection acceptance of *malkut Shamayim*. The scholars were, of course, better qualified and also had more occasion to identify such texts than the folk in general. A passage in praise of the learned links their acceptance of *malkut Shamayim* with their daily study of Torah.[165]

We saw above that, according to the rabbis, other scriptural passages besides Ḳeri'at Shema' refer to the acceptance of *malkut Shamayim* and commitment to the miẓwot. These passages are the Ten Commandments (Exod. 20:2 ff.) and Leviticus 18:2 ff.[166] Exodus 20:2–3 is interpreted as follows: "He [God] said to them [Israel], 'I am He Whose Kingship you accepted upon yourselves in Egypt;' [and when] they said, 'Yes,' He continued, 'Now, just as you accepted My Kingship upon yourselves, accept [now] My decrees.' " A very similar interpretation is given by R. Simeon b. Yoḥai to Leviticus 18:2–3. Most likely these interpretations are projections in Haggadah of the daily acceptance of *malkut Shamayim* through Ḳeri'at Shema'; at the same time, however, the scriptural passages so interpreted may well have taught acceptance of *malkut Shamayim* and commitment to the miẓwot here and now. Certainly the Ten Commandments carried such an implication. Coupling the first statement there—"I am the Lord thy God"—with the third commandment, the rabbis teach that he who is accustomed to swear in vain or falsely does not accept upon himself the full kingship of God (מלכות שמים שלמה), and he who is not thus accustomed does accept upon himself the full kingship of God.[167] Indeed, the tradition persisted that the Ten Commandments contained the same themes as the Ḳeri'at Shema', a tradition probably going back to the priests' service in the Temple where the Ten Commandments were recited preceding the Ḳeri'at Shema'.[168]

Not only the Shema' and the Ten Commandments referred, in accordance with rabbinic interpretation, to the acceptance of *malkut Shamayim* and commitment to the miẓwot, but other scriptural texts as well. This is borne out by R. Simeon b. Yoḥai's interpretation of Leviticus 18:2–3. The Sifre seems to indicate that the scholars, at least, sought out texts of that kind, and that these texts, "when reflected upon," gave them additional opportunities to accept *malkut Shamayim* and to commit themselves to the miẓwot.

D. The Berakot of the Shema'

In the morning liturgy the berakah immediately preceding the Shema' begins as follows: "With abounding love hast Thou loved us, O Lord our God. Great and exceeding compassion hast Thou had for us. O our Father, our King, for our father's sake, who trusted in Thee, and whom Thou didst teach the statutes of life, be also gracious to us and teach us."[169] In *Siddur R. Saadia Gaon* the text is slightly different, but there, too, the idea is expressed that God has loved us and has had compassion for us "and taught us the statutes of life," the statement closing with the plea that He continue in this wise to be gracious to us.[170]

This berakah, second in the order of the berakot which precede the Shema', is called in the Babli (the Babylonian Talmud), because of the opening words, 'Ahabah Rabbah.[171] The Yerushalmi, however, calls it Birkat Torah.[172] That name, according to Elbogen, corresponds with the content of the berakah which, he says, consists of thanksgiving for the giving of Torah.[173] But the berakah takes for granted that God gave the Torah. The concept embedded in the berakah is study of Torah, not the giving of Torah, the thought being that God teaches us now, and at all times, by means of the words of the Torah and that the very understanding of the Torah is a gracious gift from God. When we study Torah, and understand what we study, it is God himself Who is our Teacher: "Thou didst teach the statutes of life"; "Be gracious to us and teach us"; and further on, "Enlighten our eyes in Thy Torah, and let our hearts cleave to thy miẓwot."[174] When we study and acquire knowledge of Torah, therefore, we are the objects of God's "abounding love." Precisely the same idea is expressed in the parallel berakah said before the Shema' in the evening: "With everlasting love Thou hast loved the house of Israel, Thy people; Torah and miẓwot, statutes and judgments hast Thou taught us."[175] In each case, the berakah immediately before the Shema' begins with giving thanks to God for teaching us Torah and for the knowledge gained through study, both of which are felt to be manifestations of God's love.[176] Anticipating the recital of the Shema', this section of the berakah stresses that aspect of Ḳeri'at Shema' which constitutes study of Torah.

A statement in 'Ahabah Rabbah also anticipates the recital of the Shema' as an acknowledgment of *malkut Shamayim*. Our version of that statement amplifies slightly the one in *Siddur R. Saadia Gaon*, which reads: כי בנו בחרת מכל עם ולשון וקרבתנו לשמך להודות לך וליחדך.[177] Let us consider, for a moment, the last phrase of this statement. Elsewhere we have demonstrated that מודים אנחנו לך in the 'Amidah refers to the acknowledgment of God, and that this phrase is linked in rabbinic literature with the acceptance of *malkut Shamayim*;[178] moreover, the two ideas are explicitly linked in the long berakah after the Shema' in the phrase: הודו והמליכו ואמרו וכו׳.[179] Acknowledgment of God is similarly linked with the acceptance of *malkut Shamayim* in the phrase, להודות לך וליחדך, except that now, in the word וליחדך, there is a particular reference to the Shema'. The section of the berakah which precedes the whole statement, and which consists of a plea for the restoration of Israel, varies greatly in the different versions, and that fact, as well as the content of the section, indicates that it is a later interpolation.[180]

Let us now consider the first phrase of the statement—כי בנו בחרת מכל עם ולשון. The idea here does not contain a rabbinic concept of the chosen people, for there is no such rabbinic concept. Always, without exception, a rabbinic value concept is represented in rabbinic literature by a substantive; that is, by a conceptual term which can abstract and classify. But the idea present here is not represented by a conceptual term in rabbinic literature, and that means that it is always tied to another idea which does possess a conceptual term. Here it is tied to the concept of *malkut Shamayim*, the emphasis being on that concept and not on our having been chosen. We thank God because He has permitted us or enabled us to acknowledge His kingship.

Furthermore, as used in the liturgy, the verb בחר in the present tense always signifies "to take delight in," "to love," rather than "to choose." In the daily berakah after the recital of the psalms,[181] for example, the word הבוחר cannot possibly mean that God has chosen the psalms from among other writings;[182] likewise, in the berakah before the Hafṭarah that word certainly does not convey the idea that God has chosen the Torah from among other possible Torot. The words הבוחר בעמו ישראל, at the end of 'Ahabah Rabbah, can only mean, therefore, that God loves or takes delight in Israel, a meaning that seems to be corroborated by the text in *Siddur R. Saadia* which does not have the redundant באהבה.[183] Although the idea is similar to that of the closing formula of the parallel berakah in the evening, the wording here expresses gratitude for God's love in enabling us both to study Torah and to acknowledge His kingship.[184]

'Ahabah Rabbah, unlike the berakot we discussed above, is not occasioned by a phenomenal experience. This berakah is called forth by an act yet to be performed by the individual, the very anticipation of the act being an experience in itself. In anticipating the act of study, the individual feels that God Himself is the teacher, and in anticipating the acceptance of *malkut Shamayim* he has a sense of a high privilege being conferred by God; and both anticipations blend in a single berakah of gratitude for God's love in a unitary experience of worship. Notwithstanding allusions to Israel's past in this berakah, it is the individual who has this experience of worship—the individual in his role as a representative of Israel. In early times, according to Ginzberg, the individual most likely recited the Shema' and its berakot immediately upon arising in the morning[185] and hence by himself and not with the community at prayer.

Formally, the berakah just before the Shema' and the berakah just after it are not independent berakot, since they do not have an opening formula. Indeed, they are constituents of a chain of berakot, the first of which, as we shall see, is touched off by a phenomenal experience and does have an opening formula; that is why, no doubt, the Yerushalmi gives the berakot adjacent to the Shema' as instances of berakot "joined to the preceding berakah."[186] On the other hand, the Tosefta certainly implies that these berakot are not "joined to the preceding berakah," and later authorities stress that implication.[187] This view, it seems to us, takes cognizance of the orientation of these berakot, for both 'Ahabah Rabbah and the berakah following the Shema' are oriented to the Shema', and it is that orientation, rather than their position in the chain of berakot, which determines their character. In fact, there is a rabbinic rule to the effect that the successive order of the berakot of the Shema' is not mandatory, the rule itself being based on the practice of the priests in the Temple who said 'Ahabah Rabbah alone before the Ten Commandments and Ḳeri'at Shema'.[188] Our point is that, although 'Ahabah Rabbah and the berakah following the Shema' are constituents of a chain of berakot, their real character derives from their association with the Shema'.

'Emet we-Yaẓẓib, the berakah following the Shema', is at once oriented to the Shema' and a meditative experience in its own right. Ideas of the Shema' are given a new turn in the berakah.

Rules of the Halakah enable the individual to achieve a meditative experience in this case, too. "He who recites the Shema' in the morning," states a baraita in the Yerushalmi, "ought to make mention of (להזכיר) the Exodus from Egypt in 'Emet we-Yaẓẓib. Rabbi [Judah the Prince] says, 'He ought to make mention there of the Kingship [of God] [*malkut*].' Others say, 'He ought to make mention of the division of the Red Sea and the plague of the first-born.' R. Joshua b. Levi says, 'He ought to make mention of all these [matters] and ought to say [at the end], Rock of Israel and his Redeemer.' "[189] As Lieberman has indicated, there was a period when it was not yet the established practice to specify the division of the Red Sea and the plague of the first-born,[190] apparently because, we should say, they are only details of the Exodus itself. The idea-content of the meditative experience had to do with the Exodus and with *malkut*.

The impetus to recall the Exodus from Egypt in the berakah is given by the last verse in the third paragraph of the Shema': "I am the Lord, your God, Who brought you out of the land of Egypt, to be your God" (Num. 15:41). This is to be inferred from the baraita just quoted. In mishnaic times, the third paragraph of the Shema' was recited only in the morning and not in the evening;[191] accordingly, the baraita states that he who recites the Shema' in the morning ought to make mention of the Exodus, the inference being that when the third paragraph is not recited, there is no reason to make mention of the Exodus in the berakah.[192]

If we turn now to the berakah itself, we find that the Exodus is referred to not only explicitly but, in fervent words, by implication. The Exodus is an event the significance of which is conveyed by the concept of *ge'ullah*, redemption. Phrases which contain only forms of the root of the conceptual word *ge'ullah* refer to the Exodus merely by implication, but they are phrases which are highly connotative and charged with significance: גואלנו גואל אבותינו and גאל ישראל or צור ישראל וגואלו.[193] Specific references to Egypt, too, contain forms of the conceptual word, as in ממצרים גאלתנו.[194] We may say, then, that, although the Exodus is recalled in the Shema', it is the berakah which expresses the significance of the Exodus; and this was probably already the case in very early times, for Ginzberg has shown that the first statement in the baraita goes back at least to the period of the schools of Shammai and Hillel.[195] Incidentally, since the Exodus is an instance of *ge'ullah*, the connotation of *ge'ullah* is redemption from servitude or oppression, and not, as some modern writers would have it, redemption from sin.

The idea of *malkut*, too, is given a new turn in the berakah. *Malkut* as a technical term, Ginzberg points out, may refer to God either as King of the world or as King of Israel, and he adds that, both in the morning and the evening, what the berakah after the Shema' speaks of is the sovereignty of God over Israel.[196] That berakah also indicates, however, that it is the acceptance of *malkut Shamayim* which gives rise to the fresh awareness of God's kingship over Israel. "*'Emet*, it is true," declares the berakah, thus first affirming the experience of Ḳeri'at Shema', "it is true: the God of the world is our King, the Rock of Jacob."[197] On the other hand, there is now an emphasis on the idea of God as the Protector of Israel, the Rock of Jacob, and hence an emphasis on the concept of God's love rather than on that of *malkut Shamayim*.

In the berakah after the Shema', the redemption from Egypt is felt to be an event which took place in the individual's own day, and not only an event of the remote past. "True it is," the individual says, "that Thou art indeed the Lord our God, and the God of our fathers, our King, King of our fathers, our Redeemer, the Redeemer of our fathers."[198] In the text as given in *Siddur R. Saadia*, there is almost a demarcation between the event as an experience of the present and the event as a happening in the past: גואלינו וגאל את

אבותינו.[199] There is indeed so strong an awareness of the redemption, so poignant a sense of the event as a present actuality, that in the evening berakah references to details of the Exodus are couched in the present tense: העושה לנו נסים וכו׳.[200] We have here, then, a meditative experience which is extraordinarily vivid.

The belief that God brought Israel out of Egypt, we have demonstrated elsewhere, is a rabbinic dogma.[201] A rabbinic dogma is a matter of belief, not a matter of personal experience, a belief that an event did take place or will take place. Often, however, the dogma is mitigated by the endeavor to render the event of the past, imaginatively, a matter of personal experience. The Passover Seder is such an attempt, its theme being, in the words of the Passover Haggadah, that "in every generation, a man is duty-bound to look upon himself as though he personally had gone out of Egypt."[202] But this quotation from the Passover Haggadah and from the Mishnah[203] is not just the theme of the Passover Seder; it is a halakah, and it is stated in general terms. It reflects a meditative experience on the part of the individual, not at the Passover Seder alone, but one which is achieved every day in the berakah after the Shema', except that now the background is different. In place of the imaginative reliving of the Exodus through the cumulative effect of the Passover Seder, the consciousness of God as King, Protector, and Redeemer of Israel rises now out of the previous experience of Ḳeri'at Shema'.[204]

In subject-matter, the First Berakah in the series is entirely unrelated to Ḳeri'at Shema'. It has not only a closing formula, as do the other two berakot, but also an opening formula. Thus in the morning it opens with "Blessed art Thou, O Lord our God, King of the world, Who formest light and createst darkness, Who makest peace and createst all things";[205] and it closes with "Blessed art Thou, O Lord, Who formest the lights."[206] Already given in the Talmud,[207] the statements here are in consonance with the following phrase in the berakah, likewise, in the main, found in the Talmud, although in quite a different context: "[And in His goodness, He] renews the Creation every day continually."[208] What is expressed in all these statements is the feeling on the part of the individual who witnesses the sunrise that God creates anew every day the light of the day. The sunrise, which is a phenomenal experience, is interpreted by the berakah to be a manifestation of God's love, a present act of God's, as it were, the occasion and the berakah together constituting a unitary, experiential entity. Once more a daily event is, through a berakah, charged with significance; and once more, through that same act of worship, the individual is given a sense of kinship with the whole world, a kinship again expressed in yet another phrase: "Who in lovingkindness givest light to the earth and to them that dwell thereon."[209]

The connection between this berakah and Ḳeri'at Shema' is really only a temporal one. Sunrise marks the beginning of the period for the recitation of Ḳeri'at Shema' in the morning, as we have seen above,[210] but the sunrise is itself an element in an integrated experience of worship. Ḳeri'at Shema' and its berakot can be recited, therefore, only after the berakah on the lights has already been said. When the Shema' was recited before sunrise, however, as was done by the priests in the Temple, there was no occasion to say the berakah on the lights at that time, but only the berakah immediately preceding the Shema'.[211] Of course, it is true that ordinarily the berakah on the lights is recited as the first of a series, and this practice is, no doubt, the basis for the view that the berakot adjacent to the Shema' are instances of berakot "joined to the preceding berakah."[212]

There is reference in this berakah, also, to the Messianic redemption—a petition which consists of the phrase, "O cause a new light to shine upon Zion."[213] Saadia objects to this phrase on the ground that, as ordained by the *Ḥakamim*, the theme of the berakah is simply the light which we have every day, and he therefore omits the phrase in his *Siddur*.[214] His stricture as to the mention of a future redemption thus applies only to this berakah.[215] We have noticed, however, that petitions for redemption in the other berakot of the Shema' are later additions,[216] and Ginzberg points out that, originally, none of the berakot of the Shema' contained any reference to a future redemption.[217] Nevertheless, if we hold that the berakah on the lights has a single theme, we have to account for the presence of the Ḳedushah in this berakah. Saadia does include it here in his order of public worship,[218] although he omits it in his section on the individual's worship, for another reason.[219]

The berakot of the Shema' are formally constituents of a single series. They can be taken as members of the same series because, ordinarily, the berakah on the lights, the Yoẓer, precedes the others;

moreover, the berakot do present a conceptual continuum, since each of them is an acknowledgment, in one way or another, of God's love. But the conceptual continuum is not a basic one, for the Yoẓer does not impart an impetus to the berakah adjacent to the Shema'. Ḳeri'at Shema' represents a new experience, only temporally associated with the Yoẓer, an experience so profound and moving as to give rise to a berakah before and after it. Before Ḳeri'at Shema', the anticipation of studying Torah and at the same time of accepting upon oneself the kingship of God becomes itself a religious experience, and the individual is moved to thank God for enabling him to study Torah and for permitting him to acknowledge *malkut Shamayim*. When the Shema' has been said, the recitation gives rise to another experience, a meditative experience, in which the individual, guided by the Halakah, comes to regard the redemption from Egypt as an event of his own day. Ḳeri'at Shema' and the berakot associated with it are, in a sense, a continuous religious experience.

CHAPTER V

The Daily Tefillah (*'Amidah*)

A. The Conceptual Continuum in the Tefillah

In Palestine the Daily Tefillah, in the second century C.E., consisted of eighteen berakot,[1] and thus "Eighteen" (*Shemoneh 'Esreh*) came to be a common designation not only for the Daily Tefillah, but also for the Tefillah on the Sabbath and festivals, even though on those occasions the Tefillah consists of fewer berakot. Conforming to the practice of Babylon, however, the Daily Tefillah now has nineteen berakot, not because another was added there, but because Babylon kept to the very early practice of not combining the Fourteenth and Fifteenth Berakot, whereas in Palestine these two Berakot were made into a single berakah.[2] Of these berakot, the first three and the last three are characterized by the rabbis as "praise of God [*Maḳom*]," and the "middle" berakot as referring to "the needs of men."[3] Because the middle berakot contain petitions, the Eighteen Berakot as a whole are designated as *ha-Tefillah*, the Prayer.[4] In fact, the word tefillah, prayer, became so closely associated with the Eighteen Berakot that it was used as warrant for regarding other words in biblical texts as referring to these berakot, among such other words being the term 'Amidah.[5]

In the days of the Second Temple—as a controversy between the schools of Shammai and Hillel indicates—the six berakot characterized as "praise" were already the fixed elements of every Tefillah.[6] Two in the last group of berakot, indeed, were originally part of the Temple service itself.[7] Undoubtedly, therefore, the Tefillah was ordained by the Men of the Great Synagogue, as the rabbis explicitly say.[8] On the other hand, the Talmud also records that Simeon Ha-Paḳoli arranged the Eighteen Berakot in their successive order "before R. Gamaliel at Jabne."[9] The sources are not contradictory, however, as Ginzberg has pointed out, but only tell of different stages in the development of the Tefillah, the berakot not having had the present order until Simeon so arranged them.[10] Lieberman also draws the conclusion that before Jabne it had been permitted to enlarge the Tefillah by saying more than the Eighteen Berakot.[11] Moreover, arranging the berakot must have involved a general editing of them, although in a manner which still left the wording of the berakot not entirely fixed. Numerous variants in the texts of the early versions testify to the fluid character of the berakot for centuries after the tannaitic period, so far as the wording was concerned.

A conceptual continuum results from the form of the Tefillah, a form through which the berakot express a series of successive experiences.[12] The form of the Tefillah allows one concept, God's love, to be carried over from one berakah to the next. Beginning with, "Blessed art Thou, O Lord our God and God of our Fathers, God of Abraham, God of Isaac and God of Jacob, the great, mighty and awesome God, the most high God," and closing with, "Blessed art Thou, O Lord, the Shield of Abraham,"[13] the First Berakah, designated in the Mishnah as 'Abot (Fathers or Patriarchs),[14] is the only one in the series which has both an opening and a closing formula. Every berakah which follows is "a berakah which is joined to the immediately preceding berakah," and hence has only a closing formula. A meditative, nonphenomenal experience of worship, and in that respect not like the First Berakah either in the Birkat ha-Mazon or in the berakot of the Shema', 'Abot represents an experience of God's love that imparts an impetus to a further act of worship and the latter, in turn, imparts an impetus to still another act of worship, and so on.[15] There need be no given limit to such a series, as we saw in an earlier section, for each berakah is a unitary entity in itself;[16] that is why the Tefillah could consist, at various times, of more than eighteen berakot or of fewer. What needs explanation is, essentially, not the length of the series in the Tefillah, but rather the occasion for the Tefillah. What kind of an occasion can it be that gives rise to a nonphenomenal, meditative religious experience, the experience expressed in 'Abot? The answer involves other aspects of the Tefillah and we shall come to it in due course.

A berakah in the Tefillah may embody other value concepts beside the concept of God's love. For example, the Fifth Berakah, closing with "Who delightest in *teshubah* [repentance]," fuses the concepts of God's love and *teshubah*; and the Sixth, closing with, "Who dost abundantly [i.e., again and again] forgive," fuses the concepts of God's love and forgiveness.[17] In these and many similar instances, the presence of other concepts in a berakah only emphasizes God's love, and the conceptual continuity is, therefore, also emphasized all the more. This cannot be said now of the Third and of the Twelfth Berakot; in both of these, the inclusion of other concepts not present in those berakot originally tends to weaken the conceptual continuum.

The Third Berakah, Ḳedushat ha-Shem,[18] consists, in the Palestinian version, of a brief statement (the first four words of which are given in the Sifre)[19] on the holiness of God and the berakah closes with "Blessed art Thou, the holy God."[20] The statement "Holy art Thou and awesome is Thy Name, and there is no God beside Thee"[21] does not attempt to express any specific experience. We shall see later that a vivid awareness of God's holiness involves the presence of at least ten Jews: a *parhesya'* in the case of a heroic act of *ḳiddush ha-Shem*, and a *ẓibbur* in the case of a liturgical act of *ḳiddush ha-Shem*.[22] If it does not relate to an actual experience, however, the Third Berakah, in its Palestinian version, does make a fitting close to the series of berakot here "in praise of God." This Third Berakah is thus bound with the first two meditative experiences even though it is not a meditative experience in itself. What is more, it does not interrupt the conceptual continuum. The concept of *ḳedushah*, holiness, has an association with God's love, and that association is reflected in the Third Berakah on New Year and on the Day of Atonement. On those days the Palestinian version is recited, but with the addition of the proof-text "And the Lord of hosts is exalted in judgment, and the holy God is sanctified in *ẓedaḳah*" (Isa. 5:16).[23] This verse was chosen not only because the first half was taken to refer to the "ten days between New Year and the Day of Atonement," the days when God "is exalted in judgment,"[24] but also because the second half goes on to speak of God's charity or mercy at that very period of judgment, for according to the rabbis, *ẓedaḳah* stands for charity or love in this verse,[25] and indeed in almost every verse in which the word occurs.[26] The holy God is made holy, sanctified in His charity at judgment. In the brief Palestinian version, a version to which no other concept has been added, the concept of holiness in the Third Berakah has, then, an association with God's love, since the verse, as the rabbis interpret it, only carries out the holiness theme of the berakah.[27]

Finkelstein has called attention to the difference in the Third Berakah between the Palestinian version and the non-Palestinian versions. He rightly concludes that, since the Palestinian version contains no reference to the Ḳedushah and the others do contain such references, the Ḳedushah was not part of the Third Berakah when the Palestinian version was formulated and that the others are later versions formulated after the Ḳedushah had been inserted.[28] We must add, however, that the non-Palestinian versions differ in a striking manner from each other as well; they differ in the character of their references to the Ḳedushah. In the version where the reference consists of וקדושים בכל יום יהללוך, "And holy beings praise Thee daily," reciting the Ḳedushah was regarded as simply telling of the praise of the angels; whereas in the version where the reference consists of ולנצח נצחים קדושתך נקדיש, the words קדושתך נקדיש correspond to נקדש את שמך, the words with which the whole section on the Ḳedushah begins, and both these phrases alike refer to the Ḳedushah as an act of worship and as an act of *ḳiddush ha-Shem*.[29] After the Ḳedushah was attached to the Third Berakah, there apparently was a period when the Ḳedushah was not an act of worship in itself but merely an enlargement of the Third Berakah, an addition to the original statement on God's holiness in the berakah, telling by means of biblical verses of how the angels praise God by reciting, "Holy, holy," etc.; it is this enlargement of the berakah which is reflected in the version containing the phrase "and holy beings praise Thee daily." But the Ḳedushah also crystallized into an act of worship in itself, an act of *ḳiddush ha-Shem* (as we shall see in the next chapter), and in time a reference to that act of *ḳiddush ha-Shem* was put into the Third Berakah itself. This berakah was thereby given a character which makes it different from all the other berakot of the Tefillah. All the other berakot express various aspects of God's love; the concept of *ḳiddush ha-Shem* expressed in the Third Berakah does not refer to an act by God but to an act by man. It is only the cumulative effect of the preceding berakot which overcomes this break in the conceptual continuum.[30]

Except for phrases added later, the Twelfth Berakah, like the rest, was formulated in the period of the Second Temple. It contains a petition for the uprooting of "the arrogant kingdom [מלכות זדון]"—an epithet for Rome, and earlier for Syria, as Ginzberg has shown.[31] Proof that this petition was the principal theme of the berakah is to be found in the closing formula of the old Palestinian version, for that formula consisted only of the words "Blessed art Thou, O Lord, Who dost subdue the arrogant (מכניע זדים)."[32] When the era of "the arrogant kingdom" is over, the age of perfect justice and peace will begin, the days of the Messiah or the world to come, and hence not God's justice alone is the concept embodied here but God's love as well. True, the petition and the berakah have reference only to the prelude of the new and perfect world order, but the prelude necessarily implies the sequel, and this is made evident in the Tefillah of Rosh ha-Shanah. In a prayer there, the phrase "when Thou makest the arrogant government [ממשלת זדון] to pass away from the earth" is followed directly by the statement "and Thou, O Lord, shalt reign, Thou alone, over all Thy works."[33] Evident, too, in that prayer is the fusion of God's love and His justice: "Then shall the righteous see and be glad; the upright shall exult and the pious rejoice in song, and iniquity shall close its mouth, and all wickedness shall be wholly consumed like smoke, when Thou makest the arrogant government to pass away from the earth."[34] What is implicit in the Twelfth Berakah of the Daily Tefillah is but given explicit expression in the prayer on Rosh ha-Shanah. Both contain the same idea; and not only the striking expression "the arrogant kingdom [or government]" which is common to both but, more especially, the closing formula of the Twelfth Berakah, bears witness that this idea was the theme of the Twelfth Berakah from the very beginning.

The petition of the berakah was expanded, however, to include references to Jewish separatists and to *minim*, sectarians.[35] If these dissident groups, among them some of the Judeo-Christian sects, were placed in a category with Rome as enemies of Israel, it was because they had demonstrated their antagonism to the nation as a whole in the period following the destruction of the Temple and denied Israel's belief in a national redemption.[36] The feeling against them expressed itself at Jabne when Samuel the Little, at the behest of R. Gamliel, formulated the berakah against the *minim*, a formulation which, as Lieberman explains, really meant amending the existing berakah so as to have it make specific mention of the *minim*.[37] A concept was thus inserted into the berakah which had not been present there before, the concept of *minim*. When this added concept was emphasized it became the major theme of the berakah.

On that score Palestine differed from Babylon. In Palestine, the *minim* were only an incidental theme in the berakah; in Babylon, on the other hand, they became, in effect, the major theme. Ginzberg shows that the very manner of referring to the Twelfth Berakah is indicative. In the Yerushalmi, it indicates that the main theme of the berakah is "subduing the arrogant," while in the Babylonian Talmud it indicates that the theme of "subduing the arrogant" is secondary to that of the *minim*.[38] Again, in the various versions of a Midrash on the Tefillah, the haggadot on the Twelfth Berakah have for their theme (as Ginzberg points out) enemies of Israel, "the arrogant," and never the *minim*,[39] and that Midrash, he demonstrates, is of Palestinian origin.[40]

The insertion of the *minim* into the Twelfth Berakah did not inevitably make for a break in the conceptual continuity, but it did make such a break or interruption possible. There was no interruption so long as the added concept remained an incidental theme, and this was the case in Palestine. On the other hand, when the added concept is emphasized and made the major theme of the berakah (as was the case in Babylon) the chain of experience inherent in the Tefillah is broken, and only the cumulative effect of the preceding berakot overcomes the break in the conceptual continuum.

We have left for the last, in this discussion of the Twelfth Berakah, the consideration of two halakot: a halakah in the Yerushalmi and a related halakah in the Babylonian Talmud. A baraita in the Yerushalmi states that a leader who has omitted two or three berakot in the Tefillah is not made to go back and say them "*except* when he has not said, 'Who quickenest the dead' [the Second Berakah], or 'Who dost subdue the arrogant' [the Twelfth Berakah], or 'Who buildest Jerusalem' [the Fourteenth Berakah], [for] I conclude he may be a *min*."[41] A suspicion of being a *min* thus attaches not just to him who has omitted the Twelfth Berakah but to a person who has omitted any one of the three berakot named here; the berakot are mentioned in accordance with their order in the Tefillah and the phrase "I conclude he may be a *min*" follows the last berakah named, the Fourteenth, and hence must refer to the omission of any one of these berakot. Evidently, then, the three berakot have a character in common. Furthermore, since each can become a means for testing whether the leader is a *min*, the character which is common to all of them must have to do with rabbinic dogma. Now we found, in an earlier discussion, that the concept of the days of the Messiah and the other hereafter concepts are not pure value concepts, but are rabbinic dogmas which possess a degree of specificity which the value concepts do not have, pointing to such specific events as the ingathering of the Diaspora and the building of Jerusalem.[42] This explains why the berakot named in the baraita relate to rabbinic dogma. Specific events indubitably constitute the themes of the Second and Fourteenth Berakot, future events pointed to by hereafter concepts. Those berakot involve rabbinic dogma because they embody not only the concept of God's love but also concepts of the hereafter, the days of the Messiah or the world to come. That is likewise true of the Twelfth Berakah for, as we saw, its major theme is the uprooting of "the arrogant kingdom," a specific event of the future which is the prelude to the days of the Messiah or the world to come. When the baraita speaks of the Twelfth Berakah, it refers, as do similar references in the Yerushalmi, to the original, major theme of the berakah.

The halakah in the Babylonian Talmud declares that if the leader has omitted (טעה) any of the berakot of the Tefillah he is not removed, but if it be the "Birkat ha-Minim he is removed, [for] we apprehend lest he be a *min*."[43] Here, as in the Yerushalmi, the apprehension is lest a *min* be the leader in the Tefillah, but otherwise the halakot are different. By naming no berakot other than the Twelfth, the Babylonian halakah reveals that, unlike the Yerushalmi, its ground for apprehension is something other than the leader's omission to say berakot embodying concepts concerning the hereafter. It is simply a matter of the *min* having given himself away by omitting the berakah which contains a prayer for the destruction of his sect, and that is why he is to be removed forthwith. Once again the

Babylonian Talmud has made the added concept of the *minim* the major theme of the Twelfth Berakah.

A Yelammedenu (a homily beginning with an inquiry regarding a halakah) passage combines the halakah in the Yerushalmi with the Babylonian halakah and also contains an idea not found in either. We may divide the passage, for the purpose of analysis, into three parts. In the first part, which largely employs the phraseology of the Babylonian halakah, only the Birkat ha-Minim is named, but now the leader who omits it is to be made to go back to the berakah, as the Yerushalmi teaches.[44] The passage continues with an idea not expressed in either the Yerushalmi or the Babylonian halakah: "And he is to recite it even against his will. And why do we make him go back? We apprehend lest he be a *min*; if he indeed holds a heretical doctrine, [by reciting the berakah] he utters a curse against himself to which the congregation responds, 'Amen.' "[45] A statement then follows which is reminiscent of the Yerushalmi but which mentions only the Fourteenth Berakah: "And so, too, he who has not said 'Who buildest Jerusalem' is made to go back [for] we apprehend lest he be a *Kuti* [Samaritan]."[46] The first and the last parts of the passage are palpably post-talmudic; the first part because it utilizes the crystallized halakot of *both* the Yerushalmi and the Babylonian Talmud, and the last part because it reflects a development of the post-talmudic period. Instead of completing the list given in the Yerushalmi, the last part of the Yelammedenu passage names only the Fourteenth Berakah and makes no mention of the Second, "Who quickenest the dead," and yet *Masseket Kutim*, a Palestinian (Yerushalmi) treatise,[47] indicates that the *Kutim* not only refused to acknowledge Jerusalem but also denied the quickening of the dead,[48] the dogma in the Second Berakah; if, therefore, the Yelammedenu gives as a test for a *Kuti* the recitation of the Fourteenth Berakah alone, the passage must have been composed in the post-talmudic period when the Samaritans had come to accept the dogma of the quickening of the dead.[49] Indeed, the entire passage is post-talmudic, the middle part as well, for the middle part is based on the first part, giving a reason for the halakah stated in the first part.

The Yelammedenu passage depicts the Twelfth Berakah, when uttered by a *min*, as a curse directed against himself. This is an idea which is not to be found either in the Babylonian halakah or in the Yerushalmi. According to the former, the leader suspected of being a *min* is to be removed and hence he is not to be permitted to say the Twelfth Berakah at all. According to the Yerushalmi, the leader is suspected of being a *min* if he has omitted the Second, the Twelfth, or the Fourteenth Berakah; in that case he must go back and say whichever of these three he has omitted. All three are tests of a *min* because all three contain dogmas, embodying the concepts of the days of the Messiah or the world to come. No distinction is made in the Yerushalmi between these berakot, and the Twelfth Berakah is not singled out as different in kind from the others, as a berakah which is a denunciation. Nevertheless, although only the Yelammedenu passage depicts this berakah as a denunciation, we need not conclude that the idea is altogether post-talmudic. It may have been an interpretation already placed upon the berakah in talmudic times—not by the rabbis, to be sure, but by the folk.[50] Be that as it may, we do find such an interpretation of the berakah by post-talmudic authorities, some of whom clearly take it for granted that the term Birkat ha-Minim is a euphemism for ḳilelat (denunciation of) ha-Minim.[51]

B. Prayer, Berakah, and the Self

Tefillah, we noticed in the preceding section, is a word which stands for both the 'Amidah and for prayer in general.[52] Tefillah also applies more specifically to the middle section of the 'Amidah, the section that follows the berakot of praise. This the rabbis indicate when, in support of their statement that the petitions of the Tefillah ought to be preceded by praise of God, they interpret *rinnah** in I Kings 8:28 to be *tehillah*, praise, and then say that the word tefillah which follows *rinnah* in that verse means *baḳḳashah*, petition or request.[53]

Prayer is petition of a special kind. To pray is "to beseech compassion" from God—*le-baḳḳesh raḥamim*.[54] Thus the rabbis declare, "Anyone who can beseech compassion for his fellow and does not beseech is called a sinner," and they cite as proof I Samuel 12:23: "Far be it from me that I should sin against the Lord by ceasing to

* Literally, "song," hence praise. Usually translated "cry."

pray [*le-hitpallel*] for you."[55] Just as the word Tefillah stands for the entire 'Amidah, so also does the Talmud characterize the Tefillah itself as *raḥame*,[56] referring by that word alone to the beseeching of compassion from God.[57] A tefillah, then, is the beseeching of compassion from God, an appeal to His *middat raḥamim*, to His love or mercy.

But the 'Amidah has a dual character. Not only does the section of praise consist of berakot, but every petition in the 'Amidah concludes with a berakah and hence the term "Eighteen Berakot" as a designation for the daily 'Amidah.[58] It is not our purpose, at present, to account for the rabbinic nomenclature: we are simply pointing out that the designations for the 'Amidah reflect its dual character of tefillah and berakah.

Between a berakah and a prayer there is a fundamental distinction. A berakah refers to something which has already taken place, or else to something felt as taking place in the present. On the other hand, a prayer or petition refers to something which one hopes will take place. R. Ze'ira makes this distinction between a berakah and a prayer when he contrasts a phrase in the Ḳiddush of the Sabbath, the Ḳiddush being a berakah, with a similar phrase in the Tefillah of the Sabbath. The Ḳiddush contains the phrase "Who has sanctified us by Thy miẓwot," whereas the Tefillah contains the phrase "O sanctify us by Thy miẓwot." Why? Because the Tefillah is "the beseeching of compassion."[59]

Every petition in the 'Amidah closes with a berakah. Yet a petition is tefillah, beseeching God for a particular manifestation of His love or compassion. On the other hand, a berakah, we repeat, is usually an expression of gratitude for a particular manifestation of God's love, a manifestation experienced either in some phenomenal manner or through meditation; the berakah itself is an element in that experience, interpreting and enhancing it. On the surface, therefore, a petition which closes with a berakah appears to contain a basic contradiction: something which has not been experienced is prayed for and apparently immediately afterwards it is acknowledged in gratitude as something that has already been experienced. There is no contradiction, however. What is necessary now is a clearer apprehension of a psychological factor we have spoken of before: namely, the larger self and its role in the consciousness and experiences of the individual. It is the larger self which is expressed in prayers and berakot relating to needs men have in common. In the prescribed prayers and berakot, private needs are by no means ignored but the greater emphasis is placed on the common needs.

A prayer or berakah in which the individual refers to himself in the first person singular expresses a private need. This is the case, for example, in the following prayer to be said by a person upon entering a town: "May it be Thy will, O Lord my God, that I enter in peace [לשלום]."[60] Similarly, again speaking in the first person singular, the individual, after having entered the town safely, is to say, "I thank Thee, O Lord my God, that Thou hast enabled me to enter in peace. May it likewise be Thy will to bring me forth in peace."[61] In like vein, and once more employing the first person singular, the individual is to thank God after having come forth from the city, and is also to say a prayer for his safe return home.[62] Part of a section dealing with prayers and thanksgiving of the same personal character,[63] the halakot just cited have Ben ʻAzzai as authority and very likely reflect a period of Roman violence and lawlessness. We must add that the phrases of thanksgiving here, although not containing a berakah formula, nor even the root *brk*, are regarded as berakot; they are referred to as such when the texts or the variants introduce them with the word "*mebarek*," "says a berakah."[64]

In contradistinction to these prayers and berakot, the entire ʻAmidah, including the petitions, is recited in the first person plural. The needs mentioned in the petitions are common needs, either those of mankind in general or of the whole people of Israel: knowledge and understanding, repentance, forgiveness by God, health, good crops, and the rebuilding of Jerusalem, to mention several. Because they relate to common needs, the "middle" berakot, those containing petitions, are designated at one place in the Yerushalmi as "the needs of men [צרכן של בריות]."[65] But the Tannaim, Ginzberg has pointed out, usually designate the middle berakot as "his needs [צרכיו]"[66]—that is, the needs of the individual. Now these needs relate to mankind as a whole or to Israel as a people. Not only are they not private needs, but at the moment of prayer they may not even be relevant to the individual, as is the case, for example, of the person in good health when he is reciting the Eighth Berakah with its petition for recovery from illness. Again, the Tenth Berakah is called "the Ingathering of the Exiles,"[67] and it closes with "Who gathereth the dispersed of His people, Israel" (after Is. 56: 8), yet it was, of course, recited in Palestine as well as in the Diaspora. How is it that the individual can regard common needs as "his needs," even when they are not at the time his own needs at all?

The concept of man, its near alternate, *'olam* (world),[68] and the concept of Israel are value concepts. They do not represent external objects, basically, but are concepts of valuational experience and hence, their concretizations, like all concretizations of value concepts, are expressions of the self. Ordinarily the awareness of the self is not conceptualized, and even when expressed, must rely on the pronouns "I" and "my"; the concepts of man and Israel, however, have the special quality of supplying in their concretizations the awareness of the self with conceptual expression. On such occasions, the self is enlarged: a person is both himself and at the same time man, all men, or himself and all Israel. When, for example, after a meal, a man thanks God for feeding "the whole world," he refers, in his experience of worship, not just to "the whole world" but to himself as well. Similar in character are the petitions and berakot of the 'Amidah, except that they are more subtle expressions of the larger self. Not an actual experience, but the sheer knowledge of a common need of man is now the occasion for an individual's petition and he regards the common need as his need. Once more the awareness of the self is an awareness of the larger self. The pronoun used in those petitions and berakot is the first person plural, the plural standing not for a given number of individuals but for himself and all men, for man. We may put the entire matter more simply but not altogether correctly by saying, as we did earlier, that, when reciting such berakot, the individual senses himself to be a representative of man or of Israel.

The problem of the larger self is a fundamental problem, but a consideration of the 'Amidah may at least illumine some aspects of it. The key to the problem is to be found in the way the pronouns "we" or "us" are used by the individual. Ordinarily, when the individual says "we" he refers to himself and other individuals. Self-awareness, at such times, implies that the individual is also aware of other individuals. But this is not the case when the larger self comes into play. Then the word "we" as used by the individual refers to himself and, it is true, to others but not to others as individuals. The "others" are now undifferentiated; they are man or Israel, or any group within man or Israel, again not as individuals, but as man or Israel having, for the time, a distinguishing characteristic. For example, when the individual uses "we" or "us" in the petition of 'Ahabah Rabbah, the berakah before the Shema', he refers at that moment to himself and others, the "others" here being all of Israel. When, however, he says "we" and "us" in the petition for recovery from sickness, he is referring to himself and to man as characterized by sickness, to the undifferentiated group of men who are sick.[69] This is not identification of himself—if he is well—with those who are sick. On the one hand, the sick are not particular individuals with whom he can identify himself, and on the other, he is bound, on such an occasion, to be conscious of his own good health. The larger self allows an individual to be aware, poignantly aware, that there are others who are sick; the awareness is so strong that he associates himself with them, though at the same time retaining his self-identity. It is precisely in a petition of this kind, a petition not relevant to the individual qua individual and yet one in which he says "we" and "us", that the character of the larger self is best revealed. Self-identity is retained and the material circumstances of the individual have not changed; nevertheless, the self has become larger, more inclusive: large enough to include indefinite others and a consciousness of their needs.

There is no loss of self-identity either, even when the "others" are all men or all Israel. When reciting 'Ahabah Rabbah, for instance, the individual associates himself with all Israel in anticipating the recital of the Shema', but there can be no loss of self-identity. Acceptance of *malkut Shamayim* is incumbent upon each individual, and the commitments involved are personal commitments. The experience demands *kawwanah*, something in which no other individual can have a share. In anticipating this experience, the individual associates himself with all Israel but completely retains his self-identity. "We" and "us" in 'Ahabah Rabbah are expressions of the larger self.

We have noticed that the rabbis designate the 'Amidah as tefillah, "the beseeching of compassion" from God. A petition in the

'Amidah is no less a whole-souled prayer for a particular manifestation of God's compassion than is a prayer concerning a private need. Indeed, so completely in keeping with the character of true prayer are the petitions in the 'Amidah that a petition there reflects changing needs. The petition of the Ninth Berakah, the Mishnah says, is to include a prayer for rain,[70] and the insertion of this prayer, according to a baraita, is to depend "upon the nature of the seasons and upon the nature of the localities."[71]

Because they embody the concept of man or of Israel, the petitions in the 'Amidah are more than just petitions, however. They act as meditations, as well, being meditations of one type in petitions embodying the concept of man and largely of a second type in those embodying the concept of Israel. Petitions of the first type, those referring to the common needs of man, are, besides prayers, reminders to the individual that here and now man possesses the very things prayed for—that is, such a petition reminds the individual that there is a group within man, an undifferentiated group and not a given number of men, which at this moment possesses the thing prayed for. But to possess a thing which has been prayed for is to possess a gift from God, and hence the individual now says a berakah, thanking God for a particular manifestation of His love or compassion. The petition for a common need culminates in a meditative experience—an experience in which the individual, becoming aware of a manifestation of God's love, expresses that awareness in a berakah which itself enhances the experience.[72]

Although the individual associates himself in these petitions with others, that association, let us remember, is always with undifferentiated others. He associates himself with man, not with any definite group of men. Not being differentiated as individuals, the others may now be man with this distinguishing characteristic, now man with some other characteristic. Thus, in the petition for the recovery of the sick, the individual associates himself with man as characterized by illness, whereas in the berakah at the end of that petition he associates himself with man as characterized by being healed. The Fourth Berakah, again, is an instance, apparently, in which both petition and berakah involve the same "others." Here, before the petition, the individual recites an ascription which explicitly names man as the recipient of God's favor: "Thou favorest *'adam* [man] with knowledge, and teachest *'enosh* [another word for man] understanding."[73] In the petition, which employs the first person plural, he prays for "knowledge, understanding and discernment," (since these may fail man at any moment unless given anew by God)[74] and in the berakah he thanks God Who is "the gracious Giver of knowledge."[75] But the others in the petition may well include the witless, and if so, the others there are simply man, and not man as characterized by understanding or knowledge.

What has been called here the larger self is, essentially, the individual's awareness of a relationship between himself and others. In this consciousness of relationship, the awareness of the self is a stable element, for the individual always retains his self-identity in petitions and berakot. The awareness of others, on the contrary, is an unstable element: the others, we have just observed, may have now one character and now a different character. In fact, since the others may be either man or Israel, a petition may embody the concept of Israel whereas the berakah in which the petition culminates may embody the concept of man. For example, the petition in the Fifth Berakah reads: "Cause us to return, O our Father, to Thy Torah; draw us near, O our King, unto Thy service, and bring us back in complete repentance to Thee [before Thee]";[76] and "us" here manifestly refers to Israel, since Israel alone possesses the Torah. This petition, however, culminates in the following berakah: "Blessed art Thou, O Lord, Who delightest in [or, accepts] repentance";[77] but now the reference is to all who repent, to man as distinguished by repentance, for God accepts everyone who repents, Jew or Gentile.[78]

Sometimes the early Palestinian version of such a culminating berakah refers to man, and the later Babylonian version refers, instead, to Israel. That is the case with the Nineteenth Berakah, the early Palestinian version reading "Who makest peace"[79] where the Babylonian version reads "Who blesseth His people Israel with peace."[80] In all the versions, however, the petition of this berakah refers to Israel, for the petition takes its departure from the priests' blessing (Num. 6:24–26) preceding it, and the blessing itself is introduced in the verse immediately preceding with the words "On this wise ye shall bless the children of Israel."[81] Again, the Eighth Berakah concludes in the early Palestinian version with "Who healest the sick,"[82] and in the later Babylonian version with "Who healest the sick of His people Israel";[83] but in this case, the petition of the berakah has no specific reference to Israel and therefore we have every reason to assume that, in the early Palestinian version, petition and culminating berakah are of a piece, and hence that petition, as well as the berakah, refer to man.

In a previous section we found that the recitation of a berakah is an element in a moral experience, since a berakah interprets an event or situation as being a manifestation of God's love, and God's love is characterized as *raḥamim*, *ẓedaḳah*, and *gemilut ḥasadim*, all moral or ethical concepts.[84] When a berakah is recited, therefore, the scope of morality is made to extend beyond the range of purely human relations; not only that, but the individual's entire moral life is thereby strengthened, for any concretization of a moral concept, even if it consists simply of an interpretation of an event by the individual, in some degree strengthens that moral concept's very drive toward concretization.

A berakah in which the individual associates himself with man is a moral experience in a double sense. Besides interpreting a situation or a phenomenon as a manifestation of God's love, it calls into play a concept, man, which has moral implications with respect to human relations. At times, to be sure, the word "man" is no more than a description of a biological species, but at other times it has, on the contrary, a universalistic, valuational connotation.[85] *'Adam*, man, say the rabbis, "is a term of love, and a term of brotherhood, and a term of friendship"; [86] similarly, to call Ezekiel "the son of man" (Ezek. 2:1) is tantamount to calling him "the son of upright people, the son of righteous people, the son of those who do deeds of *gemilut ḥasadim*."[87] Statements such as these, conveying the moral connotations of the concept of man, are concretizations of the concept in Haggadah, in speech. When man is one of the concepts embodied in a berakah, it is again, of course, concretized in speech, yet not in speech alone; it is now a factor in a moral and emotional experience in which the dominant feeling is gratitude for a manifestation of God's love, and the moral implications of the concept of man are thus apprehended in a living rather than a literary context. An individual reciting a berakah in which he associates himself with man becomes aware not only of God's love but of a relationship to all men, a relationship "of love, of brotherhood, of friendship." We have here another instance of the organismic integration of concepts, another example of how a number of value concepts may combine in a unitary yet many-toned experience.[88]

Most of the berakot of the 'Amidah in which the individual associates himself with Israel embody concepts of the hereafter, the days of the Messiah or the world to come; these berakot represent a fusion of such concepts with the concept of God's love. Several berakot of this type we have already discussed: the Second Berakah ("Who quickenest the dead"), the Twelfth Berakah ("Who dost subdue the arrogant"), and the Fourteenth Berakah ("Who buildest Jerusalem").[89] By reason of the hereafter concepts which they embody all three berakot, we saw, have to do with rabbinic dogma. Concepts of the hereafter are not pure value concepts, for instead of being only suggestive or connotative, they point to specific events, events that, it is believed, will take place in the future; in fine, a hereafter concept represents a rabbinic dogma.[90]

What is true of the berakot just mentioned is also true of other berakot in the 'Amidah. Specific events regarded as certain to take place in the future constitute the themes of the Seventh Berakah (the redemption of Israel), the Tenth (the ingathering of the exiles), the Eleventh (the restoration of the judges, i.e., the Sanhedrin),[91] the Fifteenth (the flourishing of the sprout of David),[92] and the Seventeenth (the dwelling of the *Shekinah* in Zion and restoration of the Temple service).[93] All these future events are subsumed under the concept of the days of the Messiah or the world to come. Furthermore, these particular events of the future relate to the restoration of Israel and to that of the Temple in Jerusalem. When the individual recites petitions and berakot having those events as themes, therefore, the pronouns "us" and "we" mean that he now associates himself with Israel.[94]

Such petitions and berakot have a distinctive character of their own. We depicted that character when we dealt with the Third Berakah of the Birkat ha-Mazon, a berakah which is practically identical, in R. Saadia's version, with the Fourteenth Berakah of the 'Amidah.[95] A rabbinic comment on Psalm 31:24—"The Lord preserveth the faithful [*'emunim*]"—we found, indicates that still another concept is embodied in these berakot, the concept of *'emunah*. "They say: Who quickenest the dead, though the resurrection of the dead has not yet come; they say: Redeemer of Israel, though they are not yet redeemed; they say: Who buildest Jerusalem, though Jerusalem is not yet built. The Holy One Blessed be He says: Israel was redeemed for only a little while and then went into servitude, and [yet] they have faith [*ma'aminim*] in Me that I shall redeem them in a time to come."[96] *'Emunah* connotes faith or trust in God's word or promise, and the preordained events referred to in the 'Amidah, being matters of dogma, are taken as so many promises of God.[97] This is not to say that the petitions having these preordained events as their themes are not whole-souled petitions; on the contrary, the promised events are profoundly longed for and the petitions express that longing. What the embodied concept of *'emunah* does is to make of these petitions, even as they are being uttered, a meditative experience as well. So unbounded is the trust in God that present circumstances for the moment fade away and there is a pervasive consciousness that the promised event is indeed taking place right now. These meditative experiences culminate, therefore, in berakot employing the present tense: "Who gatherest the dispersed of His people Israel"; "Who buildest Jerusalem."

Rabbinic dogmas are concerned with events which, in a literal sense, are beyond the range of an individual's experience, but which become, especially during the recitation of the pertinent berakah, something akin to experience. "In the berakah after the Shema', the redemption from Egypt is felt to be an event that has taken place in the individual's own day, and not only as an event of the remote past."[98] Similarly, the closing formula of both berakot on the Torah uses the present tense—"Who givest the Torah"—thereby expressing the feeling that the Torah is being given "this day."[99] Now, sober reflection upon these events certainly did not place them literally within the range of the individual's experience. Rabbinic injunctions to recollect those events, it must be noticed, qualify the duty to recollect them with the phrase "as though"; "as though he [the individual] personally had gone forth out of Egypt";[100] and with respect to *mattan* (the giving of) *Torah*, "as though you received them [the statutes and ordinances] from Mount Sinai this day" and "as though you heard them this day."[101] In sober discussion of the 'Amidah, likewise, the promised events were regarded as imminent, but certainly not as a present reality.[102] It is primarily in berakot, acts expressing and enhancing religious experience, that these things, events ordinarily depicted as having taken place in the past and promised events of the future, take on the character of contemporary happenings. Events that are matters of dogma, of belief, lose their dogmatic character and become matters of personal experience. They become personal experiences, however, when the individual associates himself with Israel, for this is the case with all berakot having such events as themes.

These berakot help us to realize that, although berakot are in the category of Halakah, they also have a character of their own. In halakic discussions of the promised events of the future, or of the Exodus from Egypt and the giving of Torah, there is a clear awareness of future and of past, and the categories of time are not to the slightest degree obliterated. Haggadah, too, holds fast to the categorics of time. In contrast, a berakah tends to interpret an event or situation as, in some sense, a present experience of God, and the other categories of time, when not obliterated in a berakah, always implicate the present.[103] Not being entirely subject to the categories of time, an experience expressed in a berakah has thus a mystical character, a character which we shall describe as "normal mysticism" when we take up the general problem of the rabbinic experience of God.

The Thirteenth Berakah was already in tannaitic times a composite of several berakot. From the Tosefta it is apparent that although originally there was a berakah in the 'Amidah concerning the *zeḳenim*, elders, and another berakah concerning the *gerim*, proselytes, the two were soon combined by expanding the petition in the former to include *gerim*.[104] A baraita in the Yerushalmi records a somewhat different tradition, namely, that the berakah on *zeḳenim* and the one on *gerim* should be included in "the Trust (*Mibṭaḥ*) of the *ẓaddiḳim* (righteous)";[105] this can only mean that the petition in the Thirteenth Berakah ought to refer not only to the *ẓaddiḳim* but also to the *zeḳenim* and to the *gerim*, the *ẓaddiḳim* being taken here as the major theme of the berakah.[106] In *Siddur R. Saadia Gaon*, the berakah reads as follows: "Towards the righteous and the pious and the true proselytes, may Thy mercies be stirred, O Lord, our God; and grant a good reward unto all who trust in Thy Name, and may they not be put to shame. Blessed art Thou, O Lord, the Stay and Trust of the righteous."[107]

Ẓaddiḳim, zeḳenim, gerim, and similar terms in the texts of the berakah are all value concepts.[108] A *ẓaddiḳ* may also be a *ḥasid* (pious),[109] and a *ger* may likewise be a *ẓaddiḳ*; hence such terms do not designate groups but are valuational characterizations of individuals. A person who prays for the welfare of these individuals does so, however, not because he may happen to know some of them, but because all of them are of especial concern to him when, as now, he associates himself with all Israel. That association is either explicitly expressed or else simply alluded to in the different versions of this berakah; in *Siddur R. Saadia* it is implied in the additional plea for "a good reward unto all who trust in Thy Name," but in the other versions it is expressed explicitly—as in our present version which adds to that plea "and set our portion with them," and as in the early Palestinian version which reads "and grant us a good reward."[110] "Us" refers to the person reciting the berakah and to the "undifferentiated others" with whom he is now associated, whereas the *ẓaddiḳim*, the *gerim*, etc., are the differentiated others who are the burden of the petition.

As given in the Yerushalmi, the closing formula of the berakah, we noticed, is "the Trust (*Mibṭaḥ*) of the *ẓaddiḳim*." Obviously God is also the Trust of the *zeḳenim*, the *gerim*, and all the others mentioned in the petition. He is, indeed, the Trust of all Israel, of "all who trust in Thy Name." The closing formula mentions the major theme of the berakah, the *ẓaddiḳim*, but in affirming that God is the Trust of the *ẓaddiḳim* it also affirms, by direct implication, that He is the Trust of all Israel. In fine, when the individual closes the berakah with the phrase "the Trust (*Mibṭaḥ*) of the *ẓaddiḳim*" he is expressing, as well, his own heart-felt trust in God. Embodied in that phrase is the concept of *biṭṭaḥon*, a term which connotes reliance on God for welfare and security,[111] and which is, therefore, to be distinguished from the kindred concept of *'emunah*, the trust in God's word or promise.

An expression of *biṭṭaḥon*, however, need not be only the culmination of a petition for welfare and security. Reliance on God is an abiding consciousness and hence may be expressed in a berakah of praise alone, one that does not contain a petition. Such an expression of *biṭṭaḥon* is the First Berakah in the 'Amidah, a berakah in which that concept is fused with the concepts of God's love and *'Abot* (Patriarchs). Being the First Berakah it has an opening as well as a closing formula,[112] and yet, because the concepts are fused, the berakah is a unitary entity. The two formulas are dependent on each other for their full meaning. In consonance with the opening formula, "Blessed art Thou, O Lord our God and God of our Fathers, God of Abraham, God of Isaac and God of Jacob," the closing formula praises God as "the Shield of Abraham" (in accordance with Gen. 15:1) and thus gives pre-eminence to the first Patriarch.[113] But if "Shield" as a metaphor for God's protecting love refers back to "God of Abraham," it also refers back to the phrase "our God and God of our Fathers"—God protected the Patriarchs and He protects us now, as well. Insofar as the First Berakah relates to the individual's own experience, therefore, it expresses gratitude for God's protection here and now; in other words, it is an expression of *biṭṭaḥon*.[114] This theme of *biṭṭaḥon* is emphasized in the Palestinian version by the phrase "our Shield and the Shield of our Fathers, our Trust (*Mibṭaḥenu*) in every generation,"[115] a phrase that immediately precedes the closing formula. In our version the same idea is expressed by the words "O King, Helper, Savior,[116] and Shield," words that, again, immediately precede the closing formula. The term "the Shield of Abraham" in the closing formula hence implies, at least, God's protection in the present, too. We ought to add that the section in our version affirming that God remembers the deeds of the Patriarchs and that He is bringing a redeemer to their children's children is not even hinted at in the Palestinian version; the themes of this section are not integral to the berakah.[117]

Biṭṭaḥon is, indeed, an abiding consciousness, but it will not become a crystallized experience without an occasion of some sort. That occasion, however, need be no more than a reminder and the occasion for the First Berakah, we shall see, is precisely of such a character.

The Tefillah or 'Amidah makes high demands upon the individual. In the first place, there must be the awareness on the part of the individual of a relationship between himself and others, but this in itself presents no difficulty when the concepts of Israel and of man are elements of the common value complex. Moreover, the very idea that one is saying the Tefillah also contributes to this expression of the larger self, as we can see from the "short Tefillah." This short Tefillah consists of a single petition which culminates in the berakah "Blessed art Thou, O Lord, Who hearkenest unto prayer," the closing formula of the Sixteenth Berakah. The short Tefillah is to be said instead of the regular Tefillah when a person journeys in dangerous territory.[118] The danger is limited to the individual, yet in the various formulations of the petition for safety the individual associates himself with the people of Israel: "Save, O Lord [הושע השם], Thy people, Israel";[119] or "Hearken to the prayer of Thy people, Israel";[120] or "Thy people's needs are many. . . . May it be Thy will, O Lord our God, that Thou give to each one according to his needs."[121] Despite the particular danger to which he is exposed, the individual prays not for personal deliverance but for the people as a whole; he is, after all, saying what constitutes the Tefillah in these circumstances, and that very idea makes his personal need subordinate. 'Abaye later put into words what had long been the general view when he said, "A person ought always to associate himself with the *ẓibbur* [community]."[122]

A major difficulty, however, is the length of the regular Tefillah. True, the conceptual continuum which unites all the berakot enables a person to carry over the experience of God's love from berakah to berakah. On the other hand, that experience was made difficult to achieve when the Tefillah was recited from memory by the effort to recollect the correct phrases, and the longer the Tefillah, the greater the difficulty. The early Tannaim differed, therefore, with respect to the recitation of the Daily Tefillah by the individual, there being no difficulty, of course, when it was recited at the synagogue service by the leader.[123] As against Rabban Gamaliel, who holds that the individual ought to recite the full Eighteen Berakot every day, R. Joshua says, "the substance [or an abstract, מעין] of the Eighteen" and R. 'Aḳiba says, "if the Tefillah is fluent in his mouth" he ought to recite the full Eighteen, but if not, the substance of the Eighteeen.[124] Ginzberg has demonstrated that the statements of R. Joshua and R. 'Akiba relate to everybody and not only to him who is at the time harassed or distracted.[125] R. Joshua holds that the individual may, if he wishes,[126] recite merely an abstract of the Tefillah every day, but R. 'Aḳiba evidently holds that only if it is difficult for the individual to recollect the full Tefillah ought he to recite an abstract. With respect to the abstract itself, Rab taught that it is to consist of "the end of each and every berakah," including the closing formula of each of them, while Samuel taught that the middle section is to be condensed and made into one berakah but that the first three and the last three berakot are to be recited in full.[127]

Keeping to a fixed text over a long period of time likewise makes a heartfelt Tefillah difficult. Reciting the same words day after day doubtless results in fluency, but it may also result in saying the Tefillah mechanically and by rote. The individual who fulfills R. 'Aḳiba's requirement and who recites the Tefillah fluently may simply be reciting it in this way. R. Eliezer hence takes issue here with R. 'Aḳiba and with him alone, as Lieberman shows conclusively.[128] When R. Eliezer says, "He who makes his Tefillah *ḳeba'*, his Tefillah is not supplication,"[129] he means by *ḳeba'*, accordingly, keeping to a fixed text of the Tefillah over a long period of time.[130] This interpretation is borne out by the statements in the Yerushalmi which follow upon R. Eliezer's dictum. R. 'Abbahu in the name of R. Eleazar explains the dictum as merely a warning that reciting the Tefillah should not become as casual as reading a secular document—that is to say, *ḳeba'* does not mean that one must change the text of the Tefillah every day but that the same text must not be kept to over a long period of time. R. 'Aḥa' in the name of R. Jose declares that one should say something new in the Tefillah every day; R. Eleazar said a new Tefillah every day—that is, he changed the text of the middle part, which is supplication, every day; and R. 'Abbahu said a new berakah every day—that is, he changed a text in the berakot "of praise" daily, as well.

If we take *ḳeba'* in R. Eliezer's dictum to refer to "any fixed form" and thus interpret the dictum to mean that the individual must not employ any fixed form at all when he is saying his Tefillah, we are forcing R. Eliezer into a contradiction; a fixed form of the short Tefillah was formulated by R. Eliezer himself.[131] But it can hardly be supposed that R. Eliezer objects to form as such. Were that so, he would disapprove, too, of all the berakot, of any formulated berakah.

Actually, his dictum, it seems to us, implies just the opposite. When he says that the Tefillah must be supplication he can only be referring to the *petitions* of the Tefillah; if these are not heartfelt, we take him to be saying, the formulated culminating berakot[132] are not heartfelt and consequently the Tefillah as a whole does not represent an experience. He points to a difficulty, one that is inherent in the nature of a prescribed liturgy. To overcome the difficulty by eliminating the forms, however, is to do away with the possibility of profound spiritual experiences, the nurture and expression of a rich variety of value concepts, the cultivation of the larger self.

An individual's prayer which wells out of his own immediate or special need, all must grant, is heartfelt. But such a prayer does not merely "well out" of one's need; to pray at all, an individual must have the assurance that God is near, and that He hearkens to prayer. Now, the berakot of the Tefillah can bring not only the assurance but the experience of God's nearness and the experience, too, that He answers prayer. It was the practice, therefore, to attach personal petitions to the Tefillah, or else to insert them, and that practice surely testifies that the saying of the Tefillah was not a matter of rote. Rather, it brought the individual a genuine experience, an experience which enabled him to give voice to his own personal need.

A baraita rules that a person may "say words" after the Tefillah,[133] these "words" being, as Lieberman points out, thanksgivings and supplications.[134] The rule given here raises no problem, since what is added by the individual comes at the end of the Tefillah and thus does not affect the conceptual continuum of the berakot. But another baraita states that a man may insert a petition for his own needs in "Who hearkenest unto prayer," the Sixteenth Berakah,[135] and the Amoraim, while acknowledging this statement, nevertheless go further and say that he may insert a petition for a particular need toward the close of any relevant berakah.[136] Those who hold that insertions of this kind are permissible feel, we assume, that such personal petitions are entirely incidental to a berakah and so do not interrupt the conceptual continuum. In any case, we may draw the same conclusion from all these halakot; namely, that the experience achieved in saying the Tefillah helped to evoke nonformalized private prayer.

C. The Occasions for the Tefillah

The First Berakah of the Tefillah is an expression of *biṭṭaḥon*, of reliance on God.[137] *Biṭṭaḥon* is an abiding consciousness; it enables a man to initiate and carry through his daily enterprises and also to meet adversity. Nevertheless, *biṭṭaḥon* remains implicit unless it is meditated upon and put into words, as in a berakah. When expressed in a berakah, *biṭṭaḥon* becomes a unitary meditative experience, and such a unitary meditative experience is the First Berakah. But every berakah needs a stimulus of some sort, an occasion, and hence the First Berakah, too, needs an occasion. Since *biṭṭaḥon* is an abiding consciousness, the occasion here, however, need be only a reminder.[138] True, the reminder is for the recital of the Tefillah as a whole, but the Tefillah is a series of berakot united in a conceptual continuum, and the reminder directly recalls, therefore, the first of that series, the First Berakah.

Certain periods of the day are the reminders for saying the Tefillah. The Mishnah rules that the Tefillah is to be said at three different periods of the day. According to the *Ḥakamim* (a group of scholars), it may be said in the morning until midday and in the afternoon "until the evening,"[139] whereas the evening Tefillah has no fixed time (*ḳeba'*).[140] Asking, "Why did they state [i.e., in the Mishnah] that the morning Tefillah [may be recited] until midday," and repeating a similar question with regard to the afternoon Tefillah, the Tosefta supplies an explanation for the rules of the Mishnah. The morning Tefillah may be said until midday, explains the Tosefta, because the communal sacrifice of the morning (שחר) was offered until midday and the afternoon Tefillah, Minḥah, may be said until the evening because the communal sacrifice of the afternoon (בין הערבים) was offered until the evening.[141] It was because there was no communal sacrifice in the evening that there is no fixed time (*ḳeba'*) for the evening Tefillah which, consequently may be said at any time during the night.[142] But the Amoraim interpret this rule, too, in such fashion as to establish further the time-correspondence between the daily sacrifices and the Tefillah. R. Tanḥuma interprets the rule to mean that the time for the evening Tefillah corresponds to the time for the all-night consumption of the limbs and fat pieces on the altar,[143] and a supplementary interpretation in the Babli takes the rule to be also in accord with the opinion that the saying of the evening Tefillah is an optional matter.[144] The Mishnah itself, however, makes no mention of the correspondence in time between the daily sacrifices and the Tefillot, although it certainly takes such correspondence for granted.[145]

For a moment let us digress to draw attention to the implication of the view that saying the evening Tefillah was an optional matter. Such a view clearly implies that the Tefillah was not strictly a mode of communal worship but rather a mode of worship for the individual; were it primarily a mode of communal worship, at no time could the saying of the Tefillah be something left altogether to the individual.[146] The same implication is present in the wide latitude of time for the evening Tefillah given in the Mishnah.

As the occasions for the Tefillah, the designated periods of the day differ from every other occasion that serves as the initiating stimulus for a series of berakot. In all the other instances of a conceptual continuum, the First Berakah interprets the initial stimulus or occasion and the occasion becomes thereby an element in the total unitary experience expressed by the First Berakah. We observed this to be the case in the First Berakah of the Birkat ha-Mazon, a berakah which interprets the meal just eaten as a manifestation of God's bounty and love;[147] and again in the case of the First Berakah of the berakot of the Shema', a berakah which interprets the light of the new day as a manifestation of God's love.[148] Now, the designated periods of the day are likewise related to common phenomena. They constitute the three common divisions of the day: the morning, when the sun is in the east; noon, when the sun is at the zenith; the evening, when the sun is in the west. The occasions for the Tefillah, then, are none other than phenomena in common experience. Indeed, R. Samuel b. Naḥman declares that it is because of these three changes in the position of the sun every day that a man ought to say the Tefillah three times every day.[149] But the identical Tefillah is said at all three periods of the day,[150] and hence the First Berakah cannot be an interpretation of each one of them in turn. Being factors of common experience, however, the periods of the day can act as reminders to recite the Tefillah, if the First Berakah is of such a character that merely a reminder will suffice. Since the First Berakah embodies the concept of *biṭṭaḥon*—an abiding consciousness—a reminder is altogether sufficient for the berakah to become a meditative experience.

In the days of the Temple, an era of sacrificial worship, the present order of the first three berakot, beginning with 'Abot, had already become an established tradition.[151] This indicates that the occasion for the Tefillah was not, in fact, the daily communal sacrifice; had it been, the First Berakah would certainly have referred to the sacrifices. Correspondence in time between the daily communal sacrifices and the saying of the Tefillah implies, therefore, not that the communal sacrifice is the occasion for the saying of the Tefillah, but, on the contrary, that the saying of the Tefillah is to be a reminder of the communal sacrifice—and this, even in the days of the Temple.

A comparison of the statements in the Mishnah and the Tosefta cited above leads to the same conclusion. We noticed that the Mishnah, although taking for granted the correspondence in time between the daily sacrifice and the saying of the Tefillah, makes no mention of that fact. Why? Because the Mishnah states a rule with respect to the reminders for saying the Tefillah and the matter of the time-correspondence does not add anything to the rule itself. The Tosefta, on the other hand, bases its statement on the rule in the Mishnah and adds a reason for that rule, namely, the time-correspondence between the saying of the Tefillah and the daily sacrifice. But what halakic bearing does this statement have? What does the Tosefta actually add? Surely the statement in the Tosefta does not mean simply to reaffirm the halakah in the Mishnah, a halakah which the statement quotes. If the Tosefta teaches anything new, it cannot be something with regard to reminders for saying the Tefillah but with regard to recollecting the daily sacrifices. The Mishnah states a rule with regard to reminders for saying the Tefillah; the Tosefta adds to this rule the halakah that saying the Tefillah is to be a reminder of the daily communal sacrifices.[152]

Rabbinic statements implying a correspondence between the Tefillah and the sacrifices do not refer to any correspondence in subject-matter. That is evident when we examine, for example, the statements of R. Joshua b. Levi and R. Jose b. R. Ḥanina as given in *Berakot* 26b and the discussion there. R. Joshua says that the Tefillot were ordained "as against" (*keneged*) the daily communal sacrifices, but in support of this statement the Talmud brings the passage of the

Tosefta on the correspondence of the time of the Tefillot to that of the daily sacrifices.[153] R. Joshua's view that the Tefillah corresponds to the daily communal sacrifice is thus supported only by the baraita as to the correspondence in time. R. Jose makes no reference to the sacrifices at all. He says that the *'Abot* (Patriarchs) ordained the Tefillot, and in support of that statement the Talmud brings a baraita to the effect that Abraham ordained the Tefillah of the morning, Isaac that of the afternoon, and Jacob that of the evening.[154] Later, in order to harmonize R. Jose's statement with the Tosefta, the Talmud explains R. Jose to mean that the Tefillot were ordained by the *'Abot* but that the rabbis attached the Tefillot (אסמכינהו) to the sacrifices.[155] Even in the statement as amended, then, the content of the Tefillah as whole is one thing and the connection with the sacrifices quite another. Similarly, in all the versions of the various statements given here[156] and in other statements on the number, the time, or the form (Eighteen Berakot) of the Tefillot,[157] the daily sacrifices are not connected with the subject-matter of the Tefillah as a whole.

D. Worship in the Heart

'Abodah as worship refers either to the sacrificial worship in the Temple, or else pejoratively to the manner of worshipping any idol; in either case, the worship consists of actions of some kind.[158] But the rabbis extended the scope of 'abodah as proper worship, the worship of God, to include berakot and the Tefillah, the acceptance of *malkut Shamayim* and study of Torah; in other words, they developed forms of nonsacrificial worship.

Berakot are characterized as 'abodah in a rabbinic interpretation of a biblical verse and through a halakah. The berakot on bread and on water are equated with 'abodah in an interpretation of Exodus 23:25.[159] A halakah states that just as an offensive-looking or ill-smelling priest is unfit to participate in the 'Abodah (of the Temple), so ill-smelling hands make one unfit to say the berakah[160] and thus the Birkat ha-Mazon, most likely, is in this halakah equated with 'abodah.[161]

Directly associated with the daily communal sacrifices by reason of correspondence in time, the Tefillah is characterized as 'abodah in a far more emphatic manner than is any other form of nonsacrificial worship. In the halakah just cited, the berakah is characterized as 'abodah by being made analogous to the 'Abodah of the Temple, but there is no direct connection between the two. The Tefillah, however, is directly connected with the 'Abodah of the Temple; it is connected with the 'Abodah not only through the halakah which makes of the Tefillah a reminder of the 'Abodah, but also through related halakot—through the halakot that permit the evening Tefillah to be said at any time during the night since it is not a reminder of the 'Abodah, and that, for the same reason, make recitation of the evening Tefillah an optional matter.[162] Stemming from a correspondence in time, these halakot imply that the Tefillah and the 'Abodah are of a piece, a much more emphatic manner of characterizing the Tefillah as 'abodah than by the method of analogy. What the halakot can only imply, R. Joshua states more explicitly when he says that the Tefillot were ordained "as against" the daily communal sacrifices; it is a statement characterizing the Tefillah as 'abodah but which is supported, again, by reference to the time-correspondence between the two.[163]

A famous passage in the Sifre not only characterizes the Tefillah as 'abodah but indicates the distinction between the Tefillah and sacrificial worship. Taking Deuteronomy 11:13 as saying "to love the Lord your God and to worship Him [*le 'abedo*] in all your hearts," the Sifre declares that "to worship Him in all your hearts" can refer only to the Tefillah, since the sacrificial worship takes place not in the heart of the individual [but on the altar], and the passage closes (after adducing further proof from Ps. 141:2 and Dan. 6:11, 21) with the statement "just as the 'Abodah of the altar is called 'abodah, so the Tefillah is called 'abodah."[164] A version of the passage is found in the Yerushalmi and there the Tefillah is specifically designated as '*abodah ba-leb*, worship in the heart.[165] The passage in the Sifre and its variants say in so many words that the Tefillah is 'abodah, but that it is nonsacrificial worship. Despite the time-correspondence and despite halakot which connect the Tefillah with the sacrificial worship, the Tefillah—by reason of its content—is to be distinguished from sacrificial worship.

It is unlikely that any form of nonsacrificial worship, including the Tefillah, was explicitly referred to as 'abodah before the cessation of the sacrificial worship. Each form of nonsacrificial worship has its own name, such as berakah or tefillah, and that name, being a value concept, is a sufficient characterization of the form. After the Temple was destroyed, however, and sacrificial worship was no longer possible, the nonsacrificial forms of worship were felt to be, in a sense, surrogates for the sacrificial worship and it was for that reason, apparently, that they were also characterized as 'abodah. Being the reminder of the daily sacrifices, "of one piece" with 'abodah, the Tefillah was especially singled out as the surrogate for the sacrifices. Simply to characterize the Tefillah as 'abodah, therefore, was not enough and the Tefillah was further related to the daily sacrifices, as we shall see immediately, by being invested with their character and function. But the rabbis could not have equated the Tefillah and the other matters with 'abodah, even at a later time, had these things not already been from the very beginning, i.e., in the days of the Temple as well, forms of nonsacrificial worship.

In addition to being a reminder of the daily communal sacrifices because of their time-correspondence, the Tefillah was conceived, after the destruction of the Temple, as being itself an offering given in place of those sacrifices. The afternoon Tefillah, Minḥah, is designated, according to R. Samuel b. Naḥman, "a pure oblation" in Malachi 1:11, where it is depicted as a pure oblation (*minḥah*) which is offered to God everywhere, in every land.[166] Further, the Tefillah acts as a surrogate for other Temple sacrifices as well. Hosea 14:3 was interpreted to mean: We render in place of bullocks the words of our lips, the Tefillah;[167] and this interpretation cannot refer to the daily communal sacrifices, for the latter were lambs, not bullocks.

By a play on the word *kebes*, lamb, Bet Shammai taught that the daily communal sacrifices, consisting of lambs (Num. 28:3), "press down" the iniquities of Israel, whereas Bet Hillel, also playing on the same word, taught that these sacrifices "wash off" the iniquities.[168] Bet Hillel's metaphorical teaching is tantamount to saying that the daily sacrifices atone for Israel's sins, an idea elaborated by R. Judan b. R. Simon who declares that the morning sacrifice atoned for the sins committed at night and the evening sacrifice for the sins committed during the day.[169] Another source describes the atoning function of the two daily sacrifices by calling them two daily intercessors or advocates.[170] When R. Joshua says that the Tefillah was ordained "as against" the daily sacrifices,[171] he apparently suggests that the Tefillah, acting as a surrogate, likewise has an atoning function. Similarly, when the rabbis speak of the Tefillah (of Minḥah) as recited "in place of the sacrifice,"[172] they evidently imply that this Tefillah, like the sacrifice, has an atoning function. Indeed, Hosea 14: 3 once more is taken to mean that the Tefillah is a surrogate for all sacrifices of atonement, the verse being interpreted as follows: When the Temple was standing we brought a sacrifice in atonement, but now we have only the Tefillah.[173]

The concepts of 'abodah and tefillah interpret the same entity. They illustrate, but in a singular manner, how, in an organismic complex, different value concepts may interpret the same act or entity. In this section the rabbinic statements and the halakot we have cited are concretizations of the concept of 'abodah; and it is to be noticed that such statements and halakot embodying the concept of tefillah as well are based on one thing, namely, the time-correspondence between the Tefillah and the daily communal sacrifices. In all the previous sections, however, we discussed the content and form of the Tefillah and found that the many halakot cited there were concretizations of the concepts of tefillah and berakah. The concepts embodied in the content and structure of the Tefillah, therefore, are those of tefillah and berakah; in that respect the Tefillah is like all other instances of organismic thought wherein the concepts involved are embodied in the content.[174] That is not the case when the concept of 'abodah interprets the Tefillah as a sacrifice; we then have the singular instance in which a value concept interpreting an act is not involved in the content of that act.

In an organismic complex, sometimes one concept is stressed above another concept, and sometimes the stress is the other way around.[175] According to a tannaitic interpretation of Deuteronomy 12: 5, the prophets and *zeḳenim* ordained that Israel recite the Tefillah three times every day and thus say, "Restore Thy *Shekinah* to Zion and the order of Thy 'Abodah to Jerusalem, Thy city."[176] Here the concept of 'abodah is distinctly stressed above that of tefillah. Yet, in a statement containing similar phrases, tefillah is expressly stressed above 'abodah. Moses foresaw, say the rabbis, that the Temple would be destroyed and the bringing of the first fruits would cease, and he therefore ordained that Israel recite the Tefillah three times every day, "for the Tefillah is dearer to God than all the good deeds and all the sacrifices."[177] "The Tefillah," says R. Eleazar simply, "is greater than the sacrifices."[178]

'Abodah and tefillah are posed against each other in a halakic discussion.[179] On the one hand, the Tefillah (of Minḥah) is "in place of sacrifice" and hence ought not to be said later than the designated time of the sacrifice; on the other hand, it is *raḥame*, the beseeching of compassion from God, and, therefore, ought to be said whenever one wishes to do so. R. Joḥanan ruled that the principle applying in the case of a sacrifice—"When its day has passed, the sacrifice of the day is void"—does not apply here, and that when one has forgotten to say the Tefillah of Minḥah at its designated time it may be said later. What primarily characterizes the Tefillah is its content.

Besides the berakot on bread and water, the Birkat ha-Mazon, and the Tefillah, there are also other matters which are designated by the rabbis as 'abodah: Ḳeri'at Shema'[180] and study of Torah.[181] Like Ḳeri'at Shema', study of Torah can be made an occasion for the experience of God and, in fact, Ḳeri'at Shema' is only a special instance of study of Torah.[182] When these matters are characterized as 'abodah, the term 'abodah can refer only to nonsacrificial worship. But what is the distinctive character of nonsacrificial worship? We have found that in the act of saying a berakah before eating a morsel of bread an individual expresses his awareness of God's love, and that the berakah enhances that awareness. This is likewise true of the act of saying a berakah on water. In each case, the berakah and the occasion for reciting it constitute a unitary entity, an integral experience of God's love. Essentially, the Birkat ha-Mazon and the Tefillah also represent unitary experiences of God's love, although here that concept connects a series of berakot, all of which, after the First Berakah, are meditative experiences of God's love. Acceptance of *malkut Shamayim* through Ḳeri'at Shema' and the study of Torah involves an altogether different experience, but once more a unitary experience of God is achieved—this time as the result of meditating upon and studying an integrated literary entity. These various experiences are characterized as 'abodah because they have a character in common, each of them representing a unitary experience of God mediated by a concept.

If this is the distinctive character of nonsacrificial worship, then every berakah may be characterized as 'abodah, for every berakah represents a unitary experience of God mediated by a concept. True, the rabbis do not designate every berakah as 'abodah, but that is because no purpose was to be served by doing so. Nothing is actually added when a berakah is characterized as 'abodah: no special function is assigned to it, nor is it otherwise distinguished from the berakot in general. It was enough to designate a few berakot as 'abodah in order to establish the idea that all berakot were to be regarded as nonsacrificial worship, as surrogates for the worship in the Temple, and the few chosen are those that are said most often.

Nonsacrificial worship is normal mysticism. We shall discuss normal mysticism at some length in Chapter VII; in order to compare nonsacrificial with sacrificial worship, however, we must indicate how the various forms of nonsacrificial worship exhibit characteristics of normal mysticism. In a berakah the experience of God is mediated, usually, by the concept of God's love, and sometimes by that of God's justice, but these concepts are very much akin to almost parallel concepts informing universal human morality, akin, that is, to normal human experience.[183] Moreover, among the very berakot specifically designated as 'abodah are berakot which are joined to commonplace things, daily acts; normal occurrences being thus occasions for worship.[184] In Ḳeri'at Shema' the experience of God is mediated by the concept of *malkut Shamayim*, the experience being a meditative one in which the individual makes "Him King above and below and in the four winds of heaven."[185] Instructions enabling a person to achieve this experience are intended for the people as a whole, for the normal man, and are not directions aiming toward visions or locutions.[186] Nonsacrificial worship is normal mysticism, religious experience which is not isolated from normal human experience, mystical experience which does not involve such sensory phenomena.

Sacrificial worship of God can take place only in the Temple at Jerusalem. Some tannaitic sources assume that the pilgrims who came to the Temple on the festivals could experience there *gilluy Shekinah*, a revelation of God in some visible manner.[187] The *Ḥakamim* of the Mishnah reject that assumption, however, and their view is reflected in both Talmuds as well.[188] According to the general view it seems, therefore, that a pilgrim who "stood by" his sacrifice as it was being offered in the Temple had no experience of *gilluy Shekinah*, and, by the same token, neither did the representatives of the people as a whole who "stood by" as the daily communal sacrifices were being offered.[189] All agree, however, that in the future sacrificial worship will be associated with *gilluy Shekinah*. The petition quoted above, "Restore Thy *Shekinah* to Zion and the order of Thy 'Abodah to Jerusalem," reflects the assumption that when the 'Abodah will be restored, *gilluy Shekinah* will also be restored at the Temple.[190]

Since the rabbis firmly believed that ultimately the 'Abodah would be restored to Jerusalem, they obviously regarded the Tefillah as having a sacrificial character only for the time being. Because of the time correspondence, the Tefillah serves now as a reminder of the daily communal sacrifices, but basically it is in itself not a sacrifice. Sacrificial worship of God is associated with *gilluy Shekinah*, whereas the Tefillah, like the berakot and Ḳeri'at Shema', is nonsacrificial worship or normal mysticism.

CHAPTER VI

The Element of Community in Worship

A. Aspects of *Kiddush ha-Shem*

The rabbinic term for community is *ẓibbur*. It is a concept of relationship, referring to the group as a corporate entity, a collectivity, in contradistinction to the individual member. Since the contradistinction holds whether the *ẓibbur* be large or small, the word *ẓibbur* may stand either for the entire people or for a local community. When the rabbis speak, for example, of "the sacrifices of the *ẓibbur*,"[1] they refer to the Temple sacrifices brought in behalf of the entire people;[2] on the other hand, when they speak of the *ẓibbur* at prayer, they definitely refer to a local community.[3]

Being a concept of relationship, *ẓibbur* is a cognitive concept.[4] In concrete valuational situations, cognitive concepts are fused with value concepts,[5] and *ẓibbur* is a cognitive concept often fused with the value concept of Israel. When the word *ẓibbur* is used, the value concept of Israel is made concrete, embodied in a living human group. Thus, when the word *ẓibbur* is applied to Israel as a whole, the Talmud indicates, it excludes those who are no longer living.[6] When the word is applied to a local community, it is used in so concrete a sense as to refer, frequently, to a face-to-face group.[7]

We must, however, distinguish between a mere aggregate of individuals and a *ẓibbur*. A *ẓibbur* is a corporate entity, that is to say, it has a character which is often expressed in corporate acts. A corporate act is an act which, as a unitary entity, is performed by the *ẓibbur* but in which the individual members participate in definite and varied ways. Further, despite only sharing in the preformance of the act, each individual has an experience of the act as a whole. On the other hand, when the word *ẓibbur* is used without any reference to a corporate act, the word refers to Israel as a whole or to the community as a whole—to either as a corporate entity which is not differentiated into particular individuals.

In the case of the "sacrifices of the *ẓibbur*," participation by all the members of the *ẓibbur*, meaning by all Israel, was obviously not possible, and could therefore only be symbolized. Present at these daily Temple sacrifices were weekly representatives of the people of Israel as a whole—priests, Levites, and laymen,[8] and these representatives "stood by" the sacrifice as it was being offered.[9] To stand by a sacrifice was a duty laid upon the person bringing the sacrifice;[10] the representatives were thus deputies, agents acting in behalf of all the living members of the people.[11] The point is that the deputies consisted of representatives of all three divisions of Israel, so that symbolically the entire people participated.

In nonsacrificial worship, the type of worship we are discussing in this chapter, acts of communal worship require a face-to-face group. We shall see how, in a number of such acts, the face-to-face *ẓibbur*, in the very process of a corporate act, brings to its members a vivid awareness of God's holiness. The *ẓibbur* enables the individual to achieve an experience of worship he could not otherwise have achieved.

A corporate act of worship bringing to the individual a consciousness of God's holiness is a concretization of *ḳiddush ha-Shem*. Now *ḳiddush ha-Shem* involves not only an act itself but the effect which the act produces upon others, and these two factors are not readily apparent in an act of worship, precisely because it is a corporate act. When *ḳiddush ha-Shem* is not an act of worship, however, the two factors are obvious, as the following halakah indicates. Even to save his life, declares R. Ishmael, a Jew must not commit an act of idolatry in public, *be-farhesya'*, for it says, "Ye shall not profane My holy Name, but I will be hallowed among the children of Israel" (Lev. 22:32).[12] The verse here speaks of profaning the Name, *ḥillul ha-Shem*, and of hallowing the Name, *ḳiddush ha-Shem*, the act in either case, according to R. Ishmael's interpretation, being *be-farhesya'*, "among the children of Israel." Another baraita teaches that "among the children of Israel," taken in conjunction with

Numbers 16:21, refers to the presence of at least ten Jews, and so the Talmud defines *be-farhesya'*, "in public," to mean an act which is beheld by at least ten Jews.[13]

From the halakah just cited we can apprehend the significance of *ḳiddush ha-Shem*. *Kiddush ha-Shem*, we learn, consists of an act which produces a consciousness of God's holiness in the beholders, since it is "among the children of Israel" that the hallowing of the Name of God occurs. Obviously the heroic act and the effect which that act produces have something in common. The heroic act, whatever else it may be, is an ultimate acknowledgment of God. Its effect, therefore, on the beholders, must be a concurrence with, almost a participation in, that acknowledgment. There is a consciousness of God's holiness in the beholders because the martyr, through his heroic act, demonstrates his own consciousness of God's holiness.[14]

Further, the halakah helps us to differentiate between corporate acts on the one hand, and acts which require what is merely an aggregate of individuals, on the other. A heroic act of *kiddush ha-shem* takes place *be-farhesya'*—that is, in the presence of at least ten Jews. An act of corporate worship, we shall see, also requires at least ten Jews. In a corporate act, however, every individual present is an active participant, and hence the ten constitute a *ẓibbur*. On the other hand, the individuals beholding a heroic act of *kiddush ha-Shem* are not active participants in that act, and hence are only a public, a mere aggregate of individuals. A corporate act of *ḳiddush ha-Shem* in worship is the act of a *ẓibbur*, whereas a heroic act of *ḳiddush ha-Shem* is the act of an individual which takes place *be-farhesya'*, in public. This is not to say, of course, that "the public" can be dispensed with. *Be-farhesya'* is a requisite if the act of martyrdom is to be *ḳiddush ha-Shem*, an act that produces a consciousness of God's holiness in fellow-Jews.[15]

Kiddush ha-Shem is not limited to an act of martyrdom on the part of a Jew and to the effect of such an act upon its Jewish beholders. Among the other aspects of *ḳiddush ha-Shem* is one in which a righteous act by a Jew toward a Gentile elicits from the Gentile an acknowledgment of the God of the Jews, albeit a qualified acknowledgment, and this aspect of *ḳiddush ha-Shem*, too, has a bearing on corporate worship. Stories on this aspect of *ḳiddush ha-Shem* are found in the Yerushalmi, some having a circumstantial character and some being evidently folk tales. There is a circumstantial character, for example, to the story of R. Jonathan and his Roman neighbor. It tells how R. Jonathan, before deciding a case dealing with property infringement, first corrected a similar infringement of his own against the property of his Roman neighbor, and how the Roman, impressed by R. Jonathan's integrity, thereupon exclaimed, "Blessed is the God of the Jews!"[16] A story with a folk-tale quality is the one about R. Samuel b. Sisraṭai and the empress.[17] R. Samuel had found a jewel belonging to the empress and, having heard it proclaimed that the finder would be rewarded should he return it within thirty days, and be decapitated should he return it after that time, R. Samuel returned the jewel after thirty days. When the empress asked him his reason for the delay, he replied that it was in order to make evident that what he did was not out of "fear of thee, but out of fear of God [*Raḥamana'*]"; whereupon the empress declared, "Blessed is the God of the Jews!" In a similar tale, 'Abba' 'Osha'yah likewise returns to the empress her lost ornaments and jewelry,[18] but the moral of this story is more subtle. Here the empress says that these articles belong to the finder, adding that she has other such things which are more valuable. 'Abba' 'Osha'yah replies, however, "The Torah has decreed we must return [the valuables]," and once more the response is, "Blessed is the God of the Jews!" Another story regarding the return of a lost jewel has to do with Simeon b. Shaṭaḥ.[19] To ease his daily labor his pupils bought a donkey for him from a Sarḳi (a member of a trading tribe), and found a pearl hanging from its neck. Simeon ordered his pupils to return the pearl, and when they demurred, he said to them, "Do you think Simeon b. Shaṭaḥ is a barbarian? Simeon b. Shaṭaḥ would rather hear [the Sarḳi say], 'Blessed is the God of the Jews' than have all the wealth of this world."[20] (There is still another story on the same theme in this collection, also with Gentiles exclaiming, "Blessed is the God of the Jews!")[21]

These stories in the Yerushalmi undoubtedly reflect a dominant attitude of the Jews during much of the rabbinic period. The Jews were very anxious to have the Gentiles acknowledge God, incomplete as that acknowledgment had to be by persons who still remained Gentiles. Simeon b. Shaṭaḥ's statement, though perhaps apocryphal, does indicate how keenly leading scholars felt on this matter. In like manner, the stories about R. Samuel and 'Abba' 'Osha'yah reflect numerous less dramatic occasions when there was *ḳiddush ha-Shem* as a result of a righteous act by a Jew toward a Gentile. But all the stories, and not only the folktales, reflect something else as well. In all the stories, the Yerushalmi has the Gentiles, in every instance, make the same declaration, "Blessed is the God of the Jews," and this declaration identifies the incident as an instance of *ḳiddush ha-Shem*. Actually, however, "Blessed is the God of the Jews" is a declaration which does not commit the Gentile at all. What suggests an acknowledgment of God here is the form of the declaration, the form being very reminiscent of a berakah. We shall find, indeed, that there is a genuine berakah which consists solely of an acknowledgment of God, and that this berakah is part of a corporate act of worship. The declaration or formula placed in the mouths of the Gentiles reflects that berakah. In other words, the berakah associated with *ḳiddush ha-Shem* was already so well known that a formula resembling it identified acts of another type as acts of *ḳiddush ha-Shem*. All this does not mean that a new type of *kiddush ha-Shem* emerged, but only that the literary formula which identified that type presupposed an actual berakah consisting solely of an acknowledgment of God.[22]

B. Baraku

Ḳiddush ha-Shem in noncorporate acts is always an outcome of a specific situation. Even when *ḳiddush ha-Shem* is avowedly sought for, as in the story of Simeon b. Shaṭaḥ or in that of R. Samuel, the act of *ḳiddush ha-Shem* is made possible because of a specific situation. *Ḳiddush ha-Shem* in corporate acts, that is, in acts of worship, likewise is an outcome of a situation, namely, the presence of a *ẓibbur*. A *ẓibbur* is not deliberately formed for the purpose of making a corporate acknowledgment of God. An acknowledgment of God under such circumstances would undoubtedly tend to be something contrived and artificial. A *ẓibbur* is formed in the first instance to enable the individual to engage in certain acts of worship incumbent upon him as an individual.[23] There is thus a *ẓibbur* to start with. Because a *ẓibbur* had already been formed, it could also engage in a corporate act of *ḳiddush ha-Shem*.

A mishnah, *Megillah* IV.3, gives a list of the occasions requiring the presence or the participation of at least ten Jews. First in that list is the public recitation of the Shema', but it is described as פורסין את שמע, a phrase to which many different meanings have been variously assigned.[24] On the basis of the evidence in other tannaitic passages,[25] however, there can be little doubt that the phrase refers to a kind of responsive recitation, the leader reciting the first part of a verse in the Shema' and the *ẓibbur* apparently repeating that part and completing the verse.[26] The public recitation of the Shema' was, therefore, a corporate act; that is, an act in which every member of the *ẓibbur* was an active participant. It had to be a corporate recital, we should say, for the simple reason that in early tannaitic times the Shema' was known by many only imperfectly. Calling attention to the baraita (*Berakot* 47b) which defines an *'am ha-'areẓ* (one who is ignorant and negligent of the law) as one who does not recite the Shema', Ginzberg points out that there were Jews who could not recite the Shema',[27] and that this was especially true in Galilee until toward the close of the tannaitic period.[28] The corporate recital enabled the untutored to join in Ḳeri'at Shema' and was a pedagogic device as well, by means of which they could learn the Shema'.[29]

But there is also a corporate act associated with the Shema' and its berakot, and with another occasion named in the mishnah, the public reading of the Torah, to which the mishnah makes no explicit reference. It is an act of worship so simple as to require almost no previous training at all, and it embodies the concept of *ḳiddush ha-Shem*. This corporate act of worship the Gemara assumes to be the one referred to in the mishnah, probably for several reasons. In the first place, the rabbis of the Talmud, as we have demonstrated elsewhere, always endeavor to establish, or rather to make explicit, the nexus inherent in the laws;[30] here they posit *ḳiddush ha-Shem* as the uniting principle which several of the occasions mentioned in the mishnah have in common. Moreover, *ḳiddush ha-Shem* actually does relate to those occasions because they do make possible corporate acts of *ḳiddush ha-Shem*. Second, certain acts of worship, including the corporate recital of the Shema',[31] are not intrinsically corporate in character—that is, the act need not be corporate but may be accomplished by the individual in private; yet the mishnah does not qualify its statement that not less than ten be present on, or participate in, the various occasions listed. The presumption is, therefore, that the mishnah lists only those acts of worship which are intrinsically of a corporate character, and that is precisely the category to which belong such acts of worship as constitute *ḳiddush ha-Shem*.

The uniting principle adduced in the Gemara is a maxim-like interpretation of verses employed by the rabbis to elucidate the concept of *ḳiddush ha-Shem*.[32] In this interpretation *ḳiddush ha-Shem* consists of acts of worship, for the maxim teaches that words which are acts of *ḳiddush ha-Shem* may not be said (at worship) by less than ten.[33] What these acts of worship are is not specified in this passage of the Gemara because they are presumed to be specified in the mishnah; they are, however, named or referred to or discussed by Rashi and other commentaries on the passage, commentaries which reflect an authentic tradition. Rashi names the Ḳaddish, Baraku and, by inference, the Ḳedushah,[34] and we shall see that it is just these acts of worship, and no others, which constitute *ḳiddush ha-Shem*. Asheri refers to "Baraku and Ḳaddish," as occasions when an individual says "a word involving *ḳedushah*" and thus "sanctifies the Name among 'ten.'"[35] Elsewhere in the Talmud itself, an authority characterizes the Ḳedushah by the very maxim and the supporting verses which the Talmud here employs for the interpretation of the mishnah.[36] Finally, *Masseket Soferim*, a post-talmudic tractate, in a section which is practically a quotation of the mishnah, asserts that Ḳaddish and Baraku may not be said in the presence of "less than ten."[37] The acts of worship constituting *ḳiddush ha-Shem* are thus Baraku, the Ḳaddish, and the Ḳedushah.

Baraku is associated, in the synagogue service, with Ḳeri'at Shema'. Because there were Jews who could not recite the Shema' by themselves in early tannaitic times, the recitation of the Shema' was made the act of a *ẓibbur*, one of whom functioned as the leader. The leader also recited, in behalf of the *ẓibbur*, the berakot which precede and follow the Shema',[38] again doubtless because of the untutored in the *ẓibbur*. But the presence of the *ẓibbur* makes possible still another act of worship, one that constitutes *ḳiddush ha-Shem*. Before engaging in the berakot preceding the Shema', the leader says, "Bless ye [*baraku*] the Lord Who is blessed," and the rest of the *ẓibbur* responds with, "Blessed is the Lord Who is blessed for ever and ever."[39] Unlike Ḳeri'at Shema' and its berakot, this act of worship is intrinsically of a corporate character, for it is an act which no individual can accomplish in private. When the leader calls on the others to bless or acknowledge God, he merely initiates the act of hallowing God's Name, the act itself being accomplished when the others actually do acknowledge God. True, since the leader issues the call and hence initiates the act, he is regarded as the one who sanctifies God's Name—witness Asheri's reference to him above; nevertheless, there is no *ḳiddush ha-Shem* until the others respond. Being thus intrinsically corporate, this act of worship remained the act of a *ẓibbur* even when Ḳeri'at Shema' and its berakot ceased to be so.

The response of the *ẓibbur*, "Blessed [*baruk*] is the Lord Who is blessed forever and ever," is a berakah. Although a berakah is usually couched in a formula, Ginzberg has pointed out that there are also instances when a berakah is to be recognized as such by virtue of the idea it expresses.[40] We observed an instance of this type, above, in the berakah of Benjamin the shepherd,[41] and we have another clear instance in the response to Baraku—"Blessed is the Lord." Does not a berakah, however, always express a specific experience of God? What experience of God does the berakah in Baraku reflect?

A berakah which is the response of a *ẓibbur* reflects experience of God, but it is a berakah *sui generis*.[42] The *ẓibbur* consists of individuals to whom God's love is made apparent, through berakot, many times every day. Each berakah expresses and enhances a specific experience of God's love. A berakah which is the response of the *ẓibbur*, however, voices an awareness of God rising not out of a specific experience but out of all of them, an awareness of God Whom the individuals experience on so many different occasions, and in so many different ways, every day. Even a corporate act of worship may reflect a specific experience; it is only in a corporate act of *ḳiddush ha-Shem* that a *ẓibbur* gives expression to an encompassing awareness of God—in a word, to a consciousness of God's holiness itself. In such an act of worship a *ẓibbur* achieves what no individual can achieve. It confirms the personal experience of God by every individual in the *ẓibbur*. If it is to do so in a berakah, that berakah must express a general consciousness of God.[43]

To express this consciousness, the corporate act of worship can have recourse only to general ideas—here to the idea that God is "blessed for ever and ever," and in the Ḳedushah, as we shall find, to the idea that God is everywhere. A corporate act of *ḳiddush ha-Shem* consists, accordingly, of an acknowledgment of God in general terms, although such an acknowledgment can only emerge out of many specific experiences of God. Nor should we be misled into thinking that the general ideas in the acknowledgment contain philosophic implications. The acknowledgment is a berakah, and the general idea, too, is introduced with a form of *baruk*. What is expressed is a consciousness of God which rises out of many and repeated experiences, and not a philosophic abstraction. The abstract terms attempt to express a sense of the holiness of God, an awareness of God not restricted now to any single experience of God.[44]

Baraku and its response are associated also with the public reading of the Torah, another matter listed in *Megillah* IV.3 as requiring the presence of not less than ten. To arrive at the nature of this association, however, we must first describe some features of the public reading of the Torah.

Public reading of the Torah takes place at the services in the morning and at Minḥah on the Sabbath and on fast days; on Monday, Thursday, and on the festivals, only in the morning.[45] Depending on the occasion, from three to seven (or more) are called up to read from the Torah.[46] The reading in later times was done by a man skilled in the practice, although in early times, when the sections were shorter, each of those called up read his own section.[47] According to the Mishnah, a berakah before beginning the reading of the Torah was recited by the first man to read, and another berakah was recited by the last man upon the completion of the entire reading;[48] but it later became the custom for every man called up to recite both berakot, the one before and the other after the reading of his particular section.[49]

The public reading of the Torah is a corporate act on the part of the *ẓibbur* as a whole. Not only do men from the *ẓibbur* participate by being called up to the Torah and by reciting the berakot, but the rest of the *ẓibbur* too is involved. The *ẓibbur* responds with "Amen" to each berakah on the Torah, and the reader must not begin to read until this response has been completed;[50] the members of the *ẓibbur* must refrain from talking during the reading, even to discuss a point of Halakah;[51] it is forbidden for anyone to leave while a section is actually being read.[52] Since it thus involves the *ẓibbur* as a whole, the public reading of the Torah is a corporate act; further, as we shall now see, it is an act which is intrinsically corporate. Manifestly, public reading of the Torah is public instruction, but it is also more than that; the berakot indicate that it is part of an experience of worship. Detailed halakot as to the writing and as to the preparation of the parchment of the scroll to be used for public reading[53] again imply that this reading is not simply public instruction. Such a scroll of the Torah, moreover, is highest in the hierarchy of holy objects.[54] Public reading of the Torah on Sabbaths and festivals, and on several other occasions, goes back, say the rabbis, to an ordinance of Moses.[55] All this is sufficient to demonstrate that participation in public reading of the Torah is something different from an individual's study of Torah. We may say, then, that public reading of the Torah is not merely a corporate act on the part of the *ẓibbur*, but is one which is intrinsically corporate in character.

The berakot on the Torah are an essential feature of this corporate act.[56] The berakah preceding the reading is, in some respects, akin to 'Ahabah Rabbah.[57] Like 'Ahabah Rabbah, it is an anticipatory berakah, called forth by an act yet to be performed. Like 'Ahabah Rabbah, once more, it contains the idea of "the chosen people," the idea now being expressed in the phrase "Who has chosen us from all the peoples."[58] Here, however, this nonconceptualized idea is tied to the concept of *mattan* (the giving of) *Torah*, for the full phrase reads, "Who has chosen us from all the peoples and has given us His Torah," and the emphasis now is on the concept of *mattan Torah*, a concept already concretized in the very selection about to be read. That selection, as it is read, is felt to represent a gift from God, and so when the reading is over another berakah is recited, similar to the first and expressing and enhancing this experience.[59] The corporate act is a unitary act of worship, beginning with a berakah on the Torah, continuing with the reading of a section of the Torah felt to represent a gift from God, and closing with another berakah on the Torah.

But this unitary act of worship does not stand alone. Immediately before reciting the first berakah on the Torah, the man who has been called to the Torah says the Baraku and the rest of the *ẓibbur* replies with the response.[60] The association between Baraku and the first berakah on the Torah is so early as to have been taken for granted in tannaitic times.[61] Nevertheless, there is no integral relation between Baraku and the first berakah on the Torah—for one thing, because the first berakah begins a unitary entity in its own right, and for another, because Baraku constitutes an act of *ḳiddush ha-Shem*, whereas the act of public reading of the Torah, as has been remarked by post-talmudic authorities,[62] does not. The association of Baraku with the public reading of the Torah is entirely due to the circumstance that the public reading of the Torah is intrinsically a corporate act, an act which the individual cannot engage upon alone. Because a *ẓibbur* is present for the reading of the Torah, a corporate act of *ḳiddush ha-Shem*, the Baraku, can precede the reading.[63]

C. The Ḳaddish

The Ḳaddish is a corporate act of *ḳiddush ha-Shem*, and its response is very similar to the one in Baraku. From various statements in rabbinic literature, it is evident that the Ḳaddish was associated originally with public lectures by the rabbis having Haggadah as the subject matter.[64] At the end of such lectures, if there were at least ten men present, there would take place a corporate act of worship. The leader, most likely the lecturer himself, would say, "May His great Name be magnified and sanctified [*we-yitḳaddash*] in the world which He hath created according to His will, and may He make His kingship recognized ["His kingship to reign"—וימליך מלכותיה] during your life and during your days, and during the life of all the house of Israel, speedily and at a near time and say ye, Amen."[65] This part of the Ḳaddish is a prayer by the leader that in the lifetime of his hearers God's Name may be sanctified "in the world": that is, that the whole world may acknowledge God, which means also that His kingship will be recognized by all.[66] The entire idea in this prayer, including the words "magnified and sanctified" which epitomize it, stems from Ezekiel 38:23: "And I will magnify Myself and sanctify Myself, and I will make Myself known in the eyes of many nations; and they shall know that I am the Lord."[67]

When the people say "Amen" to this prayer, as they are bidden to do, they are naturally reminded that they themselves ought to acknowledge God here and now. Immediately after saying "Amen," therefore, they add, "Blessed be His great Name forever and ever."[68] Almost identical with the berakah in Baraku, this statement, too, is an acknowledgment of God in general terms and is a berakah in content, if not in form. Prayer and response now constitute a corporate act of *ḳiddush ha-Shem*,[69] and hence the rubric "Ḳaddish," taken from the second epitomizing term, *we-yitḳaddash*. Since the act of *ḳiddush ha-Shem* has been consummated by the response, the rest of the paragraph is probably a later addition, as indeed its partly Hebrew, partly Aramaic character seems to indicate. The Ḳaddish proper—that is, the prayer and the response—are in Aramaic, for the Ḳaddish came at the end of lectures to the Aramaic-speaking public.[70]

Later it became the practice to recite the Ḳaddish at public worship at the end of each section of the liturgy, and public worship as a whole thus came to be an occasion for acts of *ḳiddush ha-Shem*. A conjunction of two separate acts of *ḳiddush ha-Shem* occurs at the morning service when Baraku is preceded by Ḳaddish, a conjunction so striking that it was repeated at the end of that Tefillah ('Amidah) for possible latecomers, according to *Masseket Soferim*.[71] Providing for similar circumstances, Rashi too says that latecomers can have Baraku recited, preceded by the Ḳaddish.[72] Actually, however, Ḳaddish before Baraku is by no means an introduction to Baraku, but, as post-talmudic authorites have declared, is rather a corporate act of *ḳiddush ha-Shem* which closes the first section of the liturgy at public worship.[73] Originally, then, the presence of the folk at public lectures, and hence the presence of a *ẓibbur*, provided an occasion to say the Ḳaddish, and later the very presence of the *ẓibbur* at worship likewise provided occasions for reciting the Ḳaddish; in both developments the recital of the Ḳaddish is the outcome of an occasion,[74] something which is true of all acts of *ḳiddush ha-Shem*. Since in rabbinic literature the Ḳaddish is associated with public lectures, it is obviously not associated with the list given in *Megillah* IV.3.

D. The Ḳedushah

After the public recital of the Shema', and so conforming to the order in the liturgy, *Megillah* IV.3 lists the recital of the Tefillah or

'Amidah by the "deputy of the *ẓibbur*"[75]—that is, by the leader—as another act requiring not less than ten. Repeated by the leader at the synagogue service in behalf of those who knew the Tefillah only imperfectly,[76] the Tefillah becomes a corporate act when the *ẓibbur* as a whole responds with "Amen" to each berakah.[77] Since the individual can recite it privately, however, even the reciting of the Tefillah aloud[78] is not an act of worship which is intrinsically corporate.

When the leader, in repeating the Tefillah, reaches the Third Berakah, which is called Ḳedushat ha-Shem,[79] and which has for its theme, as the name implies, the holiness of God, there takes place, according to an express declaration, a corporate act of *ḳiddush ha-Shem*, the Ḳedushah.[80] Like other liturgical acts of *ḳiddush ha-Shem*, the Ḳedushah here consists essentially of two parts. The first is a declaration of intention to "extol and sanctify Thee" (נעריצך ונקדישך) as do the holy seraphim,[81] or, in a simpler version, to "sanctify Thy Name in the world" as it is sanctified in heaven.[82] Specifically stressed in *Masseket Soferim*,[83] this declaration is the introduction to the Ḳedushah proper, and is said by the *ẓibbur* and then repeated by the leader.

In all the versions, the conclusion of the declaration of intention introduces the Ḳedushah proper with the words, "As it is written by Thy prophet, 'And one called unto another and said.' . . ." This quotation of the opening phrase of Isaiah 6:3 concludes the introduction to the Ḳedushah. Now the Ḳedushah itself begins, the *ẓibbur* picking up the verse precisely where the leader has left off: "Holy, holy, holy is the Lord of hosts; the whole world is full of His Glory." But the Trisagion ("thrice-holy") does not close the Ḳedushah. To these words of the seraphim in heaven, according to the Ḳedushah, there is an antiphonal response by other celestial beings, and this response is a phrase in Ezekiel 3:12. The leader refers to these beings and introduces the antiphonal response after the Trisagion has been recited by the *ẓibbur* by saying, in the simple version, "Those over against them say, 'Blessed [*baruk*].'" The *ẓibbur* now responds with the whole phrase from Ezekiel 3:12, "Blessed [*baruk*] is the Glory of the Lord from His place."[84] Only the verses presented here (Isa. 6:3 and Ezek. 3:12) are germane to the Ḳedushah; the verses which now follow these are later additions.

We are led to this conclusion not alone by a consideration of the various ways in which the particular verses are introduced or connected,[85] but by the character of the Ḳedushah as a midrashic interpretation.

A midrashic interpretation, we have demonstrated elsewhere, is always a unitary entity,[86] and the Ḳedushah is fundamentally a midrashic interpretation. Two verses (Isa. 6:3 and Ezek. 3:12) are brought together and so interpreted that they become integral elements of a new idea, an idea that would not be complete were either of the verses omitted. In Scripture, each of these verses has for its context a description of a mystical experience of God on the part of a prophet, a phenomenal experience in which celestial beings utter praise of God; in Isaiah, the celestial beings are six-winged seraphim, and in Ezekiel, they are, apparently, the *ḥayyot* and *'ofannim* (the "living creatures" and "wheels" of Ezek. 1:5 ff. and 1:15 ff.).[87] In the Ḳedushah, not only is the praise in Ezekiel 3:12 made an antiphonal response to the praise in Isaiah 6:3, but both verses are taken as embodying the same rabbinic concept. Both verses, in speaking of "the Glory of God," use a form of the word *Kabod*, and that word in rabbinic usage is a term for God limited to *gilluy Shekinah*—that is, to visual or auditory revelations of God.[88] Does God, then, reveal Himself to the celestial beings? He does not, as a comment by the leader in the Musaf Ḳedushah tells us. After the praise of seraphim, the leader says, "His *Kabod* [meaning God] fills the world,[89] [yet] His servitors [the *ḥayyot*] ask one another, 'Where is the place of His *Kabod*?'"[90] Because the question has been raised, there must be an affirmation, an acknowledgment of God, and this acknowledgment, emphasizing the presence of God by mentioning "His place," is made by the *ḥayyot* and *'ofannim* themselves in the form of a berakah. In other words, it is necessary for the *ḥayyot* to acknowledge the presence of God because neither they who carry the Throne see Him, nor by implication, do the seraphim who are more distant, even though the latter know and proclaim that God may reveal Himself anywhere. The Ḳedushah thus integrates the aforementioned verses into a midrashic interpretation which concretizes the concept of *gilluy Shekinah*, and which teaches that God is everywhere and that the scene of His revelation may be anywhere, any place, in the world.[91] The verses in the

Ḳedushah which at present follow the praises of the seraphim and the *ḥayyot*, however, do not embody the concept of *gilluy Shekinah*, are not integral elements of the midrashic interpretation,[92] and hence can only be later additions.

In its declaration of intention, "We will sanctify Thy Name," the introduction characterizes the Ḳedushah which follows it as an act of *ḳiddush ha-Shem*. The declared intention is realized when the *ẓibbur* recites a berakah[93] affirming that God is everywhere, and hence a berakah which consists of a general acknowledgment of God. Moreover, as in the other corporate acts of *ḳiddush ha-Shem*, this liturgical act, too, takes place because a *ẓibbur* has already been formed, this time because of the need to hear the repetition of the 'Amidah or Tefillah by the leader. On the other hand, there is an aspect to the Ḳedushah which makes it different from what we have come to regard as a corporate act of *ḳiddush ha-Shem*. An act of *ḳiddush ha-Shem* has, as background, experience of God on the part of the individuals of the *ẓibbur*, specific and daily experience. The Ḳedushah in the 'Amidah, however, does not arise out of such a background. It is, after all, only a representation of the angels' praises, and hence its sanctification of God is conceived to be, in the very declaration of intention, but an act which imitates that of the angels.[94]

In the early amoraic period authorities still differed as to whether or not the Ḳedushah in the 'Amidah was to be regarded as a corporate act of *ḳiddush ha-Shem*. The question is a halakic one, and is an instance of how a value concept depends on the Halakah for concretization. It is a halakic question because it involves a decision as to whether the individual may recite the Ḳedushah in the 'Amidah by himself or whether he may not. As inferred in the Talmud, R. Joshua b. Levi, a Palestinian, says he may not, whereas R. Huna', a Babylonian, says he may, and the Talmud goes on to cite R. 'Adda' b. 'Ahabah, a countryman and contemporary of R. Huna', who not only agrees with R. Joshua b. Levi but who also characterizes the Ḳedushah as *dabar shebi-ḳedushah*—that is, as a corporate act of *ḳiddush ha-Shem*.[95] According to Ginzberg, it is not possible that the text here contained, originally, any reference to R. Joshua b. Levi or to any other Palestinian.[96] The fact remains, however, that R. Huna' does not regard the Ḳedushah as intrinsically a corporate act.

At that period, therefore, the Ḳedushah in the 'Amidah could not have been preceded by a declaration of intention characterizing the Ḳedushah as a corporate act of *ḳiddush ha-Shem*.[97]

The only form of the Ḳedushah in which no extraneous verses were added to the midrashic interpretation is the Ḳedushah of the Yoẓer (the first of the two benedictions preceding the Shema'). Now it is true that a good many literary embellishments crept into the Yoẓer in the course of time, and that these vary from version to version.[98] But it is also true that the Ḳedushah proper has remained intact and furthermore, that the idea introducing the Ḳedushah is the same in all the versions. It is merely necessary to disengage the idea from the embellishments.

The introduction relates the Ḳedushah to the theme of the berakah in the Yoẓer. Found in all the versions, the phrases "[Who] createst holy ones" (בורא קדושים) and "[Who] formest ministering angels" (servitors—יוצר משרתים) continue the theme of the berakah with the very words, יוצר and בורא, employed in the berakah itself. Moreover, just as the present tense of these verbs in the berakah implies a renewed creation every day, an implication made explicit there,[99] so does it imply, in the phrases on the angels, the daily creation of new angels. Again, in all the versions the introduction concludes with a statement leading directly to the Ḳedushah proper to the effect that the angels say the Ḳedushah in unison.* These elements, which all the versions have in common, are constituents of a single

* See Baer, *op. cit.*, pp. 78 f. The key phrase in the concluding statement is וכלם מקבלים . . . ונותנים רשות זה לזה; see the notes, *ibid.*, p. 79. From the sources cited there, *Targum Jonathan* on Isa. 6:3 and *Tanḥuma, Ẓaw*, par. 13, it is evident that מקבלים refers to "receiving permission from one another," and this accords with the phrase that follows, "and give permission to one another"; this receiving and giving permission to each other to say the Ḳedushah meant that the angels said it in unison. But our present text is certainly not clear. How was it possible to receive עול מלכות שמים, the yoke of the kingship of Heaven, "from one another"? The entire idea is even more difficult. The yoke of the kingship implies positively acceptance of miẓwot and negatively the denial of idolatry, as we have seen; and what have the angels to do with either? The early liturgy had, undoubtedly, a far more simple introduction. Very likely what we have in *Targum Jonathan* and in the *Tanḥuma* is not the *source* of the introduction in the Yoẓer (although Rashi on Isa. 6:3 says that it is), but on the contrary, it is part of the actual introduction itself, taken bodily from the early liturgy. Usually a midrashic interpretation, though only stimulated by a biblical text, retains the tense of the biblical text, but that is not the case here. Whereas Isa. 6:3 is in the past tense, *Targum Jonathan*

idea, as the parallels to that idea in rabbinic literature demonstrate. Such parallels contain the idea that angels who say *shirah* (i.e., the Ḳedushah)[100] are created every day.[101]

Despite the similarity in theme between the berakah of the Yoẓer and the introduction to the Ḳedushah, the Ḳedushah unquestionably represents an addition—although an early addition—to the Yoẓer. The berakah is called forth by the sunrise; it interprets the light of the new day as a manifestation of God's love, and the occasion and the berakah together are an integrated unitary entity. Meditation brings the Ḳedushah into the context of the Yoẓer, to be sure, but only as something additional, and hence as something which is not alluded to either in the opening or in the closing formula of the berakah.[102] Yet, if the Ḳedushah has been inserted into the Yoẓer, it is also completely in consonance with it. The Yoẓer depicts the world as being created anew every day by God; the Ḳedushah, in its rabbinic interpretation, depicts God as being everywhere in that world. It was a problem, however, how to demarcate the Ḳedushah, which is praise of God, from its introduction which, though necessary, is only narrative. This problem was solved, it would seem, by R. Judah who, the Tosefta reports, singled out the verses of the Ḳedushah (Isa. 6:3 and Ezek. 3:12) and said them together with the leader out loud, the rest of the Yoẓer being said apparently by the leader alone.[103] Incidentally, the embellishments in the Yoẓer, too, probably stem in part from the later endeavor to render the narrative in the introduction, as well, a means of praising God.

---

reads: ומקבלין דין מן דין ואמרין, an act in the present tense, and hence referring to a daily act such as is depicted in an introduction forming part of the Yoẓer. In the *Tanḥuma*, more of the old liturgical introduction is given, though it is interrupted by some explanatory material. Beginning with the phrase in *Targum Jonathan* but now in mishnaic Hebrew, the introduction here contains also the idea that the angels say the Ḳedushah in unison: [וקרא זה אל זה ואמר] נוטלין רשות זה מזה . . . פתחו כולם כאחד ועונין וכו' The word פתחו means to begin, and it should, of course, read פותחין to conform with נוטלין and עונין, which are in the present tense. The word עונין means to recite in a loud voice (see below, n. 103, the reference to the ראבי"ה). Moreover, a phrase in *Targum Jonathan* on Ezek. 3:12—דמשבחין ואמרין—also presupposes the Ḳedushah, most likely that of the Yoẓer. The entire phrase is something which has been added by the *Targum Jonathan*. Again, whereas the preceding verbs of the verse are given in the past tense, and so in accordance with the Hebrew, this phrase is in the present tense. We have here, evidently, part of the introduction to the second verse of the Ḳedushah.

The Ḳedushah of the Yoẓer is not *dabar shebi-ḳedusha*—at least it was not such in the tannaitic period. From the account in the Tosefta, it is clear that the *ẓibbur* did not say the verses in the Ḳedushah together with the leader and that originally only R. Judah did so. At that time, apparently, it was felt that the Ḳedushah in the Yoẓer was of a piece with the narrative, rather than an entity in itself, and R. Judah did no more than to bring the Ḳedushah into bolder relief.

Recital of the Ḳedushah in the Yoẓer, including the introduction, is ordained by the Halakah. We might suppose, therefore, that the events pictured in the Ḳedushah and in its introduction, events depicted in a section of prescribed liturgy, are matters of dogma. But rabbinic dogmas, we have shown elsewhere, are few in number, and the events spoken of in the Yoẓer are not among them.[104] Far from being dogma, the Ḳedushah in its setting here is only one among a number of divergent representations in rabbinic literature of the *shirah* (song) of the angels.* It is difficult for the modern man to recapture the category of thought and feeling which permits divergent and even contradictory concretizations of the same value

* According to the Yoẓer, the angels "continually declare the Glory of God and His holiness," whereas a baraita in *Ḥullin* 91b states that they say it only once a day, or once a week, or once a month, or once a year, or once in seven years, or once a Jubilee, or "once in the world." *Targum Jonathan* on Isa. 6:3 interprets the Trisagion ("holy, holy, holy") to mean that God is holy in the highest heavens and upon the earth, and forever and ever. Another source interprets it to mean that mankind (הבירות) do not see Him, that the ministering angels do not see Him, "that even the *ḥayyot* carrying His throne do not see the *Kabod*" (*Seder Eliahu*, ed. Friedmann, p. 163). The same source also states that two rows of angels sanctifying God say the Trisagion from the rising of the sun until its setting, and from the setting of the sun till its rising they say, "Blessed be," etc. (*ibid.*, and pp. 34, 84, 156, 193). According to the Talmud in *Ḥullin* 91b–92a, however, three groups of angels say the Trisagion, one group saying, "Holy," the second saying, "Holy, holy," and the third group saying the entire Trisagion and finishing the verse; and it also states that the *'ofannim* say, "Blessed be," etc. It is not likely that the *merkabah* hymns were intrinsically related to the Ḳedushah. "All these hymns end with the *trishagion* of Isa. 6:3 and are therefore *Ḳedushah*-hymns. In many of them, however, this refrain is introduced quite artificially and without any reference to the text of the hymn itself" (G. G. Scholem, *Jewish Gnosticism, Merkabah Mysticism, and Talmudic Tradition* [New York, 1960], p. 21, n. 2). A comparison between the interpretation of the Trisagion in *Targum Jonathan* to Isa. 6:3 and the use of the Trisagion in Christian liturgy has been made by Mann, "Changes in the Divine Service," etc., *Hebrew Union College Annual*, IV, 263 f. See also his discussion there of the Ḳedushah de-Sidra', pp. 267–277.

concept—in this case, the value concept of *ḳiddush ha-Shem*. We have described it in earlier works as the "category of significance," and also as "indeterminacy of belief."[105] Belonging to this category are the events portrayed in the Ḳedushah and its introduction, notwithstanding their halakic framework. Indeed, they afford an instance of the interrelation of Halakah and Haggadah.

The Ḳedushah of the Yoẓer is earlier than that of the 'Amidah and, with respect to the liturgy, is the original Ḳedushah.[106] It was inserted early in the tannaitic period, for by the time of R. Judah it was already an integral part of the liturgy. Not on that account alone, however, do we hold it to be earlier than the Ḳedushah of the 'Amidah. In the Yoẓer, the Ḳedushah is made continuous with the berakah of the Yoẓer, as we have noticed; in the 'Amidah, it so obviously interrupts the berakot that it must have been inserted after the berakot were established, and inserted for a specific purpose. In the Yoẓer, the two verses of the Ḳedushah are seen to be elements of an integrated midrashic interpretation; in the 'Amidah, other verses follow the midrashic interpretation, verses which can only be later additions to the original Ḳedushah, since they are not integrated with the midrashic interpretation.[107] Decidedly a later composition, too, is the introduction to the Ḳedushah of the 'Amidah; although the midrashic interpretation itself is in accord with a tannaitic tradition,[108] the idea in this introduction is distinctly not in line with tannaitic statements on the same theme. While the introduction, in effect, declares that Israel will imitate the angels by saying the *shirah* of the angels, tannaitic sources state that Israel says *shirah* all the while (בכל שעה), whereas the ministering angels say *shirah* less often, opinions here ranging from *shirah* once a day to once in time;[109] that Israel mentions God's Name after two words, evidenced in the Shema', and the angels only after three, evidenced in the *shirah*;[110] that the angels do not say *shirah* until after Israel has said [the Shema'];[111] and that all these things indicate that Israel is more beloved of God than the ministering angels.[112] The introduction to the Ḳedushah in the 'Amidah appears, therefore, to be non-tannaitic and a later addition. In fact, we found above that it was not in the Ḳedushah during the period of the early Amoraim.[113]

First, then, the Ḳedushah came to be an integral part of the Yoẓer, and only subsequently was it also inserted into the Third Berakah of the 'Amidah. Since the introduction to the Ḳedushah in the Yoẓer is associated with the theme of the Yoẓer, and since that theme, the creation of the new day, is irrelevant to the Third Berakah of the 'Amidah, the midrashic interpretation alone was inserted there. In other words, the Ḳedushah in the 'Amidah originally consisted merely of: (*a*) the second part of Isaiah 6:3, (*b*) a reference to the *ḥayyot*,[114] and (*c*) the last part of Ezekiel 3:12, these being the sole elements of the midrashic interpretation and sufficient to convey a complete rabbinic idea, a unitary thought. But now a change began to take place in the character of the Ḳedushah. Recited without its introduction in the Yozer, the Ḳedushah in the 'Amidah took on an independent character, and the biblical verses, while recognized as the praises of the angels, also became more clearly a means of worship in themselves. It was possible, moreover, to regard them as being intrinsically a means of corporate worship, for the folk, having undoubtedly followed the example of R. Judah,[115] continued to say the verses out loud when they were made part of the 'Amidah, so that, as far as the action of the *ẓibbur* was concerned, the Ḳedushah resembled corporate acts of *ḳiddush ha-Shem* already established. The berakah in the Ḳedushah, a berakah expressing a general acknowledgment of God, completed the resemblance. In the early amoraic period, accordingly, some held that the Ḳedushah in the 'Amidah was a corporate act of *ḳiddush ha-Shem*, *dabar shebi-ḳedushah*, although there was also a contrary opinion.[116] Of course, when the declaration of intention was added, the Ḳedushah in the 'Amidah definitely assumed the character of *dabar shebi-ḳedushah*.

Several circumstances enable us to surmise the reason for the insertion of the Ḳedushah into the 'Amidah. It was at first recited in the 'Amidah only on the Sabbath and on the festivals, and even then, only at the Shaḥarit service. In Palestine the Ḳedushah in the 'Amidah was limited to these occasions until well into geonic times.[117] Now the Fourth Berakah on the Sabbath and on the festivals, the Ḳedushat ha-Yom, refers to the hallowing of the day, either of the Sabbath or of the festival, while the theme of the berakah which precedes it—that of the Third Berakah—is Ḳedushat ha-Shem, the holiness of God. To differentiate between these two aspects of the concept of *ḳedushah*, something especially necessary because the

Ḳedushat ha-Shem was so brief,[118] the Ḳedushah, with its vivid representation of the holiness of God, was inserted into the Third Berakah. Since in the tannaitic (and early amoraic) period, the 'Amidah as a whole was not recited on Friday night,[119] the first opportunity to differentiate between the Ḳedushat ha-Shem and the Ḳedushat ha-Yom occurred at the Shaharit service (the morning liturgy), and hence the practice of reciting the Ḳedushah in the Shaḥarit 'Amidah. It was not inserted into the other 'Amidot of the day since its quasi-pedagogic function had already been fulfilled, and it was not inserted into the week-day 'Amidah since that 'Amidah naturally does not contain the Ḳedushat ha-Yom. Because it was said only on certain occasions, the Ḳedushah in the 'Amidah was thereby accentuated and the *ẓibbur*, who recited it aloud, were all the more likely to regard it as *dabar shebi-ḳedushah*.

Geonic sources and cognate material, adduced and interpreted by Ginzberg, reveal how the hegemony of Babylon in the geonic period further affected the character of the Ḳedushah in the 'Amidah and determined the occasions when that Ḳedushah was to be recited. Babylonian mystics had provided an introduction to the Ḳedushah in the 'Amidah, the כתר formula, and had inserted the Ḳedushah, together with that formula, into every 'Amidah, on week-days as well.[120] The Palestinians were obliged to accept the Babylonian practices but they divested the Ḳedushah of the mystical *merkabah** idea.[121] In place of the Babylonian formula, they employed the introduction characterizing the Ḳedushah as *ḳiddush ha-Shem* and as an act whereby Israel engages in the practice of the angels.[122] It seems likely, therefore, that the Ḳedushah in the 'Amidah did not have the Palestinian introduction either until the geonic period; and if that was indeed the case, the introduction, by putting into words what had hitherto been left uncrystallized, gave the Ḳedushah an imitative character which it had not originally possessed.[123]

E. Berakot as *Gemilut Ḥasadim*

A passage in the Midrash tells of occasions when a person acting as deputy of a *ẓibbur* thereby performs an act of *gemilut ḥasadim*.[124] Those occasions are the public recitation of the Shema', the recital

* The "chariot" of Ezek. 1:4 ff., relating to theosophic speculations.

of the Tefillah by the leader, the recital of the Birkat Ḥatanim (benedictions said at a wedding), and the recital of the Birkat 'Abelim (benedictions said at a house of mourning); he who is the deputy of the *ẓibbur* on any of these occasions performs an act of *gemilut ḥasadim* when the others in the *ẓibbur* do not know how to serve as the deputy or leader.[125] A corporate act of *ḳiddush ha-Shem* is never, under any circumstances, an act of *gemilut ḥasadim*, for it is never done in behalf of others. None of the acts named here, therefore, is an act of *ḳiddush ha-Shem.*

A berakah which is part of a corporate act of *ḳiddush ha-Shem* is, in fact, altogether different from any other berakah. It consists solely of a general acknowledgment of God, and hence it does not embody, as do all the other berakot, the concept of God's love or that of His justice. A corporate act of *ḳiddush ha-Shem*, furthermore, is intrinsically corporate in character, but this feature is possessed by a number of other corporate acts as well. Thus, of the acts named in the midrash referred to above, Birkat Ḥatanim and Birkat 'Abelim are, we shall soon see, intrinsically corporate in character, although, as we have noticed, the public recitation of the Shema' and the recital of the Tefillah by the leader are not. All four acts are in the list of things enumerated in *Megillah* IV.3 as requiring the presence of "not less than ten."[126]

Birkat 'Abelim consists of a series of berakot said in the presence of mourners, and Birkat Ḥatanim, of a series of berakot said at a wedding.[127] These two series, Lieberman has shown, were once closely related: the halakot on the one series largely corresponded with the halakot on the other, and the form of the one series largely paralleled the form of the other. Birkot 'Abelim were said first in the synagogue or in the open place of the town (רחבה), and were repeated in the house of the mourners, where they were said during the first two days (not necessarily in conjunction with a meal);[128] similarly, Birkot Ḥatanim were said first at the *ḥuppah* (i.e., at the wedding) and were repeated in the home of the groom (*bet ḥatanim*), again not necessarily in conjunction with a meal.[129] On each of those occasions three berakot were said, the series in the Birkat 'Abelim and the series in the Palestinian version of Birkat Ḥatanim each containing three berakot.[130] When Birkat 'Abelim was said after a meal during the first two days of mourning, the three berakot were so combined with Birkat ha-Mazon that the result was a special form of the Birkat ha-Mazon for mourners.[131] For all the remainder of the seven days, however, the only one of these berakot retained together with its closing formula as a substitute for a regular berakah in the Birkat ha-Mazon was that which closed with "Who comfortest His people in His city";[132] and similarly, the only berakah of the Birkat Ḥatanim which was said after a meal during all the seven days was that which closed with "Who makest His people joyful in His city."[133]

The parallelism between Birkat 'Abelim and Birkat Ḥatanim thus, in a degree, extended to the actual phraseology. We have just pointed out one instance. Another is the phrase, "Who hast formed man," which was at one time part of the First Berakah of the Birkat 'Abelim as well as part of the First Berakah of the Birkat Ḥatanim.[134]

All these halakic and literary similarities stem from an unusual conceptual kinship between the two sets of berakot. Both Birkat 'Abelim and Birkat Ḥatanim contain berakot which are concretizations of *gemilut ḥasadim*,[135] berakot representing acts of *gemilut ḥasadim* that are incumbent upon the *ẓibbur* as a whole. Other acts of *gemilut ḥasadim* are often conditioned by the wealth or superior position or skill possessed by the benefactor: that is to say, are acts on the part of an individual.[136] In the midrash cited above, we had an example of such a benefactor in the person who serves as the leader in a corporate act of worship when none of the others can serve in that capacity. At the same time, this very midrash also indicates that Birkat Ḥatanim and Birkat 'Abelim themselves have to do with acts of *gemilut ḥasadim*, and that these acts require a *ẓibbur*. It speaks of ten who gathered to enable a bride to be married and of ten who gathered in the house of a mourner (to comfort him), and in both instances the act which required the presence of the ten was the saying of the appropriate berakot.[137]

Comforting mourners was a deed of lovingkindness incumbent not only on the friends of the mourners[138] but also on the *ẓibbur* as a whole. Pointing to the role of the *ẓibbur* are the place where the Birkat 'Abelim is first said and the content of the Second and Third Berakot. Birkat 'Abelim is first said in the synagogue or in the open square of the town, the meeting places of the *ẓibbur*, and this can only mean that the saying of these berakot is incumbent on the *ẓibbur* as a whole. But if Birkat 'Abelim is to be a means of comforting the mourners, it must contain words of comfort addressed directly to them. Such is precisely the case with the Second Berakah of Birkat 'Abelim. Characterized as relating to the mourners, it begins by addressing them as "our brethren, who are worn out and crushed by this bereavement," continues with phrases of comfort, the burden of the berakah, to the effect that "such is the path from the Six Days of Creation," and concludes with, "Our brethren, may He Who comforteth [בעל הנחמות] comfort you—Blessed art Thou, O Lord, Who comfortest mourners."[139] This is indeed a peculiar berakah, for it begins not by addressing itself to God, as is true of berakot and prayers generally, but to the mourners.[140] It is not intended to be a berakah in the usual sense, however. What we have here is a statement and a berakah combined—a statement of comfort addressed to the mourners, and then a brief prayer and a berakah. Said in the first instance by the *ẓibbur* in the synagogue, or rather by the deputy on behalf of the *ẓibbur*, the words of comfort together with the prayer and the berakah constitute an act of *gemuilt ḥasadim* on the part of the *ẓibbur* as a whole.

The Third Berakah of Birkat 'Abelim complements the Second. Characterized as relating to the comforters, it addresses them directly, describes them as those who engage in deeds of lovingkindness, and after a prayer that they be rewarded, concludes with the berakah, "Blessed art Thou, O Lord, Who rewardest the good deed [משלם הגמול]."[141] This is a counterpart of the Second Berakah, for the Third, too, begins by addressing itself not to God but to men—this time to the comforters. The comforters are members of the *ẓibbur* who, having just performed an act of *gemilut ḥasadim* by means of the Second Berakah, are addressed by the deputy, now not in his capacity as a deputy but as an individual. The Third Berakah complements the Second Berakah: it refers to the Second, designates the Second as an act of *gemilut ḥasadim*, reflects the same situation as does the Second: that of the *ẓibbur* as a whole comforting the mourners. Since this act is incumbent upon the *ẓibbur* as a whole—witness the locale of the act, the synagogue—the act is intrinsically corporate in character. When the act was repeated in the house of the mourners, the character of the act had already been established and hence Birkat 'Abelim requires "not less than ten."

Birkat 'Abelim was a conceptual continuum. The First Berakah closed with, "Blessed art Thou, O Lord, Who quickenest the dead," but it also possessed, according to Rashi, an opening formula: "Blessed art Thou, O Lord, our God, King of the world, the great God," etc.[142] Every berakah which followed, in contradistinction to the First, had a closing, but no opening formula, and thus was "a berakah which was joined to the immediately preceding berakah." The occasion for the First Berakah was an event which the other berakot in the series reflected as well, namely, the death of a member of the community. Such an event called forth a berakah with the same closing formula as that of the Second Berakah of the Tefillah, a formula embodying the concept of God's love and the rabbinic dogma of *teḥiyyat ha-metim*, the resurrection of the dead.[143] The verbs in the formula were in the present tense because, like the other hereafter concepts, the resurrection was felt to be a promise of God, and the trust in God, *'emunah*, made resurrection seem like a present reality.[144] As in every series of this kind, the concept of God's love was carried over from one berakah to the next; nor was that conceptual continuum broken when the mourners were addressed at the beginning of the Second Berakah and the comforters at the beginning of the Third, for there were other unifying factors that overcame those interruptions. All the berakot in the series were united because, in one way or another, they were concerned with the same event and, in addition, the Third Berakah, as a complement of the Second, was continuous with the Second.[145]

Although an element in a conceptual continuum, the Second Berakah was an act of *gemilut ḥasadim* rather than a berakah of the usual character. The First Berakah expressed a religious experience on the part of the *ẓibbur*, an experience evoked by the death of one of its members. But the Second Berakah did not express a specific religious experience on the part of the *ẓibbur* despite the berakah formula at the end. Just as both the statement of comfort and the prayer which followed it referred to the mourners, so did the berakah at the end refer to the mourners. It is also possible that the berakah at the end referred to mourners in general, but in any case, though said by the deputy in behalf of the comforters, this berakah did not include the comforters at all. Unlike the berakot in the Tefillah and other berakot, the berakah here did not employ the first person plural[146] either in the prayer or in the berakah at the end, but only the second person plural and the third person plural. We must conclude, therefore, that the berakah formula expressed, not a specific religious experience, but at best, only generalized experience. The Third Berakah, on the other hand, may well have represented felt, specific experience, since it was said by the deputy as an individual, and since he was at the same time one of the comforters.

The parallelism exhibited by Birkat Ḥatanim and Birkat 'Abelim is due to their conceptual kinship. Like comforting mourners, to gladden the bride and the groom is a deed of lovingkindness and again, one that is incumbent not only on the friends[147] but also on the *ẓibbur* as a whole. Here, too, this role of the *ẓibbur* is indicated by the circumstances under which Birkat Ḥatanim was first said, and especially by the content of one of the berakot.

In Palestine, as we noticed, Birkat Ḥatanim was said first at the *ḥuppah* and was repeated in the home of the groom (*bet ḥatanim*);[148] the wedding, accordingly, was not held in the home. It was held, undoubtedly, in the presence of the *ẓibbur*, for he who said the berakot was the *ḥazzan*, a paid official of the *ẓibbur*.[149] The *ẓibbur* as a whole engaged in an act of *gemilut ḥasadim* when, through the *ḥazzan* as deputy, it prayed for the bride and groom. "O make these loved companions greatly to rejoice, even as of old Thou didst gladden Thy creature in the Garden of Eden—Blessed art Thou, O Lord, Who makest bridegroom and bride to rejoice."[150]

There is a striking contrast between this act on the part of the *ẓibbur* and the acts of *gemilut ḥasadim* toward the bride and groom on the part of individuals. Individuals, among them the scholars, would sing bridal songs, praising the bride as being beautiful and graceful, or would dance and at the same time perform feats of jugglery to amuse her, and one scholar even carried the bride on his shoulder as he danced.[151] In contrast, the act of *gemilut ḥasadim* performed by the *ẓibbur* is a religious act, consisting of a prayer which closes with a berakah. Incumbent on the *ẓibbur*, said first in the presence of the *ẓibbur* as a whole by the *ḥazzan* of the *ẓibbur* acting as its deputy, Birkat Ḥatanim was thus originally an intrinsically corporate act. As with Birkat 'Abelim, the character of Birkat Ḥatanim was established by the context in which those berakot were said in the first instance. Wherever Birkat Ḥatanim is said, therefore, it requires not less than ten.

In Babylon, Birkat Ḥatanim consisted of the seven berakot we say to this day, whereas in Palestine it consisted of but three berakot, the full text of which has been lost.[152] The berakah we quoted is the Fifth Berakah in the Babylonian series, not counting the berakah on wine, the use of wine here being optional.[153] It seems to us, nevertheless, that in this Fifth Berakah we have either the original Third, and last, Berakah of the Palestinian series, or else one very much like it; and that, indeed, the Fifth Berakah closes a series of three berakot which, again, either represent the original Palestinian series or else are berakot in every way similar.

The two berakot preceding the Fifth read seriatim as follows:[154] "Blessed art Thou, O Lord our God, King of the world, Who hast formed man in his [man's] image, in the image [and] likeness of his form,[155] and hast prepared unto him, out of his very self [ממנו], a perpetual fabric [בנין עדי עד, i.e., woman][156]—"Blessed art Thou, O Lord, Creator of man" (Third Berakah); "May she who was barren [Zion] be exceeding glad and exult, when her children are gathered within her in joy—Blessed art Thou, O Lord, Who makest Zion joyful in her children" (Fourth Berakah). Now the Third Berakah begins with the identical phrase with which the First Berakah in the Palestinian series also began[157] and is very similar in content and style to a Palestinian morning berakah.[158] The closing phrase of the Fourth Berakah, furthermore, is certainly reminiscent of the closing phrase of the only berakah in the Birkat Ḥatanim said in Palestine after a meal during all the seven days.[159] Such a relationship to Palestinian berakot indicates that the Third and Fourth Berakot, though found in the Babli, are not purely Babylonian. This is also true, most likely, of the Fifth Berakah, for it is associated with the two preceding berakot in a unitary series characterized by a conceptual continuum.

We base our remarks on the conceptual continuum in this series upon Rashi's interpretation.[160] Since it opens the series of the three berakot having to do with the occasion—the marriage itself—the Third Berakah has both an opening and a closing formula, while the Fourth and Fifth, being dependent berakot, have, each of them, only a closing formula. The theme of the Third Berakah is the manifestation of God's love in the creation of man, and that idea is so phrased as also to relate the present marriage to that of the first man and woman, and to convey the thought of the permanence of mankind as well.[161] Included, too, in the closing formula—"Blessed art Thou, O Lord, Creator of man"—is the gratitude felt by the members of the *ẓibbur* that they themselves were created by God. The Fourth Berakah begins with a prayer for the restoration of Zion in accordance with the rabbinic emphasis on Psalm 137: 5–6: "If I forget thee, O Jerusalem. . . . If I set not Jerusalem above my chiefest joy"; and closes with a berakah in which the restoration of Zion is represented as taking place in the present. This type of berakah, we have so often noticed, reflects an "as if" experience, for the prayer is in effect a meditation, and the meditation on what is regarded as a promise of God results in the feeling that the restoration is taking place right now.[162] Like the Fourth, the Fifth and last Berakah in this series of three similarly begins with a prayer and closes with a berakah, and now the prayer is for the happiness of the bride and groom. But the berakah here, "Who makest bridegroom and bride to rejoice," a berakah said by the *ẓibbur* through its deputy, does not express a specific experience of the *ẓibbur*, a present experience, and all that we said about the Second Berakah in Birkat 'Abelim applies equally to this berakah. The rejoicing of the bride and groom is an experience which is theirs alone, one in which the *ẓibbur* cannot share. At best, the berakah expresses, as in the case of the Second Berakah of Birkat 'Abelim, not a specific religious experience of the *ẓibbur*, but only generalized experience. Both berakot alike are acts of *gemilut ḥasadim* rather than berakot of the usual character. We must add, however, that the Fifth Berakah, like its parallel, does not altogether lose its character as a berakah. All of the three berakot, including the Fifth, are elements in a conceptual continuum, wherein the concept of God's love is carried over from one berakah to the next, and all of them have reference, in one way or another, to the same event.[163]

A berakah embodies a number of other concepts, not only that of berakah. It usually embodies the concept of God's love, or else that of God's justice, and frequently, as in the Tefillah and Birkat ha-Mazon, the concept of man; all of these are moral or ethical concepts, though those of God's love and God's justice are interpretive only. A berakah is thus an instance of how "a number of value concepts may combine in a unitary yet many-toned experience."[164] A distinction is to be drawn, however, between the role of berakah and that of the other concepts in any berakah. The term berakah alone usually designates the act as a whole. The act as a whole is a concretization of the concept of berakah; although other concepts are also concretized when the act is performed, the other concretizations are concomitant concretizations. In other words, when a berakah is said, an act of worship takes place and such an act of worship usually carries with it ethical concomitants.

But Birkat 'Abelim and Birkat Ḥatanim, while designated by name as berakot, are also designated as *gemilut ḥasadim*.[165] They are called *gemilut ḥasadim* because in each series there is one berakah which is an act of *gemilut ḥasadim* as well. So far as these two berakot are concerned, the concretization of *gemilut ḥasadim* is not simply a concomitant of the act of worship; the ethical concept, in fact, so predominates that the character of these berakot is different from that of all others, and instead of expressing felt, specific religious experiences, they express generalized experience. Because in both cases, the berakot in the series are not only integrated but are all related to the same event, the entire series is designated as *gemilut ḥasadim*.

Birkat 'Abelim and Birkat Ḥatanim demonstrate to what degree worship can implicate ethics. It is possible for a berakah to be also an act of *gemilut ḥasadim*, and to stamp with this dual characterization an entire series of berakot. On the other hand, it is also possible for a berakah to be an act of worship alone, and to have no ethical concomitants at all—as we noticed in the berakot of *ḳiddush ha-Shem*.[166] Both extremes are acts of worship which are intrinsically corporate.

F. Birkat ha-Zimmun

Birkat ha-Zimmun is an act of worship incumbent on three (or more) men who have eaten a meal together,[167] an act which, on such occasions, precedes Birkat ha-Mazon.[168] When the company consists of at least three and fewer than ten, one of them acting as leader says, "We will bless [*nebarek*] Him of Whose bounty we have eaten," and the others respond with, "Blessed [*baruk*] is He of whose bounty we have eaten and by Whose goodness we live."[169] The response is then repeated by the leader.[170]

The response is a berakah, for the act as a whole is designated in the Tosefta[171] and in the Talmud[172] as Birkat ha-Zimmun; moreover, the response begins with "*baruk*" and is introduced in the call with the word "*nebarek.*" We have here a berakah, therefore, similar in several respects to the berakah in Baraku. Like the latter,[173] the berakah in Birkat ha-Zimmun is not couched in the formula of a berakah and, again like the berakah in Baraku, it is a berakah said in response to a call. So far as form is concerned, Birkat ha-Zimmun as an act of worship thus strongly resembles Baraku, a corporate act of *ḳiddush ha-Shem.* It is even likely that at one time, the leader's call in Birkat ha-Zimmun was the same as the call in Baraku.[174]

Nevertheless, Birkat ha-Zimmun is not a corporate act, much less a corporate act of *ḳiddush ha-Shem.* A corporate act requires a *ẓibbur,* the presence of at least ten men, whereas here the minimum is three. Besides, the berakah in Birkat ha-Zimmun is not a general acknowledgment of God, as is the berakah in an act of *ḳiddush ha-Shem,*[175] but one that is related to an event, the meal just eaten, and one that embodies the concept of God's love—"Of Whose bounty we have eaten and by Whose goodness we live." We can only conclude that Birkat ha-Zimmun represents a special case, that it is an act of worship which is a group act but not a corporate act.

If the group consists of ten men, the leader is to say, "We will bless our God of Whose bounty," etc., and the rest of the group is to respond with, "Blessed be our God of Whose bounty," etc.[176] Birkat ha-Zimmun is hence now to include the Name of God,[177] and, accordingly, *Megillah* IV.3 lists among the acts requiring "not less than ten" the inclusion of the Name of God in the Zimmun. It is not *derek ereẓ* (*'oraḥ 'ar'a,* in the Aramaic), says the Gemara in accounting for this inclusion, to mention the Name of God when there are less than ten present.[178] That statement applies, of course, to a group act only, and it thereby implies a distinction between a group act and one that may be taken to be an act of a *ẓibbur.*

In passing, it is well to recognize that no single principle unites all the matters which are listed in *Megillah* IV.3 as requiring "not less than ten." The Gemara accounts for some of the acts of worship named there on the ground of *ḳiddush ha-Shem*, as we saw earlier in this chapter, and here the Gemara accounts for another act of worship on the ground of *derek ereẓ*. If a principle other than *ḳiddush ha-Shem* is explicitly stated to be the ground for having not less than ten in an act of worship, we certainly have no right to assume that such an act is also *ḳiddush ha-Shem*. Moreover, an act listed as among those requiring not less than ten is by no means necessarily an act of *ḳiddush ha-Shem*. Birkat 'Abelim and Birkat Ḥatanim are definitely not acts of *ḳiddush ha-Shem*, let alone the matters in the list which are not acts of worship at all.[179]

The question is: Does Birkat ha-Zimmun change its character when there are ten and become an act of corporate worship, an act of a *ẓibbur*, or does it always retain its special character and remain an act of merely a group, no matter how large the group comes to be? Bearing on this question are statements in *Berakot* VII.3, a mishnah which is interpreted by both the Babli and the Yerushalmi in much the same way. According to the Babli,[180] the mishnah contains two opposing opinions: on the one hand, the opinion of R. Jose, who teaches that the larger the size of the gathering, the more numerous are to be the epithets for God in Birkat ha-Zimmun, the wording depending on whether the gathering is that of three, ten, a hundred, a thousand, or ten thousand; and, on the other hand, the opinion of R. 'Aḳiba, who teaches that Birkat ha-Zimmun is to remain the same "whether there are ten or ten myriads."[181] The Yerushalmi says, in effect, much the same thing as the Babli except that, according to the Yerushalmi, the opinion that Birkat ha-Zimmun is to remain the same "whether there are ten or ten myriads" is that of the *Ḥakamim*.[182]

On the basis of these interpretations, it appears that, according to R. 'Aḳiba or the *Ḥakamim*, Birkat ha-Zimmun is no longer a group act when there are ten but an act of worship intrinsically corporate in character. Like other corporate acts of worship, no matter how many are present providing there are at least ten, the wording remains the same. Indeed, R. 'Aḳiba,[183] as the Babli interprets him, by offering Baraku as an analogy and thus equating Birkat ha-Zimmun with another intrinsically corporate act of worship, actually identifies Birkat ha-Zimmun as a corporate act of worship when there are ten or more present. The Yerushalmi does so also, but by indicating that the ten or more constitute a *ẓibbur*.[184] R. Jose's view, however, is otherwise. Since he teaches that the formula changes in accordance with the size of the gathering, he must hold that ten or more do not constitute a *ẓibbur* in the case of Birkat ha-Zimmun. He maintains, we take it, that because Birkat ha-Zimmun is merely a group act when there are three, it always possesses that character. This view allows any berakah which is a response by a *ẓibbur* to have a consistent, distinctive character. Such a berakah is a general acknowledgment of God, an act of *ḳiddush ha-Shem*. A berakah that is a general acknowledgment of God confirms the past and varied experiences of God of the individuals who compose the *ẓibbur* reciting that berakah. In contrast, the berakah of Birkat ha-Zimmun expresses a specific experience of God which the individuals reciting the berakah have just had in common.

Even in a corporate act, there must be an expression of the individual, of each and every member of the *ẓibbur* engaged in the act. A corporate act requires not only that ten or more must be present, but that each and every man present must act. This is just as true when the deputy acts on behalf of the *ẓibbur* as when the members of the *ẓibbur* themselves say a berakah.

When a deputy acts on behalf of the *ẓibbur*, every member of the *ẓibbur* is to respond, "Amen."[185] What that response implies is especially evident when the act is not intrinsically corporate, as in Birkat ha-Mazon[186] and in the Tefillah.[187] Since such acts are incumbent on the individual in any case, and may be accomplished by him in private, the deputy acts not for the *ẓibbur* as a whole but for each individual in the *ẓibbur*, and it is as though the individual himself has said the berakah when he responds, "Amen." "Amen" cannot have a different implication even when it is a response in acts intrinsically corporate, as in Birkat 'Abelim and Birkat Ḥatanim. Acts of *ḳiddush ha-Shem* are a class by themselves, for in these acts each member of the *ẓibbur* himself says the berakah. According to R. Jose's teaching, however, there is one act resembling the act of a *ẓibbur*, Birkat ha-Zimmun, in which the individual has an even larger role; the very form of that act, in his opinion, depends on the number of individuals who participate.

CHAPTER VII

Worship as Normal Mysticism

A. From *Gilluy Shekinah* to Normal Mysticism

There are verses in the Psalms in which the psalmist speaks of having had a visual, sensory experience of God in the Sanctuary, or else in which he expresses the expectation or hope of having such an experience. "So have I beheld Thee [חזיתיך] in the Sanctuary, to see Thy strength and Thy glory."[1] "I shall behold [אחזה] Thy face in righteousness; I shall be satisfied, when I awake, with Thy likeness."[2] "My soul thirsteth for God, for the living God: 'When shall I come and see the face of God?' "[3] A visual experience of God is, in rabbinic terminology, an experience of *gilluy Shekinah* (revelation of God), a term which stands also for other sensory experiences of God.[4]

The rabbis, too, say that *Shekinah* "dwelt" or "rested" (*sharetah*) in the Tabernacle and in the First Temple.[5] In other words, they regarded the Tabernacle and the First Temple as locales of *gilluy Shekinah*. With respect to the Second Temple, opinions differed, some holding that *Shekinah* did not,[6] and others holding that *Shekinah* did,[7] dwell there. In an early controversy between the Sadducees and the Pharisees, the halakah taught by the Sadducees implies that in the Holy of Holies there is permanent and steady *gilluy Shekinah*, whereas the halakah taught by the Pharisees seems to imply that *gilluy Shekinah* may take place there, not that it necessarily will occur.[8] Ultimately at the basis of these various statements and halakot is the association of *gilluy Shekinah* with the sacrificial worship of the Temple, an association reflected in the petition "Restore Thy *Shekinah* to Zion and the order of Thy 'Abodah to Jerusalem."[9] Some tannaitic sources even assume, if our interpretation is correct, that there was *gilluy Shekinah* at the time a sacrifice was being offered; they assume that the pilgrim to the Temple on the festivals could, apparently, experience *gilluy Shekinah* when he stood by his sacrifice as it was being offered.[10] But whatever the opinion held with regard to *gilluy Shekinah*—that it occurred at the sacrificial service, or that it occurred only occasionally and then in the Holy of Holies—everybody felt that *gilluy Shekinah* and the sacrificial service at the Temple were ultimately associated. Everybody felt that the sacrificial service took place in, so to speak, the proximity of God, a proximity that, when all conditions were fulfilled, would be made visibly manifest.

As we saw in a preceding chapter, nonsacrificial forms of worship had already been developed in the days of the Second Temple; and these acts of worship were designated by the same word as designates the sacrificial worship of the Temple—'abodah.[11] The new forms of worship, in which there is no *gilluy Shekinah*, were called for, it seems to us, by the rabbinic value complex which had crystallized during the days of the Second Temple. The concept of *gilluy Shekinah* is not fully compatible with this value complex as a whole. "Standing for the revelation of God to human senses, particularly the sense of sight, it represents a mixture of the valuational and the cognitive, and it is therefore not a pure value-concept."[12] The rabbinic value complex called for acts of worship fully in consonance with the character of the value complex as a whole; moreover, it called for acts of worship in which as many value concepts as possible would be given expression. We are saying no more than that it is in the very nature of institutions to express the dominant character and the content of the value complex of the folk.

Although not a pure value concept and therefore restricted in its application,[13] *gilluy Shekinah* is nonetheless a component part of the value complex. It is a concept that connotes the experience of God's nearness, albeit in a visual and sensory manner. Now the awareness of God's nearness is also an element in the experience of God involved in the Tefillah and in the berakot, nonsacrificial forms of worship. In this awareness there is no *gilluy Shekinah*, no sensory experience and so, of course, the concept of *gilluy Shekinah* is not concretized in these acts. Nevertheless, a relationship between the nonsensory experience and *gilluy Shekinah* is certainly discernible: in both there is awareness of God's nearness and in both God is external to man. The new forms of nonsacrificial worship were developed not only in accordance with the dominant character of the value complex but were also affected by the concept of *gilluy Shekinah*. Indeed, the dominant character of the value complex doubtless also shaped, to a degree, the character of the concept of *gilluy Shekinah* itself.

Different as is nonsacrificial from sacrificial worship, there is nevertheless a link between them, and that link is the Tefillah. There is a time correspondence between the saying of the Tefillah and the offering of the daily communal sacrifices in the Temple, the Tefillah being thus a reminder of the daily communal sacrifices. The Tefillah was ordained "as against" those sacrifices. After the destruction of the Temple, the Tefillah, as their surrogate, like them atones for Israel's sins. The Tefillah is "in place of the sacrifice." All these matters, which we have discussed earlier,[14] tend to give the Tefillah the character of a sacrifice. On the other hand, the Tefillah is obviously nonsacrificial worship, for it consists of berakot. Furthermore, its sacrificial character is only temporary. Related to the daily sacrifices, yet itself nonsacrificial worship, the Tefillah constitutes a link between sacrificial and nonsacrificial worship.

Practices accompany the saying of the Tefillah which can only be reminiscent of an experience of *gilluy Shekinah*. They point to the special character of the Tefillah as a surrogate for the daily communal sacrifice, for they derive from the association of the sacrifices with *gilluy Shekinah*, and hence themselves constitute a link between *gilluy Shekinah* and awareness of God without visual experience. A person saying the Tefillah is to face and to direct his heart toward Jerusalem, the Temple, and the Holy of Holies;[15] if he cannot determine the proper direction, he is simply to direct his heart toward the Holy of Holies.[16] At the beginning and at the end of the First Berakah ('Abot) one is to bow, and again at the beginning and the end of the Eighteenth Berakah (Hoda'ah)[17]—the bowing at the First Berakah being apparently an obeisance in greeting, and the bowing at Hoda'ah being an obeisance accompanying מודים אנחנו לך, "We acknowledge Thee."[18] Although these obeisances suffice for an ordinary person, they are not enough for those of exalted rank. According to one version of a tradition, the high priest is to bow at the end of every berakah, and the king, at the beginning and at the end of every berakah, while another version requires the latter practice of the high priest and directs the king to kneel throughout the Tefillah.[19] After a person has recited the Tefillah, he steps back three steps, bowing and inclining his head to his left and then to his right.[20] The background of these practices is the association of the sacrificial worship (for which the Tefillah is a surrogate) with *gilluy Shekinah.* "He who is reciting the Tefillah (*ha-mitpallel*) ought to regard himself as though *Shekinah* were in front of him, as it says, 'I have set the Lord always before me' " (Ps. 16:2).[21] Rashi applies this talmudic dictum to the practice at the leave-taking,[22] but it is no less applicable to the other practices accompanying the recital of the Tefillah.

Since there is no *gilluy Shekinah* when the Tefillah is recited, these practices but express and accentuate the awareness of God's nearness. "Can you have a God nearer than that?" ask the rabbis in telling of how God hears even a whispered Tefillah.[23] The rule forbidding one to raise his voice when reciting the Tefillah[24]—a rule which teaches how to express in a practice the awareness of God's nearness—is thus quite in consonance with all the other rules and practices as to the reciting of the Tefillah. All of them teach how to express in various practices the awareness of God's nearness.

A berakah is an acknowledgment of God's love in a living context. Such a living context is provided by the occasion for the berakah, the occasion and the berakah which interprets it combining to form a unitary, experiential entity. We have characterized this as an experience of God mediated by the concept of God's love, *middat raḥamim*, but we can now better appreciate what the experience of God in these contexts implies. The berakah formula expresses not only an awareness of God's love in a particular situation but also awareness of God's nearness. "Blessed art Thou, O Lord," are the words of the berakah formula, and these words, as Rab teaches, accord with the verse "I have set the Lord always before me" (Ps. 16:2).[25] When the individual addresses God with the words of the berakah, he feels that God is before him, and hence he can use the pronoun, "Thou." Other than by some such figure of speech, there is no way to express the nonsensory awareness of God's nearness. That kind of awareness has not been conceptualized. To convey the idea of God's nearness, therefore, the rabbis often use *Shekinah*, the name for God which is part of the term *gilluy Shekinah*, the conceptual term which connotes the visual experience of God's nearness.[26]

Just as the Tefillah involves the awareness of God's nearness, so does the berakah. The same verse, Psalm 16:2, accords with the individual's experience when he says a berakah as when he recites the Tefillah. The fact is that the Tefillah consists of berakot; it is a particular form of the type of worship represented by a berakah.

This type of worship is normal mysticism. It is mystical because awareness of God's nearness is a mystical experience—experience that is not conceptualized and hence private, not communicable to others. And because awareness of God's nearness is not an experience that can be conveyed to others, it cannot be demonstrated or proved. On the other hand, it is no more questioned by the individual than is the experience of the self, another noncommunicable experience. Awareness of God's nearness is, indeed, as steady and on-going an experience as the awareness of the self. At worship and on some other occasions, awareness of God's nearness becomes more acute, quite as the awareness of the self is more acute at some times than at others.

Nonsacrificial worship is not exclusive mysticism, however, but *normal* mysticism.[27] Awareness of God when reciting the Tefillah or saying a berakah is, to a certain degree, communicable, primarily by means of the concepts of God's love, *middat raḥamim*, and God's justice, *middat ha-din*. These concepts are not only terms in the common vocabulary of the folk, elements of ordinary speech, but are also very much akin, as we have noticed,[28] to the parallel concepts of universal, human morality. Awareness of God, though a mystical experience because actual awareness of His nearness is not communicable, is at the same time a normal experience because awareness of His love and His justice *is* communicable. Experience of God in a nonsacrificial act of worship is, in fact, marked by a paradox. Awareness of God's nearness, the noncommunicable factor, is then made more acute than ordinarily by the awareness of God's love, a communicable factor. Of course, the value concepts in an act of worship are not limited to those of God's love and, sometimes, God's justice, and when other value concepts are involved as well, concepts such as *biṭṭaḥon* or Torah, they enrich the entire experience of worship.

Normal mysticism enables a person to make normal, commonplace, recurrent situations and events occasions for worship. The food he eats, the water he drinks, the dawn and the twilight are joined to berakot acknowledging God's love. These daily commonplace situations are not only interpreted in the act of worship as manifestations of God's love, but they arouse in the individual, in the same act of worship, a poignant sense of the nearness of God.

Antecedents of the normal mysticism of the rabbinic period are to be found in the Bible and particularly in the Psalms, where the nearness of God, God's justice and His love are recurrent themes. The nearness of God expressed in the berakah formula accords, as the rabbis taught, with "I have set the Lord always before me" (Ps. 16:2). The First Psalm is entirely devoted to the theme of God's justice. He whose "delight is in the law of the Lord" is rewarded, for "he shall be like a tree planted by streams of water," whereas the wicked are punished and are "like the chaff which the wind driveth away"; and the psalm closes with, "For the Lord regardeth the way of the righteous, but the way of the wicked shall perish." The Twenty-third Psalm tells of both God's love and His nearness. "The Lord is my shepherd; I shall not want. . . . Yea, though I walk through the valley of the shadow of death, I will fear no evil, for Thou art with me; Thy rod and Thy staff, they comfort me." Even the use of the word *baruk* (blessed) in an acknowledgment of gratitude for God's love is biblical: "Blessed [*baruk*] is the Lord, Who hath not given us as a prey to their teeth" (Ps. 124:6). Indeed, the berakah formula itself—"Blessed art Thou, O Lord"—is a clause in Psalm 119:12.

But *middat raḥamim* (God's love), *middat ha-din* (God's justice) and berakah, the noun forms, are not biblical terms. They are rabbinic terms, and this means that the ideas for which these terms stand were fully crystallized only in the rabbinic period. Represented by abstract terms, terms which may be used to abstract and classify, the rabbinic concepts are more applicable than the nascent concepts which were their biblical antecedents.[29] What is more, as elements in the common vocabulary, they can be employed by the ordinary man, and not only by the gifted, temperamentally sensitive man. Thus, everybody can now make even commonplace things significant, let alone matters like the giving of Torah, by interpreting them as manifestations of God's love. The new development is most strikingly exemplified, however, by the rabbinic concept of berakah. That concept's drive toward concretization impels everybody, the gifted and the ordinary alike, to make of anything interpreted as a manifestation of God's love a stimulus for an act of worship.

In one respect, we ought to add, the normal mysticism of the rabbis does not represent a new development, but remains altogether the same as in the Bible. Nonsensory awareness of God's nearness is conceptualized neither in the Bible nor in rabbinic literature.

We discussed earlier another form of nonsacrificial worship, Ḳeri'at Shema', as a special instance of the study of Torah.[30] In Ḳeri'at Shema', the individual accepts upon himself God's kingship and commits himself to His miẓwot. Normal mysticism in this experience does not involve awareness of God's nearness but a sense of His kingship and an awareness that the entire world is His kingdom. Acceptance of *malkut Shamayim*, God's kingship, is in this mystical experience accomplished by a meditative act, an act whereby the individual makes God "King above and below and in the four directions of the world." Here, too, normal mysticism is marked by a paradox. A communicable aspect of the experience is expressed in the term *malkut Shamayim*, and in the figure of "above and below and in the four directions" which makes that term more definite, yet the experience as a whole wherein God is made King is private, noncommunicable. That experience requires *kawwanah*, "direction of the heart," on the part of the individual, a state of mind completely personal and noncommunicable.[31]

In Haggadah, acceptance of *malkut Shamayim* and commitment to the miẓwot are associated with *gilluy Shekinah*. When God reminded Israel that they had accepted His kingship in Egypt, according to one passage, they replied, "Yes," whereupon He continued, "Now, just as you accepted My kingship upon yourselves, accept [now] My decrees—'Thou shalt have no other gods before Me' [Exod. 20: 3]."[32] Here God first demands confirmation by Israel that they accepted *malkut Shamayim*, and then He demands of them acceptance of His decrees, the Ten Commandments. This portrayal of an auditory manifestation of *gilluy Shekinah* is a projection in Haggadah of the acceptance of *malkut Shamayim* and of the miẓwot as experienced in Ḳeri'at Shema'.[33] There is no suggestion of *gilluy Shekinah*, however, in the actual experience of Ḳeri'at Shema' itself.[34] That experience is normal mysticism.

Although *malkut Shamayim* is a rabbinic term, the concept has an antecedent in the Bible—for example, "The Lord reigneth" (Pss. 93:1, 97:1, and 99:1). But the rabbinic term, an abstract term, enables the individual now to abstract the idea from biblical statements, to meditate on the idea and to transmute its implications, the kingship of God and commitment to the miẓwot, into a fresh emotional experience. Miẓwot, on the other hand, is already used in the Bible as a conceptual term—for example, "This miẓwah which I command thee this day" (Deut. 30:11); "And remember the miẓwot of the Lord" (Num. 15:39). Yet, as we shall see in the next chapter, when used by the rabbis, miẓwot, too, has a new connotation which is at times distinctly moral.[35] To *kawwanah* as a rabbinic term, we shall give separate treatment in a later section of this chapter.

Elements of the experience of worship are factors in the valuational life of the individual not only in conjunction with acts of worship. By being interpreted as a manifestation of God's love or God's justice, every event acquires significance, an event in the individual's own life, as well as an event in the contemporary world or in the nation's history.[36] In any heartfelt prayer and in repentance, there is an acute awareness of God's nearness. Occasions for performing miẓwot, many of them of an ethical character, are frequent. Precisely because the elements of normal mysticism occur in numerous other contexts besides that of worship, the mystical experience of worship itself can only be characterized as normal mysticism.

In each instance, however, something is added in the context of worship. Since a berakah refers to a personal experience, the experiential quality of the concept of God's love and God's justice is accentuated there. Recital of the Tefillah brings a more acute awareness of God's nearness than does a private prayer, so that it became the practice to attach purely personal petitions to the Tefillah.[37] In accepting *malkut Shamayim*, commitment to the miẓwot may indeed be only a general commitment; nevertheless, that entire, exalting experience, a daily orientation to one's duties and opportunities, adds its sanction to every specific miẓwah to be performed.

Acts of worship, we have noticed, call into play the larger Ordinarily, the awareness of the self is not conceptualized, and when expressed must rely on pronouns such as "I" or "my." in the acts of worship, by and large, the awareness of the self conceptualized through the concept of man or that of Israel, and this is achieved by the individual without loss of his self-identity. There is an enlargement of the self in a living, experiential context. A person is both himself and man, all men, or himself and all Israel. When awareness of the self is conceptualized in an act of worship, the individual associates himself with others, with undesignated, undifferentiated others. It is not a matter of identifying himself with others for, on the one hand, the individual always retains his self-identity[39] and, on the other hand, the "others" with whom he associates himself are not specified individuals. In sum, the larger self is, essentially, the individual's awareness of a bond, a relationship, between himself and others. All this does not mean that no room is left for the ordinary self. Not only may purely private petitions be attached to the Tefillah, but there are even forms of berakot of an entirely personal character.[40]

For the larger self, events ordinarily depicted as having taken place in the past or conceived as certain to take place in the future assume the character of contemporary happenings.[41] In halakic discussions of the Exodus from Egypt and the giving of Torah, or of the promised events of the future, past and future are never, to the slightest degree, obliterated. Haggadah, too, holds fast to the categories of time. When, however, the larger self is called into play in berakot, in acts of worship, these events of the past and the promised events of the future lose their orientation in time, and they are apprehended, instead, as manifestations of God's love in the present. Such a psychological phenomenon cannot be characterized as other than mystical. Since, however, it is not accompanied by visions or locutions, it can only be a phenomenon of normal mysticism.

B. Interrelation of Worship and Ethics

In the course of our discussions thus far, a number of ethical concomitants of worship have come to light, some of which we designated as such[42] and others which we did not.[43] In fact, rabbinic worship implicates ethics to such a degree that some berakot are themselves acts of *gemilut ḥasadim*.[44] We can now demonstrate that rabbinic worship as a whole implicates ethics, that rabbinic worship is interrelated with the great emphatic trends of ethics and morality: namely, with the emphasis on love, the emphasis on universality, and the emphasis on the individual.[45]

In worship there is the experience of God, an experience mediated by concepts, and there is also the awareness of the self, usually conceptualized but also sometimes unconceptualized. Again, worship consists of specific acts, such as the saying of specific berakot or the acceptance of *malkut Shamayim*. Each emphatic trend is interrelated, in some manner, with all of these aspects of worship. That is most clearly discernible, perhaps, with respect to the emphasis on love. There is an emphasis on love in the experience of God because the great majority of the berakot concretize the concept of God's love. Awareness of the self is conceptualized through the concept of man and that concept, we saw, has the connotation of love. Specific berakot in Birkat Ḥatanim and Birkat 'Abelim constitute acts of *gemilut ḥasadim*, deeds of lovingkindness.

We found above that the emphatic trends tend to coalesce.[46] In worship that tendency is especially to be discerned in the way the emphasis on universality coalesces with the other emphatic trends. Emphasis on universality rises to expression in the concept of *malkut Shamayim*, God's kingship, a kingship of absolutely universal scope. Yet that kingship is to be accepted twice daily by each individual, and by him alone. Further, the same concepts emphasizing love also emphasize universality. God's love is universal and is manifested to all mankind.[47] The concept of man not only has the connotation of love but also that of universality.

The emphasis on the individual is particularly noticeable when we consider the specific acts of nonsacrificial worship. In contrast to the daily communal sacrifice, which was "the sacrifice of the *ẓibbur*," the Tefillah, although the surrogate for that sacrifice, is intrinsically not a corporate act but one that is incumbent upon the individual. Most of the other berakot, too, are to be said by the individual. Even in those nonsacrificial acts that are intrinsically corporate, every individual has his particular role, and we have just spoken, also, of the stress laid on the individual in the acceptance of *malkut Shamayim*.

We may put the entire matter in another way. The many acts of worship employ a large number of value concepts—not only those already mentioned here but numerous others, such as *'olam* (world), Israel, *ger* (proselyte), *ẓaddiḳ* (righteous man), *rasha'* (wicked man), *ge'ullah* (redemption), *biṭṭaḥon* (trust), *teshubah* (repentance), *shalom* (peace), to give only a partial list. Since the value concepts are organismically interrelated, the emphatic trends rise to expression in the sphere of worship just as they do in the other spheres of valuational experience. Indeed, various acts of worship employ, among other concepts, the very concepts which enabled us to describe the emphatic trends in our earlier discussion. Because the value concepts are organismically interrelated, acts of worship are not only experiences in normal mysticism but acts which are fraught with ethical concomitants and motifs. It is no wonder, therefore, that some acts of worship, as we shall see in the final chapter, have profound implications for personal morality.

The prophets exhibit a negative attitude toward sacrificial worship. Isaiah includes prayer as well in his condemnation: "Yea, when ye make many prayers, I will not hear" (Isa. 1:15). Did the rabbis, in developing the forms of nonsacrificial worship, go contrary to the message of the prophets? Before an answer can be given, that message itself must be stated, and stated correctly. Of modern writers, Yehezkel Kaufmann alone, it seems, has plumbed to the depth of that message and his presentation alone is free from ideological anachronisms.

Classical prophecy teaches that God requires morality and ethical sensitivity of man, and not worship. "I hate, I despise your feasts, and I will take no delight in your solemn assemblies. Yea, though ye offer Me burnt-offerings and your meal-offerings, I will not accept them; neither will I regard the peace-offerings of your fat beasts. . . . But let justice well up as waters, and righteousness as a mighty stream. Did ye bring unto Me sacrifices and offerings in the wilderness forty years, O house of Israel?" (Amos 5:21–25).[48] "For I desire mercy [*ḥesed*; lovingkindness], and not sacrifice, and the knowledge of God rather than burnt-offerings" (Hosea 6:6, and cf. *ibid.*, 4:1 f.).[49] "To what purpose is the multitude of your sacrifices unto Me? saith the Lord; I am full of the burnt-offerings of rams, and the fat of fed beasts; and I delight not in the blood of bullocks, or of lambs, or of he-goats. . . . Wash you, make you clean, put away the evil of your doings from before Mine eyes, cease to do evil. Learn to do well; seek justice, relieve the oppressed, judge the fatherless, plead for the widow" (Isa. 1:11–17).[50] "Wherewith shall I come before the Lord, and bow myself before God on high? Shall I come before Him with burnt-offerings, with calves a year old?. . . . It hath been told thee, O man, what is good, and what the Lord doth require of thee: only to do justly, and to love mercy [*ḥesed*], and to walk humbly with thy God" (Micah 6:6–8).[51]

At the same time, many details of the Temple cult and worship, far from being negated by the prophets, are taken entirely for granted by them. Cultic matters, in fact, sometimes figure in their utterances in a positive manner. Amos speaks of the land of the Gentiles as "an unclean land" (Amos 7:17), and he regards it as a sin that the Nazarites were given wine to drink (*ibid.*, 2:11).[52] When Hosea speaks of "the Lord's land," "the house of the Lord," "the feast of the Lord" (Hosea 9:3–5), he thereby designates these matters as sacred in his eyes, too, and not only in those of the folk, for he also prophesies, "I will drive them out of My house" (*ibid.*, v. 15).[53] Isaiah, too, regards the Temple as the house of the Lord. In his very reproof, he says, "Who hath required this at your hand, to trample My courts?" (Isa. 1:12); the Temple stands in the center of his vision of universal justice and peace (*ibid.*, 2:2–4); the entire background of his vision in 6:1 ff. is the Temple and its cult—the song of the seraphim, the cloud of incense, the altar, the tongues, the ritual of cleansing.[54] The Temple and the worship in the Temple are likewise sacred matters to Jeremiah. He underscores his reproof when he says, "Yea, in My house have I found their wickedness" (Jer. 23:11); the Temple is God's throne of glory: "Thou throne of glory, on high from the beginning, thou place of our sanctuary" (*ibid.*, 17:2); he prophesies that the vessels of "the house of the Lord" will, in the end, be "restored to this place" (*ibid.*, 27:22); he tells of the glad events of the future, of chants and offerings of thanksgiving "in the house of the Lord" (*ibid.*, 33:11); he declares, "Neither shall there be cut off unto the priests the Levites a man before Me to offer burnt-offerings, and to burn meal-offerings, and to do sacrifice continually" (*ibid.*, v. 17), and he speaks of "the Levites the priests" as "My ministers" (*ibid.*, vv. 21–22).[55] How is this positive attitude of the prophets toward the Temple and toward worship to be reconciled with their even more forceful negative stand on worship?

First of all, we must recognize that sacrificial worship in Israel was utterly different, in conception, from pagan worship.[56] Pagan cultic worship is magical and mythological. In pagan religions the cult has an intrinsic value. The fate of the gods themselves depends on it. This basic pagan conception of cult and worship is not even alluded to by the prophets. They apparently need do no more than remind the people that God has no need for food and drink, and therefore has no need for sacrifices, an idea explicitly expressed in Psalm 50:8–13. To be sure, the prophets thereby argue against a widespread pagan idea, but their argument does not touch on the magical and mythological core at the center of all the forms of pagan worship. They inveigh neither against totemistic sacrifice, an ancient form of pagan folk worship, nor against other ideas of pagan worship, the ideas informing cult and sacrifice in Egypt, Babylon, and Canaan, the civilizations of which constituted the cultural milieu of Israel. In Egypt, cult and sacrifice were based on the idea of the death of the gods and their rebirth, and the food was the magical-mystical crystallization of the power of the god and his life; in Babylon, the sacrifice meant mystical strengthening of the divine powers in their war against the demons, and the sacrifice was similarly conceived in Canaan. But in the prophets' denunciations of the views of the folk on worship, not one of these ideas is mentioned. We can only conclude, hence, that in the religion of the folk, too, there was no mystical and mythological conception of sacrificial worship.[57] Their assumption was that God does not need the sacrifice, and the prophets' light mockery—"to what purpose?"—was sufficient to bring that assumption to the fore as something which was self-evident. If the prophets went beyond the folk, it was partly due to the ideas which they received from the folk.

The prophets insisted that only morality and ethics have intrinsic value and this idea was the prophetic innovation.[58] It is neither a metaphysical idea nor a "humanistic" one. According to the prophets, God requires morality and ethical sensitiveness of man: lovingkindness, justice, righteousness, truth, humility. It is this sphere alone that man shares with God, for the qualities of God are lovingkindness and justice. What of sacrificial worship? That, too, was ordained by God as an act of lovingkindness toward man; it is a symbol of God's love and His covenant with man, for God Himself has no need of sacrifices and offerings. Had man proved himself morally worthy, his sacrificial worship would have been acceptable to God. When Jeremiah declares that the people "have not attended unto My words," and therefore, "your burnt-offerings are not acceptable, nor your sacrifices pleasing unto Me" (Jer. 6:19–20), there is the inference that the offerings and sacrifices would have been "acceptable" and "pleasing" had the people "attended unto My words." The negative attitude of the prophets toward sacrificial worship is always associated with denunciations of the immorality of those who bring the sacrifices, the immorality consisting, in the main, of those violations of social ethics so often found among all peoples to this day—perversion of justice, bribery, oppression of the poor, exploitation, cynicism, lying, fornication, and so on. Such violations of ethics and social morality on the part of those who bring offerings to God make of those offerings a travesty. On the other hand, the same prophets occasionally refer to the cult and the Temple in a positive manner because they regard the cult, too, as ordained by God.

For all their depth and passion, the prophets did not crystallize into a conceptual term their awareness that morality constitutes a sphere in itself. This was achieved in rabbinic thought where, as we have seen, the term *derek ereẓ* refers to ethics and morality as a whole. Rabbinic thought, in this regard, developed out of the prophets.[59] Nor is that the only development in rabbinic ethics which goes back to the prophets. Deriving from the emphasis of the prophets on the ethical sphere are the great emphatic trends of the rabbinic value complex: the emphasis on love, universality, and individuality, an emphasis which sometimes found expression in a new ethical concept, as in *gemilut ḥasadim*. Even the prophets' implication that man shares with God the ethical sphere is reflected in rabbinic thought. The rabbis teach that man ought to imitate God, "to walk in the ways of Heaven," and the imitation of God is to consist primarily in the imitation of God's lovingkindness—mercy, compassion, graciousness, patience, forbearance.[60] It goes almost without saying that when there is a conflict of laws in the Halakah, the ethical is given right of way.[61]

In accord with this rabbinic emphasis on the ethical sphere, an emphasis deriving from the prophets, are the acts of nonsacrificial worship. Interrelated with ethics, these acts of worship not only give expression to the great ethical trends but also embody a large number of ethical concepts. The berakot and the other acts of worship thus have the effect of sensitizing the individual, during the experience of worship, to the ethical sphere.[62]

The rabbis' interpretations of sacrificial worship enable us better to recognize the point at which the rabbis do diverge from the prophets. Like the prophets, the rabbis, too, declare that God does not need the sacrifices, that "there is no eating and drinking for Him"; indeed, sometimes the rabbis marshal argument after argument in support of that teaching.[63] In keeping with the view of the prophets, also, is the rabbinic teaching that the sacrifices are ordained by God, and are for man's benefit, not for God's.[64] Again, the rabbis are at one with the prophets when they negate the belief that the sacrifices can be a means of propitiating God.[65] The rabbis certainly diverge from the prophets, however, when they also interpret the sacrifices symbolically. Drawing their lessons from the less costly as opposed to the more costly sacrifices, and from other aspects of the sacrificial ritual, the rabbis find in these things calls to repentance, good deeds, study of Torah, deep humility, and a sense of sin.[66] According to these interpretations, sacrificial worship, like nonsacrificial worship, is interrelated with ethics. At this one point, then, the rabbis differ from the prophets, even though in other respects the rabbis' teachings concerning sacrificial worship are much the same as those of the prophets.

If the rabbis differ at this one point from the prophets, it does not mean that they failed to absorb the message of the prophets. The contrary is true. Just because they absorbed the basic teaching of the prophets as to the primacy of the ethical sphere, the acts of nonsacrificial worship developed by the rabbis are fraught with ethical concomitants and ethical motifs. The rabbis were able to develop such new forms of worship because, we make bold to say, they had a conceptual advantage over the prophets. The awareness that morality constitutes a sphere in itself was not expressed by the prophets in a conceptual term, and they could present that idea only by placing specific moral matters on one side and sacrificial worship on the other. The rabbis crystallized and gave expression to the message of the prophets. In *derek ereẓ* they possessed a term referring to ethics and morality as whole, and they had no need to present morality and worship as contrasts. They could, therefore, take heed of the emphasis of the prophets on morality and give it expression in worship as well as in other fields.[67]

C. What Normal Mysticism Is Not

"Normal mysticism" is a descriptive term only,[68] calling attention to certain phenomena in rabbinic worship. Instead of enumerating these phenomena when we have occasion to discuss them as a whole, we epitomize them either by the term "normal mysticism" or else by that of "religious experience." Normal mysticism is the term used when we wish to stress the idea that the religious experience of the rabbis was associated with ordinary daily living, since the term "mysticism" by itself usually designates a far different type of religious experience.

A brief comparison of these two types of religious experience, of mysticism with what we have called normal mysticism, will serve to bring into bolder relief several features of normal mysticism. Such a comparison is all the more in place because it is often assumed that actual religious experience, the experience of God, is limited to mysticism in the accepted usage of the word. On the other hand, the character of rabbinic religious experience is obscured when it is described in terms which seem to us inadequate or incorrect, and it is well to deal with these matters, as well.

In her brilliant work on mysticism, Evelyn Underhill characterizes mysticism as "the art of establishing [man's] conscious relation with the Absolute."[69] "Union with the Divine" is a quest; the goal is not to be achieved without strenuous search, and the Mystic Way itself is constituted of various states or phases.[70] It is only in the final state that union is achieved, a state in which "the Absolute Life is not merely perceived and enjoyed by the Self, as in Illumination, but is one with it":[71] a state, in other words, of "communion between the soul and the Absolute," when "a mysterious fusion of divine and human life takes place."[72] Before such fusion or communion can take place, the Self must "surrender itself, its individuality, and its will, completely."[73] The Self is remade: the mystic life "abolishes the primitive consciousness of selfhood, and substitutes for it a wider consciousness; the total disappearance of selfhood in the divine, the substitution of a Divine Self for the primitive self."[74] From "this ineffable meeting-place, which is to the intellect an emptiness, and to the heart a fulfillment of all desire, . . . the normal self is separated by all the 'unquiet desert' of sensual existence."[75] But the Self can "become detached from the 'things of sense' " by purgation—that is, by discipline and mortification, fasting and solitude.[76] Complete surrender of selfhood, "self-naughting," occurs, however, in the process of a "passive purgation," a process accomplished in the soul "whether she will it or no."[77]

At some points mysticism and normal mysticism seem to converge, yet at these points, too, more is dissimilar than similar. Mysticism seems to have something in common with normal mysticism when we are told that for "the primitive consciousness of selfhood" mystic life substitutes "a wider consciousness." This statement reminds us of those occasions at worship when the individual associates himself with Israel or with mankind, occasions when he posseses a larger self, "a wider consciousness." That enlargement of the self is possible psychologically because the self is less an entity than a continuous process making for an entity; the self can be enlarged because it is not static.[78] But mysticism speaks an altogether different language when it characterizes selfhood as "primitive" and says that it is subject to "substitution." More, we see that "a wider consciousness" means one thing when it refers to the association of the individual with mankind and an entirely different thing when it refers to "a conscious relation with the Absolute." At this point, too, another parallel between mysticism and normal mysticism breaks down: the obliteration of the categories of time. In normal mysticism, we may remember, there are occasions when the categories of past and future are obliterated and only the present is retained. Since mysticism is union with the Absolute, however, all the categories of time are obliterated in an experience felt to partake of eternity rather than of time. In normal mysticism, the present is retained because what is experienced is an event, and an event can be experienced only in the present. Furthermore, these events (such as the Exodus from Egypt and certain promised events of the future) to be events at all, must normally be oriented in time: that is, when not experienced in worship, they must either be regarded as having taken place in the past or else assumed to be events of the future; and they are indeed so oriented when not experienced in acts of worship.

There is no "self-naughting" of any kind in normal mysticism, and neither is there purgation. Association with Israel and with man is nothing other than self-awareness conceptualized in the concepts of Israel and of man. In such relationships with Israel and with man, self-awareness is never lost, for the individual always retains his self-identity.[79] The general prevalence of value concepts in normal mysticism makes, in fact, for the opposite of "self-naughting." Value concepts, we noticed in an earlier chapter, not only constitute a vital aspect of a man's personality, but project, whenever concretized, his entire personality, his own particular individuality. When, therefore, in an act of worship, an individual interprets a situation by means of value concepts (among which there is always the concept of God's love or God's justice), he expresses at the same time his own individuality. By the same token, the prevalence of value concepts in normal mysticism makes for the opposite of purgation. Instead of detaching a man from "the things of the senses," religious experience, through the concepts of God's love, *nes* and berakah, makes of the things of the senses, in themselves ordinary and commonplace, things fraught with significance.[80]

Since they make for self-expression, not for "self-naughting," rabbinic acts of worship are emphatically not a means of communion or fusion with the divine. On the contrary, God is felt to be other than the self—"Blessed art *Thou*." Even in *gilluy Shekinah* there was no communion. *Gilluy Shekinah* is a concept connoting a sensory awareness of God's nearness, but it does not connote fusion or communion with Him. Sacrificial worship as described in the Bible, too, was not communion, modern theories to the contrary notwithstanding.[81] Kaufmann once again brings us back to what the Bible itself has to say. The sacrifices referred to in the modern theories, the *shelamim*, were eaten "*before* the Lord," and not *with* the Lord (see Deut. 12:7, 18; 14:23, 26; 15:20; 27:7); further, it is not required that a sacrifice to God be brought out of the tithes, yet any person eating the tithe, and even drinking "the wine or strong drink" bought with the money of the tithe, is likewise spoken of as eating "before the Lord" (*ibid.*, 14:26).[82] "Before the Lord" can only be, therefore, an expression implying nearness to God, as Kaufmann says,[83] an implication very similar to the connotation of *gilluy Shekinah*. Communion is no more a biblical idea that it is a rabbinic idea. It is the central idea of the mystery cults, where "the characteristic rite is sacramental—an act of communion and reunion with the daemon."[84] What is experienced in all the forms of Jewish worship considered here is not communion but God's nearness.[85] Conceptualized in *gilluy Shekinah*, the awareness of God's nearness remains unconceptualized, as we have seen, in normal mysticism.

Although not conceptualized, and hence not an experience that can be conveyed to others, nonsensory awareness of God's nearness is not entirely ineffable. In the total experience of worship represented by a berakah, the berakah itself expresses an awareness of a manifestation of *middat raḥamim*, God's love. Normal mysticism is marked by a paradox, we pointed out earlier in the chapter, awareness of God's nearness, the noncommunicable factor being made acute in the total experience of worship by the consciousness of God's love, a communicable, conceptualized factor.[86] Thus, also with respect to ineffability, normal mysticism is different from mystical union with the divine, that "ineffable meeting-place which is to the intellect an emptiness."

Awareness of God's nearness is not to be confused with the idea of God's immanence, an error made by some modern writers. "God is not external to anyone, but is present in all things, though they are ignorant that He is so," says Plotinus in telling of God's immanence.[87] The mystic, accordingly, is able to discover a " 'divine' essence or substance, dwelling at the apex of a man's soul."[88] Especially in keeping with the idea of communion, the doctrine of God's immanence may also imply the idea of "the Creative Logos."[89] It is almost unnecessary, by now, to point out that all such ideas are contradicted by the experience of normal mysticism, and indeed, by that of *gilluy Shekinah* as well. In both there is awareness of God's nearness, and in both God is felt to be entirely external to man.[90]

Underhill tells us that "we can gauge something of the supernormal vitality" of the great mystics by the magnitude of what they accomplished in a practical way, and that "the things done" by them "are hardly to be explained unless these great spirits had indeed a closer, more intimate, more bracing contact than their fellows with that Life 'which is the light of men.' "[91] Normal mysticism is not limited to the few who have special gifts of temperament. It is the experience of the ordinary man as well as of the gifted man; rather, it is the experience of the gifted man which has also become the experience of the ordinary man. The effectiveness of normal mysticism, too, can be gauged by "the things done," but these practical results of normal mysticism can only be in the field of morality and ethics, a field cultivated by normal mysticism.

As a term professing to represent the Jewish experience of God, "monotheism," so widely used today, is certainly inadequate and may be misleading. The term is inadequate because it does not distinguish between the Jewish experience of God and a cult such as that of Aten in Egypt which, as Albright justly remarks, "was a true monotheism."[92] The term may be misleading when it fosters nonrabbinic interpretations of rabbinic statements. If Judaism can be equated with monotheism, then it ought to be possible to relate philosophical ideas of monotheism to biblical and rabbinic texts; we must remember, however, that when medieval Jewish philosophers attempted to do this very thing, they had to employ the method of allegorical interpretation, a completely arbitrary method.[93]

In polytheism, worship of a deity centered around a concrete object, usually an image. A particular image might be regarded as only *a* manifestation of a deity, but this consideration by no means interfered with the worship of the image itself. Thus, an Egyptian text declares, "Honor [the] god in his way, [honor] him who is made of precious stones and formed of copper, just as water takes the place of water," and the meaning seems to be that, although the image made of precious stones and copper is only temporary and will be replaced by another image, another manifestation, "as water takes the place of water," the present image itself is to be honored and worshiped.[94] The particular image plays so great a cultic role that, among the Romans, one image of a deity may be superior to another image of the same deity, depending on the locale. "The cult-titles of this Jupiter, Optimus Maximus, the best and the greatest, seem to raise him to a position not only far above his colleagues, but above all other Jupiters in Latium or elsewhere, and presumably above all other deities. They thus suggest a deliberate attempt to place him in a higher position than even the Jupiter Latiaris of the Mons Albanus, whose temple had been rebuilt in the same period."[95] On the other hand, as can here be seen, making one representation of a deity "the best and the greatest" is perfectly compatible with the idea that other representations of the deity worshiped elsewhere—that is to say, other images—are also manifestations of that deity. Similarly, Ishtar and Adad were worshiped in many different places in Mesopotamia, and the same was true of Baal and Anath in Canaan.[96] "As a result of this phenomenon," says Albright, "we find in Canaanite an increasing tendency to employ the plural *'Ashtarôt*, "Astartes," and *'Anatôt*, "Anaths," in the clear sense of 'totality of manifestations of a deity.' "[97] The plural forms also indicate, however, that the various representations of a deity in as many different localities were all regarded as manifestations of the deity; conversely, without such representations or images, it would not have been possible to worship the same deity in different localities.

An image, then, was not an incidental matter in polytheism but an essential element in worship. The image was felt to be a manifestation of a deity. Images made it possible to worship the same deity in different localities. Placing a specific image in a specific locality could be a means of making that particular manifestation of a deity "the best and the greatest." Polytheism did allow for the view that "the domain of a high god is universal," and even for a monotheistic view in which "Marduk of Babylon is successively identified with a whole list of male deities," or in which "all the important deities are listed successively as parts of the body of Ninurta."[98] Nevertheless, it is obvious that, according to these views too, the images of the various deities listed are also to be worshiped, so that, as far as worship was concerned, polytheism was not affected by these views.

Monotheism was established for a brief period in Egypt as a solar monotheism, "with the solar formula, 'who rejoices on the horizon in his quality [literally, name] as light which is in the solar disk.' "[99] The sun-god himself cannot be separated from his "quality," from the light which is in the solar disk, and the worship of the sun-god thus involves the worship of an object, the sun. The association of the sun with the sun-god is even closer, apparently, than the one between a deity and any particular image of it.

There can be no gainsaying that the worship of images or of sundry concrete things is a characteristic element of polytheism, be the other elements in polytheism what they may. Similarly, there can be no gainsaying that the worship of Aten involves the worship of the sun itself. All such worship, including specifically the worship of the sun and the moon and other heavenly bodies,[100] the rabbis stigmatized as *'abodah zarah*, strange and abhorrent worship. Now the Halakah provides for the avoidance of any possible contact with *'abodah zarah*,[101] but that is not all. The negation of *'abodah zarah* is actually an aspect of an experience of worship. Acceptance of *malkut Shamayim* when reciting the first verse of the Shema' implies also the negation or exclusion of *'abodah zarah*.[102] The monotheism of the rabbis (and of the Bible, as well), demands the exclusion of the faintest taint of idolatry, and we wash away that fact when we put Judaism and idolatrous religions in the same category.

Philosophic monotheism may be either theistic or pantheistic. A nonrabbinic interpretation is placed on the first verse of Ḳeri'at Shema' as a result of associating rabbinic monotheism with philosophical theism. The first of the three sections of Ḳeri'at Shema' is Deuteronomy 6:4–9, and that is followed by the second section, Deuteronomy 11:13–21, which in turn is followed by the third section, Numbers 15:37–41. According to Maimonides, "The section beginning, 'Hear, O Israel' [Deut. 6:4–9] is recited first because it sets forth the duties of acknowledging the Unity of God, loving Him, and studying His words [מפני שיש בה צווי על ייחוד השם ואהבתו ותלמודו]."[103] Maimonides has here interpreted the acceptance of the kingship of God to mean the acknowledging of the unity of God, for the commentaries all take it for granted that the source of the statement is *Berakot* II.2,[104] where the reason for first reciting "Hear, O Israel" (Deut. 6:4–9) is declared to be "so that a person shall first accept upon himself the yoke of the kingship of Heaven [God], and after that accept upon himself the yoke of mizwot."[105] For Maimonides and for other medieval authorities affected to a lesser degree by medieval philosophy, this interpretation was undoubtedly a valid one;[106] the fact remains, however, that it *is* an interpretation and that for the ordinary man it over-intellectualizes what is primarily a mystical experience.

Moreover, the interpretation has led to a basic misconception. In 'Ahabah Rabbah, which is the berakah preceding the recital of the Shema', the phrase להודות לך וליחדך anticipates the acceptance of *malkut Shamayim* through the recital of the Shema'. It refers to the acknowledgment of God and links that acknowledgment with the acceptance upon oneself of God's kingship by the recitation of the Shema'.[107] Influenced by the notion, however, that the first verse of the Shema' teaches the idea of the unity of God, modern translators have so misunderstood the phrase as to make it say, "That we might give thanks unto Thee and proclaim Thy unity."[108] Acceptance of *malkut Shamayim* has thus been transformed into the proclamation of God's unity, a proclamation of a form of philsophic monotheism.

Philosophic pantheism, too, is monotheism, as in Stoic thought where God is conceived as the all-pervading Soul of the world or as the creative Reason of the world. Stressing unduly in several rabbinic passages what we call "auxiliary ideas,"[109] modern scholars often point to such passages as expressions of the Stoic doctrine that God is the Soul of the univ rse.[110] But this brings us back to the doctrine of the immanence of God, and we have already seen how that doctrine runs counter to the rabbinic experience of God. In this case, rabbinic texts have been misinterpreted because no differentiation was made between pantheistic monotheism and rabbinic monotheism. Once more as a representation of the rabbinic experience of God, the term "monotheism" was definitely misleading.

D. *Kawwanah*

The term *kawwanah* is used in several different ways in rabbinic literature, ways which are closely related yet which are to be distinguished from each other. These various aspects of the concept of *kawwanah* constitute fairly distinct conceptual phases.

One phase of the concept is to be found chiefly in the context of worship, and in that phase *kawwanah* connotes devotion, concentration, the sustained focusing of attention. This was exemplified in an earlier chapter when we discussed Ḳeri'at Shema'. By reciting the first verse of the Shema' "with direction of the heart—כוונת הלב,"

the individual accepts upon himself "the yoke of *malkut Shamayim*, the kingship of God."[111] To aid the individual in this meditative experience there is also the rule that when saying *'eḥad*, the last word in the verse, the individual is to make God king "above and below and in all the four directions."[112] *Kawwanah* here is associated with the concept of *malkut Shamayim*; by directing his heart or mind the individual achieves the experience of accepting "the yoke of *malkut Shamayim*," and it is the concept of *malkut Shamayim* which gives that experience its idea-content. But to limit the need for *kawwanah* to the first verse of the Shema', as R. Me'ir does, could only be the result of reckoning with the limited powers of the ordinary man.[113] According to the opinion of other authorities, the whole of the Shema' must be recited with *kawwanah*, sustained concentration,[114] and this opinion means that a person must attempt to achieve not only the experience of accepting upon himself *malkut Shamayim* but that of accepting upon himself "the yoke of the miẓwot" as well.[115] Although both R. Me'ir's teaching and that of the other authorities stress the need for *kawwanah*, the other authorities refer to an experience in addition to the one referred to in R. Me'ir's teaching. *Kawwanah*, then, does not point to the actual content of these experiences. It is characteristic of this phase that, while *kawwanah* is a necessary element in an experience of worship, the content of such an experience is not given in the concept of *kawwanah* but in the other concepts which are involved in that experience.

As we shall soon see, rabbinic teachings concerning *kawwanah* in the saying of the Tefillah or in the recitation of the berakot, the other forms of worship, likewise usually have to do with *kawwanah* in the sense of concentration or the sustained focusing of attention. Once more, as in Ḳeri'at Shema', *kawwanah* is a necessary element in these experiences of worship but does not determine the content of those experiences. Both the Tefillah and the berakot embody the concept of God's love and it is that concept which, concretized in one specific experience after another, largely gives such experiences their idea-content.

At the same time that we recognize the role of the other concepts in the various forms of worship, however, we must by no means relegate *kawwanah* to an inferior role. *Kawwanah* in this phase amounts to nothing less than the deliberate cultivation of an inward experience. True, the other concepts involved in an experience of worship determine its idea-content, but it is *kawwanah* which makes any experience of worship possible at all. In other words, without conveying the idea-content of an experience of worship, *kawwanah* is as large a factor in such an experience as concepts which do express the idea-content.

A person saying the Tefillah ought to "direct his heart": that is, say the Tefillah with *kawwanah.*[116] A man's mood at the time, however, may make it impossible for him to concentrate. One authority teaches, therefore, that a man ought to gauge himself, when the time for prayer comes, as to whether he can "direct his heart" or not, and if he feels that he cannot, he ought not to say the Tefillah;[117] while another authority, in a similar vein, declares that he whose mind is unquiet (at the time for prayer) ought not to say the Tefillah.[118] From still another passage in the Talmud, the inference is to be drawn that he who says the Tefillah without "directing his mind" is to repeat the Tefillah and say it with *kawwanah,*[119] an inference made by Maimonides who adds, "A Tefillah said without *kawwanah* is no Tefillah."[120]

Kawwanah in the saying of the Tefillah does not mean only the awareness of performing a miẓwah, as may be the case with the recital of Ḳeri'at Shema',[121] but refers to concentration on the ideas of the Tefillah. That is borne out by the passages just cited and by other statements and practices. "He who says the Tefillah must direct his heart in all of them [all the berakot], but if he is unable to direct his heart in all of them, he must at least direct his heart in one."[122] "He whose dead lies [unburied] before him is exempt from Ḳeri'at Shema' and from [saying] the Tefillah,"[123] the reason being, as Ginzberg shows, that under these circumstances a person cannot direct his heart.[124] Again, artisans working on a precarious perch, such as a tree-top, are not permitted to say the Tefillah since, as Rashi explains, "The Tefillah is *raḥame* [the beseeching of compassion from God] and needs *kawwanah.*"[125] When R. Eliezer declares, "He who makes his Tefillah *ḳeba'*, his Tefillah is not supplication,"[126] his objection to *ḳeba'*, manifestly, is on the ground that it makes *kawwanah* in the supplications of the Tefillah impossible. In fact, various practices are recorded which are intended to avoid *ḳeba'* and these are patently just so many attempts to keep the ideas of the Tefillah fresh, as an aid to *kawwanah*; this is especially evident in the practice of changing the text of the berakot "of praise" daily, and not only that of the supplications.[127] On the other hand, R. Ḥanina b. Dosa, according to a story told about him, achieved the acme of concentration while keeping, apparently, to a fixed text of the Tefillah. It is told of him that though once a serpent stung him while he was saying the Tefillah, he did not even pause because, as he explained later, his mind had been so concentrated on the Tefillah that he had felt no sting.[128] There are men, however, who are not able to concentrate at all unless they can at least hear the words of the Tefillah. To him who could not direct his heart were he to say the Tefillah in a whisper, it is, therefore, permitted to make his voice heard.[129] In all the texts quoted or cited here, *kawwanah* in the saying of the Tefillah can only refer to concentration on the ideas of the Tefillah, and we shall find that *kawwanah* has the same connotation also in those texts on the Tefillah we shall have occasion to discuss later.*

With respect both to Ḳeri'at Shema' and the Tefillah there are, as we have just seen, rules requiring that they be said with *kawwanah*, with concentration. These rules are necessary because neither the Shema' nor the First Berakah of the Tefillah interprets specific occasions. Certain periods of time constitute the occasions for

* *Kawwanah* in the sense of concentration is associated not only with tefillah as worship (the 'Amidah) but also with tefillah as prayer in general, and hence with personal or private prayer and petition. Thus, according to R. Me'ir, when one of two men in the same mortal danger has been saved and the other has not, the reason is that the one who has been saved had prayed with *kawwanah* and therefore his prayer was answered, whereas the other had not prayed with *kawwanah* and therefore his prayer was not answered (*Rosh ha-Shanah* 18a, and Rashi, *ad loc.*). There is a view, too, that the very ability to have *kawwanah* in the Tefillah is an indication that one's petition will be answered—see 'Abba Saul's statement in *Tos. Berakot* III.4, ed. Lieberman, p. 12, and the versions and variants there, and see *Tos. Kif.*, I, 29, top; apparently, then, so far as the petition is concerned, that relates to specific desires or needs of an individual. In specific personal petitions, however, there lurks the danger that the consciousness of saying them with *kawwanah* may make of them not true prayers at all, and the rabbis warn against that danger. They declare that if one is long at prayer and expects his petition to be answered because he has said it with *kawwanah*, his petition will not be answered, and indeed, he will be punished instead. (See *Berakot* 32b and Tosafot *ibid.*, *s.v.* כל; *Berakot* 55a and Rashi, *ad loc.*; *Rosh ha-Shanah* 16b and Tosafot *ibid.*, *s.v.* ועיון.) When *kawwanah* passes over into theurgy, we no longer have true prayer. עיון תפלה applies both to true prayer and to improper prayer (see the remarks in Tosafot) because the sheer effort at concentration is characteristic of both.

(reciting) the Shema' and the Tefillah, and since those occasions serve only as reminders, they do not determine the actual content of either form of worship. In other words, these forms of worship are not directly stimulated by external occasions, and the experience of worship in both is entirely a matter of *kawwanah*, of concentration upon ideas.

When a berakah interprets a specific occasion, however, *kawwanah* is not a matter of concentration upon an idea alone. In such cases, the occasion constitutes the stimulus for the berakah. Saying a berakah of that kind with *kawwanah*, therefore, is largely a matter of focusing attention upon the occasion or stimulus for the berakah; hence rules concerning *kawwanah* in the saying of such berakot consist of rules calculated to make a person more aware of the occasions for those berakot. For example, there are two different berakot for the fruit of trees and for the fruits of the earth, the one on the fruit of trees calling attention to its occasion by the words "Who createst the fruit of the trees," and the one on the fruits of the earth, including vegetables, calling attention to its occasion by the words "Who createst the fruit of the earth."[130] These rules are given in an anonymous statement in the Mishnah but other tannaitic authorities discriminate further between the occasions. Maintaining that the berakot to be said ought to vary in accordance with the species,[131] R. Judah disagrees with the anonymous opinion and states that the berakah on vegetables ought to be "Who createst the various kinds of herbs";[132] similarly, and holding to the same principle, the Tosefta has a different berakah in each case for seeds, for herbs, and for vegetables which are not herbs.[133] Far from being "legalism," such refinements are, on the contrary, examples of how focusing attention on the specific occasion makes for *kawwanah* in the saying of the berakot. When a person has to select a berakah in order to interpret an occasion, his attention is called to the specific character of the occasion, and the occasion then becomes all the more a stimulus for the berakah—that is, all the more poignant a factor in a religious experience.

A berakah and its occasion constitute a unitary experiential entity, as we have observed before, but that is true only when a person directs his heart. "In all the berakot," says the Gaon R. Samuel b. Ḥofni, "the person saying the berakah ought to direct his heart in regard to what he is saying the berakah for, from the beginning of the berakah."[134] This rule, too, reflects experience. When a person directs his heart from the beginning of the berakah, saying the berakah has the effect of enhancing the experience of God's love as manifested in the occasion for the berakah.

Kawwanah in worship, though referring to concentration upon ideas, is not intellectual concentration. Those ideas express emotional experiences, religious experiences. As we have observed so often, the idea in a berakah refers to an experience of God's love, the ideas in the Tefillah, to a chain of such experiences, and the ideas in the Shema', to the acceptance of God's kingship. The ideas here embody value concepts, and through *kawwanah* those value concepts are concretized in fresh experiences. Because *kawwanah* itself is a value concept, it can be an integral element in all these experiences.

A consideration of a passage in Sifre Deuteronomy, par. 335 (ed. Friedmann, p. 140b) will help us to recognize the difference between intellectual concentration and *kawwanah*. The passage declares that a man's eyes, heart, and ears "ought to be directed to the words of the Torah"; continuing, by quoting Ezekiel 44:5, "Son of man, set thy heart, and behold with thine eyes, and hear with thine ears all that I say unto thee concerning all the ordinances of the house of the Lord", the passage underlines its initial statement with the lesson, "If in the case of the Temple which could be seen by the eyes and measured by the hand, eyes, heart and ears must be directed, how much more so, in the case of the words of the Torah which are as mountains hanging on a hair." Concentration, as advocated in this passage, is intellectual concentration, the subject matter being at once difficult and fine-spun—"as mountains hanging on a hair." Nor is the emphasis on the heart (mind), the eyes, and the ears accidental, for in intellectual concentration just these organs were involved since attention was focused either on a book or on a lecture. In contrast, *kawwanah* does not refer to an intellectual problem at all, but to an experience or an act.

All of this may very well be reflected in the difference between the form of the root *kwn* indicating intellectual concentration and the one which indicates *kawwanah*. In the passage we have just considered, the verb is passive: "ought to be directed" (מכוונים). When *kawwanah* is referred to, however, the verb is active: "ought to direct his heart" (לכוין את לבו). The noun *kawwanah* itself, furthermore, is formed from the active verb, not from the passive. At the same time, it must not be forgotten that both *kawwanah* and the form indicating intellectual concentration derive from the same root, *kwn*, and hence that they are, to some degree, related.

In the phase of *kawwanah* we have just discussed, *kawwanah* refers to concentration upon the ideas in acts of worship. Although *kawwanah* is a necessary element in all such acts, the specific character of an act of worship is determined not by *kawwanah* but by the ideas concentrated on. In that respect, this phase of *kawwanah* represents a departure from the usual manner in which a value concept functions, for as a rule a value concept embodied in an act determines, at least as one of several such concepts, the specific character of that act. There is, however, another phase of the concept, another connotation of *kawwanah*, that of intention, which either by itself determines the specific character of an act, or else does so in combination with other value concepts.

Halakah has given the phase of *kawwanah*, which connotes intention, wide and varied application. We shall cite several examples. A person engaged in an act of formal acquisition must not merely intend to perform the formal act, such as making a furrow in the field, but must intend to acquire the object in question;[135] in marriage, cohabitation is not sufficient, but both parties must intend marriage;[136] in *ḥaliẓah*, the act of taking off the shoe (Deut. 25:9) must be performed with the intention of *ḥaliẓah* on the part of both the man and the woman concerned, else the *ḥaliẓah* is not valid.[137] A writ of divorce is valid only if it is written with the intention of using it for a particular, specified woman.[138] In vows, the bearing of the vow is determined not only by the actual words uttered but also by the intention of the person when he makes the vow.[139] It is this phase of *kawwanah*, too, which is involved in the question as to whether miẓwot must be performed with *kawwanah*, and we shall shortly take up that topic.

Higger distinguishes between *kawwanah* as intention and *maḥashabah* (having an idea in mind) by pointing out that the latter refers to a future act, the execution of which is indefinite.[140] *Maḥashabah* also refers to instances of an intention which may be expressed in words. That usage of the term is to be found in cases of sacrificial offerings,[141] but it is not limited to those instances.[142]

Kawwanah possesses still another conceptual phase. In that phase, *kawwanah* refers to the deliberate cultivation of an inward experience, and is in that regard similar to the conceptual phase we discussed first: the phase in which *kawwanah* refers to concentration upon ideas. Now the inward experience, a meditative experience, is not something that can be expressed in words or ideas but is sheer experience of God, for the moment unconceptualized and hence not communicable at all. Were such an experience of God, unmediated as it is by any concept, an experience complete in itself, it would not have been possible in normal mysticism. But it is not a unitary experience for, as we shall see, it is always associated with another experience, one that is expressible in a concept. What starts out as altogether incommunicable mysticism soon becomes an experience in normal mysticism.

A mystical experience of God is associated with the Tefillah. It was the practice of the pious men of former generations (*ḥasidim ha-rishonim*) before saying the Tefillah, to wait for an hour "in order to direct their heart to God."[143] Their practice was to direct their hearts to God, yet that experience but prepared them to say the Tefillah. A brief experience of a similar character takes place when the individual, as he is about to say the Tefillah, faces Jerusalem and directs his heart toward the Temple and the Holy of Holies—that is, toward the *Shekinah*.[144] The orientation is not primarily just a physical orientation, but a means of cultivating an acute awareness of God's nearness, of His immediate presence.[145] The practice derives, we have tried to indicate, from the association of *gilluy Shekinah* with the sacrifices in the Temple, the Tefillah being a surrogate for the sacrifices;[146] moreover, there is the rule that they who are unable to determine the proper direction need but direct their hearts toward "their Father Who is in heaven."[147] Here what begins as incommunicable mysticism almost immediately becomes normal mysticism: the sheer experience of God's presence leads directly to the awareness of God's love as expressed in the conceptual continuum of the Tefillah.

In the haggadot found in *Rosh ha-Shanah* III.8, a physical orientation is likewise represented to be a means of cultivating an awareness of God's near presence. This mishnah interprets Exodus 17:8–13 to teach that "when Israel looked upward and subjected their heart to their Father Who is in heaven,"[148] they prevailed, and that when they did not, they were slain in battle; similarly, continues the mishnah, but now interpreting Numbers 21:4–9, "When Israel looked upward and subjected their heart to their Father Who is in heaven," they were healed (of the serpents' bites), and if not, they decayed.[149] Now these haggadot immediately follow a halakah dealing with *kawwanah* in the performance of a miẓwah, the halakah and the haggadot being juxtaposed, as Bertinoro has pointed out, because both have to do with *kawwanah*.[150] The phrase "when Israel looked upward . . ." embodies, therefore, the concept of *kawwanah*. But this phrase, whatever else it contains, refers to an act, a physical orientation, an orientation which is thus akin to the one required before saying the Tefillah; indeed, the phrase resembles a statement made with regard to the Tefillah—"He that says the Tefillah ought to direct his heart upward (למעלה)."[151] Looking upward is represented in these haggadot as an act of orientation informed by *kawwanah*, and hence as an act which made for an experience of God's immediate presence.

For the meaning of the remainder of the phrase—"and subjected their heart to their Father Who is in heaven"—the word "subjected," משעבדין, is decisive. To say that the Israelites subjected their hearts to God is to say that they acknowledged in their hearts the kingship of God.[152] The need in both cases for such an acknowledgment of God's kingship is supplied by the respective backgrounds of the haggadot. According to an oft-repeated rabbinic tradition, derived from Exodus 17:8, Israel was obliged to do battle with Amalek in punishment for having sinned and for having neglected the study of Torah and the doing of miẓwot,[153] while in the passage on the serpents, the Bible itself says, "And the people spoke against God, and against Moses" (Num. 21:5).* These haggadot speak, then, of an experience which begins as an incommunicable awareness of God's immediate presence but which becomes an experience mediated by a concept, the concept of *malkut Shamayim*, God's kingship.

The juxtaposition of the halakah and the haggadot confirms what we have been saying here, namely, that the various aspects of *kawwanah* are phases of a single concept. In *Rosh ha-Shanah* III.7,

* In relating that the Israelites subjected their hearts to God, the haggadot tell us that they now acknowledged God's kingship and were no longer rebellious.

the Mishnah declares that, "If one was passing behind a synagogue, or if his house was near a synagogue, and he heard the sound of the *shofar* or the reading of the *megillah*, if he directed his heart, he fulfilled his obligation, but if not, he did not fulfill his obligation—even though the one heard and the other heard, the one directed his heart but the other did not direct his heart."[154] *Kawwanah* as described in this halakah refers to intention, for by the words "directing the heart" the Mishnah here means having the intention to fulfill the miẓwah regarding the hearing of the *shofar* or the miẓwah of the reading of the *megillah*. The Mishnah so far, however, has only stated the law. In order to extol *kawwanah*, therefore, the Mishnah places the two haggadot on *kawwanah* right after this halakah; by implication, *kawwanah* as described in the halakah too is extolled, even though *kawwanah* there refers to the intention to observe a miẓwah and not, as in the haggadot, to the cultivation of an experience of God's immediate presence. In all these phases of *kawwanah*, a man "directs his heart" or his mind, and hence all these phases possess a character in common. That common character permits the rabbis to use *kawwanah* as a single concept despite the fact that the very instances they refer to at any given time embody different phases of the concept.

Somewhat expanded, the same halakah is given in the Tosefta.[155] There *kawwanah* is extolled in a statement which is connected with the halakah itself, yet there, too, the general concept is employed in much the same manner as in the Mishnah. The halakah in the Tosefta concludes by stating, "All depends upon the direction of the heart,[156] as it says, 'Thou wilt direct their heart, Thou wilt cause Thine ear to attend' [Ps. 10: 17], and it [also] says, 'My son, give Me thy heart and let thine eyes observe My ways' [Prov. 23: 26]." But the first verse quoted here, although referring to " the direction of the heart," to *kawwanah*, is not directly related to the halakah in this passage, and consequently the passage gives no clue as to how this verse, Psalm 10: 17, is to be interpreted. It is in another tractate of the Tosefta that this verse is interpreted, and there the verse is taken by 'Abba Saul to mean that when the individual has *kawwanah* in the saying of the Tefillah, he is thereby given an indication that his petition will be answered.[157] Once more *kawwanah* as described in the halakah is extolled by implication; whereas the halakah deals with instances of *kawwanah* as intention, the verse quoted in the halakah and extolling the efficacy of *kawwanah*, according to rabbinic interpretation, refers to *kawwanah* in the saying of the Tefillah, and thus to concentration on ideas. *Kawwanah* is again used as a single concept despite the fact that the instances involved embody different phases of the concept.

Found in several contexts is the teaching "it matters not whether much or little, if only a man directs his mind [or, heart] to Heaven," but that teaching has no reference either to a preparatory experience or to a physical act of orientation. The original setting of the statement is a mishnah (and a baraita) which teaches that so long as a sacrifice is offered with the proper intention—that is, to God—it matters not whether the sacrifice be a bullock, or only a bird, or even a meal-offering.[158] A different meaning is conveyed by the statement, however, when the rabbis detach the statement from its context in the Mishnah and quote it in connection with the study of Torah. R. Eleazar was ill and R. Joḥanan went to visit him. Finding R. Eleazar weeping, he asked, "Why do you weep? If it is because you have not studied as much Torah as you wished, we have learned in the Mishnah, 'It matters not whether much or little, if only a man directs his heart to Heaven.' "[159] The same statement is again applied to the study of Torah in the famous passage in which the rabbis of Jabneh compare their work with that of the non-scholars.[160] What can the teaching, "it matters not whether much or little, if only a man directs his heart to Heaven," mean in these contexts? We take it to mean that, besides being an intellectual activity,[161] study of Torah ought to be a mystical experience. A man has such mystical experience when he feels that what he is acquiring through study is being taught him at that very moment by God; in other words, on these occasions *mattan Torah* is not merely a dogma, an event in the past, but is felt as a present reality.[162] "It matters not whether much or little"—the experience is the same—"if only a man directs his heart to Heaven." Experience of God is here mediated by the concepts of study of Torah and *mattan Torah*.

Although the concepts of God's love and His justice are value concepts, they differ from most other value concepts in that they only interpret events or occasions.[163] What enables these concepts to be factors in day-to-day living are the berakot, or rather the halakot concerning the berakot, for those halakot call attention to the daily occasions which can be interpreted as manifestations of God's love. The question remains, however, whether such habitual interpretations can always constitute genuine experience of God's love, even with the aid of the berakah formula. This problem comes to the fore in the rabbinic views on *kawwanah*.

The material adduced in our discussions so far assumes that every individual can experience what we have called normal mysticism. There is the teaching, for example, that a man ought to gauge himself, when the time for saying the Tefillah has come, as to whether he can "direct his heart" or not;[164] obviously, the assumption is that generally an individual can "direct his heart." Again, to recall another example, it is assumed that artisans working on a precarious perch cannot have *kawwanah*, and hence the rule is that they are not permitted to say the Tefillah;[165] that rule, too, obviously also assumes that under proper circumstances, all men, artisans included, can have *kawwanah*.

But some scholars declare that, even if they try, they do not have *kawwanah* when saying the Tefillah. A scholar who admits to never having had *kawwanah* relates that on one occasion he did make an attempt, but only found himself debating in his mind as to who preceded whom in appearing before the king, a high Persian dignitary or the Exilarch.[166] Similarly, another scholar relates that he found himself counting flying birds.[167] A third scholar states that he is grateful to his head, since it bows of itself at "*Modim*" ("We acknowledge," the beginning of the Eighteenth Berakah).[168] From these examples it is apparent that rabbinic scholarship did not always go hand in hand with a capacity for normal mystical experience; untutored artisans may have had that capacity whereas some eminent scholars may have lacked it. Nevertheless, we must also recognize that the entire development of normal mysticism was largely the outcome of the experience of the scholars as a whole. Were it not for the rabbis, there would have been no Halakah, no perception of the occasions for religious experience, no permanent means for the cultivation and expression of normal mysticism.

If some scholars found *kawwanah* difficult, then this must have been all the more true of the many who were not scholars. There must have been a segment of the folk in general that found *kawwanah* difficult to achieve or who could not achieve it at all. This segment of the folk had its champions among the rabbis, especially among the Amoraim. Despite numerous rules and statements emphasizing *kawwanah*, sometimes opinion is divided on whether this or that thing "requires *kawwanah*." In such instances, the negative opinion certainly implies no objection to people having *kawwanah*; it simply states the case for those for whom *kawwanah* is difficult. Thus, when R. Jose holds, in the Yerushalmi, that the berakot of the Shema' require *kawwanah* and the anonymous opinion has it that they do not require *kawwanah*,[169] the negative opinion certainly implies no objection to the saying of these berakot with *kawwanah*. The negative opinion here simply does not impose *kawwanah* as a requirement for everybody, thereby taking into account those for whom it would be too stringent a requirement.[170]

In the Babli, this division of opinion has crystallized into two opposing general principles—a positive principle, "Miẓwot require *kawwanah*,"[171] and its negative, "Miẓwot do not require *kawwanah*."[172] According to the proponents of the positive principle, by the words "directing the heart," the Mishnah always means having the intention to fulfill a particular miẓwah,[173] and that is the way we have interpreted these words above, when we discussed *Rosh ha-Shanah* III.7; according to the proponents of the negative principle, however, by those words the Mishnah means having the intention merely of hearing the blowing of the *shofar*, or hearing the reading of the *megillah*, or reading the Shema', as the case may be, but not in order to fulfill a particular miẓwah.[174] The difference between the two views, it is to be noted, is not with regard to intention as such, but rather with regard to the *scope* of the intention. According to the negative view, for example, the Mishnah requires a person to have the intention only of blowing the proper sounds on the *shofar*, whereas, according to the positive view, the Mishnah goes further and requires that it be the intention to blow those sounds on the *shofar* because it is a miẓwah to do so.[175] Similarly, according to the negative view, the Mishnah requires a person to have the intention only of reading the Shema', an intention whereby just mechanical reading is excluded, whereas, according to the positive view, a person must have the intention of reading the Shema' in this manner because it is a miẓwah to do so.[176] Hence the intention to fulfill any particular miẓwah includes the intention to perform the required act in a particular manner. The proponents of the negative principle cannot possibly object, therefore, to the performance of such an act with the intention of fulfilling a miẓwah. They simply do not make it a requirement for everybody to have that kind of *kawwanah*, since for many it would be too stringent a requirement.[177] (In the next chapter we shall see that *kawwanah* in miẓwot, too, is associated with normal mystical experience.) A discussion in the Babli on certain details of the Passover Seder relates the two opposing principles to differences in view between tannaitic sources.[178] Apparently, already in tannaitic times, some authorities took a less rigorous stand on *kawwanah*.[179]

All the phases of *kawwanah* have a character in common. This is reflected, as we saw above, in the term "directing the heart [or, mind]," a term employed by the rabbis in regard to every phase of *kawwanah*. The term itself is biblical, despite a formal grammatical difference in the verb. "And direct your hearts unto the Lord" (I Sam. 7:3); "A generation that directed not their heart [to God]" (Ps. 78:8);[180] "If thou direct thy heart [to Him]" (Job 11:13);[181] "Neither as yet had the people directed their hearts unto the God of their fathers" (II Chron. 20:33).[182] The concept of *kawwanah*, then, has a biblical antecedent.

But the abstract noun *kawwanah* is rabbinic, not biblical. This means that the rabbinic concept possesses connotations which its biblical antecedent does not have, something also true of *middat raḥamim*, *middat ha-din*, and *malkut Shamayim*.[183] Indeed, *kawwanah* is often integrated with those three concepts. One of the connotations of *kawwanah* is concentration on the ideas in worship—that is to say, concentration on one or another of these value concepts. *Kawwanah* may also be associated with study of Torah, and in this phase, according to our interpretation, the dogma of *mattan Torah* also enters into the experience. The organismic character of the value concepts enables *kawwanah* to be integrated with other concepts as well, however. As we saw specifically when we studied the relation of *kawwanah* to miẓwot, *kawwanah* has in those instances the connotation of intention. Finally, there is a phase of *kawwanah* which refers to sheer, unconceptualized experience of God. Were that experience anything but a preparatory one, it would not have been possible in normal mysticism.

CHAPTER VIII

Miẓwot, Ethics, and Holiness

Since it is not our intention to present here all the various types of berakot, we shall discuss in this last chapter only the Birkat ha-Miẓwot, a berakah which directly affects the moral life. Embodied in the Birkat ha-Miẓwot are the concepts of miẓwot (commandments) and *ḳedushah* (holiness). Before dealing with the berakah itself we must discuss, therefore, some aspects of the concepts of miẓwot and *ḳedushah*.

A. The Concept of Miẓwot

According to the rabbis, the miẓwot of the Torah consist not only of the commandments or laws which are explicitly given in the written Torah, the Bible, but also of laws derived from the Bible and found in the oral Torah.[1] To identify all the laws implied in the Torah remains a problem, however. Although the rabbis employed definite hermeneutic rules, the thirteen *middot*, in deriving laws from the Torah, the textual methods and approach are quite the same when they designate a verse as merely *'asmakta*, "support," for a nonbiblical law.[2] What criterion, therefore, will enable us to distinguish between a biblical basis for a law and an *'asmakta*? Maimonides states that laws derived by the thirteen *middot* are to be regarded as biblical only if the rabbis themselves declare them to be so. Naḥmanides, on the other hand, brings proof to the contrary, namely, that all matters derived by means of the thirteen *middot* are to be regarded as biblical unless the rabbis characterize a derivation as an *'asmakta*.[3] Obviously, if these great authorities could differ so radically, there is not always a clear demarcation between laws regarded as rabbinic and laws regarded as implicit in the Bible.

To be sure, in the famous statement by R. Simla'i cited earlier,[4] the miẓwot "delivered unto Moses on Mount Sinai" are characterized as fixed in number, the number being six hundred and thirteen. Again, however, Naḥmanides differs from Maimonides and others who based their lists of laws, or codes, on that number. To quote Schechter: "Nachmanides questions the whole matter, and shows that the passages relating to this enumeration of laws are only of a homiletical nature, and thus of little consequence. Nay, he goes so far as to say, 'Indeed the system how to number the commandments [miẓwot] is a matter in which I suspect all of us [are mistaken] and the truth must be left to him who will solve all doubts.' "[5]

The point we are making is that there is no clear demarcation between the laws felt to be implied in the Bible and laws that are purely rabbinic. But a word ought to be added with regard to what appears to be the vast number of the miẓwot in any case. To quote Schechter once more: "Even a superficial analysis will discover that in the times of the Rabbis many of these commandments were already obsolete, as, for example, those relating to the arrangements of the tabernacle and to the conquest of Palestine; whilst others concerned only certain classes, as, for instance, the priests, the judges, the soldiers and their commanders, the Nazirites, the representatives of the community, or even one or two individuals in the whole population, as, for example, the king and the high priest. Others, again, provided for contingencies which could occur only to a few, as, for instance, the laws concerning divorce or levirate-marriages. The laws, again, relating to idolatry, incest, and the sacrifices of children to Moloch, could hardly be considered as coming within the province of the practical life of even the pre-Christian Jew."[6] Schechter concludes by saying, "A careful examination of the six hundred and thirteen laws will prove that barely a hundred laws are to be found which concerned the everyday life of the bulk of the people."[7]

The rabbinic dogma of *mattan Torah*, the giving of Torah, includes within its scope the oral as well as the written Torah. After stating that Moses learned the Mishnah or oral Torah directly from God, a baraita tells of how Moses taught the oral Torah to Aaron, and then to the sons of Aaron, and then to the elders and then to the people as a whole.[8] Another tannaitic passage refers specifically to the mizwot, declaring that all the mizwot were ordained at Sinai, and not only the general principles but the details as well.[9]

As we have pointed out elsewhere,[10] the concept of Torah modifies the dogma, of *mattan Torah.* Torah was, quite like the other value concepts, an indeterminate concept which was made determinate when concretized in new laws and in new interpretations. It is the concept of Torah rather than the dogma of *mattan Torah* which endows Midrash with divine sanction, even with divine origin, and Midrash consists of what is avowedly the work of the rabbis, namely, the interpretation of the Bible together with the laws resulting from the interpretation.[11] " 'But if ye will not hearken unto Me' [Lev. 26: 14]—if ye will not hearken unto the Midrash of the *Ḥakamim.*"[12] If mizwot recognized as derived from the Bible by the rabbis themselves are nevertheless characterized as mizwot of God, it was not necessary always to make a clear demarcation between laws regarded as implied in the Bible and laws acknowledged to be essentially rabbinic.

Sometimes, indeed, the rabbis taught that "the words of the *Ḥakamim,*" the purely rabbinic laws, are more "weighty" than "the words of the Torah." The legislative authority of the rabbis is usually based on Deuteronomy 11: 17: "According to the Torah which they shall teach thee, and according to the judgment which they shall tell thee, thou shalt do; thou shalt not turn aside from the sentence which they shall declare unto thee, to the right hand nor to the left."[13] A tannaitic comment on "thou shalt not turn aside from the sentence which they shall declare unto thee," after stating that this phrase refers to the tradition handed down from one man to another, adds: "Weighty [חמורים] are the words of the *Ḥakamim,* for he who transgresses their words is like him who transgresses the words of the Torah—indeed, the words of the *Ḥakamim* are more weighty than the words of the Torah, for among the latter there are light and weighty [mizwot], whereas the words of the *Ḥakamim* are all weighty."[14] Now this statement, and others in a similar vein,[15] do not altogether agree with the Halakah, for in the Halakah "the words of the Torah" are often applied with greater strictness than "the words of the *Ḥakamim.*" For example, a doubtful case in a matter of biblical law is decided in accordance with the stricter practice, whereas a doubtful case in a matter of rabbinic law is decided according to the lenient practice.[16] But when the rabbis say that "the words of the *Ḥakamim* are more weighty" they are not referring to this or that principle. They are expressing their feeling of reverence for rabbinic law in general, a feeling as profound as their reverence for biblical law.[17]

Do the rabbis, however, actually characterize as miẓwot of God laws that are acknowledged to be purely rabbinic? Here authorities differ. In *Yebamot* II.3–4, the phrase *'issur miẓwah*, is applied to certain marriages (incest of second degree) prohibited by rabbinic law, and 'Abaye interprets the word miẓwah here to mean that "it is a miẓwah to obey the words of the *Ḥakamim*."[18] The same idea is more fully stated in the Yerushalmi on our mishnah: "It is a miẓwah of the Torah to obey the words of the *Soferim* [i.e., *Ḥakamim*]."[19] According to both statements, apparently, the phrase in *Yebamot* II.3–4 refers to Deuteronomy 11:17: "Thou shalt not turn aside," etc., and the rabbinic laws are thus associated with miẓwot of God, albeit indirectly. Alon thinks it likely that by miẓwah here the Mishnah itself has in mind *miẓwat Zeḳenim* (elders=*Ḥakamim*), and he cites passages containing this term.[20] The term *miẓwat Zeḳenim*, we ought to add, certainly indicates that the rabbinic laws are to be regarded as distinct from "the words of the Torah,"[21] as does likewise the term, *'aberah de-rabbanan*.[22] Even so, there is a passage, with versions elsewhere, which explicitly teaches that *miẓwot Zeḳenim* are to be associated with "words of the Torah," although again by virtue of Deuteronomy 11:17. "A man ought not say, 'I shall not fulfill *miẓwot Zeḳenim* since these are not [miẓwot] of the Torah.' The Holy One Blessed be He says to him: No, My son, but fulfill thou all that they decree, for it says, 'According to the Torah which they shall teach thee' [Deut. 11:17]."[23] The passages adduced in this paragraph, then, relate the rabbinic laws or ordinances to the miẓwot of the Torah by means of the biblical law in Deuteronomy 11:17, and hence do no more than to associate rabbinic law with "the words of the Torah."

But there are also authorities who go much further, and who deliberately and unmistakably characterize rabbinical ordinances as miẓwot of God. They do so in their wording of the Birkat ha-Miẓwot on matters that are nonbiblical. As given in the Yerushalmi, Rab's wording of the berakah on the Ḥanukkah light reads: "Blessed art Thou, O Lord our God, King of the world, Who has sanctified us by His mizwot, and commanded us concerning the mizwah of kindling the light of Ḥanukkah."[24] Although a rabbinical ordinance (מדבריהם), as the discussion in the passage itself brings out, the kindling of the Ḥanukkah light is twice characterized in this berakah as a mizwah of God—first implicitly in the general formula, and again explicitly in the phrase "And commanded us concerning the mizwah." The same passage[25] also allows us to see how a form of the Birkat ha-Mizwot which only associates a rabbinical ordinance with the mizwot of God differs from the form which characterizes that ordinance to *be* a mizwah of God. On the first day of Sukkot, both R. Joḥanan and R. Joshua b. Levi in reciting the berakah on the *lulab* (palm frond) said, "And commanded us concerning the taking of the *lulab* [על נטילת לולב]"; on the rest of the days, however, since the taking of the *lulab* on those days (elsewhere than in the Temple) was a rabbinical ordinance, R. Joshua changed the formula to say, "and commanded us concerning a mizwah of the *Zekenim* [על מצות זקנים],"[26] whereas R. Joḥanan retained on those days, too, the formula of the first day. Another version, after stating that R. Joḥanan agrees that the taking of the *lulab* after the first day is a rabbinical ordinance, gives as the reason for his practice the following interpretation: " 'The words of the wise [*Ḥakamim*] are as goads . . . they are given from One Shepherd' [Koheleth 12:11]—the words of the Torah and the words of the *Ḥakamim* are given from One Shepherd."[27]

When a person is about to fulfill a mizwah with *kawwanah*, he has a heightened awareness of a relationship between himself and God. The mizwah, he feels, represents a communication which has been directed to him by God. In such an experience, the particular mizwah which the individual is about to perform is not merely a practice transmitted to him by previous generations but is a command from God here and now. Such an experience, in other words, belongs in the category of normal mysticism.

This mystical experience of the rabbis is reflected in rabbinic literature in various ways. By saying or implying that the individual heard the mizwah at Sinai, some statements, so to speak, transport the individual to Mount Sinai and thus relate an occasion in the present to the dogma of *mattan Torah*, a dogma positing an event in the past. For example, the rabbis, in purely halakic contexts, speak of a miẓwah as something "on which he [the individual] is sworn from Mount Sinai."[28] Again, in reference to the thief, the Mekilta says, "[His] ear had heard, 'Thou shalt not steal' [Exod. 20:13], and yet he went and stole."[29] Such statements certainly accord with the well-known haggadah that the souls of those who were not yet born were present at Sinai,[30] yet it is hardly possible that the halakic statements were based entirely on the haggadah. Both the halakic statements and the haggadah reflect, it seems to us, the consciousness of the rabbis as they were about to perform a miẓwah—namely, that the miẓwah was given to them directly by God, and hence they associated that consciousness with the dogma of *mattan Torah* itself.

We noticed that Rab and R. Joḥanan, in their berakot, designate rabbinical ordinances as miẓwot of God, but that R. Joshua b. Levi, in his berakah, designates a rabbinical ordinance as a miẓwah of the *Zeḳenim*. A difference so basic can only imply a difference in experience, Rab and R. Joḥanan having the consciousness, as they pronounce the berakah, that such a miẓwah is given them now directly by God, a consciousness not possessed by R. Joshua b. Levi. Haggadot reflect this difference in experience. There is a baraita, for example, which relates the rabbinical ordinances directly to the whole dogma of *mattan Torah* and calls them miẓwot which are to be instituted in the future. It declares that the covenant was made not only with those who stood at Mount Sinai but also with the generations to come (not mentioning souls at all), and with the *gerim* who would be converted in the future; and it adds that the covenant was made not only with respect to the miẓwot received "from Mount Sinai," but also with respect to miẓwot to be instituted in the future, such as the reading of the *megillah*, meaning, with respect to rabbinic ordinances as well.[31] On the other hand, there is also the haggadah, as we have seen, which designates the rabbinical ordinances as *miẓwot Zeḳenim* and which, while associating them with "words of the Torah," does so indirectly and by virtue of Deuteronomy 11:17.

In an earlier work we show that when the rabbis speak of acknowledging God, they refer to experience of God, and that when they speak of denial of God, or of one "who denies the root," they refer to willful rebellion against God, to willful rejection of Him on the part of one who had known, had experienced Him.[32] Now the rabbis say that no one transgresses a mizwah "until he denies the root," applying that phrase in a number of instances: to him who denies the Ten Commandments, to him who deals falsely with his neighbor "in a matter of deposit," to him who utters slander, to him who lends money on interest.[33] If the rabbis assume denial of God to be a condition for the transgression of a particular mizwah, it can only be because for them the fulfillment of a mizwah involves an experience of God.

To fulfill a mizwah with *kawwanah*, a person must have the consciousness that the particular mizwah he is performing has been given him directly by God. Many, apparently most, of the rabbis retained this consciousness even when about to fulfill a rabbinical ordinance. Making for this attitude, we may safely say, was the awareness that much of what was regarded as biblical law was itself the work of the rabbis. There were others, however, who found that, while they could associate avowedly rabbinical ordinances with biblical law, they could do so only indirectly.

Mizwot is a conceptual term which is found in the Bible, but once more it is a term whose rabbinic connotations differ from the biblical. In the Bible, while the word often refers to commandments of God,[34] it also refers, as Greenberg has shown, to the commands or admonitions of a king, parent, or teacher, or those of "any other superior."[35] In rabbinic literature, the tendency is to limit the term to the mizwot of God, even *mizwot Zekenim* being either characterized as, or associated with the mizwot of God.[36] But the rabbinic concept possesses another connotation as well. We shall notice that the rabbinic concept of mizwot sometimes has a moral or ethical connotation.

B. Mizwot and the Ethical Concepts

In this section we shall discuss several ways in which the ethical concepts dealt with in earlier chapters[37] interweave with the concept of mizwot. We shall find that these ways of interweaving relate to the role of emphasis in organismic thought.

Most often, an ethical concept is associated with the concept of miẓwot in such fashion that both interpret an act or a situation as a whole. This is true even when the word miẓwah itself has an ethical connotation, the connotation of *ẓedaḳah*. Men are described as doers of miẓwah, meaning doers of *ẓedaḳah*,[38] and a plea for charity may often be phrased as, "Give me miẓwah."[39] Miẓwot likewise can connote charity, as in the halakah in the Yerushalmi which limits what a man may give away in miẓwot.[40] But though miẓwah and miẓwot may thus, in many instances, connote *ẓedaḳah*, that connotation does not displace the primary meaning of miẓwot. In the very passage of the Yerushalmi just cited, the discussion there indicates that charity is a miẓwah in the same sense as are the other miẓwot; indeed, the Tosefta declares that *ẓedaḳah* and *gemilut ḥasadim* are equal in importance to all the [other] miẓwot taken together.[41] An act of charity, in fine, is interpreted by two concepts at once: the concept of *ẓedaḳah* and the concept of miẓwot.

"The Sons of Noah," or mankind in general, were given, the rabbis say, seven miẓwot, and they are: To institute law and justice (*dinin*), not to blaspheme God (*birkat ha-Shem*) and not to worship idols (*'abodah zarah*), not to commit incest (*gilluy 'arayot*), murder (*shefikut damim*), or robbery (*gezel*), and not to eat the meat of a living animal.[42] We have here a formulation of what we have recognized above to be the rabbinic category of universal ethics.[43] Acts of incest, murder, and robbery, when designated as such, are thereby interpreted by negative ethical concepts, and when they are characterized as violations of miẓwot they are interpreted by the concept of miẓwot as well. To eat the meat of a living animal is to violate a miẓwah but it is also the opposite of the ethical concept of *raḥamim*, the scope of which includes animals.[44] The one positive miẓwah in the list is the instituting of law and justice, and that is characterized by the term *dinin*, an ethical value concept. If the rabbis include in the list also matters relating to God, it is because, as we shall see later, the relationship to God was a primary factor in their ethical consciousness.

In another formulation of universal ethics, the rabbis say, "Because of eight things is the world destroyed: Because of *dinin*, idolatry, incest, murder, profanation of the Name (*ḥillul ha-Shem*), because of foul things a person utters, arrogance (*gassut ruaḥ*), scandal-mongering (*lashon ra'*), and some say also because of covetousness."[45] This list contains, in addition to most of the matters mentioned in the other formulation, more acts or types of acts, the names for which constitute negative ethical concepts. But all the matters here are also designated, by implication, as violations of mizwot, the concept of mizwot being embodied in the statement. "Because of eight things is the world destroyed" contains the concept of God's justice;[46] by the same token, the statement also embodies the concept of mizwot, for when God rewards, it is for the performance of a mizwah, and He punishes when a mizwah has been violated.[47] A statement in the Mishnah similarly embodies the concepts of God's justice and mizwot, but now there is posited God's reward for refraining from unethical conduct. Pointing to Deuteronomy 12:23–25, verses which prohibit the eating of the blood of a slaughtered animal "that it may go well with thee and with thy children after thee," the Mishnah draws the following lesson: If a man receives reward for refraining from eating blood, something a man loathes, all the more will he receive reward, he and his generations after him, for refraining from *gezel* and *'arayot* (forbidden marriages), things which he may desire or covet.[48] Acts of *gezel* and *'arayot* are then interpreted not only by the negative ethical concepts which designate these acts but also by the concept of mizwot embodied in the statement.

Acts prohibited by a biblical verse are, of course, governed by a negative mizwah. When such acts are also designated by a negative ethical concept, they are being interpreted both by an ethical concept and by the concept of mizwot. Acts of *'ona'ah* are a case in point, and these acts are of two kinds: *'ona'at mamon* and *'ona'at debarim*. *'Ona'at mamon* refers to certain instances of fraud or overreaching in business transactions,[49] acts prohibited according to rabbinic interpretation, in Leviticus 25:14: "And if thou sell aught unto thy neighbor, or buy of thy neighbor's hand, ye shall not wrong ['*al tonu*] one another."[50] The last part of the verse is practically repeated in verse 17: "And ye shall not wrong [*we-lo' tonu*] one another, but thou shalt fear thy God"—and since verse 17 makes no reference to "money" the rabbis say that it refers to *'ona'at debarim*, injury or wrong through words.[51] Among the many instances given of *'ona'at debarim* are those of merely pretending to buy an article, saying to a person who has repented, "Remember your former deeds," or to a proselyte, "Remember the deeds of your fathers";[52] and saying, after the manner of Job's friends, to a person who is afflicted or ill or has buried his sons, "Remember, I pray thee, who ever perished, being innocent, or where were the upright cut off," etc. (Job 4:6 f.).[53] It is proved in various ways that *'ona'at debarim* is worse than *'ona'at mamon*. The former is the greater wrong, says one authority, since the verse prohibiting it adds, "But thou shalt fear thy God," whereas the verse prohibiting *'ona'at mamon* does not do so.[54] The former affects the man himself, the latter (only) his property, says another.[55] Still another points out that *'ona'at mamon* can be made good but *'ona'at debarim* cannot.[56]

From the discussion in the last paragraph it is patent that acts of *'ona'ah* were interpreted both as violations of miẓwot of the Torah and as unethical acts, the unethical quality of the acts being designated as *'ona'ah*. But we have also adduced material bearing on the role of the ethical term. Those who have dealt with the ordinances or rules on *'ona'ah* found in the Mishnah and the Talmud have recognized that these ordinances constitute a remarkable foliation and development of the biblical precepts underlying them.[57] What has apparently altogether escaped attention, however, is the tremendous role played by the rabbinic term *'ona'ah*, the conceptual term itself, the noun-form. Thus, Lazarus, while evidently approving of the rabbinic term *'ona'at mamon* as an expression of the idea in Leviticus 25:14, regards *'ona'at debarim*, the rabbinic term expressing the idea in Leviticus 25:17, as "a rather infelicitous term";[58] and this, after he himself had demonstrated that the biblical *lo' tonu* defies consistent translation.[59] The fact is that the rabbinic word *'ona'ah*, too, defies translation into a modern idiom. *'Ona'ah* is a rabbinic concept which has as its antecedent the biblical *lo' tonu*. Because the rabbinic concept is represented by an abstract conceptual term, a classifying noun-form, *'ona'ah*, the range of the rabbinic concept is much wider than that of its biblical antecedent,[60] the rabbinic concept including within its scope such widely different matters as fraud in a business transaction and a husband causing his wife to shed tears.[61] Both *'ona'at mamon* and *'ona'at debarim* are subconcepts of *'ona'ah*, aspects of *'ona'ah*.

If *'ona'ah* is not translatable, there is a reason for that. So far as the individual instances of *'ona'ah* are concerned, these can, of course, be described in any modern idiom. What modern idioms cannot do, since they lack equivalents for *'ona'ah*, is to unify all these instances, to give them all a similar significance, to interpret them as a whole. There is simply no modern ethical concept which can designate at the same time such diverse matters as fraud and *Schadenfreude*.

'Ona'ah is a striking example of what an ethical concept does when it designates an act. By designating an act, the ethical concept not only classifies it but gives significance to the act as well. More correctly, the significance is not given to the act but is inherent in it, since the ethical concept, being a value concept, is embodied in the act.

Certain mizwot themselves, that is, the laws apart from the acts enjoined or prohibited by the laws, may be characterized, and hence interpreted, by means of an ethical concept. The verses, "Whether it be cow or ewe, ye shall not kill it and its young both in one day" (Lev. 22:28) and "If a bird's nest chance to be before thee . . . thou shalt not take the dam with the young," etc. (Deut. 22:6 f.) are interpreted in several rabbinic sources to mean that God has compassion on the animals. From Leviticus 22:27 f. those sources conclude that just as God has compassion on mankind so He has compassion on the animals, and from Deuteronomy 22:6 f. that "just as the Holy One blessed be He has bestowed His compassion [*raḥamim*] on beasts" so also has He compassion on fowl.[62] *Targum Jonathan* on Leviticus 22:28, in the spirit of this teaching, renders that verse as follows: "O My people, ye Children of Israel, just as I am compassionate in heaven, so be ye compassionate on earth: cow or ewe, ye shall not kill it and its young both in the same day."[63] When this law is observed, *Targum Jonathan* says in effect, a man is both performing a mizwah and acting with *raḥamim*, compassion.

In all of the instances so far cited, both an ethical concept and the concept of mizwot interpret an act or a situation as a whole. Acts so interpreted have a dual significance, a phenomenon of interpretation fairly common in organismic thought where a situation usually embodies several concepts.[64] Thus, in addition to the concept of mizwot and an ethical concept, an act may also embody the concept of the sons of Noah, a concept which is practically an alternative to the concept of man, and the act has thereby been given a universal significance. Similarly, when an element in the interpretation is the concept of God's justice, that concept adds its own significance to the interpretation of the act as a whole. When two value concepts interpret an act as a whole, therefore, the several concepts do not contradict but supplement each other. Organismic interpretation usually endows an act with a significance that is many toned.

Usually when an act as a whole is interpreted by two concepts at once, neither of the concepts is stressed above the other. But this form of organismic interweaving of concepts is by no means the sole form. One of the concepts interpreting a situation as a whole may be stressed on one occasion, and the other on another occasion; in the case of the Shema', for example, at one time the study of Torah is stressed, and at another time the acceptance of *malkut Shamayim*.[65] It is also possible to stress one concept as against the other, as does that halakah on the saying of the 'Amidah which stresses the concept of tefillah as against the concept of 'abodah.[66] Organismic thought allows room for differences in temperament, in point of view and in circumstances. On the one hand, organismic thought makes for rich significance by allowing full play to all the value concepts embodied in a situation; on the other hand, by permitting now one concept to be stressed and now another, organismic thought allows room for the predilections of the individual and for special circumstances.

We have presented a number of illustrative instances in which an act is interpreted at the same time both by the concept of miẓwot and by an ethical concept, and in which neither concept is stressed above the other. We shall soon see that the association between the two concepts is not lost even if one of them should be stressed. At present, however, we wish to indicate that when the idea of God's command is emphasized by the concept of *gezerot*, *gezerot* may exclude an ethical concept. *Gezerot* and miẓwot are closely related, so closely related that the verb *ẓwh* is sometimes used in connection with the word *gezerah*, as Albeck has shown.[67] *Gezerot* refers, therefore, to commands or decrees, and often to the commands or decrees of God.[68]

Taking issue especially with *Targum Jonathan*, R. Jose b. Bun ('Abun), a Palestinian Amora, characterizes Leviticus 22:28 and

Deuteronomy 22:6 f. as *gezerot* of God. He says that those who declare that the qualities of the Holy One Blessed be He consist (primarily) of mercy or love (שעושין למדותיו של הקב״ה רחמים), "do not do right," and then he adds, "Those who translate [Lev. 22:8], 'O My people, ye Children of Israel, just as I am compassionate in heaven, so be ye compassionate on earth: cow or ewe, ye shall not kill it and its young both in the same day [*Targum Jonathan* to Lev. 22:8],' do not do right, for they render the *gezerot* of the Holy One Blessed be He [to be] mercy."[69] The basis for this statement is the rule in the Mishnah that if a man says in the Tefillah, "Thy mercy extends to a bird's nest," he is to be silenced;[70] the rule here forbids including in the Tefillah any plea wherein the law in Deuteronomy 22:6 f. is interpreted as an evidence of God's mercy.[71] The term *gezerot* (of God) in R. Jose b. Bun's statement, therefore, refers both to the law in Leviticus 22:28 and to the law in Deuteronomy 22:6 f. As a characterization of those laws, *gezerot* implies so strong an emphasis on the idea of God's command as to exclude other considerations. If the organismic complex allows room for such emphasis on that idea, however, it also allows room for the interpretation to which R. Jose objects, an interpretation of Leviticus 22:28 and Deuteronomy 22:6 f. discussed a few pages back. That is why, despite R. Jose's explicit objection, *Targum Jonathan*'s rendering was retained by the rabbis. Incidentally, R. Jose b. Bun's comment on the rule in the Mishnah does not represent a consensus, for other interpretations of that rule are also given.[72]

When a law is characterized as a *gezerah* of God, the idea of God's command is so strongly emphasized as often to exclude either an ethical concept or else some other matter. R. Jose b. Bun designates certain laws as *gezerot* of God in order that they may not be taken as embodying the ethical concept of *raḥamim*. R. Eleazar b. Azariah, a Tanna, uses the verb *gazar* to emphasize the idea of God's command, likewise in order to exclude something.[73] "A man should not say, 'I have no desire to wear a garment of mixed stuff, I have no desire to eat pig's meat, I have no desire for forbidden sexual connections'; but [he should say], 'I do have the desire, [but] what shall I do, since my Father Who is in heaven has so decreed [*gazar*] for me.'" This teaching R. Eleazar finds in the proof-text, "I have set you apart from the peoples, that ye should be Mine" (Lev. 20:26), a text which enables him also to conclude his teaching with the following statement: "[A man] thus [both] keeps himself aloof from the transgression and accepts upon himself *malkut Shamayim* [the kingship of God]." This concluding statement is overlooked by modern writers critical of R. Eleazar's teaching. To obey a law solely because it is felt to be a *gezerah* of God is not obedience in a spirit of arid formalism, as they would have it. Such obedience, instead, is accompanied by a religious experience, the acceptance of *malkut Shamayim*.[74]

There are points in common between this passage which we shall call B, and another passage in the Sifra cited earlier,[75] which we shall call A. Mentioned in both passages are the laws against eating pig's meat and wearing garments of mixed stuff; Rashi in his glosses on a version of A also designates the laws there as *gezerot*.[76] Furthermore, the context in A implies that those laws are possessed by Israel alone. In B a similar thought is conveyed by the proof-text, "I have set you apart from the peoples," a verse relating, according to R. Eleazar b. Azariah, to distinctive laws which set Israel "apart from the peoples." Finally, the *gezerot* in A, too, exclude something, although only as a means of drawing a contrast. As against the universal laws mentioned there—laws in the Torah which other peoples possess as well—are *gezerot*, laws which are *not* universal but which are possessed only by Israel.

We shall cite one more instance. The law in Numbers: 19 ordains that persons who had in some manner been in contact with the dead and a house in which a death had occurred be purified by the ashes of a red heifer in water. That law is introduced with the words, "This is the statute [*ḥuḳḳat*] of the law" (Num. 19:2). On the basis of these words, R. Joḥanan b. Zakkai declares, "A dead person does not make unclean nor does the water purify, but it [i.e., the law] is a *gezerah* of the King of the kings of kings."[77] By designating the law here as a *gezerah* of God the idea of God's command is so strongly emphasized as to exclude the thought that contact with the dead makes a person intrinsically unclean or that the water of the red heifer has an intrinsic power of purification.[78]

When the term *gezerah* is used so as to emphasize the idea of God's command, it often excludes something, including an ethical concept, as these examples demonstrate. On the other hand, we saw that the concept of mizwot is often associated with ethical concepts, so much so that the words mizwah and mizwot may also connote *zedakah.* We shall now see that there are statements or principles which do stress the concept of mizwot, but that even in such instances the association between mizwot and the ethical concepts is not lost.

"Greater is he who does because he is commanded," says R. Ḥanina in regard to mizwot, "than he who does without being commanded."[79] In several passages this statement definitely emphasizes the concept of mizwot as against ethical concepts, and yet the association between mizwot and the ethical concepts is not really lost. As an answer to the question of how far one must go in *kibbud 'ab wa-'em*, honoring father and mother, a story is told of a Gentile in Ashkelon by the name of Dama b. Netinah who refused a fabulous profit because he did not wish to disturb his sleeping father; God rewarded him when a red heifer was born in his herd for which he asked and received the sum he had felt obliged to refuse while honoring his father.[80] After telling this story, one of the sources in the Babli adds: "And R. Ḥanina said, If he who does without being commanded thus [is rewarded by God], he who does because he is commanded is all the more [certain to be rewarded]—for R. Ḥanina said, 'Greater is he,' " etc.[81] Nevertheless, it remains true, first, that *kibbud 'ab wa-'em* is both a mizwah and an ethical concept; second, that, according to the rabbis, when God rewards, it is for the performance of a mizwah;[82] and that, hence, in this story which tells of a reward for an act of *kibbud 'ab*, the association between mizwot and ethical concepts is not lost. This conclusion holds with respect to another instance where R. Ḥanina's principle is applied. When God saw that the sons of Noah did not keep the seven mizwot which they had accepted on themselves, He made those mizwot no longer mandatory, so that even if the sons of Noah do observe them the reward is only that given to him who does without being commanded, for R. Ḥanina said, "Greater is he," etc.[83] Here, too, an element of reward nevertheless remains, and hence here, too, there remains an association between mizwot and ethical concepts.[84] (We must add that statements of R. Ḥanina's principle occur only in the Babli.[85] A better version of the story about Dama ben Netina is found in the Yerushalmi,[86] and that version contains neither R. Hanina's remark nor his principle.)

A principle enunciated by Raba stresses the idea of God's command inherent in miẓwot, although the stressing is achieved through an implication. The miẓwot, he says, were not given (to Israel) as a means of enjoyment,[87] a statement which calls forth Rashi's gloss, "But were given for a yoke on their necks."[88] Raba's principle is a legal principle and it means that legally the observance of the miẓwot is not considered enjoyment, rather than that such observance ought not to bring enjoyment.[89] The principle is applied to matters such as blowing the *shofar*[90] and sitting in the *sukkah*.[91] In a discussion on the *'erub*,* this principle is also applied, however, to going to a house of mourning and going to a wedding feast,[92] acts of *gemilut ḥasadim*.[93] Here we have a principle which stresses the idea of God's command, yet one which maintains the association between miẓwot and the ethical concepts.

According to Lazarus' interpretation,[94] Raba's principle is a general ethical idea which has been restricted by its halakic application. He declares that Raba's statement "originally and in much earlier times had a wider meaning," that it was "directed against the hedonist view of life." He goes on to say, "The pleasure derived from the fulfilment, especially from the glad fulfilment, of commands had probably become an Epicurean subterfuge, which the ethical spirit of the Rabbis desired to render unavailing, so that men might fulfil duty for its own sake. Here, as in so many cases, the Kantian conception of duty and its contrariety to inclination suggests itself." But where, we ask, is the motive of "duty for its *own* sake" to be found in Raba's principle? On the contrary, the principle plainly says that the miẓwot were "given," and it does not say that they were given for their own sake. A philosophical, non-rabbinic criterion for ethics has here been read into a rabbinic text. Lazarus also misinterprets the principle when, according to him, "'the expression is restricted to its legal sense." He limits the halakic application to "the use of an object in the execution of a ceremonial law." A rabbinic text is always misconstrued when given a philosophical interpretation.[95]

* The establishment, before the Sabbath, of a symbolical domicile by an individual at some point within the limit of permitted locomotion on the Sabbath, in order that he might go beyond that limit on the Sabbath for the purpose of performing a mizwah.

The concept of mizwot, we have found, is often associated with ethical concepts. Acts as a whole may be interpreted at the same time by both the concept of mizwot and an ethical concept, for in the organismic valuational process not one, but several concepts may be embodied in an act or in a situation. The organismic process, however, also allows one concept occasionally to be emphasized over another; there are thus some statements or principles which primarily emphasize the concept of mizwot, sometimes even as against the ethical concepts. Nevertheless, in these instances as well, the association between mizwot and the ethical concepts is maintained; it is only when the idea of God's command is expressed through the concept of *gezerot* that an ethical concept may be excluded.

An act as a whole may be interpreted by both the concept of mizwot and by an ethical concept, and yet be an act in which the ethical concept is emphasized. This occurs when such an act is regarded as a mizwah that supersedes the other mizwot, as an overriding mizwah. A well-known instance is the saving of a life on the Sabbath, the principle in the Mishnah being that the Sabbath is to be superseded when the danger to life is possible or even uncertain.[96] The rule applies, of course, to all the other mizwot, not to the Sabbath alone.[97] It is a rule which enjoins acts prompted by *rahamim*, compassion,[98] as against the observance of other mizwot.

Nor are the ethical concepts emphasized only when it is a question of saving a life. A high priest or a Nazarite is not permitted to attend to the burial of even near relatives, since any contact with a corpse makes him ritually unclean, yet he is required to attend to the burial of a *met mizwah*, the corpse of one whose relatives are not known.[99] Were he both a high priest and a Nazarite and, furthermore, on his way to slaughter his paschal lamb (which cannot be eaten if a person is unclean), attending to the burial of a *met mizwah* supersedes all.[100] An overriding mizwah, the obligation concerning a *met mizwah* is imposed, the Talmud says, because of *kebod ha-beriyyot*, the honor of mankind,[101] that is to say, because of an ethical value concept. Similarly, acts of *gemilut hasadim* may be overriding mizwot: A baraita teaches that the study of Torah is to be interrupted for the sake of participating in a funeral escort or in a wedding procession.[102]

All these instances are, of course, prime examples of the association between the concept of miẓwot and the ethical concepts.

A bond unites the rabbis with the prophets, as was observed in the previous chapter.[103] Further evidence of that bond is the parallel between the prophets' interpretation of acts and the rabbinic interpretation. The prophets, feeling themselves to be messengers of God, have, of course, a different approach and their ethical vocabulary, too, is somewhat different from that of the rabbis. Nevertheless, despite these differences, the parallel is close enough to enable us to use rabbinic concepts in order to describe the prophets' message. A few verses will suffice as illustrations: "It hath been told thee, O man, what is good and what the Lord doth require of thee: Only to do justice [*mishpaṭ*], and to love mercy [*ḥesed*], and to walk humbly with thy God" (Micah 6: 8). Acts designated by the ethical concepts of *mishpaṭ* and *ḥesed* are acts which "the Lord doth require of thee," that is to say, they are miẓwot of God. "Thus hath the Lord spoken, saying: Execute justice [*mishpaṭ*], and do [acts of] mercy [*ḥesed*] and compassion [*raḥamim*] every man to his brother" (Zech. 7: 9). This verse similarly allows us to characterize as miẓwot of God actions designated by the ethical concepts of *mishpaṭ*, *ḥesed*, and *raḥamim*. Hosea 4: 2 refers to acts designated by negative ethical concepts and verse 3 embodies the concept of God's justice—"Swearing and lying, and killing, and stealing, and committing adultery! They break all bounds and blood toucheth blood. Therefore doth the land mourn, and every one that dwelleth therein doth languish."

C. *Ḳedushah* and the Moral Life

Ḳedushah is a complex concept. Not only is it composed of phases, like other concepts studied here, but the phases themselves are complex. Besides, it also possesses a subconcept in *ḳiddush ha-Shem*, several aspects of which were discussed in Chapter VI.

One phase of *ḳedushah* refers to a sphere in which it is sensed as a mystical quality of certain objects, days, and persons. If these are felt to possess a mystical quality it is because they are regarded as being God's own, as belonging to God in a special sense. That sphere of *ḳedushah* is conceived, furthermore, as consisting of various hierarchies of *kedushah*, each hierarchy being arranged in an ascending order of things designated as *kedushot*. At the same time, in a number of instances, though not in all, this mystical quality results from human acts, acts of a kind which in other contexts have no such mystical association. We shall exemplify these matters as briefly as we may.

"There are ten *kedushot*," says the Mishnah, and it then proceeds to describe the particular hierarchy of holy areas, beginning with the lowest, the Land of Israel, and ascending to the highest, the Holy of Holies.[104] In a version of this tannaitic tradition, the Land of Canaan is declared to be holier than Trans-Jordan, the reason being that "the Land of Canaan is fit for the House of the *Shekinah*," whereas Trans-Jordan is not.[105] Another tannaitic source affirms that "the *Shekinah* does not reveal itself outside the Land,"[106] a statement which refers to God's communications to the prophets. The reason for the holiness of the Land of Israel, such statements indicate, is that only there are there forms of *gilluy Shekinah*. The hierarchy of the holy areas relates to the closeness of those areas to the Holy of Holies, the locus of *gilluy Shekinah* in the Temple.[107]

Related to the hierarchy of holy areas is that of the sacrifices and the tithes. The highest grade in this hierarchy is designated as *kodshe kodashim*, the most holy.[108] Among such sacrifices or offerings are those which are to be eaten by the priesthood, but only by the males and only "inside of the enclosures [literally, curtains]."[109] Lower than this grade are the sacrifices designated as *kodashim kallim*, that is, sacrifices holy in a lesser degree.[110] A common characteristic of the various kinds of sacrifices placed in this category is that all of them may be eaten in any part of the city of Jerusalem.[111] The area where the sacrifice or offering is to be eaten is thus one of the factors bearing on the gradations in this particular hierarchy, the wider area indicating a lower degree of holiness. That criterion is reflected in the *kodashim kallim* taken by themselves. The first-born of the clean cattle is to be eaten by the priests only, whereas the tithe of cattle may be eaten by any person, and yet, because both may be eaten in any part of Jerusalem they are in the same category, that of *kodashim kallim*.[112] On the other hand, the grade of *kodshe kodashim*, restricting as it does the eating of such sacrifices as may be eaten to male priests, indicates that another factor has a bearing on the gradations in this hierarchy, namely, whether the holy thing be among the *mattenot kehunah*,[113] the gifts or prerogatives of the priesthood. Both *ḳodshe ḳodashim* and *ḳodashim ḳallim* are, of course, offered in the Temple, although here, too, a distinction is made between the two grades with respect to the place where they are to be slaughtered.[114]

Included in the *mattenot kehunah* are *ḳodshe ha-gebul*, the holy things, such as *terumah*, the priest's share of the crop, and *ḥallah*, his share of dough, which are set apart and consumed outside the Temple and Jerusalem.[115] A passage in the Sifre, stressing the idea that the *ḳodshe ha-gebul* are included in *mattenot kehunah*, but also distinguishing between the *ḳodshe miḳdash*, the offerings in the Temple, and *ḳodshe ha-gebul*, identifies *ḳodshe ha-gebul*, practically in so many words, as the third grade in the hierarchy below *ḳodashim ḳallim*. To all three, to *ḳodshe ḳodashim*, *ḳodashim ḳallim*, and *ḳodshe ha-gebul*, the passage applies the same formula: לגזור דין ולכרות להם ברית, a formula referring to God's confirmation of Aaron in the priesthood as against Koraḥ, and to areas where these various grades of holy things may be eaten and indicating by whom they may be eaten.[116] Since that formula is applied to all three grades, all of them are thereby characterized as *mattenot kehunah*. But the formula is applied seriatim —first to *ḳodshe ḳodashim*, then to *ḳodashim ḳallim*, then to *ḳodshe ha-gebul*.[117] Since we know that *ḳodshe ḳodashim* is the highest grade in the hierarchy and that *ḳodashim ḳallim* is the second grade, *ḳodshe ha-gebul* must, therefore, be the third grade. Again, as we have said, the passage demarcates between the offerings in the Temple and *ḳodshe ha-gebul*.[118] Since all the holy things mentioned here are *mattenot kehunah*, the demarcation can only mean that *ḳodshe ha-gebul* are lowest in the grades of *mattenot kehunah*, in other words, that they are the third grade in the hierarchy.

Having given the *terumah* to the priest and the first tithe to the Levite, a man must then set aside *ma'aser sheni*, the second tithe,[119] every year in the sabbatical period except the fourth and the sixth, when the tithe was given to the poor.[120] In conformity with Deuteronomy 14:22 ff., *ma'aser sheni* was to be consumed by the owner and his family in the city of Jerusalem. Designated in Scripture as holy, according to the Tannaim,[121] it cannot be higher than the fourth grade in the hierarchy, since the first three consist of *mattenot kehunah.* Concerning the fourth year's fruits of a young tree (Lev. 19:24), Bet Hillel and Bet Shammai differ, Bet Hillel coupling them with *ma'aser sheni,*[122] and Bet Shammai obviously regarding them as of a lower grade of holiness.[123] The first tithe, however, was not taken to be holy by most of the rabbis.[124]

Kodshe ḳodashim, ḳodashim ḳallim, ḳodshe ha-gebul, ma'aser sheni, and the fourth year's fruits of a young tree or vineyard, it was felt, all possessed the quality of *ḳedushah,* holiness. It was this felt quality alone that distinguished those things from the rest of their kind with which they had originally been intermingled, that marked off those things as being something other, something different. The quality of *ḳedushah* was thus a purely mystical quality, so much so that it could neither be described nor demonstrated. This did not mean that the sense of *ḳedushah* was weak. On the contrary, the sense of *ḳedushah* was so strong that it made possible an awareness of ascending grades. In turn, that hierarchical order almost gave to *ḳedushah* a character of substantiality, since some things were felt to possess more of *ḳedushah* than others. Now these things became *ḳedushot,* by and large, when they were dedicated to God, but no element of theurgy whatsoever was involved in the manner whereby either sacrifices or the things which were set apart became peculiarly God's own. According to an anonymous statement in the Mishnah, a sacrifice is to be slaughtered with certain ideas in mind, among them the idea that it is being dedicated to God.[125] R. Jose declares, however, that it is a proper sacrifice even if it is slaughtered with no idea in mind.[126] Again, when a person sets apart *terumah,* he is to say, "*Terumah* to God";[127] on the other hand, it is also enough if he only has such an idea in mind and utters nothing at all.[128] Theurgy is obviously out of the question in the halakah stated by R. Jose, but the other halakot likewise have nothing to do with theurgy.

In all the halakot here, we are dealing with intention, *maḥashabah* or *kawwanah,*[129] whether the intention is expressed in words, or consists of an idea in the mind, or is indicated simply by an act.[130] The intention whereby a thing is made holy is akin to the instances of intention mentioned in Chapter VII, section D—the intention required, for example, on the part of a person who performs an act of acquisition, or the intention required in a writ of divorce.[131] Indeed, in consecutive statements, authorities differing with respect to intention in the redemption of *ma'aser sheni* differ also with regard to intention in the matter of handing a writ of divorce to a woman,[132] evidently because intention in the one instance is analogous to intention in the other. The manner whereby any particular holy thing acquired its character was akin to the manner in which a number of nonholy things acquired their specific character. If the character of these nonholy things was not determined by theurgy, neither was the character of the holy things so determined.

The hierarchy of holy days, as we have indicated elsewhere, consists, in descending order, of the Sabbath, the Day of Atonement, Rosh ha-Shanah, the Three Festivals, and the intermediate days of the Festivals.[133] In the mishnaic period and for some time afterward, the first day of every month was established by a proclamation of the *bet din*, the court,[134] upon the evidence of witnesses that they had seen the new moon. As a result, it was the *bet din* that determined when the holy days would fall,[135] except, of course, for the Sabbath which is fixed. The holy days are, to be sure, "the appointed seasons of the Lord" (Lev. 23:4), but they assume that character only when they are proclaimed as such by Israel: "If ye proclaim them, they are My appointed seasons, but if [ye do] not [proclaim them] they are not My appointed seasons."[136] Distinguishing between the Sabbath and the other holy days, a tannaitic statement specifically relates the holiness of the other holy days to the decision of the *bet din*. Whereas the Sabbath has been determined by God—"But on the seventh day is a Sabbath of solemn rest holy to the Lord" (Exod. 35:2)—"the holiness of the 'appointed seasons' [קדושת מועדות] is given over [מסורה] to the *bet din*."[137] The holiness of a day is not associated, therefore, with theurgy. The Sabbath simply recurs regularly every seventh day. Although the holiness of the other days depends upon the decision of a court,[138] that decision is based on the evidence of witnesses as to the recurrence of a natural monthly phenomenon; hence, in the final analysis, the holiness of the other days, too, depends upon regular recurrences. In fact, the law is that if the first appearance of the new moon has not been seen, there is no proclamation by the court, and the month just past becomes a "full month" of thirty days.[139]

Halakah makes the holy days distinctive. It does so by prescribing acts through which the individual himself is to make the days holy, and these acts are of an entirely normal character. The *Mekilta de Rabbi Simon* speaks of such acts in commenting on the verse, "Remember the Sabbath Day to make it holy [לקדשו]" (Exod. 20:8).[140] "Remember" refers to remembering the Sabbath by reciting the Ḳiddush over a cup of wine, while "to make it holy" means that the Ḳiddush is to be recited, in the first instance, on the Sabbath Eve.[141] According to another interpretation, "remember" means to remember the Sabbath every day by designating the successive days of the week as "the first day in the Sabbath, the second day in the Sabbath," and so on until the sixth day, the designation for that day being, "the eve of the Sabbath."[142] The Sabbath Day is to be made holy by being made festive: " 'To make it holy'—with what are you to make it holy? With food and with drink and with clean clothes," so that your meals and clothes may be different on the Sabbath from what they are on week-days;[143] and the same rule is applied to the Festivals.[144] More than in any other way, however, the holy days are distinguished by the individual abstaining from work on those days. "Make it holy by [refraining from] the doing of work."[145] The gradations in the hierarchy of holy days are established, in large measure, by the halakot which prohibit anything classified as "labor." In the main, the holier the day, the more inclusive is the category of prohibited "labors."[146]

On the hierarchy of holy objects we need not enlarge here, for we have dealt with aspects of it at some length in an earlier work.[147] In descending order, that hierarchy consists of a *Sefer Torah* (a scroll of the Pentateuch), *tefillin* (four specified passages from the Pentateuch on parchment), *mezuzot* (two specified passages from the Pentateuch on parchment), *sefarim* (scrolls of Prophets and *Ketubim* [from Psalms to Chronicles]), a synagogue.[148] Failure to conform with but a single one of the many rules for the writing of a *Sefer Torah* and for the preparation of its parchment is enough to disqualify it,[149] and similar rules apply to the making of *tefillin* and *mezuzot*.[150] A number of those rules have to do with *kawwanah*, intention, and one rule in particular reminds us of *kawwanah* in the case of sacrifices and of tithes:[151] names of God in a *Sefer Torah*, *tefillin*, and *mezuzot* must be written with *kawwanah*, that is, each name must be written with the idea in mind that it refers to God.[152] Basically, however, the holiness of a *Sefer Torah* and of *tefillin* and *mezuzot* must derive from the dogma of *mattan Torah*, the belief that the Pentateuch was given by God.[153] We infer this because *sefarim* are but a degree less holy than *mezuzot*, and the holiness of *sefarim* can be accounted for only on the ground that Prophets and *Ketubim* are associated with that dogma.[154] The synagogue derives its holiness simply from its specified use as a house of prayer.[155] Neither the dogma, a matter of belief alone, nor the mere use of a building, involves theurgy.[156]

At first sight, the *ḳedushah* of persons, too, seems to present a firm hierarchical order. The highest grade of *ḳedushah* is that of the *kohanim*, the priests. Their *ḳedushah* derives from the *ḳedushah* of Aaron: "Who has made us holy with the *ḳedushah* of Aaron";[157] as descendants of Aaron they were given the *mattenot kehunah*, the holy things which priests alone are permitted to eat.[158] The other groups in Israel are holy also; for example, a child born to converts after they have been converted, says a mishnah, is born "in *ḳedushah*."[159] Between the *ḳedushah* of the priests and that of all other groups, however, the demarcation is so strong that even the Levites, so far as levitical impurity is concerned, are classified together with the Israelites.[160]

But this demarcation was challenged. It was in conflict, Alon has demonstrated, with a contrary tradition regarding both the obligation of levitical purity and the holiness of persons.[161] That contrary tradition insisted that *ḥullin*, ordinary food, be eaten in levitical purity;[162] by the same token, the contrary tradition tried to extend the *ḳedushah* of the priests to all Israel.[163] This view is epitomized in a brief passage cited by Alon. It is a passage that insists on "the washing of the hands" before eating *ḥullin*, and it concludes with, "Not to the priests alone was *ḳedushah* given, but to all—to the priests and to the Levites and to the Israelites."[164] Doubtless because most people found it too difficult to observe all the laws of levitical purity in their everyday life, the demarcation remained;[165] nevertheless, the contrary tradition did prevail with respect to a number of laws.[166] Among them is the practice of "the washing of the hands" before a meal,[167] a practice specifically informed by the idea that the *ḳedushah* of the Israelite is like that of the priest.

Since one value concept can be stressed as against another in the process of their organismic integration, the rabbinic value complex allowed room both for the demarcation between the priests and the people and for the opposition to that demarcation. In the demarcation, the concept of *kehunah* was stressed as against the concept of Israel,[168] whereas in the opposition to the demarcation, the concept of Israel was stressed as against that of *kehunah*.[169] The opposition to the demarcation, however, was not limited to laws and statements involving those concepts alone. It also called upon and stressed, as against the concept of *kehunah*, the concept of Torah, although now the opposition to the demarcation is more explicit on some occasions than on others. "A *mamzer* [bastard] who is a *talmid ḥakam* [learned] precedes a high priest who is an *'am ha-'areẓ* [unlearned]."[170] "Torah is greater than the *kehunah* and than the *malkut* [kingship], for the *malkut* is acquired through thirty qualifications and the *kehunah* through twenty-four, but Torah is acquired through forty-eight things," etc.[171] The knowledge and practice of Torah renders one who is not a priest "worthy to offer up a burnt-offering upon the altar."[172]

Ḳedushah as concretized in a hierarchical order is only one phase of the concept. In another phase *ḳedushah* is inseparable from personal conduct and, instead of connoting a hierarchical order, has several connotations of its own, a complex of connotations. In this phase, *ḳedushah* means the holiness acquired through the observance of the miẓwot; it means the imitation of God in deeds of lovingkindness and in like matters; it means separation or refraining from the cardinal sins: murder, sexual sin, and idolatry.[173] But deeds of lovingkindness and refraining from specific sins are themselves miẓwot. The several connotations of this phase of *ḳedushah* are interconnected, interrelated, as is the case in general with the different phases of a concept. Indeed, the various connotations of *ḳedushah* in this phase may themselves be viewed as phases of *ḳedushah*.

Ḳedushah is acquired through fulfilling the miẓwot. " 'Ye shall be holy' [Lev. 19:2]—that refers to the holiness [conferred by] all the miẓwot."[174] " 'Be holy' [Num. 15:40]—for as long as you fulfill the miẓwot you are sanctified, but if you neglect them, you will become profaned."[175] "With every new miẓwah which God [*ha-Maḳom*] issues to Israel He adds to them *ḳedushah*."[176]

This phase of *ḳedushah* seemingly has some elements in common with the phase wherein *ḳedushah* connotes a hierarchical order, but only apparently so. Thus, we have noticed that when *ḳedushah* connotes a hierarchy, *ḳedushah* is felt to be a mystical quality which almost possesses the character of substantiality. Something quite similar seems to be conveyed by the statement, "With every new miẓwah which God issues to Israel He adds to them *ḳedushah.*" But another statement, in like manner apparently attributing substantiality to *ḳedushah*, enables us to recognize that now this mystical quality has a moral implication. The angels, says R. 'Abin ('Abun), were given only one *ḳedushah*, since as heavenly beings they are not subject to the evil *yeẓer*, whereas earthly beings, men, because they are subject to the evil *yeẓer*, were given two *ḳedushot*, and "would that they might stand up with [the help of] two *ḳedushot.*"[177] The mystical quality remains, but now, so far as it relates to man, it implies the moral strength to withstand temptation.[178]

In hierarchical *ḳedushah*, what is holy is regarded as belonging to God in a special sense, as being God's own. Now, however, a similar idea is given an entirely different turn; in fact, the idea is inverted. Because Israel belongs to God in a special sense it is incumbent upon them, obligatory for them, to be holy. " 'Ye shall be holy, for I, the Lord, am holy' [Lev. 19:2]— 'Ye shall be holy'—why? Because I am holy, for I have attached you to Me, as it is said, 'For as the girdle cleaveth to the loins of a man, so have I caused to cleave unto Me the whole house of Israel' [Jer. 13:11]."[179] The same point is made in a passage which Schechter renders as follows: "Another Rabbi remarked, 'God said to Israel, Even before I created the world you were sanctified unto me; be ye therefore holy as I am holy'; and he proceeds to say, 'The matter is to be compared to a king who sanctified [by wedlock] a woman unto him, and said to her: Since thou art my wife, what is my glory is thy glory, be therefore holy even as I am holy.' "[180] The import of the command, "Be holy," must not escape us. That command marks a vital difference between hierarchical and nonhierarchical *ḳedushah*. Rather than just a mystical quality alone, *ḳedushah* is now something which must be achieved through effortful personal conduct. To achieve holiness is obligatory upon Israel because they are God's own and God is holy. It follows, therefore, that only when the individuals in Israel are holy men are they indeed God's own. The verse "And ye shall be holy men unto Me" (Exod. 22:30) is interpreted by R. Ishmael to say, "When you are holy men, then you are Mine."[181] How Israel is to achieve holiness is not stated in these passages. But we already know that Israel achieves holiness through the miẓwot, and we shall soon see how such efforts to achieve holiness are profoundly affected by the idea that God is holy.

To demonstrate that the *ḳedushah* acquired through the fulfillment of the miẓwot differs from hierarchical *ḳedushah* we have shown that what appear to be elements in common between these two phases of *ḳedushah* are only seemingly in common. At one point, nevertheless, these two phases of *ḳedushah* are completely congruent. The act whereby a holy thing in hierarchical *ḳedushah* is made holy is at the same time an act that is a miẓwah, and hence also belongs to the nonhierarchical phase of *ḳedushah*. Now we have recognized that such an act, often merely expressing intention, is entirely devoid of theurgy. In other words, the only type of miẓwah which could possibly have had theurgical associations is definitely nontheurgical, for there is no question of theurgy at all with regard to the rest of the miẓwot. The *ḳedushah* achieved through fulfilling the miẓwot is throughout, therefore, nontheurgical. Instead, it is an experience in normal mysticism, an experience of a close relationship with God, so close that passages can tell of how God has attached Israel to Himself, and of how Israel was "sanctified unto" God even before the creation of the world. Such an experience of relationship can take place, of course, only when a miẓwah is fulfilled with *kawwanah*. Indeed, *kawwanah* in this connection, we have noticed, itself implies an awareness of a relationship with God, a consciousness that a particular miẓwah is a communication by God here and now.[182]

There is a phase of *ḳedushah* which does not have even an apparent resemblance to any element in hierarchical *ḳedushah*. Schechter has called this phase or aspect of *ḳedushah* the imitation of God.[183] " 'Ye shall be holy, for I the Lord am holy' [Lev. 19:2]. These words are explained by the ancient Rabbinic sage Abba Saul to mean 'Israel is the *familia* [suite or bodyguard] of the King [God], whence it is incumbent upon them to imitate the King.' "[184] Another statement by Abba Saul tells of the nature of this imitation. "*I and He*, that is, like unto him [God]. As he is merciful and gracious, so be thou [man] merciful and gracious."[185] Similarly, a passage in the Sifre teaches: "As the Holy One blessed be He is called merciful and gracious, so be thou merciful and gracious, giving free gifts to all; as the Holy One blessed be He is called righteous, so be thou righteous; as the Holy One blessed be He is called loving [*ḥasid*], so be thou loving."[186] An obligation rests upon Israel to imitate God in these ways because they are His *familia*, and they must, therefore, like Him be holy. The close relationship of Israel with God is expressed in other metaphors as well, and once more that relationship is given as the reason for the imitation of God. God, according to the rabbis, investigated within Himself, and found eleven qualities, those mentioned in Psalm 15:2 ff.: "He that walketh uprightly, and doeth charity [צדק]," etc. And He asks of Israel nothing but that they imitate these eleven qualities, basing His request on the ground that "ye are My children and I am your Father, ye are My brothers and I am your Brother, ye are My friends and I am your Friend, ye are My beloved and I am your Beloved."[187]

A motive behind an act of charity or a deed of lovingkindness may be the imitation of God. "The profession of the Holy One blessed be He is the practice of charity and deeds of lovingkindness, and Abraham who will command his children and his household after him 'that they shall keep the way of the Lord' [Gen. 18:19] is told by God, 'Thou hast chosen My profession.' "[188] A famous statement in Soṭah 14a specifies the deeds of lovingkindness in which a man ought to imitate God. Schechter renders that passage as follows: "Walk in the attributes of God (or rather make his attributes the rule for thy conduct). As he clothes the naked [Gen. 3:21], so do thou clothe the naked; as he nurses the sick [Gen. 18:1], so do thou nurse the sick; as he comforts the mourners [Gen. 25:11], so do thou comfort the mourners; as he buries the dead [Deut. 34:5], so do thou bury the dead."* To do charity and to perform these deeds of lovingkindness, as we know, are miẓwot.

* Schechter, *Aspects*, pp. 202 f. See also A. Marmorstein, *Studies in Jewish Theology* (London, 1950), pp. 113 f. The following is taken from a cento formed by E. Hatch (*The Influence of Greek Ideas on Christianity*, ed. F. C. Grant [New York, 1957], p. 155) of passages from Epictetus: "Every one of us may call himself a son of God. Just as our bodies are linked to the material universe, so by virtue of reason our souls are linked to and continuous with Him, being in reality parts and offshoots of Him. He Himself is within us, so that we are His shrines, living temples and incarnations of Him. We and He together form the greatest and chiefest and most comprehensive of all organizations. If once we realize this kinship, no mean or unworthy thought

Besides standing for the imitation of God by man, *kedushah* in this phase also has the connotation of love. Whether related to God or to attitudes and acts of man in imitation of God, holiness in this context refers only to acts and attitudes which express love.[189] But in another context, too, *kedushah* is associated with God's love. In the 'Amidah for New Year and the Day of Atonement, the Third Berakah closes with Isaiah 5:16, since that verse, as interpreted by the rabbis, contains the idea that God is sanctified in His charity at judgment. The verse was taken as saying, "And the Lord of hosts is exalted in judgment, and the holy God is sanctified in *zedakah*."[190] In view of the connotation of love in the context of the imitation of God, such an added association of *kedushah* with God's love indicates that *kedushah* is among the concepts in which the emphasis on love rises to expression. The question is, however, under what circumstances does this phase of *kedushah* emerge, for the concept of *kedushah* may also refer to hierarchical *kedushah*. We shall attempt to answer that question in the next section.

There remains one more phase of nonhierarchical *kedushah* to be considered. Because that phase is posed against acts designated as *tum'ah* [defilement], we must first touch on several matters concerning the concept of *tum'ah*.

Tum'ah is the obverse of the concept of *kedushah*. When *tum'ah* refers to levitical impurity it is the obverse of hierarchical *kedushah*, and that relationship manifests itself, among other ways, in a certain similarity of structure. Like hierarchical *kedushah*, this type of *tum'ah* too possesses hierarchical orders.[191] The structural similarity, however,

---

of ourselves can enter our souls. The sense of it forms a rule and standard for our lives. If God be faithful, we also must be faithful: if God be beneficent, we also must be beneficent. If God be highminded, we also must be highminded, doing and saying whatever we do and say in imitation of and union with Him." In Epictetus' view, the imitation of God is the result of coming to the recognition that "our souls are . . . in reality parts and offshoots" of God; that is to say, the imitation is due to a proper knowledge of the universe, to a rational or intellectual factor. According to the rabbis, as we shall see in the next section, it is in an emotional experience, the mystical experience of *kedushah*, that the individual dedicates himself to the imitation of God. Of course, the rabbis would be unalterably opposed to the idea expressed by Epictetus that the human being is an incarnation of God. That notion leads him also to say, "We and He together form the greatest and chiefest and most comprehensive of all organizations." Such a statement would strike the rabbis as being extremely presumptuous, to put it mildly.

serves only to emphasize the antithetical character of the two concepts. Thus, in the case of *ḳedushah*, a person must act in such fashion that a higher degree is achieved if possible, and not a lower;[192] in the case of *ṭum'ah*, on the other hand, it is ordinarily not permitted to allow a thing already levitically unclean to become *ṭum'ah* of a higher degree.[193] At the same time, the prohibitions relating to *ṭum'ah* apply only to the Temple, the sacrifices, and the *terumot* and *ma'aser sheni*, but not to *ḥullin*, ordinary food; hence a person is permitted to eat and drink *ḥullin* that is levitically impure.[194]

But there is also *ṭum'ah* which is nonhierarchical. On the basis of biblical verses, a passage in the Sifra[195] specifically designates three acts as *ṭum'ot*—the *ṭum'ah* of *'abodah zarah*, the verse being, "To defile My sanctuary, and to profane My holy Name" (Lev. 20:3), and referring to the worship of Moloch; the *ṭum'ah* of *gilluy 'arayot*, the verse being, "That ye do not any of these abominable customs, which were done before you, and that ye defile not yourselves therein" (*ibid.*, 18:30), and referring to adultery and prohibited sex relations; the *ṭum'ah* of *shefikut damim*, the verse being, "And thou shalt not defile the land which ye inhabit, in the midst of which I dwell" (Num. 35:34), referring to murder. In each instance, the verse employs a verb with the root *ṭm'* (defile), thereby allowing the rabbis to draw the conclusion that the act referred to is *ṭum'ah*. As Tosafot says, those acts are not "real *ṭum'ah*" but are simply alluded to in the Bible linguistically as *ṭum'ah*.[196] What the rabbis characterize here as *ṭum'ah* is not hierarchical *ṭum'ah* but the three cardinal sins.[197] In other words, *ṭum'ah* here is moral *ṭum'ah*.

When posed against nonhierarchical or moral *ṭum'ah*, *ḳedushah* connotes the idea of separation from moral *ṭum'ah* or abstention from such acts. That idea is contained in a rabbinic comment on Leviticus 19:2: "Speak unto all the congregation of the children of Israel, and say unto them: Ye shall be holy; for I the Lord your God am holy." The comment paraphrases this verse as follows: "The Holy One blessed be He said to Moses, 'Say to the children of Israel: My sons just as I am separated [פרוש], so be ye separated [פרושין]; just as I am holy, so be ye holy.' "[198] An interpretation in the Sifra likewise paraphrases "Ye shall be holy" as "Be ye separated."[199] These rabbinic renderings of Leviticus 19:2 relate that verse to what immediately precedes it, namely, to the chapter in Leviticus containing a catalogue of the prohibited sexual relations.[200] All the prohibited sexual connections there, "all the *'arayot,*" are characterized in the Sifra on Leviticus 18:30 as *ṭum'ah.*[201] In this context, then, *ḳedushah* means abstaining from all the prohibited sexual connections, these things being *ṭum'ah.* That is also the connotation of *ḳedushah* in rabbinic interpretations of Exodus 19:6 and Leviticus 20:26. To quote Schechter:[202] "The Rabbis interpret the verse, 'And ye shall be unto Me a kingdom of priests and a holy nation' (Exod. 19:6) with the words, 'Be unto Me a kingdom of priests separated from the nations of the world and their abominations.'[203] This passage must be taken in connection with another, in which, with allusion to the scriptural words, 'And ye shall be holy unto Me . . . and I have severed you from other people that you should be Mine' (Lev. 20:26), the Rabbis point to the sexual immorality which divides the heathen from Israel."[204] Schechter goes on to say that "the notion of impurity is further extended to all things stigmatized in the Levitical legislation as unclean, particularly to the forbidden foods."[205] Except for the forbidden foods, however, what is stigmatized as unclean in levitical legislation is treated by the rabbis as hierarchical *ṭum'ah.* Even with regard to the forbidden foods, a rabbinic statement deliberately refers to nonhierarchical *ṭum'ah* and then to hierarchical *ṭum'ah,* and unless we distinguish between the two, the statement is confusing.[206]

Every precaution was taken to preclude the remotest contact with idolatry, as is evident from the tractate *'Abodah Zarah.* In this anxiety to be "separated" from the least suggestion of idolatry, apparently some individuals practiced precautions of their own. R. Menaḥem b. Sim'ai went so far as never to look at the figures stamped on the silver coins, and that was reason enough for R. Joḥanan to refer to him as "the descendant of holy men."[207]

The idea of "separation" from sin was naturally not limited to the sins designated as *ṭum'ah.* A mishnah uses the same verb (פורש), for example, not only in reference to abstaining from *'arayot,* but also in reference to abstaining from eating blood and to abstaining from *gezel.*[208]

Ṭum'ah is the obverse of nonhierarchical *ḳedushah* just as it is the obverse of hierarchical *ḳedushah,* and yet the resemblance between the two phases of *ḳedushah* is, once more, only apparent. In the first place, nonhierarchical *ḳedushah* is not posed against "real *ṭum'ah*" but against the cardinal sins, moral *ṭum'ah*. That difference, furthermore, makes for a basic difference in the attitudes engendered by the respective phases of *ḳedushah*. Hierarchical *ḳedushah* does not rule out all possible contact with "real *ṭum'ah*," a person being permitted to eat *ḥullin* which is levitically unclean. On the other hand, nonhierarchical *ḳedushah* connotes complete separation from moral *ṭum'ah*. To imitate God by being "separated" can only imply that Israel is thus separated from moral *ṭum'ah* and made undefiled. The imitation here does not consist of acts, as in the imitation of God's love, but only of separateness.

This phase of *ḳedushah* differs from hierarchical *ḳedushah* in another respect as well. At times it does not have *ṭum'ah* as its obverse at all. When *ḳedushah* connotes separateness it connotes self-restraint. The rabbis can therefore extend the concept of *ḳedushah* to include self-control in matters that are not moral *ṭum'ah*—to restraint in licit sexual relations and also to other forms of self-control or self-discipline. "Hallow thyself in what is permitted to thee," say the rabbis.[209] They employ the idea of holiness in the same way when they speak of the man who "hallows himself" in the marriage bed.[210] Asceticism as such, however, is regarded as *ḳedushah* only by R. Eleazar, the other authorities even disagreeing with him when he calls the Nazarite holy by reason of the Nazarite's abstention from wine.[211]

We can now see how closely interrelated are the various phases of nonhierarchical *ḳedushah*. The phase in which *ḳedushah* means the holiness acquired through the fulfillment of the miẓwot is inseparable from the other two phases. Imitation of God refers to specific acts of *ẓedaḳah* and *gemilut ḥasadim*, acts that, for a man, are miẓwot. Separateness is the withdrawal from the three cardinal sins, moral *ṭum'ah*, and from the forbidden foods, all of which matters are negative miẓwot. The mystical quality inherent in nonhierarchical *ḳedushah*, we noticed, implies moral strength to withstand temptation, and we can now recognize the relevance of that implication. Such moral strength is called upon when the temptation is to withhold from an act of kindness or to surrender to an immoral desire. In the next section we shall discuss the occasions in which all these phases of *ḳedushah* come to the fore.

Despite its dependence on the Bible, the rabbinic concept of *kedushah* has definite characteristics of its own. But the problem of the relation to the Bible involved here is a very complex one, requiring an extended discussion. It will suffice now to point to several matters that are solely rabbinic. Stressing the concept of Torah as against that of *kehunah* (priesthood); the phase of *kedushah* in which the imitation of God consists of doing *zedakah* and *gemilut hasadim*; the extension of the concept of *kedushah* to include self-restraint even in matters legally permitted—all these are purely rabbinic.

Thus far we have discussed phases of the concept of *kedushah*—connotations of the concept which do not possess abstract conceptual terms of their own but which are all represented by the term *kedushah*. *Kiddush ha-Shem*, however, is a subconcept of *kedushah*, an aspect of *kedushah* sufficiently crystallized to be represented on its own account by a conceptual term. Although we dealt with concretizations of *kiddush ha-Shem* in Chapter VI, we are only now in a position to indicate its relation to the concept of *kedushah*.

Kiddush ha-Shem means, literally, hallowing God's Name. There is *kiddush ha-Shem* in a heroic act of martyrdom before a *parhesya'* (ten or more Jews);[212] in a righteous act by a Jew toward a Gentile which elicits the response, "Blessed is the God of the Jews";[213] in the corporate act of worship consisting of the Baraku and its response,[214] and in several other corporate acts of worship.[215] Since these are acts of *kiddush ha-Shem*, presumably they are acts whereby God's Name is hallowed. But these are acts which call forth an explicit or, in the case of the *parhesya'*, an implicit acknowledgment of God. In what sense is God's Name hallowed when an acknowledgment of God is called forth?

A general acknowledgment of God is associated with the denial of idolatry. The concurrence of the *parhesya'* with the martyr's denial of idolatry is therefore tantamount to an acknowledgment of God on their part. Idolatry is also negated, however, by the concept of *tum'ah*. We must remember that idolatry is *tum'ah*, and that *tum'ah* is the obverse of *kedushah*. An idol itself is an original cause of an entire order of hierarchical *tum'ah*.[216] A person or thing in physical contact with an idol thereby becomes unclean,[217] and similarly a person who has entered the house of an idol and benches brought into that house become unclean.[218] *Ṭum'ah* here constitutes a denial, the strongest denial possible, that whatsoever is worshiped other than God is a deity. To acknowledge God is to affirm that it is God alone Who is holy. God's Name is "hallowed," therefore, when an act calls forth an explicit or implicit acknowledgment of God. An acknowledgment of God is an affirmation of the *ḳedushah* of God.

In the struggle against idolatry, the people of Israel as a whole were pitted against the Gentile world. This, it seems to us, is reflected in the character of these acts of *ḳiddush ha-Shem*. The general acknowledgment of God is always by the *ẓibbur* or by the *parhesya'*, that is, by the community.[219]

Ḳiddush ha-Shem is a rabbinic term, but the concept has, as in all such instances, its biblical antecedent.[220] The difference between the rabbinic concept and its biblical antecedent, however, is striking, as Avraham Holtz has shown in a recent study.[221] According to the Bible, whereas the people of Israel have the power to profane the Name of God, it is God alone Who can sanctify His Name. Most of the aspects of *ḳiddush ha-Shem*, including *ḳiddush ha-Shem* in a *parhesya'* and in a *ẓibbur*, are thus purely rabbinic.

D. The Experience of *Ḳedushah*

A miẓwah is performed with *kawwanah*, we saw, when the individual feels that the miẓwah represents a communication which has been directed to him by God. "In such an experience, the particular miẓwah which the individual is about to fulfill is not merely a practice transmitted to him by previous generations, but is a command from God here and now."[222]

During the process of performing a miẓwah with *kawwanah*, a person has an experience of *ḳedushah*. It is a mystical experience and yet, being normal mysticism, it is in some degree describable. The miẓwah as a communication from God is felt to be a priceless privilege. Having been given that privilege, the individual has a consciousness, not of union with God, but of belonging to God, of being God's own. At the same time, this entire emotional experience is pervaded through and through with a sense of dedication. The individual dedicates himself to imitate God in acts of *zedakah* and *gemilut hasadim* and to abstain from moral *tum'ah*. A mystical experience is thus also a source of moral energy, and the more often the experience occurs the greater will be the latent ethical motive power; in other words, experiences of *kedushah* are character-building experiences. It will be noticed, of course, that in describing the mystical experience of *kedushah* we have simply set down the rabbinic ideas already discussed in the previous section, the ideas concerning the *kedushah* of the mizwot, the nonhierarchical phase of *kedushah*. Those rabbinic ideas can only reflect the actual experience of that phase of *kedushah*.

An experience of *kedushah* is always associated with an act of worship. The consciousness that the mizwot are a priceless privilege evokes a berakah, an expression of gratitude for God's love as manifested in the conferring of that privilege. The berakah here, however, embodies not only the concepts of God's love and berakah, but also those of *kedushah* and mizwot. Again, as in all berakot, one of the elements of the experiential entity consists of an occasion, the occasion now being an act about to be performed or a holy day. But here the occasion has a dual role; not only is it the stimulus for the berakah but it also serves as a reminder of the mizwot in general. We shall shortly take up the Birkat ha-Mizwot, the berakah said when the occasion is an act about to be performed, leaving perhaps for future consideration the Kedushat ha-Yom and the Kiddush, berakot said when a holy day is the occasion.

The concept of *kawwanah* is a factor in the experience of *kedushah*, as much a factor as any of the other concepts involved. Nevertheless, like *kawwanah* in the other forms of worship,[223] the concept of *kawwanah* here, too, is not a constituent of the idea content of the experience. *Kawwanah* is a factor in the experience as a whole solely by virtue of making the concept of mizwot a vital factor, the result being that the concept of mizwot, and not that of *kawwanah*, is a constituent of the idea content. The question is whether, for those who cannot achieve *kawwanah*, the concept of mizwot has any meaning at all. In the Babli, we saw above,[224] the division of opinion on this matter crystallizes into two opposing general principles—a positive principle ("mizwot require *kawwanah*") and a negative principle ("mizwot do not require *kawwanah*"). The proponents of the negative principle obviously feel that the concept of miẓwot retains a certain meaning even for those who cannot achieve *kawwanah*. The latter can at least have the intention of observing the miẓwot, can have the intention of hearing the blowing of the *shofar*, or of hearing the reading of the *megillah*, or of reading the Shema', as the case may be. Probably, in one way or another, this intention of fulfilling a miẓwah may at times be an element in an experience of *ḳedushah*, but an element in a correspondingly weak experience. Only the positive principle—"miẓwot require *kawwanah*"—accords with a morally energizing experience of *ḳedushah*.

E. Birkat ha-Miẓwot

Acts designated as miẓwot include acts ordained by the rabbis, as we pointed out in the first section of this chapter. The berakah on the kindling of the Ḥanukkah light cited there is hence typical of the Birkat ha-Miẓwot, even though the act referred to in that berakah is a rabbinic ordinance. "Blessed art Thou, O Lord our God, King of the world, Who has sanctified us by His miẓwot, and commanded us to kindle the light of Ḥanukkah."[225] Up to and including "and commanded us [*weẓiwwanu*]," the formula remains the same for all the Birkot ha-Miẓwot, and only the words which follow refer to this or the other specific act. (Some of these specific acts are referred to by a verb,[226] as here, and others by a gerund.)[227]

The rule is that the Birkat ha-Miẓwot is to precede the act which is the occasion for the berakah.[228] This rule is called for so that the recitation of the berakah together with the act may constitute a unitary entity. The berakah is an expression of gratitude for the privilege of having been given a command here and now by God—"and commanded us," as the berakah declares. A consciousness of the command naturally must precede the fulfillment of the command. But the consciousness of the command continues to inform also the fulfillment of the miẓwah otherwise the performance itself would lack *kawwanah*. There is no break in mood from the moment the berakah is begun until the command has been fulfilled;[229] that is to say, the recitation of the berakah and the act which follows constitute a unitary experience. As the plural "us" in the berakah indicates, that experience engages the larger self. Once again the individual associates himself with all of Israel whilst retaining his own self-identity.[230]

Kawwanah encompasses every detail of the act enjoined by the mizwah. Even the quality of the object employed in such an act can express *kawwanah*. Interpreting ואנוהו in Exodus 15:2, R. Ishmael says, "And is it possible for [a man of] flesh and blood to make lovely his Creator? But [it means] I will be lovely to Him in [performing] mizwot: I will make before Him a lovely *lulab*, a lovely *sukkah* [booth], lovely *zizit* [fringes], lovely *tefillin*."[231] The concept of *kawwanah* is integrated in this statement with that of *hiddur mizwah* (doing a mizwah in the handsomest way).[232]

In contradistinction to the last part of the berakah and its reference to a specific mizwah, the words, "And Who has sanctified us by His mizwot," speak of the mizwot in general. These words, too, nevertheless relate to the act about to be performed, since what they say has relevance, at the moment, to that particular act. Nor should the past tense in which the phrase is couched lead us to think otherwise. The phrase conveys several things, all of them associated with *kedushat mizwot*, the holiness conferred by mizwot.[233] One of the ideas implied by the phrase is that God adds *kedushah* to Israel with every new mizwah which He issues to them,[234] an idea referring to the individual who fulfills any given mizwah, as Maimonides says.[235] To the individual about to fulfill a mizwah, therefore, the phrase "And Who has sanctified us by His mizwot," past tense and all, suggests an experience of *kedushah*; indeed, the past tense encourages him by reminding him of past experiences of that kind. In any case, the phrase certainly relates to the particular mizwah in which he is engaged. The other ideas conveyed by the phrase—*kedushah* as the imitation of God in acts of love and *kedushah* as abstaining from moral *tum'ah*—suggest to the individual, in like manner, the moral idea content in the hoped-for experience of *kedushah*.

According to a view in the Yerushalmi, a berakah (i.e., the Birkat ha-Mizwot) ought to be said at the fulfilling of every mizwah,[236] and the same rule, somewhat differently worded, is found in the Tosefta as an anonymous statement.[237] This rule, on the face of it, would seem to apply to ethical acts too since, as we saw in the last chapter, ethical acts are also characterized as mizwot.[238] A medieval authority, on the ground that a berakah ought to be said when observing any of the positive miẓwot, did go so far as sometimes to say the Birkat ha-Miẓwot when he gave charity and on similar occasions.[239] One of the earlier commentators on the Yerushalmi properly adds that this was not the general practice.[240] Obviously the rule in regard to saying a berakah when fulfilling any of the miẓwot was not meant to be taken literally; it is probably a way of declaring that a berakah ought to be said at every possible occasion.

There are, in fact, occasions when the Birkat ha-Miẓwot is said and occasions when it is not said. In a *responsum*, R. Joseph Ibn Plat[241] points out that there is no one general reason which accounts for all the various occasions when the berakah is not said, but that such occasions are to be accounted for on the basis of various principles. Among the principles he adduces is one that, we should say, may apply to many ethical acts, namely, the principle that the berakah is not said when the act depends upon the acquiescence of others, for example, in the case of charity, upon the acquiescence of the recipient of charity. We are here concerned, however, not so much with the principles adduced as with Ibn Plat's approach to the problem. As a general proposition, it appears, the berakah should normally be said (a general principle quite in accord with the rule in the Yerushalmi and the Tosefta), but there are many exceptions, each exception being due to special circumstances.[242]

When it comes to ethical acts, each separate ethical act, it seems to us, constitutes an exception by virtue of its own special circumstances. In an ethical act, there is a certain emotional undercurrent or a degree of tension peculiarly its own, apart from its being a miẓwah. Were such acts subject to the Birkat ha-Miẓwot, the concept of miẓwot would be stressed as against the ethical concept which also qualifies or interprets the act, and the act would then in large part lose its own peculiar character. Instead, therefore, the ethical concept is stressed, and the stressing is achieved by omitting the berakah. All such acts are prime examples of ethical concepts being stressed rather than the concept of miẓwot, other examples of which we noticed before.[243] At the same time, of course, these acts are miẓwot as well. In an organismic complex, as we have so often observed, more than one concept may be embodied in a concretization, although one concept may be stressed rather than another.

We ought not to conclude this section without some discussion of an approach which is different from the one we have utilized. Maimonides lays down the general rule that the Birkat ha-Mizwot is said before all acts commanded by the mizwot which are "between a man and God,"[244] and hence he implies, as the *Kesef Mishneh* adds, that the berakah is not said when the act is required by a law which is in the category of "between a man and a fellow-man,"[245] another general rule. The making of a "railing," *ma'akeh*, required by a law seemingly "between a man and his fellow-man,"[246] is nevertheless given by Maimonides in the selfsame paragraph as an example of the acts requiring a berakah. There are two opposing traditions as to whether *ma'akeh* requires a berakah,[247] and Maimonides doubtless had his reasons for his opinion; if so, however, besides his general rule other factors were to be taken into consideration. Furthermore, there are acts required by laws which are obviously in the category of "between a man and God," and yet those acts do not call for a berakah; such acts, for example, as are required by the laws in Exodus 12:13.[248] There are exceptions, it would seem, to Maimonides' general rules, for taking other considerations into account is only a way of indicating that those general rules do not always apply.

When ethical acts are described by a general formula, and that general formula is the same for all ethical acts, no recognition whatsoever is given to the particular character possessed by each and every ethical act. On the other hand, a value concept, being merely connotative and not a formula, has meaning only so long as it is concretized in a particular act. Conversely, when stress is laid upon the ethical value concept embodied in an act, there is also full awareness of the circumstantial, particular character of that act.

Notes to Preface

1. L. Ginzberg, *A Commentary on the Palestinian Talmud* (New York, 1941).

2. S. Lieberman, *The Tosefta, The Order of Zera'im* (New York, 1955).

3. S. Lieberman, *Tosefta Ki-Fshuṭah, A Comprehensive Commentary on the Tosefta* (New York, 1955).

Notes to Chapter I

1. M. Kadushin, *The Rabbinic Mind* (New York, 1952), p. 23. This book will hereafter be referred to as *RM.*

2. M. Kadushin, *Organic Thinking* (New York, 1938), p. 194. This book will hereafter be referred to as *OT.*

3. "The Efficacy of Torah," *OT*, pp. 68 ff., especially pp. 72 f.

4. *RM*, p. 11.

5. *RM*, pp. 59 f., 62 f., 68.

6. "Halakah and Its Nexus," in *ibid.*, pp. 89 ff.

7. *OT*, p. 98, where other examples are also cited. How extensively Halakah is reflected in Haggadah is apparent from the long list of such haggadot in the Index to Ginzberg's *Legends of the Jews* (Vol. VII, pp. 200 f.), a list running to several columns.

8. *Sanhedrin* IV. 5.

9. *Bereshit R.* XXII.9, ed. J. Theodor (Berlin, 1912), p. 216, and the sources in the note there.

10. L. Ginzberg, "Commentary to Ḳiddushin" (mimeographed, 1932), p. 142. Cf. Rashi on Exod. 21:6 in his *Commentary on the Pentateuch.*

11. "*Derek Ereẓ*," pp. 117 ff.; "Charity and Deeds of Lovingkindness," pp. 131 ff.; "Ethical Dicta," pp. 140 ff. (all cited from *OT*).

12. *Ibid.*, pp. 192 f.

13. *RM*, pp. 113 ff., 132.

14. M. Kadushin, *The Theology of Seder Eliahu* (New York, 1932), p. 25.

15. In mishnaic times there was, however, wide divergence in law, an organismic characteristic (*RM*, pp. 93 f.).

Notes to Chapter II

1. See Chap. III, nn. 101–02, below.

2. *'Abot* I.18, V.7, VI.6; *Yer. Sanhedrin* XI, 30c; and *passim.*

3. *Pe'ah* I.1; *Yebamot* XV.1; *'Abot* I.12; and *passim.*

4. *'Abot* II.7; *Ḳiddushin* IV.5; *Baba Ḳamma* X.1; and *passim.*

5. *Soṭah* IX.15; *'Abot* VI.1; *'Arakin* 16b; and *passim.*

6. *'Abodah Zarah* II.1; *'Abot* V.9; *Tosefta Pe'ah* I.2; and *passim.*

7. *Yebamot* VI.5; *Ketubbot* V.1; *Soṭah* IX.13; and *passim.*

8. *Giṭṭin* V.8; *Makkot* III.15; *Shabbat* 32b; and *passim.*

9. *Rosh ha-Shanah* II.8; *Sanhedrin* XI.5; *Shebuot* 21a; and *passim.*

10. Only *shefikut damim* (the abstract form) is solely rabbinic.

11. M. Kadushin, *Organic Thinking* (New York, 1938), pp. 138–139. This book will hereafter be referred to as *OT.*

12. *Ibid.*, pp. 132 f., 136 f., and the references in the notes. On *ẓedaḳah*, see also M. Kadushin, *The Rabbinic Mind* (New York, 1952), p. 297, and the notes and references there. This book will hereafter be referred to as *RM.*

13. *Sukkah* 49b. Parallels: *Tos. Pe'ah* IV.19, ed. S. Lieberman (New York, 1955), pp. 60 f.; *ibid., Yerushalmi,* I.1, 15b–c; *Kohelet R.* VII.2.
According to Maimonides, Hilkot *'Ebel* XIV.7, there is a gradation in *gemilut ḥasadim* itself, comforting the mourners taking precedence over visiting the sick—see Lieberman, *Tosefta Ki-Fshuṭah*, I (New York, 1955), p. 191.

14. *OT*, pp. 148 f.

15. *'Alub* has the connotation not only of humility but of humiliation; see M. Jastrow, *A Dictionary of the Targumim, The Talmud Babli and Yerushalmi, and the Midrashic Literature* (New York, Berlin, and London, 1926), p. 1080, *s.v.* עלוב.

16. *Yer. Pe'ah* I.1, 15b. See n. 19 below.

17. This is the way Maimonides seems to interpret the ordinance; see his *Mishneh Torah*, Hilkot *Mattenot 'Aniyyim* VII.5.

18. Yer. *Pe'ah, loc. cit.*; the first time a fifth of the principal and after that a fifth of the profits.

19. *Ibid.* R. Gamaliel cites this ordinance to R. Yeshebab who had divided all his property among the poor. The term miẓwot here, therefore, refers to charity. See *Midrash Debarim Rabbah*, ed. S. Lieberman (Jerusalem, 1940), p. 36, n. 10.

20. *Ketubbot* 50a.

21. *Ibid.*, and parallels.

22. Above, n. 19.

23. *Ketubbot* 50a. Here in one report the Tanna is not named and in another he is R. Yeshebab.

24. *Baba Meẓi'a* 3a, bottom, and parallels: אין אדם מעיז פניו.

25. *Sanhedrin* 74a. R. Ishmael permits private, but not public avowal of idolatry, to save one's life and this holds, apparently, with respect to other matters as well (on the basis of his proof-text). See also *Sifra, Aḥare* (on Lev. 18:5), ed. I. H. Weiss (Vienna, 1862), 86b.

26. H. Graetz, *History of the Jews* (Hebrew translation by S. P. Rabinowitz) (Warsaw 1898), II, 254 f.

27. *RM*, pp. 1–8.

28. A. N. Whitehead, *Religion in the Making* (New York, 1926), p. 87.

29. M. Lazarus attempts to depict Jewish ethics on the basis of this Kantian principle,

and he calls it "the principle of Jewish ethics"; see his *Ethics of Judaism*, Part I (English translation, Philadelphia, 1900), pp. 107 ff., especially pp. 132 f., 137 f., and 157 f. He can do so only by a free, homiletic interpretation of biblical verses and rabbinic dicta; see, for example, *ibid.*, pp. 14 f., 64, 117, 122 f., 128, 137 f., 158; (on p. 159, and earlier on p. 17 where the source is given, the important כאלו, "as if," is omitted—"as if he becomes a partner of God"); p. 278 f. Nevertheless, Lazarus makes a very valuable contribution. He emphasizes the awareness on the part of the rabbis of the ethical sphere, their great sensitiveness to moral and ethical problems of the individual and society, something that later writers have obscured by the insistence on a "logic of revealed religion" or similar ideas. A fine exposition and evaluation of Lazarus' work is given in Julius Guttman, הפילוסופיה של היהדות (Hebrew translation, Jerusalem, 1951), pp. 314 f.

30. Below, p. 243, n. 63.

31. *Bereshit R.* VI.5, ed. J. Theodor (Berlin, 1912), p. 44, and the parallels there; *Bemidbar R.* XX.1; and elsewhere.

32. *OT*, p. 137, and p. 304, n. 227.

33. *RM*, pp. 150 f.

34. *Ibid.*, pp. 38 f.

35. *Ibid.*, pp. 114–30.

36. See, for example, the interpretation of II Samuel 8:15 in *Sanhedrin* 6b.

37. *RM*, p. 55 and n. 8. The plural *Yisre'elim* is also found (*'Erubin* VI.1, *'Abodah Zarah* IV.11).

38. *RM*, pp. 40 f.

39. *Ibid.*, pp. 293 f.

40. *Ibid.*, pp. 291 f.

41. Illustrations will be found in nn. 37–40 on these terms.

42. *Menaḥot* 99a–b. Parallels: *Shabbat* 87a; *Yebamot* 62a; *Baba Batra* 14b; and see also the next note.

43. Rashi *ad loc.*; also Rabbenu Gershom *ad loc.* "The neglect of Torah" is a technical expression referring to neglect of the study of Torah: see *Tos. Shabbat* VII (VIII).5; *ibid.*, 32b; and *passim*.

The general statement is: פעמים שבטולה של תורה זהו יסודה. This is followed by an interpretation of Exod. 34:1 according to which God commends Moses for having broken the Tablets. The interpretation is not in consonance with the general statement. The latter says, "There are times" (plural), whereas the interpretation is concerned with a single occasion only, and one to which there is no parallel. Again, the idiom or technical term always refers to "neglect of the study of Torah," whereas if applied to the interpretation it would have to mean something more drastic and not refer to study at all. Furthermore, in the textual parallels only the interpretation is found, and not the general statement. The idea in the interpretation is also found in *Yer. Ta'anit* IV.8, 68c, in a substantially different form, and with a Tanna, R. Ishmael, as its author. The general statement is, then, really discrete. It contains the idea given by Rashi which is borne out by the baraita in *Ketubbot* 17a (*Megillah* 3b, 29a) where the same idiom is used. See also *'Abot de R. Nathan*, ed. S. Schechter (Vienna, 1887), Version A, Chap. IV, pp. 9a, f. and n. 16 and the references there; Version B, Chap. VIII, p. 11b.

44. *Berakot* 40a; *Giṭṭin* 62a. The proof-text is Deut. 11:15, where food "for thy cattle" is mentioned first.

45. *Mekhilta D'Rabbi Simon b. Jochai*, ed. J. N. Epstein and E. Z. Melamed (Jerusalem, 1955), p. 211; ed. D. Hoffmann (Frankfurt a. M., 1905), p. 151.

46. See G. Alon, תולדות היהודים בארץ ישראל (Tel Aviv, 1952), I, 329, citing this passage.

47. *Terumot* VIII.12. See the commentaries; also the next note.

48. *Tos. Terumot* VII.20, ed. Lieberman, p. 148, and the parallels. The passage continues with a qualifying statement, and concludes with the opinions of R. Judah and R. Simon, each of whom also specifies conditions. See Lieberman's commentary, *ad loc.* See also his *Tosefta Ki-Fshuṭah, ad. loc.*, where he discusses all the views and various later interpretations, and also to what extent the opinions in the Tosefta concur. He points out there (I, 420) that in the case of the women, no "guilty" one was specified at all, since it was a matter of sheer lust, whereas the Tosefta speaks of a case where one of the men had angered the Gentiles, but the latter did not know exactly who had done so.

49. See S. Abramson, לשוננו, קובץ מיוחד (Jerusalem, 1954), p. 63; cf. *ibid.*, pp. 64 f.; *OT*, pp. 29 f., p. 272, n. 76.

50. *Sifra, Aḥare* XIII.12, ed. Weiss, 86b. The proof-text there stresses the value concept *man.*

51. *Ibid.*

52. *Baba Ḳamma* 38a; *Sanhedrin* 59a; *'Abodah Zarah* 3a. The correct reading in all three references here is, very likely, not R. Me'ir but R. Jeremiah, as in the passage of the Sifra; see Abramson, *op. cit.*, p. 63, n. 1.

53. *RM*, p. 28, and see the discussion there on pp. 27 f. See also M. Kadushin, "Aspects of the Rabbinic Concept of Israel," *Hebrew Union College Annual*, XIX (1946), 60 and especially pp. 83–87, where we show how the element of universality acts as a check on the element of nationality.

54. *Giṭṭin* I.5. Lieberman points out that the Tosefta, *ibid.*, I.4, agrees with the Mishnah here according to the readings in the Vienna MS and other early sources; see his *Tosefeth Rishonim*, II, 69. The Erfurt MS may have been affected by the discussion in the Talmud.

55. *Giṭṭin* I.5.

56. והא לאו בני כריתה נינהו—*ibid.*, 10b, in regard to non-Jewish witnesses on a writ of divorce.

57. *Tos. Giṭṭin* I.4—again the same readings as those referred to in n. 54 above; *ibid.*, 11a.

58. Alon, *op. cit.*, p. 347, quoting Gulack. See Alon's remarks on these Gentile institutions, p. 346. His interpretation of the Tosefta passages is apparently based on the Erfurt MS.

59. See below, p. 43. Mark the dictum by Samuel in the Talmud here (*Giṭṭin* 10b): *dina' demalkuta' dina'*.

60. *Sifra Ḳedoshim* to Lev. 19:18, ed. I. H. Weiss (Vienna, 1862), p. 89b. For the inclusion of the latter part of Gen. 5:1, see the comment of R. Abraham b. David of Posquières here. A parallel is found in *Yer. Nedarim* 41c, and a version in *Bereshit R.* XXIV, end, ed. J. Theodor (Berlin, 1912), pp. 236 f.; see Theodor's note there which cites additional references in regard to the inclusion of the latter part of Gen. 5:1.

61. See the discussion in *Shabbat* 68a. The discussion there deals with the *comparative scope* of particular rules, despite the mention of "punishment," as can be seen from the instances taken up. Maimonides, however, in his commentary on the Mishnah (*ad Shabbat* VII.1), does stress "punishment"; and Edeles (*ad Shabbat* 68a, *s.v.* ודע), remarking on this contradiction to the discussion in the Talmud, offers a harmonization.

62. We can explain the widespread view that our Sifra passage contains principles intended as "the most important" (Jastrow, *op. cit.*, *s.v.* כלל גדול), or as "the most comprehensive" (G. F. Moore, *Judaism in the First Centuries of the Christian Era* [Cambridge, 1927], I, 446; II, 85), only on the ground that we are so prone today, as we have said, to look for an ultimate criterion.

63. Some instances of the conceptual term *'ahabah* in rabbinic usage are: *'Abot* V.16; *Tos. Berakot* III.7; *ibid.*, *Shabbat* VII (VIII).12; *Baba Meẓi'a* 84a; *Sanhedrin* 61b; *ibid.*, 105b; *'Abot de R. Nathan*, ed. Schechter, Version B, Chap. XXXVII, p. 49a.

64. *Bereshit R.* XXIV, end, ed. Theodor, pp. 236 f., and Theodor's notes there. See *Mekilta* (ed. J. Lauterbach [Philadelphia, 1933]), II, 291 f., where the same idea is associated—implicitly—with our verse; and see also *Tos. Sanhedrin* IX.7, *Sanhedrin* 46b, and the parallels cited in Lieberman, *Tosefeth Rishonim*, II, 159–60 (and see also Rashi's *Commentary on the Bible ad* Deut. 21:23—his explanation of the word קללת). It may well be that the version in *Bereshit R.* XXIV, end, with its additional statement, was affected by such prevalent tannaitic interpretations.

65. *'Abot* III.14, with R. 'Aḳiba as authority; *'Abot de R. Nathan*, Chap. XXXIX, ed. Schechter, p. 59b, with R. Me'ir as authority. The passage speaks first of man, then of Israel. This is how the passage is taken by *Tosefot Yom Ṭob ad 'Abot* III.14, although he also adds there some extraneous matters.

66. See W. Bacher, *Agadot ha-Tannaim* (2d ed.; Jerusalem and Berlin, 1922) (Hebrew trans.), I, Part 2, 131, n. 3, where the view of Weiss is also given, and refuted; and see also Theodor, *loc. cit.*, who has still a different view. A recent interpretation is that of Alon, *op. cit.*, p. 332, where Ben 'Azzai is regarded as the proponent of the absolute love of man as against R. 'Aḳiba who is regarded as the proponent of a realistic ethic of equality which is also love of man; and where there is even an attempt to make R. 'Aḳiba's principle apply to his stand on another occasion.

67. See the preceding note.

68. *Soṭah* 14a. On the connotation of *gemilut ḥasadim*, see above, p. 21.

69. *Tanḥuma*, ed. S. Buber (Wilna, 1885), I, 43b (*Wayyera*, par. 4), and the references and notes there. This is a later version because: (*a*) the idea that the lesson is to be found in the middle of the Torah is placed last, is tacked on; (*b*) the version has now a formal midrashic introduction and this introduction is a duplication; and (*c*) most of the proof-texts and the interpretations in the body of the statement are drawn from other midrashic sources. All this is true, as well, of the smoother variant of this version found in *Yalḳuṭ Shime'oni*, Psalms, par. 702, except for (*a*).

70. Above, p. 27.

71. *Shabbat* 31a.

72. דעלך סני לחברך לא תעביד. On Aramaic as the vernacular, see G. Dalman, *Die Worte Jesu* (Leipzig, 1930), I, 1 ff.

73. *'Abot de R. Nathan*, ed. Schechter, Version B, Chap. XXVI, p. 27a: מה דאת סני לגרמך לחברך לא תעביד. The rest of the passage here is commentary and a later addition; see Bacher, *op. cit.*, I, Part 1, 3, n. 3.

74. See the references in Theodor's note in his edition of *Bereshit R.*, p. 237.

75. Rashi *ad Shabbat* 31a, *s.v.* דעלך סני.

76. See the authorities cited in Theodor, *loc. cit.*

77. Similar in character, although not an ethical injunction, is the statement that "the entire Torah" has for its purpose "the ways of peace" (*Giṭṭin* 59b). The claim is worded exactly as in Hillel's statement—כל התורה כולה. Here, too, it can be meant only as a hyperbole; in the selfsame passage, for example, the holiness of the priests is related to its basis in the Torah, and the concept of holiness has connotations that *peace* does not have. *Shalom* (peace) does have a connotation of love—see *'Abot* I.12; *Ketubbot* 8a. This statement also, then, is an emphatic statement, recalling and strengthening the emphasis on love.

78. *Berakot* 63a—שכל גופי תורה תלוין בה. Prov. 3:6 embodies the concept of God's love: "He will direct my paths."

79. *Makkot* 23b–24a; *Tanḥuma*, ed. Buber, *Shofetim*, V, 16b, par. 10.

80. *Makkot* 24a. "Faith" is *'emunah*, and the latter concept in a rabbinic setting or interpretation has the connotation of trust in God (*RM*, p. 42).

Notes to Chapter III

1. Above, p. 19.

2. An analysis of *derek ereẓ* is given in M. Kadushin, *Organic Thinking* (New York, 1938 [to be referred to hereafter as *OT*]), pp. 117–30, and we shall draw on some of our conclusions there. The present study, however, is a more inclusive discussion of the concept.

3. *Ibid.*, p. 117.

4. *Ibid.*, pp. 118 f.

5. *Mekilta*, ed. J. Z. Lauterbach (Philadelphia, 1933), II, 129, and the parallels there.

6. *Canticles R.* I.10, end—see מתנות כהונה.

7. *OT*, p. 118.

8. On quasi-scientific concepts, see the discussion and examples in M. Kadushin, *The Rabbinic Mind* (New York, 1952 [to be referred to hereafter as *RM*]), pp. 147–49.

9. *Bereshit R.* LXXVI.3, ed. J. Theodor and C. Albeck (Berlin, 1927), p. 899. The teaching is drawn from Jacob in Gen. 32:8–9.

10. *Bereshit R.* XXXI.10, ed. J. Theodor (Berlin, 1912), p. 282, and the notes there. The teaching is drawn from the proportions of Noah's ark in Gen. 6:15.

11. *Pesiḳta de R. Kahana*, ed. S. Buber (Lyck, 1868), p. 98b; *Tanḥuma, Re'eh*, par. 15. The teaching is drawn from Job 31:40.

12. *Mekilta*, ed. H. S. Horovitz and J. A. Rabin (Frankfurt am Main, 1928), p. 38 and the references there; ed. Lauterbach, I, 86, and n. 4 there. The passage is a comment on a phrase in Exod. 12:22 and is introduced by the term ללמדך, "to teach you."

13. The note of admonition is usually present where "practical wisdom" has to do with long-range effects. "The Torah taught you *derek ereẓ*—[namely] that a man

ought not to accustom his son to meat and wine," (i.e., he ought to train his son so that the child would not develop a need for expensive food); *Ḥullin*, 84a. The other instances of *derek ereẓ* given there are admonitions of the same nature; see Rashi, *ibid.*, *s.v.* אלא בהזמנה. Another well-known example is in *Tos. Soṭah* VII.20 (*ibid.*, 44a): "The Torah taught *derek ereẓ*"—A man should first buy a house and then buy a field and then get married.

14. On subconcepts and conceptual phases, see also *RM*, pp. 16–17.

15. *Mekilta*, ed. Horovitz and Rabin, pp. 209–10.

16. *Yoma* 4b; cf. *Numbers R.* XIV.35.

17. *Baba Meẓi'a* 87a. The inference is from the dots over some of the letters of the word *'elaw*, "to him," in Gen. 18:9—"And they said unto him, 'Where is Sarah, thy wife?' " On the dotted places in the Bible, see S. Lieberman, *Hellenism in Jewish Palestine* (New York, 1950), pp. 43–46, and the references in n. 43 there.

18. See *The Treatises "Derek Erez,"* ed. M. Higger (New York, 1935); and compare *Massektot Ze'irot*, ed. M. Higger (New York, 1930). In his Introduction (Hebrew) to the latter, Higger presents a study of the various ways in which the term *derek ereẓ* is used in rabbinic literature; although that analysis differs from ours, we have found both his study and the lists given there decidedly helpful.

19. See Higger's Introduction I (English) to *The Treatises "Derek Erez."*

20. M. Friedmann, *Pseudo-Seder Eliahu Zuta* (Vienna, 1904), Introduction I (Hebrew), p. 5, bottom.

21. *OT*, p. 120.

22. *Leviticus R.* IX.3, ed. M. Margulies (Jerusalem, 1953), p. 178, and the notes there.

23. *Deuteronomy R.* V.2, in *Midrash Debarim Rabbah*, ed. S. Lieberman (Jerusalem, 1940), p. 96.

24. *Exodus R.* XLVI.1—"Moses made *derek ereẓ* known to Israel." The version in *Midrash Haggadol on Exodus*, ed. M. Margulies (Jerusalem, 1956), p. 689, has: "[Moses] taught *derek ereẓ* to Israel."

25. On the meaning of the word, see M. Jastrow, *Dictionary* (New York, Berlin, and London, 1926), *s.v.* דין II.

26. "Woe unto the men who testify to what they had not seen!" in both versions.

27. The very nature of the value concept is such that the concept is *embedded* in a situation or statement; that is why, in contrast to the concepts referring to perceived things and to defined concepts, the value concepts are so often used without employing the value term. The instances of *derek ereẓ* where the term itself is not used as a designation only illustrate this trait of the value concept. For an analysis and explanation of this phenomenon, see *RM*, pp. 3–4, 52, 54, 59–60, 111.

28. *'Abot* I.18. For the rendering here, see Bertinoro *ad. loc.* The proof-text from Zech. 8:16 is a late addition (see H. L. Strack, *Pirqe Aboth* [Leipzig, 1915], p. 12 [Hebrew] and the notes there). It is obviously, too, not a proof-text at all, for it does not actually cover the statement of R. Simeon that the world exists or is preserved by these three things.

Bertinoro also calls attention to the difference between our statement and *'Abot* I.2; in our statement, *'olam* refers to mankind, not to the cosmos (see also *RM*, pp. 150 f.), and hence the "three things" are traits of mankind in general. For a different reading and rendering, see below, p. 246, n. 41.

29. *Seder Eliahu*, ed. M. Friedmann (Vienna, 1900), p. 74—העולם מתישב. (The term "ישוב העולם is the nearest equivalent to our term 'civilization' "; L. Ginzberg's note in M. Kadushin, *The Theology of Seder Eliahu* [New York, 1932], p. 186, n. 99. This book will hereafter be referred to as *TE*).

30. *Seder Eliahu, loc. cit.* The passage continues with an enumeration of those "who were uprooted from the world" because of these things. On *ḥillul ha-Shem*, see *TE*, pp. 64 f.

31. *Sifra, Aḥare*, par. 9, ed. I. H. Weiss (Vienna, 1862), p. 86a; *Yoma* 67b (*Yalḳuṭ Shime'oni*, Leviticus, par. 587)—דין הוא שיכתבו. For examples of דין or בדין as used here, see Ben Yehuda, *Thesaurus*, II, p. 928b.

32. '*Erubin* 100b. The rooster first gains the consent of the hen. See Rashi *ad loc.*

33. Yehudah Ha-Levi, *Kuzari*, II, 48. He distinguishes there between התורות האלהיות, divine laws, and התורות המנהגיות והשכליות, social and rational laws; among the rational laws, however, is acknowledgment of God's goodness.

34. *Ibid.*

35. *Mishneh Torah*, Hilkot *Me'ilah*, end; *Moreh Nebukim* III, 26. In his *Commentary to the Mishnah, Introduction to 'Abot*, Chapter VI, Maimonides places incest not among *mishpaṭim*, as our texts do, but among *ḥuḳḳim* (and that is why, apparently, he also gives "forbidden intercourse" as an example of "transgressions against God"; see Hilkot *Teshubah*, II.9). As has been remarked by the מסורת הש"ס on *Yoma* 67b, this must have been in accordance with the texts as Maimonides had them. There is a passage in *Midrash ha-Gadol* to Gen. 26:5, ed. M. Margulies (Jerusalem, 1947), p. 447, in which *ḥuḳḳotai* is said to refer to incest, but the passage itself *may* be a reflection of Maimonides' view. On the relation of Maimonides to the *Midrash ha-Gadol*, see *Mekilta D'Rabbi Simon b. Jochai*, ed. J. N. Epstein and E. Z. Melamed (Jerusalem, 1955), Introduction, p. 54.

36. Joseph Albo, *Sefer ha-'Iḳḳarim*, I, 5, ed. I. Husik (Philadelphia, 1929), p. 72—דת טבעית.

37. According to Albo, *ibid.*, natural law may be the product of a wise man or a prophet—מסודרת מחכם או מנביא.

38. *Sifra, loc. cit.* Some of the readings in the parallel, *Yoma* 67b, give a longer list; see *Diḳduḳe Soferim ad loc.* Cf. also *Pesiḳta de R. Kahana*, ed. Buber, 38b–39a.

39. See, for example, C. G. Montefiore, *Rabbinic Literature and Gospel Teachinng* (London, 1930), p. 194. Incidentally, the word בדין is entirely misinterpreted there; see the reference above, n. 31.

40. Below, p. 57. On the entire passage, see below, p. 212.

41. A rendering of *'Abot* I.18 contained in a passage in *Deuteronomy R.* V.1 not only supports our contention but.makes it even more emphatic. '*Olam* is taken there not as mankind, but as "cosmos"; the reading is not קים, endures, but עומד, stands; and hence justice, peace, and truth are the three legs on which the world stands. "If you pervert justice, you cause the world to shake, since justice is one of its legs" (notice the reading מגלגל in *Deuteronomy R.*, ed. Lieberman, *op. cit.*, p. 95). Here it is not mankind but the entire created world that rests, in a mystical sense, on the virtues.

42. See how *ẓedaḳah*, *gezel*, etc. are designated as *derek ereẓ* (above, p. 42).

43. Subconcepts are also concepts in their own right, and are treated as such (*RM*, p. 16).

44. *OT*, p. 190.

45. See also below, p. 53.

46. "Practical wisdom" and "good manners" are subconcepts of Torah (see above, pp. 41, 42). The fourth phase is depicted as consisting of "things that are written in the Torah."

47. *Leviticus R.* IX.6 (end); ed. Margulies, p. 185. For the versions and parallels, see the note there and also the note at the beginning of the section on p. 182 there.

48. *Tanḥuma, Ḥukkat*, 12.

49. *Bereshit R.* LXX.14; ed. Theodor and Albeck, p. 813, and the parallels there.

50. Above, p. 245, n. 18.

51. "Pirke Ben Azzai," in *The Treatises "Derek Erez,"* pp. 166 f. For the many parallels, see *ibid.*, p. 165, n. 2 (I have utilized here the felicitous translation of Judah Goldin, *The Fathers According to Rabbi Nathan* [New Haven, 1955], pp. 169 f.).

52. *Ibid.*, p. 228. On שמשביח דעתו של מוכר, see the comment of R. Abraham b. David *ad Sifra, Behar, Perek* IV, ed. Weiss, *op. cit.*, p. 107d, *s.v.* ר׳ יהודה. His reference there to a "Tosefta" is a reference to our text. In our text, a person asks "grain-sellers" the price of an article (*ḥefeẓ*)! See the next note.

53. *Baba Meẓi'a* IV.10. Our text has been affected by this Mishnah. Originally, the halakah of our text dealt specifically with grain merchants, just as the halakah immediately preceding it deals specifically with wine merchants (see below, n. 57). The mishnaic phrase, however, had evidently become a cliché, and was used as such—compare R. Judah's statement in the passage of the *Sifra* cited in the preceding note with his statement as given in *Baba Meẓi'a* 58b.

54. *Baba Meẓi'a* IV.10, and *ibid.*, 58b. On *'ona'ah* as an ethical concept, see below, p. 207 f.

55. "Pirke Ben Azzai," in *The Treatises "Derek Erez,"* p. 227—דרך גזל.

56. *Ibid.*, pp. 226 f.

57. *Ibid.*, p. 227.

58. Above, p. 44 and n. 32 there.

59. *Leviticus R.* IX.3, ed. Margulies, p. 179.

60. *Seder Eliahu*, p. 56. See also *OT*, pp. 70, 73, and 126 f., for similar statements on *derek ereẓ* in this source. Cf., also, p. 248 below, n. 71, and especially the reference to *Numbers R.* XIII.15.

61. In regard to the manner of rehabilitating a field, for example, the admonitory tone is limited to the expression, "it is well to" (יפה) (see references on p. 40). Compare this with the emphatic tone in the teaching that when one goes on a journey he ought to arrive and leave in the daytime.

62. Incest is one of the negative concepts of the fourth phase, see above, p. 43.

63. Here there is another consideration as well. Not only is work a moral activity, when there is no taint of *gezel*, but it is also highly laudatory. See, for example, the many laudatory statements on work in *'Abot de R. Nathan*, ed. Schechter, Version B, Chap. XXI, pp. 22b f. In R. Eliezer's statement there, a contrast is drawn between work and *gezel*. On the rabbis' favorable attitude to business activity, see *OT*, p. 119. On the other hand, the rabbis voice disapproval when work or business crowds out study of Torah, and sometimes even advise reducing it to a minimum in favor of study; see, for example, *'Abot* IV.10.

64. The rabbis urge that a man be humble in his relations with others "and even more so" in relations with members of his household (*The Treatises* "*Derek Erez*," p. 90, Hebrew); and never to lose one's temper in one's house (*Ta'anit* 20b). Similar statements are found in *Midrash Tehillim*, ed. S. Buber (Wilna, 1891), 214b, *Giṭṭin* 6b, and elsewhere.

65. *Mekilta de R. Simeon*, ed. Epstein and Melamed, *op. cit.*, p. 108; ed. D. Hoffmann (Frankfurt am Main, 1895), p. 95.

66. *Yer. Berakot*, IX, 14b; cf. *Pesiḳta de R. Kahana*, ed. Buber, p. 104a—R. 'Abbahu's statement.

67. *Tanḥuma*, ed. Buber, *op. cit.*, I,82b; "he spoke [in the manner of] *derek ereẓ*." The synecdoche in Gen. 32:6 is lost in translation. An example given in the comment here is retained in the English "[the] cock crowed."

68. *RM*, pp. 147–149.

69. The concepts of *derek ereẓ* and *sidre 'olam* (or *sidre bereshit*) are not interchanged, even when they impinge on each other. The correct text in *Pesiḳta R.*, ed. M. Friedmann (Vienna, 1860), p. 84b, as can be seen from its parallel in *Midrash ha-Gadol* to Exodus, ed. Margulies, p. 246 (see n. 6 there), is: "the water [comes] from above them, and the bread from beneath them [i.e., from the earth]." This is designated *derek ereẓ* because the point of reference is man; but even so, this use of the term is very unusual. See the longer and earlier version in *Exodus R.* XXV.6, where the term is not used at all. Compare *Mekilta* II, p. 102, where the same idea is spoken of as a change in natural order.
In *Bereshit R.* XXXII.11, there is no reference to *derek ereẓ* in the correct text; see *ibid.*, ed. Theodor, p. 294.

70. *RM*, pp. 143 ff. on the generally consistent dichotomy of value concepts and cognitive concepts; *ibid.*, pp. 162 f. on *nes* and *sidre bereshit*; *ibid.*, pp. 232 ff. on *gilluy Shekinah*; *ibid.*, pp. 261 f. on *bat ḳol*.

71. Following are several instances where the commentators differ as to the meaning of *derek ereẓ*: "Everyone that is occupied with [שׁ״ש״נ] Bible, Mishnah, and *derek ereẓ* will be slow to sin" (*Ḳiddushin* I.10). Some take *derek ereẓ* here to refer to "work" or "occupation" and so make the statement equivalent to *'Abot* II.2 (see C. Albeck, *Commentary to Seder Nashim* [Jerusalem and Tel Aviv, 1955], p. 413); Maimonides, and following him Bertinoro, in their commentaries on the Mishnah, take it to refer to social behavior and ethics. "If there is no Torah, there is no *derek ereẓ*; if there is no *derek ereẓ* there is no Torah" (*'Abot* III.17). On this statement, see *OT*, p. 130, and the references there. The ambiguity of the concept sometimes results in different interpretations of the same mishnah even in rabbinic literature. *Derek ereẓ* in *'Abot* II.2 is interpreted as meaning "work" or "occupation" in *'Abot de R. Nathan*, ed. Schechter, Version B, p. 35b and in *Koh. R.* to *Koh.* 7:11, whereas in *Numbers R.* XIII.15 it is interpreted as meaning good deeds (cited by Albeck, *Commentary to Neziḳin*, p. 495). See also Judah Goldin, *The Living Talmud* (New York, 1957), pp. 81 f.

72. Examples of concepts which have conceptual phases are: God's justice (*middat ha-din*), with two conceptual phases—the justice due the individual and corporate justice (*RM*, p. 17); Torah, which has the phase of the efficacy of Torah (*ibid.*); *nes*, with two conceptual phases—*nes* involving spectacular things, such as changes in *sidre bereshit*, and *nes* not involving spectacular things (*ibid.*, pp. 159–162).

73. *Derek ereẓ*, as we have seen, has five phases, whereas other concepts cited (see preceding note) have only two.

74. W. Bacher, ערכי מדרש (Hebrew translation, Tel Aviv, 1923), p. 18, *s.v.* דרך ארץ.

75. *Loc. cit.*, and n. 3 there.

76. *Sifra, 'Aḥare, Perek* XI, ed. Weiss, p. 84c, and the notes and references there.

77. *Mekilta*, ed. Friedmann, p. 7a.

78. *Ibid.*, p. 83a, and n. 24 there (this is apparently directed against those who would not seek a cure, but only rely on prayer; see *Berakot* 60a, bottom, and Rashi *ad loc.*).

79. *Ibid.*, p. 63a; ed. Horovitz and Rabin, pp. 209–10.

80. *Sifre Numbers*, ed. M. Friedmann (Vienna, 1864), p. 27b, and the note there; ed. H. S. Horovitz (Leipzig, 1917), p. 100, and the note there.

81. *Sifre Numbers*, ed. Friedmann, p. 28b, top. There remain two more references cited by Bacher to be accounted for. Both are concerned with the descriptive phase of *derek ereẓ*. (*a*) It is a phenomenon of history ("a trait prevalent in all generations") that he who smites Israel will himself in the end be smitten, and the prime example is Amalek (*Mekilta*, ed. Friedmann, p. 54b–55a). Here the phenomenon depicted is itself not *derek ereẓ* but an aspect of God's justice. By drawing the proper inference "from Amalek" we arrive, according to the rabbis, at a characteristic of human history and hence of man in general; it is this element of repetition in man's history that constitutes *derek ereẓ*, for the other traits of mankind are also characterized by the element of repetition, of predictability. (*b*) R. Ishmael in *Sifre Deut.* (ed. Friedmann, p. 80b), commenting on Deut. 11.14 ("and thou shalt gather in thy corn, and thy wine, and thine oil"), says that Torah speaks here of *derek ereẓ*; and here the term refers to a person's occupation or livelihood (see Rashi on the parallel in *Berakot* 35b). See also above, p. 247, n. 63. The use of the term in these passages demonstrates again that the descriptive phase of *derek ereẓ* is not morally neutral.

82. Above, pp. 22–24.

83. *Yoma* VIII.9. Parallels and versions: *Sifra*, ed. Weiss, pp. 83a–b; *Pesiḳta R.*, ed. Friedmann, p. 185a; *Tanḥuma*, ed. Buber, I, p. 52a, and the notes there. Cf. *Yer. Nedarim* IX.41b, where the phrase "matters that are between him and God" does occur in another context, but not the "ethical formula."

84. *Sifre Zuṭṭa*, ed. Horovitz, p. 248 (cf. *Rosh ha-Shanah*, 17b).

85. *Ibid.*

86. *OT*, p. 122.

87. *Deut. R.* VI.1, ed. Lieberman, p. 103; cf. *Lev. R.* XXVII.11, ed. Margulies, p. 644 f.

88. *Exod. R.* II.2. See L. Ginzberg, *Legends of the Jews*, II (Philadelphia, 1913), 301. R. Judah the Prince, who was punished because he failed to take compassion on animals, and then was cured when he did take such compassion, quotes Psalm 145:9, "And His compassion is on all His works" (*Bereshit R.* XXXIII.3, ed. Theodor, p. 305, and the note and references there).

89. See above, p. 245, n. 27.

90. See the laws and interpretations given in Greenstone's article, "Cruelty to Animals," in the *Jewish Encyclopedia*, IV, pp. 376 ff. Many of the rabbinic laws represent interpretations or generalizations of biblical laws, as can be seen there. The rabbis maintain that the duty of relieving the suffering of animals is a biblical

injunction (צער בעלי חיים דאורייתא); cf. *Baba Meẓi'a* 32b; *Shabbat* 128b. R. Jose the Galilean, however, holds that it is a rabbinic principle (*Baba Meẓi'a* 33b; cf. *Shabbat* 154b). On kindness to animals, see above p. 29.

91. See above, pp. 43 f. *Ḥillul ha-Shem*, too, a form of blasphemy, is among the eight things because of which "the world is destroyed" (*ibid.*, p. 43, and Ginzberg's remark in *OT*, p. 300, n. 147).

92. See the material in S. Liebermann, *Greek in Jewish Palestine* (New York, 1942), pp. 77 ff., and especially pp. 81 f. There are *goyim*, Gentiles, who do not forget God and are righteous (*RM*, p. 41). On non-Jews "cancelling" an idol, see *ibid.*, p. 197.

93. There was even the term גרי אומות העולם as designation for a category of semi-proselytes (non-Jews) (Lieberman, *op. cit.*, p. 84).

94. Lieberman, *op. cit.*, pp. 76 f.

95. Maimonides regards "between a man and God" and "between a man and his fellow man" as basic general categories. When it comes to the actual organization of the laws in his Mishneh Torah, however, he does not employ these categories, but fourteen divisions of a different character; nor is his later endeavor to superimpose the two categories on the fourteen divisions very successful, since, as he says, a part of his third division deals with matters "between a man and his fellow man," and the other part concerns matters "between a man and God." He says, too, that "between a man and God" consists of matters that in the long run and indirectly also lead to matters that are "between a man and his fellow man." See his *Moreh Nebukim*, Part III, Chap. 35.

96. "The Rabbis and the Folk," *RM*, pp. 84 f. It is true that toward the end of the second century and later, the rabbinic class was more and more crystallized as a class apart. There was a tendency to free the rabbis from taxes, and there were perhaps even attempts to ensure succession to their sons. See Alon, *op. cit.*, II, 142 f.

97. Above, p. 26.

98. *Ibid.*, p. 24.

99. The phrase, "the Torah taught you *derek ereẓ*" does not introduce an actual commandment. The phrase does introduce, therefore, an *'asmakta*, "support." On *'asmakta*, see *RM*, pp. 124 f.

100. See above, p. 244, n. 13.

101. A. L. Kroeber, *Anthropology* (New York, 1948), pp. 589 f. In the rabbinic tradition, patience is associated with humility (see above, p. 248, n. 64).

102. *Ibid.*, p. 316.

103. Some of these formal ways of concretization, as well as the distinction drawn between this concept and charity, are to be found above, pp. 20–21, and n. 12 there.

104. The subject of *'ona'ah* is taken up in *Baba Meẓi'a* IV.3 ff.

105. See above, p. 48.

106. *Baba Meẓi'a* 58b–59a.

107. This was true in other spheres as well (see *RM*, pp. 211 f., and n. 36 there).

108. *Iggeret R. Sherira Gaon*, ed. B. Lewin (Haifa, 1921), p. 47, and I. H. Weiss, *Dor Dor We-Dorshaw* (4th ed.; Wilna, 1904), II, 222. See also above, p. 42.

109. *Berakot* 22a—R. Judah and his pupils.

110. *The Treatises "Derek Erez,"* pp. 265 ff., and the references there.

Notes to Chapter IV

1. On these conceptual terms, see M. Kadushin, *The Rabbinic Mind* (New York, 1952 [to be referred to hereafter as *RM*]), pp. 215 ff.

2. *Ibid.*

3. *Ibid.*, p. 15.

4. See M Kadushin, "Aspects of the Rabbinic Concept of Israel," *Hebrew Union College Annual*, XIX (1946), 85 f.

5. M. Kadushin, *The Theology of Seder Eliahu* (New York, 1932), pp. 172–76 (to be referred to hereafter as *TE*).

6. M. Kadushin, *Organic Thinking* (New York, 1938 [to be referred to hereafter as *OT*]), p. 222.

7. *Ibid.*, p. 225. When they interpret events of their own day as well, the rabbis often emphasize God's love. Thus Israel's dispersal is interpreted as an act of God's love. It was an act of charity, of love (*ẓedaḳah*) on God's part to have scattered Israel among the nations (*Pesaḥim* 87b), a statement which means, as the passage goes on to indicate, that God has assured Israel's survival since thus they cannot "all be destroyed" by any one nation. This statement has often been taken by modern writers to mean that Israel has a mission to the nations, a gross misinterpretation. See Edeles' comment, *ad loc.*, and his reference to a related passage in *'Abodah Zarah* 10b.

8. See the sources referred to in the article mentioned above in n. 4.

9. See also the characteristics of the value concept depicted above, pp. 22 ff.

10. See above, pp. 24 ff.

11. *Yer. Berakot* I.8, 3d; R. Judan's statement.

12. L. Ginzberg, *Commentary on the Palestinian Talmud*, I (New York, 1941), 178, 199; and S. Lieberman, *Tosefta Ki-Fshuṭah*, (New York, 1955), I, 7, *s.v.* שאמרו להאריך.

13. *RM*, p. 168 and n. 1 there.

14. *Berakot* VI.1–4. On these being short berakot, see *Tosefta Berakot*, I. 3 6–7, ed. Lieberman, p. 3, and see his *Tos. Kif.*, *ad loc.*, p. 9, n. 40. Cf. also the baraita in *Berakot* 46a, bottom.

15. *Berakot* 33a.

16. *Yer. Berakot* VII.1, 11a; *Yer. Megillah* IV.1, 75a (with R. Nathan as the authority in both references); *Berakot* 48b (with R. Isaac as the authority). The proof-text is: "And ye shall *serve* the Lord your God" (Exod. 23:25); and hence this berakah is service ('abodah), worship.

17. *Berakot* 40a, and Tosafot, *ibid.*, *s.v.* הבא מלח.

18. *Ibid.* 39b, and Tosafot, *s.v.* והלכתא.

19. *Yer. Berakot* VI.4, 10a, toward the bottom.

20. *RM*, pp. 113 f.

21. *Ibid.*

22. *Berakot* 35a–b. See Tosafot, *ibid.*, *s.v.* כאן לאחר ברכה, as to these verses being used in actual custom.

In *Tos. Berakot* IV.1 (and parallels), ed. Lieberman, p. 18, there is the related idea that, since "the earth is the Lord's and the fulness thereof" (Ps. 24:1), the individual who partakes of anything in this world without reciting a berakah is guilty of *me'ilah*, of diverting a sacred thing to a secular use; in this view, a berakah redeems what is partaken of, from its status as a holy thing; see Lieberman, *op. cit.*, I, *ad loc.*, 55. But this reason leaves out of account altogether the role of the individual as a member of society which is implicit in the berakah itself.

23. See above, p. 4.

24. See S. Baer, סדר עבודת ישראל (Roedelheim, 1868), p. 554.

25. *Berakot* 10a; *'Abodah Zarah* 3b.

26. *Berakot* 59b (a baraita).

27. *Berakot* IX.2.

28. *Yer. Berakot* VI.3, 10c.

29. See the three preceding references.

30. *Berakot* IX.5, ed. C. Albeck (Jerusalem and Tel Aviv, 1957), p. 32, and the note there.

31. *Sifre Deut.* on Deut. 6:5, ed. M. Friedmann (Vienna, 1864), pp. 73a–b.

32. *Ibid.*, p. 73b. A proof-text is: "For whom the Lord loveth He correcteth, even as a father the son in whom he delighteth" (Prov. 3:12).

33. It is a subconcept both of God's love and of God's justice. There are rabbinic concepts which share in two grounds simultaneously; see *RM*, pp. 28 f.

34. *RM*, p. 218.

35. On the association of *middat raḥamim* with the Tetragrammaton and *middat ha-din* with *'Elohim*, see *ibid.*, pp. 216 f.

36. For example, *Tos. Yebamot* IX.3; *Tos. Baba Ḳamma* IX.2.

37. For example, *Bemidbar R.* XX.1.

38. For example, *Bereshit R.* XXXIX.6, ed. J. Theodor (Berlin, 1912), pp. 368–9.

39. *Pesaḥim* 87b. See above, p. 251, n. 7.

40. *TE*, p. 38.

41. גומל חסדים: *Berakot* 60b, in the last berakah of the series there upon arising in the morning, dressing and so on; it is also in the "short" berakah to be recited upon recovering from illness or deliverance from peril, as given in *Berakot* 54b, both in the editions and MSS, but the codists have a different version and that version is given in the *Prayer Book*; see *Diḳduḳe Soferim*, *ad loc.*; and it is also in the "long" berakah with which the 'Amidah begins (see Baer, *op. cit.*, pp. 87 f., *Seder R. 'Amram Gaon*, ed. A. L. Frumkin (Jerusalem, 1912), I, p. 117b, and *Siddur R. Saadia Gaon*, ed. I. Davidson and others (Jerusalem, 1944), p. 18 [in the text]).

42. Other aspects of this moral experience are discussed below, pp. 112 f.

43. *Berakot* 48b.

44. *Tos. Berakot* VI (VII).1, ed. Lieberman, p. 32 and the references there.

45. This is true not only of the Birkat ha-Mazon but, in Ginzberg's words, of all "the principal prayers." "We know for certain that the principal prayers, for instance the *'Amidah* and the Benedictions of the *Shema'*, were in use at least as far back as the first century before the Common Era. Yet in the entire talmudic-midrashic literature, extending approximately from the second to the sixth century, one does not find a single principal prayer in full. . . . These prayers are cited only by initial words or have at most a sentence quoted from them. This mode of quoting surely proves the

more or less fixed character of these prayers, the assumption being that the sequel was in everyone's memory. One must not however be misled by this in concluding that at that period prayer books were in existence. The contrary may be proved by the Talmuds and has been done so by as early an authority as the Italian scholar, R. Zedekiah degli Mansi (*Shibbale ha-Leket*, p. 12) seven hundred years ago." L. Ginzberg, "Saadia's Siddur," *Jewish Quarterly Review*, N.S., XXXIII, 315 f.

46. N. 41, above.

47. Ginzberg, *op. cit.*, p. 328. He points out there that Saadia's *Siddur* has reached us in a more authentic form than that of R. Amram. "R. Amram's work has reached us in such a form that only in very rare cases are we in a position to recognize its original contents. Of course, it is not our opinion that Saadia's Siddur reached us exactly as it left his hands . . . yet with all the omissions, additions and faulty readings, one is safe in stating that on the whole the *Siddur* reached us in a fairly good state."

An essay by Louis Finkelstein, "The Birkat Ha-Mazon" (*Jewish Quarterly Review*, N.S., XIX, No. 3, 211 ff.), is devoted to the reconstruction of the original text and to the various versions of the Birkat ha-Mazon. His conclusion is "that the earliest of extant forms is not that of Palestine as recovered from the Genizah, but that of Seder R. Saadia" (*ibid.*, p. 224).

48. *Siddur R. Saadia Gaon*, p. 102. "Us and" were evidently not in the text originally; see the textual note. "The Holy One, Blessed be He, feeds the whole world" is a haggadic cliché found in *Berakot* 10a and *'Abodah Zarah* 3b.

49. This is taken for granted both by Bet Shammai and by Bet Hillel in *Berakot* VIII.7, for they differ only in case one had not said it at the place he had eaten. See Maimonides, *Mishneh Torah*, Hilkot *Berakot* IV.1.

50. See *Tos. Berakot* IV.20, ed. Lieberman, p. 25, and his comment there; and see his *Tos. Kif.*, I, 71 f., where he discusses the entire literature on this baraita. He suggests there that by חפלינ the baraita refers especially to the diversion of attention through a long conversation. "Even if it be no further than to the door" seems to be an opinion held by Maimonides alone; see his Hilkot *Berakot* IV.3, and R. Abraham b. David of Posquière's comment there.

51. *Berakot* 40b (see both references to the *Ṭur* on the margin).

52. *Ibid.* Rab is the authority who regards this berakah as halakically valid, and the Talmud, in order to make it consistent with Rab's view that a berakah must mention the name of God, has the berakah read, "Blessed be the Merciful [רחמנא], Master of this bread." On the practice in Palestine, see Lieberman, *Tos. Kif.*, I, 60.

53. This is taken as a matter of course by the Talmud, for it asks, "What does he [Rab] teach us?" (*Berakot*, *loc. cit*). We ought to add that the answer to this question is: "Even though he [the shepherd] said it in the secular vernacular."

54. Above, p. 66.

55. "World" is practically equated with the concept of man, an ethical concept connoting brotherhood; see *RM*, pp. 150 f. Worship as an expression of the larger self is a topic which we shall discuss at some length when we take up the Daily 'Amidah.

56. ברכה הסמוכה לחברתה; *Berakot* 46a, end; *Tos. Berakot* I.9, ed. Lieberman, p. 3. "Conceptual continuum" was first used by Charles Kadushin in an unpublished paper.

57. *Berakot* 49a.

58. *Siddur R. Saadia Gaon*, p. 102.

59. See above, n. 56.

60. See Tosafot to *Pesaḥim* 104b, *s.v.* חוץ and Ginzberg, *Commentary*, I, 193. Rashi, however (to *Pesaḥim, loc. cit.*), takes the berakah with the opening formula to be sufficient for all the rest, and so also does Rashbam, who uses Rashi's phraseology.

61. *RM*, p. 190. The point is also made there that "the valuational events in an individual's life are unitary but not isolated."

62. *Berakot* 49a.

63. *Ibid.*, 48b.

64. A "desirable land" (Jer. 3:19); "a good and ample land" (Exod. 3:8).

65. *Berakot* 48b and Rashi *ad. loc.* Rashi supplies the biblical verses, undoubtedly from a tradition; see the Yerushalmi referred to in the next note.

66. *Ibid.* and Rashi, *ad loc.* In *Yer. Berakot* I.9.3d, the reward of the land for Torah is adduced from Ps. 105:44–45.

67. Rab and R. Ḥisda', and probably others too, did not feel the need to practice all these rules; see Lieberman, *Tos. Kif.*, I, 38, *s.v.* ר׳ יוסי. We also noticed above (p. 253, n. 52) that Rab was satisfied with a brief berakah. But there was also very likely another factor. Finkelstein (*op. cit.*, p. 229 and n. 37 there) points out "that the insertion of the Covenant and the Torah was made by authorities of the second century," probably as a "reaction to the persecutions to which the Jews were exposed on their account." Some of the rabbis apparently did not feel that these latter-day insertions were actually integral to the meditation; see Ginzberg, *Commentary*, II, 155, beginning at וכבר.

68. See Samuel's rule in *Pesaḥim* 104a, and the text as given in R. Ḥananel (and in other early authorities). See *Diḳduḳe Soferim, ad loc.*

69. Tosafot to *Pesaḥim* 104a, *s.v.* מאי בינייהו.

70. *Berakot* 49a. According to the rule there, the closing formula must refer to only one thing, and "for the Land and for the food" seems to violate that rule. The explanation there is that the phrase means "the Land that gives forth food," and hence that the principle is not violated.

71. *Berakot* 48b and 49a. See Ginzberg, *Commentary*, II, 155 and n. 33 there.

72. *Berakot* 49a. R. Sheshet thus upholds the view of R. Jose (*ibid.*) despite the dictum of R. 'Abba (Rab).

73. *Ibid.* and Rashi, *ad loc.*

74. See Lieberman, *Tos. Kif.*, I, 52 (top), and *ibid.*, nn. 69 and 70. He regards "Have mercy" as the older version. "When Jerusalem was destroyed, they substituted 'comfort' for 'Have mercy' "; *ibid.*, n. 69. Finkelstein suggests "that the prayer for Jerusalem was composed during the Maccabean struggle when the Temple and the Altar, the importance of both of which is emphasized in the earliest form of this prayer, were under the control of the heathen" (*op. cit.*, pp. 221 f., and the references there).

75. *Siddur R. Saadia Gaon*, p. 102. See Finkelstein, *op. cit.*, p. 233, on the tautology here.

76. See Tosafot to *Berakot* 48b, *s.v.* ומתחיל; also *Ṭur 'Oraḥ Ḥayyim*, par. 188, and its source quoted in the Bet Joseph to *ibid.*, par. 187.

77. *RM*, pp. 361 ff.; on the days of the Messiah, pp. 362 f.

78. *Ibid.*, pp. 365 f. On the special character of the hereafter concepts, see *ibid.*, p. 364. The rabbinic dogmas are also not pure dogmas, nor do they constitute a creed; see *ibid.*, pp. 366 f.

79. *Ibid.*, p. 42. *'Emunah* does *not* mean belief in the existence of God. See the discussion there. An example of *'emunah* is the farmer sowing and expecting to harvest; see Tosafot to *Shabbat* 31a, *s.v.* אמונת (see also *Midrash Tehillim* to Ps. 19:8, ed. S. Buber [Wilna, 1891], p. 86a, which ought to be corrected accordingly). E. Hatch, in *The Influence of Greek Ideas on Christianity*, ed. F. C. Grant (New York, 1957), pp. 310 ff., describes how "the word Faith came to be transferred from simple trust in God to mean the acceptance of a series of propositions, and these propositions, propositions in abstract metaphysics."

80. See, for example, the passage on *'emunah* in the *Mekilta*, ed. H. S. Horovitz and J. A. Rabin (Frankfurt am Main, 1928), pp. 114 f. Notice that *'emunah* there is interchanged with *'amanah*, the common term for "trust." The word *'emunah*, too, is also used for trust or faith in men; see Jastrow, *Dictionary* . . . (New York, Berlin, and London, 1926), *s.v.* אמונה.

81. *Midrash Tehillim*, ed. Buber, p. 120b. Cf. the references there. The passage refers to berakot of this type in the 'Amidah, one of which is the Fourteenth Berakah of the Daily 'Amidah. The closing formula of that berakah—"Blessed art Thou, O Lord, Who buildest Jerusalem"—is the same as the closing formula of the Third Berakah of the Birkat ha-Mazon.

82. It is "a berakah which is joined to the immediately preceding berakah," that is, to the Second Berakah: see *Berakot* 49a.

83. *Berakot* VI.8; *Tosefta*, *ibid.*, IV.6, 7, 15 (*Berakot* 37a). The saying of "Amen" by the individual who himself recites the Birkat ha-Mazon (see the text above, p. 74) also indicates that the Third Berakah closed the series; see *Berakot* 45b, Rashi, *ad loc.*, and Maimonides, *Hilkot Berakot*, I.17. The prayer of thanksgiving in the Didache, which many scholars say was written shortly after the destruction of the Second Temple, is another indication, as has been shown by K. Kohler (*Jewish Encyclopedia*, IV, 587) and especially by Finkelstein (*op. cit.*, pp. 213 f.). Alon (מחקרים בתולדות ישראל, I [Tel Aviv, 1957], pp. 286–90) tentatively suggests that on the basis of the material in the Didache, the Second Berakah of the Birkat ha-Mazon was originally the first of the three berakot (*ibid.*, p. 290). But the First Berakah obviously must refer to the meal, else the meal does not serve as an occasion for a berakah at all; therefore, the present order is without question the original order. Further, it is not coincidental that the *second* section of the Thanksgiving in the Didache contains the phrase "for all these we thank Thee," a phrase which is found in the *Second* Berakah.

84. *Tos. Berakot* VI(VII).1, ed. Lieberman, p. 32, where all the other sources are given. The four berakot are a series derived from Deut. 8:10 and thus are "from the Torah."

85. *Ibid.* I.7, ed. Lieberman, p. 3, and the discussions and references in Lieberman, *Tos. Kif.* I, 10, *s.v.* היה חותם.

86. שגמלנו כל טוב; see the discussion in Lieberman, *Tos. Kif.*, I, 101, *s.v.* הטוב והמטיב.

87. See Tosafot to *Berakot* 49a, *s.v.* מאן. The point made here is that if the Fourth Berakah is also "from the Torah", it is similar in form to the preceding berakot. See also Lieberman, *loc. cit.*, as to R. Ishmael's view.

On a possible other version of this berakah, see below, p. 256, n. 91.

88. *Siddur R. Saadia Gaon*, pp. 102 f.

89. *Berakot* 48b, and parallels; *ibid.*, *Yer.*, I.8, 3d.

90. Albeck, *Commentary on Berakot*, Introduction, p. 10 (the berakah on good tidings; *Berakot* IX.2).

91. The berakah "Who art good and doeth good" is said not only when hearing of good tidings but on other occasions as well; see *Berakot* 59b. It is quite possible that there were several versions of the original Fourth Berakah and that one of them had as its closing formula "Who art good and doeth good"; in that case, the berakah as established simply retained this phrase too.

92. From the viewpoint of those who regard the Fourth Berakah as "from the Torah," it is so closely related to the preceding berakot as to be "a berakah, which is joined to the immediately preceding berakah," and this despite the fact that it has an opening formula (Rashi to *Berakot* 49a, *s.v.* ומאן דאמר).

93. For variations in this type of berakah, see below, pp. 100, 102.

94. See *Tos. Berakot* II.4, and Lieberman, *Tos. Kif.* I, 15–16.

95. *Yer. Berakot* II.1, 4a—זאת אומרת שאין ברכות מעכבות, and see Ginzberg, *Commentary*, I, 225–227, where he also explains that this is the view of Resh Laḳish as well (*ibid.*, pp. 165 f.) in *Yer. Berakot* I.8, 3c. See also *Ṭur 'Oraḥ Ḥayyim*, par. 60.

96. *Berakot* II.2. "Heaven" is an appellative for God; see *RM*, p. 204. On the third section of the Shema', see Lieberman, *Tos. Kif.* I, 12, *s.v.* מזכירין, and *RM*, p. 359 and the note there.

97. *Sifre* on Num. 15:39, ed. H. S. Horovitz (Leipzig, 1917), p. 126.

98. See Albeck's comment on *Berakot* II.2, and the reference there to *Sifre* on Deut. 11:13.

99. *Sifre* on Num. 15:39, ed. Horovitz, *loc. cit.* In the parallel in *Berakot* 14b, R. Simeon b. Yoḥai introduces his argument with the term בדין, "it stands to reason."

100. *Berakot* 14b.

101. *Mekilta*, ed. Horovitz and Rabin, p. 222.

102. *Ibid.* For an analysis of this and the preceding reference, see *RM*, p. 21.

103. Above, pp. 23 f.

104. *RM*, pp. 18–21, 23 (*malkut Shamayim*); *OT*, pp. 110 f. (miẓwot).

105. For a haggadic example, see *OT*, pp. 208 f. Genuinely interlocking concepts are the "hereafter concepts," but they are beliefs, dogmas, rather than value concepts; even so, they exhibit some flexibility (see *RM*, pp. 347 [on dogmas], and pp. 364 f.).

106. *Pesaḥim* IV.8, and *Tosefta*, *ibid.*, II(III).19, ed. Lieberman (New York, 1962), pp. 156 f. See also Lieberman, *Tos. Kif.*, IV (New York, 1962), 541 f.

107. Louis Finkelstein, "The Word פרס," *Jewish Quarterly Review*, XXXIII, No. 1, 36–38. On this response in Temple usage, see also I. Davidson, אוצר השירה והפיוט, II, 75, and *RM*, pp. 212 f. and the notes there. On this response as a berakah, see p. 275, n. 43. M. Friedmann, in a long note in his edition of *Sifre Deut.*, pp. 72b–73a, says that originally the Ḳeri'at Shema' was made an element of the Temple ritual in order to include the study of Torah in that ritual. It was only after Herod, whose kingship the people resented, that the idea of the acceptance of God's kingship was added to the Shema'; this idea harked back "to the words of the prophet Samuel who said, 'But the Lord your God is your King' [I Sam. 12:2]." Friedmann also implies in this connection that God's rule meant to the Jews a negation of any human

sovereignty or rule. But the acceptance of God's kingship negates idolatry and not human rule as such (see above, p. 79). Moreover, we shall soon see that the acceptance of God's kingship in Ḳeri'at Shema' does not depend, as Friedmann would have it, on the insertion of the response. Again, unless Ḳeri'at Shema' had already meant to the people the acceptance of *malkut Shamayim*, the change in the response so as to emphasize God's kingship would have been meaningless. We shall find, indeed, that there is an association between the acceptance of God's kingship and the study of Torah itself.

108. *Berakot* 13b; *ibid.*, *Yer.*, II.1, 4a.

109. See Ginzberg, *Commentary*, I, 230, *s.v.* צריך. See also Edeles on *Berakot* 13b, *s.v.* כיון.

110. *Berakot* 13b.

111. *Ibid.*, *Yer.* II.1, 4a bottom.

112. See above, p. 256, n. 106.

113. See Edeles, *loc. cit.*, who takes R. Jeremiah's approach to be that of the individual mystic as against R. Ḥiyya's, which was meant for the people as a whole.

114. See above, p. 79.

115. Notice especially the parable in the Mekilta passage cited above, p. 80; "For if they will not accept My kingship, they will not accept My decrees."

116. *Tamid* V.1. On the formulation of this tractate, see J. N. Epstein, מבואות לספרות התנאים (Jerusalem, 1957), pp. 27–31.

117. See above, p. 80. R. Phineas b. Ḥama, an Amora, even declares that at Sinai God began with, "Hear, O Israel: 'I am the Lord thy God,' " and that Israel answered, "The Lord our God, the Lord is One," and that Moses thereupon uttered the response, "Blessed" etc. (*Deut. R.* II.22). There was a widespread tradition also that in the Ten Commandments the entire Torah was included (see the supplementary notes in C. Albeck's edition and *Commentary on Ḳodashim* [Jerusalem and Tel Aviv, 1956], p. 428, top). The Ten Commandments preceded the Shema' in the service because they precede in the Bible; notice the question raised with regard to the sections of the Shema' itself in Tosafot on *Berakot* 14b, *s.v.* למה קדמה.

118. *Yer. Berakot* I.8, 3c, and *ibid.*, *Babli*, 12a. See also Rashi, *ibid.*, *s.v.* בקשו.

119. *Berakot* 12a.

120. *Yer. Berakot* I.8, 3c, and Ginzberg, *Commentary*, I, 166. As against the sectarians, mark the "widespread tradition" mentioned in note 117 above.

According to Ginzberg, the statement that the sections on Balak and Balaam ought to be recited daily was also an attempt to offset "the contention of the sectarians," some of whom claimed that these and other sections were not written by Moses but added later; and hence this statement is given here in connection with that on the Ten Commandments. R. Eleazar's interpretation, he feels, is in accordance with this view. See the entire discussion in his *Commentary*, I, 167.

121. *Berakot* 12a.

122. הן הן גופה של שמע; *Yer. Berakot* I.8, 3c.

123. Ginzberg, *op. cit.*, I, 166.

124. *Yer. Berakot*, *loc. cit.*; שעשרת הדברות כלולין בהן. See also *Deut. R.*, ed. Lieberman, p. 69 and the references there in n. 6.

125. *Tos. Berakot* II.2, ed. Lieberman, p. 6. See *idem, Tos. Kif.*, I, 15, *s.v.* שיכוין, on the sense in which this word is used here, and see also the next comment there. Cf. *Berakot* 13b. "Else it must be repeated" is evident from R. Judah's differing opinion. R. Josiah's view in the second baraita in *Berakot* 13b is similar to the anonymous opinion in the Tosefta here; see Ginzberg, *op. cit.*, I, 233.

126. *Berakot* 13b.

127. Even revising the text is classed as mechanical reading; *ibid.*, 13a. See below, p. 197.

128. The nominal form is here in the construct state. But it is also used in reference to the commitment and experience of the Shema' in the absolute state; כונה. For example, *Yer. Berakot* II.1, 4a, bottom (in a baraita); *ibid.*, 4b, top; *ibid.*, *Babli*, 13b (R. Josiah).

129. Ginzberg, *op. cit.*, p. 228, *s.v.* נישמעינה. In *Berakot* II.1, and as discussed *ibid.*, 13a, it is used in the limited sense. See Lieberman, *Tos. Kif.*, *loc. cit.*

130. Ginzberg (*loc. cit.*) cites medieval authorities who called attention to these phases.

131. *Baba Ḳamma* 92b; *Baba Meẓi'a* 107b. It is linked with the Tefillah.

132. See above, n. 16.

133. On the Shema' as a unitary entity, see above, pp. 78 ff.

134. *OT*, p. 39. Miḳra', the word used for Scripture in general, stands for Ḳeri'at Shema' in *Berakot* II.1.

135. Ginzberg, *Commentary*, II, 133.

136. *Menaḥot* 99b. Similarly, *Midrash Tehillim*, ed. Buber, p. 8b, the proof-text here being Ps. 1:2; according to Ginzberg (*op. cit.*, I, 136), we ought to read "R. Simeon" for "R. Joshua."

137. *Yer. Berakot* III.3, 6b, and Ginzberg, *op. cit.*, II, 133. Daughters are in this halakic statement excluded from study of Torah, but *Nedarim* IV.3 speaks of teaching "his sons and daughters Scripture"; compare also *Soṭah* III.4 and the controversy there. See also *Tosefot Yom Ṭob* on *Nedarim* IV.3. The Mishnah, ed. W. H. Lowe (Cambridge, 1883), p. 86a (Yerushalmi) does not read "and daughters."

138. *Yer. Berakot* I.5, 3b, and Ginzberg, *op. cit.*, I, 136 f., *s.v.* זהו שינון: because he is at the same time engaged in the study of Torah, he need not interrupt that study for Ḳeri'at Shema', which is also study of Torah.

139. *Yer. Berakot* III.3, 6b, and Ginzberg, *op. cit.*, II, 178.

140. See below, p. 90.

141. *OT*, pp. 192 ff., where a theory in explanation of this phenomenon is developed.

142. See above, pp. 68, 76.

143. *RM*, pp. 73 f.: the instances of the Exodus from Egypt and the crossing of the Red Sea.

144. *OT*, p. 197, the instances of Israel and Torah and prophecy among the Gentiles; see also the instances of Israel and Torah in *TE*, p. 25.

145. *Berakot* I.1. The statement in this mishnah refers to all priests (see Albeck's remarks in his *Commentary on Berakot*, p. 13 and p. 325 f.).

146. *Berakot* I.2.

147. *Yer. Berakot* I.8, 3c. The third passage (Num. 15:37–41) was not read at night even in the time of the Amoraim (see Lieberman, *Tos. Kif.* I, 12, *s.v.* מזכירין).

148. Ginzberg, *Commentary*, I, 162 (top).

149. *Yer. Berakot* I.8, 3c.

150. Ginzberg, *op. cit.*, I, 73 and cf. p. 63. Workingmen started their work at dawn.

151. *Tos. Berakot* I.2, ed. Lieberman, pp. 1 f., and *idem*, *Tos. Kif.*, I, 3. Besides the parallels, see the references there; *Yer. Berakot* II.3, 4c top and I.1, 2d bottom; see also Ginzberg's remarks referred to there (*Commentary*, I, 119).

152. See above, p. 84, and the note there.

153. *Sifre* to Deut. 11:13, ed. Friedmann, p. 80a. See also *Bereshit R.* XVI.5, ed. Theodor, p. 149, and the notes there.

154. On the term 'abodah as worship, see below, p. 124.

155. *Pesiḳta de R. Kahana*, ed. S. Buber (Lyck, 1868), p. 107a.

156. *Sifre Deut.*, ed. Friedmann, p. 87a, and the references there.

157. *Ibid.*, p. 74a, and the note there. A slightly different version is found in *Pesiḳta de R. Kahana*, ed. Buber, p. 102a, where the verse interpreted is Deut. 26:16 ("This day," etc.). The word for edict there is פרוזדוגמא.

158. *RM*, pp. 348 ff.

159. The call is "Hear, O Israel," and the response (the testimony) is "The Lord, our God, the Lord is One." The verse is taken as call and response in *Sifre Deut.*, ed. Friedmann, p. 72b (and see *Debarim R.*, ed. S. Lieberman [Jerusalem, 1940], p. 67, and the references in n. 4 there), the response of Jacob's sons; and again in *Deut. R.* II.22, the response of Israel to God (see above, n. 117).

160. *Lev. R.* XXVII.6, ed. M. Margulies (Jerusalem, 1956), p. 633, and the references there. See Margulies' n. 2 there, in which he rightly takes this "testifying" as referring to "Ḳeri'at Shema' which is testimony to *malkut Shamayim*." The latter part, "but if you do not," etc., is clearer in the version in *Tanḥuma*, *'Emor*, 10, and we adopted that version here.

161. *Ibid.*, p. 637, and see the notes there.

162. *Seder R. Amram Gaon*, ed. Frumkin, I (ירושלים, תרע״ב), 105a. In this edition the words דלא מהירה עלן follow here, but they are not found in the Sulzberger MS, which Marx described as the best of all the MSS of the Seder (see D. Hedegard, *Seder Amram Gaon* [Motala, 1951], p. 26 [Hebrew] and p. xxi). Moreover, those words are also not found in this quotation from the Seder given in *Ṭur 'Oraḥ Ḥayyim*, par. 61 (beginning). They were added by a copyist who attempted to explain thereby what the edict consisted of.

163. For Finkelstein's view of Ḳeri'at Shema', see his article, "The Word פרס," *Jewish Quarterly Review*, XXXII, No. 4, 378 ff., and the subsequent article quoted above, n. 107.

164. *Sifre* to Deut. 32:29, ed. M. Friedmann (Vienna, 1864), p. 138b. For שמי read שמים. In the proof-text (Deut. 32:29), the rabbis take זאת to refer to the Torah, as they do elsewhere, e.g., *Pesiḳta R.*, ed. Friedmann, 191b, where the warrant for taking the word to refer to Torah is Deut. 4:44, and so also in the examples given by Theodor, *Bereshit R.*, p. 57, bottom.

165. *Seder Eliahu*, ed. Friedmann, p. 97, and *TE*, p. 61, n. 153.

166. See above, pp. 79 f.

167. *Seder Eliahu*, ed. Friedmann, p. 132, and *TE*, p. 60, n. 151, and notice also the version in the *Yalkuṭ*, cited by Friedmann, *loc. cit.*, n. 13. Cf. also *Lev. R.* XXXIII.6, ed. Margulies, p. 770, and the reference there.

168. See above, p. 82.

169. *Daily Prayer Book*, ed. and trans. S. Singer (London, 1890), p. 39; Baer, *op. cit.*, p. 80.

170. *Siddur R. Saadia Gaon*, pp. 13 f.: ותלמדנו חקי חיים כן תחננו. See the note there, p. 13, on אהבת עולם.

171. *Berakot* 11b.

172. *Ibid.*, *Yer.*, I.8, 3c.

173. I. Elbogen, תולדות התפלה והעבודה בישראל (Jerusalem–Berlin, 1924), p. 20. Kol Bo has a similar view, and also connects the First and the Second Berakot of the Shema' in a way we can only regard as homiletical; see the quotation in the note in Baer, *loc. cit.*

174. *Daily Prayer Book*, ed. and trans. Singer, pp. 39 f.; Baer, *loc. cit.*

175. Singer, p. 96; Baer, *op. cit.*, p. 164; and so also, with a minor variation, in *Siddur R. Saadia Gaon*, p. 26.

176. On knowledge of Torah, and study itself, as gifts from God, see *OT*, pp. 45 f.

177. *Siddur R. Saadia Gaon*, p. 14; see also Singer, p. 40, and Baer, p. 81.

178. *RM*, pp. 343–346. Lieberman has pointed out in a private communication that: מודים אנחנו לך, פירושו מודים אנחנו בך, and he called attention to the many examples in J. N. Epstein, מבוא לנוסח המשנה (Jerusalem, 1948), pp. 1110–1119.

179. See *RM*, pp. 346 f., where we show that הודו here cannot mean "They gave thanks."

180. It is so regarded by L. Zunz, הדרשות בישראל (Hebrew translation) (Jerusalem, 1947), ed. C. Albeck, p. 180, and the reference in n. 45; and by Elbogen, *op. cit.*, pp. 20 f. See also L. Ginzberg, *Geonica*, I (New York, 1909), 128, n. 1, where he says, "It is hardly possible that the insertion of the *Geullah* could go back to the Talmudic time."

181. Baer, *op. cit.*, p. 75.

182. E. Garfiel, *The Service of the Heart* (New York, 1958), p. 154.

183. *Siddur R. Saadia Gaon*, *loc. cit.*

184. In *RM*, pp. 52 ff., we depict the ideas that are not represented by conceptual terms as "auxiliary ideas," and on pp. 56 f. there we give more examples of בחר as "love." When we come to discuss the Daily 'Amidah, we shall also indicate how it is possible for the berakah here to be apparently the culmination of a prayer, a petition. The pertinent paragraphs are below, pp. 110 f.

185. Ginzberg, *Commentary*, I, 171.

186. *Yer. Berakot* I.8, 3d; so also Rashi, with regard to the berakah after the Shema' (*Berakot* 46b, top).

187. *Tos. Berakot* I.9, ed. Lieberman, p. 3, and *idem*, *Tos. Kif.*, I, 10 f.

188. See *Berakot* 11b–12a. Compare *ibid.*, *Yer.*, I.8, 3c, and Ginzberg's discussion, *op. cit.*, I, 165, 168.

189. *Yer. Berakot* I.9, 3d. Cf. *Tos. Berakot* II.1, ed. Lieberman, p. 6, and *idem*, *Tos. Kif.*, *ad loc.*

190. Lieberman, *Tos. Kif.*, I, 14, *s.v.* מכת.

191. *Berakot* II.2, end and Lieberman, *Tos. Kif.*, I, 12, *s.v.* מזכירין, and also his reference to Ginzberg there.

192. On surrogates for the third section of the Shema' in the evening, see Ginzberg's view in *RM*, p. 359, n. 80. On the early date of the initial statement in the baraita, see below, next paragraph.

193. See Singer, *op. cit.*, pp. 43 f.; Baer, *op. cit.*, pp. 85 f.

194. See the references in the preceding note.

195. Ginzberg, *op. cit.*, I, 215.

196. *Ibid.*, I, 216, *s.v.* ר׳ אומר.

197. *Siddur R. Saadia Gaon*, p. 15; *Siddur R. Amram*, ed. Frumkin, I, 210; (Singer, *op. cit.*, p. 42; Baer, *op. cit.*, p. 84): אמת אלהי עולם מלכנו צור יעקב.

198. Singer, *op. cit.*, pp. 42 f.; Baer, *op. cit.*, p. 84.

199. *Siddur R. Saadia Gaon*, p. 16.

200. Singer, *op. cit.*, p. 99; Baer, *op. cit.*, p. 166; *Siddur R. Saadia Gaon*, p. 27

201. *RM*, pp. 358 f.

202. *Ibid.*, pp. 360 f., and the notes there.

203. *Ibid.* D. Goldschmidt regards it as a baraita originally; see his סדר הגדה של פסח (Tel Aviv, 1947), p. 10.

204. It was only in geonic times that there was inserted in 'Emet we-Yaẓẓib a petition for a future redemption and this was done without the sanction of the Geonim; in fact, a geonic responsum declares explicitly that a petition here is out of place, since the berakah refers only to the Exodus. (See Ginzberg, *Geonica*, I, 128, and II, 89, 91. On p. 89 there, note especially Ginzberg's brief discussion on the various versions. In *Siddur R. Saadia Gaon*, p. 16, again, there is no petition.)

205. Singer, *op. cit.*, p. 37; Baer, *op. cit.*, p. 76. It is given in the Talmud: see *Berakot* 11b, top; the phrase "Who formest light," etc., is from Is. 45:7, except that "evil" there has been changed to "all things," since the latter is felt by the rabbis to be a more favorable term (לישנא מעליא)

206. Singer, *op. cit.*, p. 39; Baer, *op. cit.*, p. 79. This too is given in the Talmud; see *Berakot* 12a.

207. See the two preceding notes.

208. Singer, *op. cit.*, p. 37; Baer, *op. cit.*, p. 76; and see *Ḥagigah* 12b. On מעשה בראשית, here rendered (though not adequately) as "the Creation," see *RM*, pp. 35 f., and n. 4 on p. 36.

209. Singer, *loc. cit.*; Baer, *loc. cit.* Finkelstein regards this berakah and others of a similar universalistic nature as having been ordained by the Men of the Great Synagogue (and hence pre-tannaitic); see his הפרושים ואנשי כנסת הגדולה (New York, 1950), p. 72; see also p. 56 and the notes there.

210. See above, p. 85.

211. See above, p. 92.

212. *Ibid.* and Ginzberg, *Commentary*, I, 191.

213. Singer, *op. cit.*, p. 39; Baer, *op. cit.*, p. 79.

214. *Siddur R. Saadia Gaon*, p. 37 and n. 6 there.

215. He has a petition for the future redemption in 'Ahabah Rabbah (*ibid.*, p. 14).

216. See above, p. 90, and n. 180; and p. 261, n. 204.

217. L. Ginzberg, *Geonica*, I, 128.

218. See *Siddur R. Saadia Gaon*, pp. 36 f. R. Sherira Gaon, who disagrees with Saadia's view, finds Saadia inconsistent here (see אוצר הגאונים, ed. B. Lewin, I [Haifa, 1928], Part I, 33).

219. *Siddur R. Saadia Gaon*, p. 13, and the note there.

Notes to Chapter V

1. The successive order of the Eighteen Berakot was established in the time of R. Gamaliel of Jabne: see the baraita in *Berakot* 28b and *Megillah* 17b, and see *Berakot* IV.3. See also L. Ginzberg, *A Commentary on the Palestinian Talmud* (New York, 1941), I, 322; III, 277. We shall soon discuss the implications of the baraita.

2. *Tos. Berakot* III.25, ed. S. Lieberman (New York, 1955), pp. 17 f., and the parallels and references there, and see S. Lieberman, *Tosefta Ki-Fshuṭah* (New York, 1955), I, 53–55. See also Ginzberg, *op. cit.*, I, 335, 337; III, 277–279.

3. *Yer. Berakot* II.4, 4d; cf. *Berakot* 34a.

4. It is so designated, for example, in the reference in the preceding note. Actually, two of the last three berakot, although characterized as "praise," contain petitions like the middle berakot.

5. *Ibid.*, *Yer.*, IV.1, 7a. Cf. *Sifre* to Deut. 3:23, ed. M. Friedmann (Vienna, 1864), p. 70b. The latter reference indicates that, while tefillah in a technical sense refers to the 'Amidah, its basic meaning is petition, that is, prayer in the sense of petition. It is used in that sense elsewhere also, for example, in *Berakot* IX.3–4.

6. See *Tos. Rosh ha-Shanah* II (IV).17, ed. S. Lieberman (New York, 1962), 320 f., and see also S. Lieberman, *Tosefta Ki-Fshuṭah*, V (New York, 1962), 1062.

7. L. Finkelstein, "The Development of the Amidah," *Jewish Quarterly Review*, N.S., XVI, No. 1, 38–41. See the entire article in that volume, pp. 1–43, and in *ibid.*, No. 2, pp. 127–170, for a detailed and suggestive treatment of the history and text of the 'Amidah. On the text of the berakot, see also J. Elbogen, תולדות התפלה והעבודה בישראל (Jerusalem and Berlin, 1924), pp. 34 ff.

8. *Berakot* 33a; cf. *Yer. Berakot* II.4, 4d, and Ginzberg, *op. cit.*, I, 327 f.; and see also Finkelstein, *op. cit.*, pp. 2 ff.

9. See the references above, n. 1.

10. Ginzberg, *op. cit.*, I, 322.

11. Lieberman, *Tos. Kif.*, I, 53. This conclusion is based on a statement in *Megillah* 18a.

12. On the conceptual continuum and on the form, see above, pp. 71 f. (Birkat ha-Mazon); 95 f. (berakot of the Shema').

13. S. Baer, *Seder 'Abodat Yisra'el* (Roedelheim, 1868), pp. 87 f., and the notes there on p. 88; S. Singer, *The Daily Prayer Book* (London, 1890), p. 44. What we have just quoted of the First Berakah lacks but a few words in order to be the original form of that berakah; we need only complete the phrase "the most high God" with "Maker of heaven and earth," so that the whole phrase from Gen. 14:19 precedes the closing formula (see Ginzberg, *op. cit.*, IV, pp. 177, 182 f. See also *ibid.*, pp. 179 f., as to the very early date of this berakah).

14. *Rosh ha-Shanah* IV.5. The Second Berakah is designated there Geburot, and the third, Ḳedushat ha-Shem.

15. See above, p. 71 f., for a detailed discussion of this form.

16. Above, pp. 76 f., 77 f.

17. On the text of these berakot, see Elbogen, *op. cit.*, p. 38; Singer, *op. cit.*, p. 46.

18. On the name, see above, n. 14.

19. *Sifre Deut.*, par. 343, ed. Friedmann, 142b.

20. See Elbogen, *op. cit.*, p. 37, and the references there.

21. קדוש אתה ונורא שמך ואין אלה מבלעדיך; see Finkelstein, "La Kedouscha et les Bénédictions du Schema," (Paris 1932, offprint from *Revue des Études Juives*), pp. 3 f., and the notes there.

22. These matters are taken up in the next chapter.

23. Baer, *op. cit.*, p. 386. He refers in the notes to *Pirḳe de R. Eliezer*, XXXV, end, where the verse is incorporated with the berakah. Ginzberg, *op. cit.*, III, pp. 21 f. gives this among a number of Palestinian practices which are followed now only during the period of New Year and the Day of Atonement, although they were practiced in Palestine originally in the course of the entire year.

24. *Berakot* 12b—R. Eleazar.

25. *Pirḳe R. Eliezer*, *loc. cit.*, and Luria, *ad loc.*; and see *Targ. Jonathan* to this verse; *Tanḥuma*, *Ḳedoshim*, par. 1, end; *Debarim R.* V.6.

26. M. Kadushin, *The Rabbinic Mind* (New York, 1952), pp. 40 f. (to be referred to hereafter as *RM*).

27. Ginzberg, *op. cit.*, IV, 200, says that in Yannai's *Ḳerobot* for New Year the content of the Third Berakah is צדקה ומשפט, and that it closes with תוגבה במשפט ותוקדש בצדקה, this line referring, as he points out, to Is. 5:16: "And the Lord of Hosts is exalted in judgment, and the holy God is sanctified in *ẓedaḳah*."

We find that the lines just preceding the one quoted by Ginzberg read as follows (*Maḥzor Yannai*, ed. I. Davidson [New York, 1919], p. 30):

מכון כסאך שתה חסד וצדקה
חלילה לך מעשות משפט בלי צדקה.

Yannai thus takes *ẓedaḳah* to be lovingkindness and charity and, accordingly, he interprets the proof-text in the Third Berakah as declaring that God is made holy, sanctified, in His charity at judgment. See also Ginzberg, *op. cit.*, IV, p. 239, and the *piyyuṭ* he quotes there.

28. Finkelstein, *loc. cit.*

29. On the Ḳedushah, see below, p. 142 ff., where we also deal with the problem of the introductory phrase.

30. We had an instance above, p. 77, of a deviation from the conceptual pattern, a deviation also overcome by the cumulative effect of the preceding berakot.

Ginzberg's theory in the fourth, and posthumous, volume of his *Commentary*—which appeared after our discussion on the Third Berakah had been written—may be summarized as follows: While it is true that the version of קדוש אתה found in the Sifre is Palestinian and is the oldest version (p. 196), it was probably only the Galilean practice (p. 172); the version of אתה קדוש, which is the Diaspora version, was originally, however, a Judean practice, and hence was probably the original version (pp. 172, 196 f.); the version of לדור ודור is geonic and was originally said only by the leader in the Tefillah (pp. 175 f., 197, 201 f., 203). This brief summary does not do justice, of course, to the many points of interest in Ginzberg's treatment; see pp. 196 ff.

31. See Ginzberg, *op. cit.*, III, 280 f., and the sources referred to there.

32. See Ginzberg, *op. cit.*, I, 324; III, 280 f.

33. Baer, *op. cit.*, p. 386, and the notes.

34. *Ibid.*; Singer, *op. cit.*, p. 239. In the same prayer, earlier: "May all creatures prostrate themselves before Thee, and may all of them form a single band to do Thy will with a perfect heart."

35. See the text of this berakah in Finkelstein, "The Development of the Amidah," *ibid.*, No. 2, p. 156. On *minim*, see the discussion in G. Alon, תולדות היהודים בארץ ישראל בתקופת המשנה והתלמוד (Tel Aviv, 1952), I, 180 ff.

36. Alon, *op. cit.*, pp. 191 f.

37. Lieberman, *op. cit.*, I, p. 54. There can be no doubt that the berakah so amended was the Twelfth Berakah, although in *Tos. Berakot* III.25 it is referred to as the one "on the separatists" (פרושין—see Lieberman, *loc. cit.*, and his reference to Finkelstein). That only means that the Twelfth Berakah had already been amended before to include mention of "separatists." See also I. Davidson, אוצר השירה והפיוט, II, 192 f.

38. Ginzberg, *op. cit.*, III, 284.

39. *Ibid.*, pp. 284 f.

40. *Ibid.*, pp. 249 f.

41. *Yer. Berakot* V.3, 9c—אני אומר מין הוא. This halakah constitutes a confirmation of the point made above, p. 98, regarding the number or limit of the berakot in a conceptual continuum. The leader is not ordinarily made to go back, for each berakah is a unitary entity in itself (but see Ginzberg, *op. cit.*, IV, 276). The Second Berakah, according to Ginzberg, originally did not contain the dogma of *teḥiyyat ha-metim*, resurrection. In *Rosh ha-Shanah* IV.5 this berakah is designated as Geburot, which is another form for Nissim (*ibid.*, p. 155). The berakah was thus not established originally because of the sectarians who denied the doctrine of resurrection; only in the course of time did the berakah of Geburot become that of *teḥiyyat ha-metim* (*ibid.*, pp. 164, 184). Originally, Geburot had but one theme, namely, God's *geburot* in saving Israel from their enemies; late in the period of the Second Temple, both the *geburot* of rain and of resurrection were added, the latter because of the aforementioned sectarians (*ibid.*). When these additions were made, the closing formula was changed to "Who quickenest the dead" (*ibid.*, pp. 167, 190). In the berakah itself all references to resurrection are post-talmudic except the one in the phrase "[Thou] sustainest the living with lovingkindness [and] quickenest the dead" (*ibid.*, pp. 187, 193). Other expressions there are likewise additions (*ibid.*, pp. 165, 184 f., 187, 188, 196).

42. Above, pp. 74 f. and the notes there.

43. *Berakot* 29a, and see *Diḳduke Soferim, ad loc.* We have stated the halakah in accordance with the rendering in *Ṭur 'Oraḥ Ḥayyim*, par. 126 (beginning).

44. *Tanḥuma, Wayyiḳra'*, par. 2; *ibid.*, ed. S. Buber (Wilna, 1885), III, 2a.

45. *Ibid.*—שאם יהא בו צד מינות.

46. *Ibid.* A *Kuti*, Samaritan, is not a *goy* (see *RM*, p. 41, and the note there).

47. M. Higger, *Seven Minor Treatises* (New York, 1930), Introduction, p. 6 (with a reference to Ginzberg, *Geonica* (New York, 1909), I, p. 73, n. 1), and p. 7 (Hebrew).

48. "Masseket Kutim," Chap. II, Higger, *op. cit.*, p. 67. See also Abraham Geiger, המקרא ותרגומיו (Hebrew) (Jerusalem, 1949), p. 85, n. 1.

49. On the doctrine of the resurrection in the Samaritan liturgy, see A. Cowley in *Jewish Encyclopedia*, X, 674a, bottom.

50. Some of the Church Fathers (Justin, Epiphanius, and Jerome) declare that three times a day, at their prayers in their synagogues, the Jews curse Jesus and the Christians (cf. H. Graetz, *Geschichte der Juden* [Leipzig, 1866], IV, 434 f.). This may refer to the Twelfth Berakah, but such a view could not have been transmitted by those who knew the berakah well, the learned.

51. See *Ṭur 'Oraḥ Ḥayyim*, par. 126, who, however, also quotes and interprets the halakah of the Yerushalmi, a quotation to which *Bet Joseph* objects because it disagrees with the Babylonian halakah. *Bet Joseph*, too, paraphrases the pupils of R. Jonah who designate the Twelfth Berakah as a denunciation and thereby distinguish between that berakah and the Second. The view of the codists is probably reflected in a late MS of the Yelammedenu passage as given in *Tanḥuma*, ed. Buber, *loc. cit.*, which contains the phrase ברכת קללת המינין—see n. 22 there. A number of scholars hold the view that the Twelfth Berakah, as formulated in the time of R. Gamaliel at Jabne (see above, p. 101 f.) was a new berakah and was not merely edited but composed at that time. Among them are Elbogen (*op. cit.*, pp. 31 f.), and Albeck (in Zunz, הדרשות בישראל (Jerusalem, 1947), pp. 480 f. n. 35).

52. Above, p. 97 and n. 5.

53. *Tos. Berakot* III.6, ed. Lieberman, p. 13, and the parallels and references there; and see Lieberman, *Tos. Kif.*, I, 30 f. I Kings 8:28 begins with ופנית אל תפלת עבדך, a phrase which is amplified, according to this interpretation, in the words: לשמע אל הרנה ואל התפלה. *Rinnah* is interpreted as *tehillah* by comparison with Ps. 33:1.

54. *Tos. Baba Ḳamma'* IX.29, ed. M. S. Zuckermandel and S. Lieberman (2nd ed; Jerusalem, 1937), p. 365; *Berakot* 34b; *Shabbat* 67a; *ibid.*, 151b; *Baba Batra* 91b; *Deut. R.* VII.11; and *passim*.

55. *Berakot* 12b.

56. *Berakot* 20b; *ibid.*, 26a; *Soṭah* 33a.

57. In explaining the halakah on the Tefillah in *Berakot* III.3, the Yerushalmi says, "In order that each and every one should beseech compassion for himself," while the Babli (*Berakot* 20b) merely says, "For it is *raḥame*," and, as Ginzberg has pointed out (*Commentary*, II, 151 f.), both are saying the same thing. Ginzberg also shows (*ibid.*, III, 149 f.) that Rashi deleted from the explanation in *Berakot* 20b all but the words "for it is [or, they are] *raḥame*" in accordance with his opinion that the Tefillah is a rabbinical ordinance.

58. Above, p. 97 and n. 1.

59. *Pesaḥim* 117b, and Rashbam, *ad loc.* Raba's statement there, preceding that of R. Ze'ira, is not a clear instance, for the Palestinian version has ונגאלו, and therefore implies a present experience (see above, p. 93). For the Ḳiddush, see Baer, *op. cit.*, p. 198, and for the Tefillah, see *ibid.*, p. 188.

60. יהי רצון מלפניך ד׳ אלהי; *Tos. Berakot* VI (VII).16, ed. Lieberman, pp. 37 f., and the parallels cited there. On "town" (כרך), see Albeck's remarks in his edition of *Seder Nashim* (Jerusalem and Tel Aviv, 1955), p. 356.

61. מודה אני לפניך; *Tos. Berakot, loc. cit.*

62. *Ibid.*

63. *Ibid.*, VI (VII).17, ed. Lieberman, p. 38, and the parallels.

64. See Lieberman, *Tos. Kif.*, I, 118, *s.v.* מתפלל, and p. 119, *s.v.* מברך. We take it that *mitpallel* is used because of the tefillah, petition, ordained by the halakah, and that *mebarek* is used because of the berakah ordained by the same halakah.

65. *Yer. Berakot* II.2, 4d.

66. Ginzberg, *op. cit.*, III, 356 f. He cites *Tos. Berakot* III.6 (ed. Lieberman, p. 13); the baraita in *Berakot* 31a (see Rashi, *ad loc.*, *s.v.* יכול ישאל); the baraita having one version in *'Abodah Zarah* 7b and another in *Yer. Berakot* IV.4, 8b, the versions containing different halakot. On the baraita in the Tosefta, see Lieberman, *Tos. Kif.*, I, 30 f.

67. *Megillah* 17b.

68. *RM*, pp. 150 f.

69. On this berakah as referring to man, see below, p. 111 f.

70. *Berakot* V.2.

71. *Ta'anit* 14b, ed. Malter (ed. minor; Philadelphia, 1928), pp. 97 f. The rendering is Malter's. See also Elbogen, *op. cit.*, p. 39.

72. Outside of the 'Amidah, this description holds also for practically all the prayers culminating in berakot which have Israel as the "others." An instance is the prayer-meditation in 'Ahabah Rabbah, which is discussed above, pp. 89 ff.

73. The ascription is of Babylonian origin, but is very early—see Ginzberg, *op. cit.*, III, p. 346; cf. Elbogen, *op. cit.*, pp. 37 f.

74. See *Seder Eliahu*, ed. M. Friedmann (Vienna, 1900), p. 70: "Were wisdom, understanding, knowledge and discernment taken away from them [men], they would be accounted as the cattle or beasts or birds." Notice that the identical words of the berakah, "wisdom, understanding," etc., are here, as it were, commented on. On "wisdom" in this berakah, see Elbogen, *loc. cit.*

75. The phrase חונן הדעת is in *Berakot* V.2.

76. Baer, *op. cit.*, p. 90, and the notes, and see also Elbogen, *op. cit.*, p. 38. On the basis of *Yer. Berakot* II.4, 4d, Ginzberg suggests that the ancient form was: "Accept our repentance (רצה בתשובתנו), and 'Turn Thou us unto Thee, O Lord, and we shall be turned; renew our days as of old' [Lam. 5:21]" (*op. cit.*, I, 324 f.). In this ancient version, too, "us" refers to Israel.

77. Elbogen, *loc. cit.* On "Who accepts" for הרוצה, see in the version of the petition given in the preceding note.

78. The repentance of the "men of Nineveh" is spoken of in *Ta'anit* II.1 as the classic example of what repentance should consist in: "Of the men of Nineveh it is not said:

And God saw their sackcloth and their fasting, but [Jonah 3:10]: 'And God saw their works, that they turned from their evil way.' " Elsewhere the rabbis speak of the equal acceptance by God of all who repent, "whether among Israel or among the nations," as a *middah*, rule (see M. Kadushin, *The Theology of Seder Eliahu* [New York, 1932]), p. 125. "Blessed art Thou, O Lord, Who hearkenest unto prayer" of the Sixteenth Berakah also refers, obviously, to man, and this point is stressed in the petition of the berakah as found in *Seder R. Amram*—see Elbogen, *op. cit.*, p. 44.

79. See the notes and references in Baer, *op. cit.*, p. 103; Elbogen, *op. cit.*, p. 48; Ginzberg, *op. cit.*, III, 250.

80. Elbogen, *loc. cit.*

81. "Unto us" (עלינו) in the first part of the petition refers to Israel, and *Siddur R. Saadia Gaon*, ed. I. Davidson and others (Jerusalem, 1941), p. 19, does not have there any other reference to Israel.

82. Ginzberg, *op. cit.*, III, 250, and the reference there; cf. *ibid.*, I, 323.

83. Elbogen, *op. cit.*, p. 39.

84. Above, pp. 67 f.

85. *RM*, pp. 150 f., where this matter is discussed; cf. *OT*, p. 137. The word *'adam* in rabbinic thought is solely a conceptual term, so much so that Adam himself is not designated as Adam by the rabbis but as "The First *'adam* [man]"—אדם הראשון. See, e.g., *Gen. R.* VIII.1, 4, 5, 15.

86. *Leviticus R.* II.8, ed. M. Margulies (Jerusalem, 1953), p. 46, and the notes there.

87. *Ibid.* Up to this point the connotations, drawn forth in this midrash refer to "the son of man," and from this point on to "the son of Buzi" (Ezek. 1:3) (see Margulies, *ibid.*, note).

88. There is no berakah in the entire 'Amidah which does not present an instance of the organismic integration of concepts. Attention has been called above (p. 84) to examples elsewhere.

89. Above, pp. 101 ff.

90. See especially *ibid.*, pp. 102 f.

91. Originally the petition here consisted solely of "Restore our judges as at first and our counsellors as at the beginning"; that is the text in *Siddur Saadia*, p. 18, which does not have the later additions. This berakah was formulated when the Sadducees controlled the Sanhedrin. On all this, see Ginzberg, *op. cit.*, III, 326 f.

92. On this berakah, see above, p. 97, and the references in n. 2 there.

93. This berakah had its origin in the Temple service, and the references to the restoration of the Service were added after the Destruction (see Finkelstein, "The Development of the Amidah," *Jewish Quarterly Review*, N.S., XVI, No. 1, pp. 38 ff., and Elbogen, *op. cit.*, pp. 44 f.). Originally, as can be seen from the material cited by Elbogen and Finkelstein, the closing formula of this berakah read: שאותך ביראה נעבוד; and this reading, in contrast to the present version, indicates how the early rabbis refrained from using the concept of *gilluy Shekinah* when it came to actual religious experience (see *RM*, pp. 235, 238 ff.).

94. The Second Berakah refers not to Israel alone but also to the righteous among the Gentiles (see G. F. Moore, *Judaism in the First Centuries of The Christian Era* [Cambridge, 1927], II, 386 [corrected in *ibid.*, III (Cambridge, 1930), 205] where R. Joshua and the halakah as formulated by Maimonides are cited).

95. Above, pp. 73 ff.

96. Above, pp. 75 f.

97. On this, see above, p. 75, and especially the notes there. *'Emunah*, as we said there, does not mean belief in the existence of God. That meaning is not rabbinic but was given the word in medieval philosophy.

98. Above, p. 93 f.

99. On the dogma of *mattan Torah*, see *RM*, pp. 348 ff., especially p. 351; on the berakot, see below, p. 140. See also the discussion above, p. 86.

100. Above, p. 94.

101. *RM*, p. 351.

102. They were indeed felt to be imminent, yet no more than that. R. Joshua b. Levi, in positing a logical order for the berakot in the 'Amidah, declares that the successive order of "the middle berakot" from the Seventh Berakah onward is due to the way these "needs" will be successively fulfilled in the future, from the redemption and onward (see *Yer. Berakot* II.4, 4d, and in Ginzberg, *op. cit.*, I, pp. 322–324, 326 f.). Similarly, the Babli accounts for the position of the Ninth Berakah by referring it to the future and linking it with "the Ingathering of the Exiles." (See *Megillah* 17b and Ginzberg's stricture, *ibid.*, p. 323. On the textual problems of the similar statement in the Yerushalmi, see *ibid.*, pp. 333 f.)

103. A good example is the First Berakah on the Torah which reads: "Who hast chosen us from all peoples and hast given us Thy Torah," with both verbs here in the past tense, and which closes with: "Who givest the Torah," in the present tense. (On the idea of "chosen" in this berakah, see below, p. 140.) For an example of implication of the present, see below, p. 117.

104. *Tos. Berakot* III.25, ed. Lieberman, p. 18, and *Tos. Kif.*, I, 54. He takes the term פליטת סופריהם to be among the early terms.

105. *Yer. Berakot* II.4, 5a; *ibid.*, IV.3, 8a, and the other parallels in *Tos. Berakot*, ed. Lieberman, p. 17.

106. That *ẓaddiḳim* is the major theme is also apparent from *Megillah* 17b and Yer. *Berakot* II.4, 5a.

107. *Siddur R. Saadia Gaon*, p. 18; cf. Singer, *op. cit.*, p. 48.

108. See Baer, *op. cit.*, p. 95, for explanations of these terms.

109. *RM*, pp. 39 f., and the notes there.

110. Elbogen, *op. cit.*, pp. 41 f.

111. *RM*, p. 43.

112. Above, p. 98.

113. See the statement of R. Simeon b. Laḳish in *Pesaḥim* 117b.

114. Cf. Ginzberg, *Commentary*, IV, 121.

115. Elbogen, *op. cit.*, p. 35. According to Ginzberg, the phrase was added—*ibid.*, p. 183.

116. As the context indicates, this word refers not to salvation but to safety, security, in the present.

117. See Elbogen, *loc. cit.* (Incidentally, the statement in Tosafot to *Berakot* 49a referred to by Elbogen here in n. 37 means that since the Shemoneh Esreh does not have a "kingship" formula, all the berakot in the series go back, "are joined," to

the First Berakah in the evening service, אל חי וקים, which does begin with the formula; the statement does not mean that the Berakah of 'Abot closed with those words, as Elbogen would have it. Tosafot goes on to say that "God of Abraham" is equivalent to the "kingship" formula.) (On this section as not being integral to the berakah, see also Ginzberg, *ibid.*, pp. 184, 192.)

118. *Berakot* IV.4 and *Tos. Berakot* III.7, ed. Lieberman, pp. 13 f., and the parallels there.

119. Mishnah *Berakot*, *loc. cit.* See Lieberman's remarks on the Palestinian texts of this petition (*Tos. Kif.*, I, p. 33).

120. *Tos. Berakot*, *loc. cit.*

121. *Ibid.* On this and the preceding reference, see Lieberman, *loc. cit.*, *s.v.* אי זה, who points out that the Tannaim in the Tosefta, as against R. Joshua in the Mishnah, hold that the short Tefillah consists of only a single berakah. R. Eliezer's petition is different in tone from the others, but there, too, ליריאיך refers to Israel. We did not cite the petition of R. Eleazar, the son of R. Zadoḳ, because it is similar to that of "Hearken", etc.

122. *Berakot* 30a; cited by Lieberman, *loc. cit.* Rashi, *ad loc.*, explains that this refers to the use of the plural in saying the short Tefillah, but adds that the prayer is thereby made more efficacious.

123. On the leader reciting the Tefillah, see below, p. 143.

124. *Berakot* IV.3.

125. Ginzberg, *op. cit.*, III, 237 f.

126. Tosafot to *Berakot* 16a, *s.v.* אפילו.

127. *Berakot* 29a; *ibid.*, *Yer.*, IV.3, 8a; and Lieberman, *op. cit.*, I, 32 f. See also Ginzberg, *op. cit.*, III, 315 ff.

128. Lieberman, *op. cit.*, I, 31 f., and the notes there. R. Eliezer's statement, he points out, properly belongs at the end of *Berakot* IV.3, as it is in the Yerushalmi edition (Venice, 1523), and it has been placed deliberately after R. 'Aḳiba's opinion so as to indicate R. Eliezer's meaning. See also his reference to Ginzberg in n. 13 there.

129. *Berakot* IV.4, but see the preceding note—העושה תפלתו קבע אין תפלתו תחנונים.

130. See Lieberman, *loc. cit.*, on this and on the rest of this paragraph.

131. Above, p. 118, n. 121, and the source there; but cf. Ginzberg, *op. cit.*, III, 354.

132. Notice that R. Eliezer employs, in his short Tefillah, the closing formula of the Sixteenth Berakah; see *Tos. Berakot* III.7.

133. *Tos. Berakot* III.6, ed. Lieberman, p. 13, and the references there.

134. Lieberman, *Tos. Kif.*, I, 31.

135. *'Abodah Zarah* 7b–8a; cf. *ibid.*, *Yer.*, IV.4, 8b. Ginzberg suggests that this halakah is of Babylonian origin (*op. cit.*, III, 360).

136. *'Abodah Zarah* 8a, and Rashi, *ibid.*, *s.v.* מעין כל ברכה.

137. Above, p. 117.

138. We saw in the last section that *biṭṭaḥon* as a meditative experience can also be the culmination of a prayer for security and welfare, and this is the case in the Thirteenth Berakah.

139. This is taken to mean until sunset by Maimonides, Hilkot *Tefillah* III.4.

140. *Berakot* IV.1. The evening Tefillah may be said at any time during the night: see Albeck's commentary on *Zera'im* (Jerusalem and Tel Aviv, 1957), *ad loc.*, and his supplementary note on p. 331; and see Lieberman, *Tos. Kif.*, I, 27, *s.v.* קבע. The morning Tefillah is to be said after dawn (see above, p. 85).

141. *Tos. Berakot* III.1, ed. Lieberman, p. 11. The basic difference between the *Ḥakamim* and R. Judah with respect to the time is in regard to the daily communal sacrifices, and the matter of the time of the Tefillah is but the result of that difference; *idem*, *Tos. Kif.*, I, p. 27, *s.v.* עד פלג.

142. *Yer. Berakot* IV.1, 7b, and Ginzberg, *op. cit.*, III, 30 f.; and see above, n. 140.

143. *Yer. Berakot*, *ibid*; *Bereshit R.* LXVIII.9, ed. J. Theodor and C. Albeck (Berlin, 1927), p. 780; cf. *Berakot* 26b.

144. *Berakot* 27b, and the pupils of R. Jonah, *ad loc.* No *ḳeba'*, as the latter interpret it, refers here to both ideas: to the idea that the Tefillah in the evening is not a matter of fixed duty and to the idea that it is not fixed as to time.

145. See above, n. 141.

146. According to Ginzberg, the opinion that the evening Tefillah was an optional matter was based on custom, for only individuals said it during the Temple days and it was not the common practice at that time (*op. cit.*, III, 170). With regard to the later practice, see *ibid.*, pp. 172 f. On the early practice, see also G. Alon, מחקרים, I (Tel Aviv, 1957), 285.

147. Above, pp. 69 f.

148. Above, p. 94.

149. *Tanḥuma*, *Ḥayye Sarah*, 5. ובמנחה should read ובערבית: see Ginzberg, *op. cit.*, III, 22, and his remarks there. The text in the *Tanḥuma* is the original statement.

150. The Nineteenth Berakah was the same for all the periods of the day until the Middle Ages (see Elbogen, *op. cit.*, p. 48).

151. Above, p. 97. At the offering of the morning sacrifice the priests said a berakah before the 'Abodah and that apparently constituted the one berakah of the Tefillah which they said in the morning (see Ginzberg, *op. cit.*, III, 28, and the note there; cf. Finkelstein (above, p. 267, n. 93).

152. The Musaf on the Sabbath and festivals, too, is a reminder despite its name. The pattern of the Tefillah remains the same, including the First Berakah, and the Musaf sacrifice is mentioned only in the Fourth Berakah, and even so only in the petition. Indeed, Ginzberg (*op. cit.*, III, 434 f.) says it is likely that in the days of the Mishnah, and in Palestine in the amoraic period as well, there was no difference between the Musaf and the other Tefillot, and that the recital of ומפני חטאינו is a Babylonian practice. He inclines to the opinion that in the Temple period there was no separate Musaf Tefillah, but that on days when there was a Musaf sacrifice, some mention of it was added in the single morning Tefillah (*ibid.*, pp. 28 f.).

153. *Berakot* 26b. In the parallel in *ibid.*, *Yer.*, IV.1, 7b, the authority is *Rabbanan* and not an individual, and instead of "ordained as against," the reading is, "They learned the Tefillot from the daily communal sacrifices—The Tefillah of the morning from the sacrifice of the morning," etc. But here, too, the association is only that of the time, for the passage continues, "They did not find what to *attach* the evening Tefillah to," and then it quotes the Mishnah which states that this Tefillah had "no *ḳeba'*."

154. *Berakot, loc. cit.* The parallel in the Yerushalmi, *loc. cit.*, has here also, "They learned the Tefillot" from the Patriarchs, meaning, that those who ordained the Tefillot found support both as to the number and as to the time for the Tefillot in the examples of the Patriarchs (Ginzberg, *op. cit.*, III, 24 ff., 30). On the question of the "baraita," see *ibid.*, p. 25, n. 30, and also *RM*, p. 128.

155. *Berakot, loc. cit.*

156. See *Bereshit R.*, *loc. cit.*, ed. J. Theodor and C. Albeck, pp. 779–80, and the sources quoted in the notes there; and Ginzberg, *loc. cit.*

157. On the number and the time: *Tos. Berakot* III.6 and the parallels, ed. Lieberman, p. 12, and *Tos. Kif.*, I, 29–30 (Daniel); *Tanḥuma, loc. cit.* (the three changes in the position of the sun). On the berakot as being Eighteen in number: *Yer. Berakot* IV.3, 7d–8a, and Ginzberg, *ad loc.*, who also gives and compares the parallels. The association of the "Eighteen" with the building of the Tabernacle is not due to the daily sacrifice, however, as Ginzberg would have it (*op. cit.*, III, 289). The "Eighteen" are the Tefillah and the Tefillah is to be directed toward the Holy of Holies (the Tabernacle), as is explicitly stated in *Berakot* IV.5–6, and as Ginzberg himself emphasizes elsewhere (*ibid.*, p. 377).

158. See *Sanhedrin* 60b. The sacrificial worship in the Temple is עבודת פנים. See also *Mekhilta D'Rabbi Sim'on b. Jochai*, ed. J. N. Epstein and E. Z. Melamed (Jerusalem, 1955), p. 210, and the references there. On actions as "cancelling" an idol, see *RM*, pp. 196 f.

159. Above, p. 65, and the references in n. 16 there.

160. *Berakot* 53b.

161. R. Naḥman, *ibid.*, quotes a baraita as tantamount to the halakah and that baraita has been variously interpreted by the post-talmudic authorities. We have taken the interpretation implied by Tosafot, *ad loc.*, and given in the דרישה to *Ṭur 'Oraḥ Ḥayyim*, par. 181, and also given in Rashi as printed with Alfasi, *ad loc.*

162. Above, p. 122, and n. 144 there.

163. Above, p. 123. Our remarks here apply as well to the parallel cited in n. 153, above.

164. *Sifre* on Deut. 11:13, ed. M. Friedmann (Vienna, 1864), p. 80a. Moore (*Judaism*, II, pp. 217 f.) errs in taking this passage and a number of others to refer to prayer in general and in doing so obliterates the rabbinic distinction between *bakkashah*, petition or prayer in general, and 'abodah, worship. See also below, p. 272, n. 176.

165. *Yer. Berakot* IV.1, 7a, and see Ginzberg, *op. cit.*, III, p. 3. On the basis of our discussion here, the concluding statement in the Sifre is not an addition, and the Yerushalmi simply has a somewhat different version. See also the version in *Ta'anit* 2a, ed. H. Malter (ed. major; New York, 1930), p. 3, and the other parallels referred to there.

166. *Tanḥuma, Aḥare*, par. 9; *ibid.*, ed. S. Buber, par. 14, pp. 34b–35a. מקטר in Mal. 1:11 is related to the קטורת, incense, of the Minḥah of the evening. Proofs are Ps. 141:2 and I Kings 18:36. See Albeck's discussion in his note on p. 331 in his edition of *Zera'im*, *s.v.* ר׳ יהודה.

167. *Pesikta de Rab Kahana*, ed. S. Buber (Lyck, 1868), p. 165b—R. 'Abbahu.

168. *Pesikta Rabbati*, ed. Friedmann, p. 84a; *Pesikta de Rab Kahana*, ed. Buber, p. 61b; and the notes in both. Buber quotes from the 'Aruk a Yelammedenu variant in which Bet Shammai says that the daily sacrifices "press down" the sins "and *Yom Kippur* comes and atones." Cf. *Rosh ha-Shanah* 17a—R. Eliezer, and see R. Ḥananel, *ad loc.*

169. *Pesikta Rabbati*, ed. Friedmann, p. 84b, and the references and notes there; *Pesikta de R. Kahana, loc. cit.* R. Judan makes this statement in support of his midrash on Isa. 1:21 which teaches that no man passed the night in Jerusalem stained by a sin. צדק in the verse is taken as צדיק.

170. *Yer. Berakot* IV.1, 7b: שני פרקליטין ליום. In *Tanḥuma, Ẓaw*, par. 13, a similar idea is conveyed in the interpretation of עולה as "ascending ('*olah*) to the Holy One blessed be He and atoning for the iniquities of Israel."

171. Above, pp. 123 f. and the version in the note there. R. Joshua's statement is in general terms and hence includes the characterization of tefillah as 'abodah.

172. *Berakot* 26a.

173. *Tanḥuma*, end *Koraḥ*; *Numbers R.* XVIII.17; see also *Tanḥuma, Wayyishlaḥ*, par. 9. Cf. *Exod. R.* XXXVIII.4.

174. Thus, in the case of Ḳeri'at Shema', given above (pp. 84 f.), the *content* embodies the various concepts. See the next note.

175. Here the characteristic is that of organismic thought in general (*OT*, pp. 197 f.).

176. Lieberman, *Tos. Kif.*, I, p. 30, and the source and note there. The petition is evidently an early Palestinian version of the petition in the Seventeenth Berakah, and is retained in the Musaf of the Ashkenazi rite at the Birkat Kohanim on the Three Festivals. Being a quotation from the Tefillah, this petition, therefore, is direct proof that the word מתפללין in these statements refers to the recitation of the Tefillah and not to prayer in general.

177. *Tanḥuma, Ki Tabo*, beginning; cf. *ibid.*, ed. Buber, V, 23a (see the preceding note).

178. *Berakot* 32b.

179. *Ibid.*, 26a.

180. Above, p. 83, and the note there.

181. Above, p. 86.

182. See the discussion above, p. 87.

183. Above, pp. 67 f.

184. Above, p. 65.

185. Above, p. 81.

186. Above, p. 257, n. 113.

187. *RM*, pp. 239 ff.

188. *Ibid.*, pp. 242 ff.

189. See the discussion below, p. 132.

190. The *Shekinah* dwelt in the Tabernacle and in the First Temple (*RM*, p. 226). Cf. also *ibid.*, p. 253, nn. 130 and 131.

Notes to Chapter VI

1. For example, *Yoma* I.7; *Zebaḥim* XIV.10. Notice that the *ẓibbur* stands in contradistinction to the individual.

2. L. Finkelstein, *The Pharisees* (2d ed.; Philadelphia, 1940), pp. 282 f., 682 f.

3. *Berakot* 7b–8a; *ibid.*, 27b.

4. In M. Kadushin, *The Rabbinic Mind* (New York, 1952; to be referred to hereafter as *RM*), pp. 151 f., we discussed another concept expressive of relation, the concept of *seder*, and found it to be a cognitive concept. Being a concept of relationship, the word *ẓibbur* does not refer only to "community." It is used in the sense of a heap or a pile: a pile of *ḥameẓ* (*Pesaḥim* 10a), and in the plural, for piles of fruit, piles of coins (*Baba Meẓ'ia* II.2). These usages indicate, once more, that *ẓibbur* is a cognitive term.

5. *RM*, p. 189.

6. *Temurah* 15b: אין הצבור מתים. See the commentaries. This is somewhat qualified in *Horayot* 6a.

7. See, for example, the way *ẓibbur* is used in *Soṭah* 39b.

8. *Ta'anit* IV.2; and see C. Albeck's comments in *Commentary to Mo'ed* (Jerusalem and Tel Aviv, 1952), p. 341, and especially his long note, *ibid.*, pp. 495 f. On the problem of מעמד, see also H. Malter's remarks in his edition of *Ta'anit* (ed. major; New York, 1930), p. 120.

9. *Sifre* on Numbers, *piska'* 142, ed. Horovitz (Leipzig, 1917), p. 188.

10. *Ta'anit* IV.2.

11. *Yer. Ta'anit* IV.2, 67d, where it is also stated that מוכיחין על עצמם שהן שלוחיהן של כל ישראל.

12. *Sanhedrin* 74a (baraita). See above, p. 25 and n. 25 there.

13. *Sanhedrin* 74b, and *Dikduke Soferim ad loc.*; cf. *Sanhedrin* I.6. See also Maimonides, Hilkot *Tefillah*, VIII.5.

14. On how the acknowledgment of God is related to a sense of God's holiness, see below, p. 231 f.

15. The לחם משנה calls attention to the plain statement of the Talmud as to *be-farhesya'*, regardless of how we interpret Maimonides' view. See his gloss on Maimonides, Hilkot *Yesode ha-Torah*, V.4, *s.v.* ואם.

16. *Yer. Baba Batra* II.11, 13c: בריך אלההון דיהודאי.

17. *Yer. Baba Meẓi'a* II.5, 8c.

18. *Ibid.* As given in the text, the story is a fragment, but see the פני משה, *ad loc.*

19. *Ibid.*

20. In the version given in *Deut. R.* III.5 (end), the donkey is bought by Simeon himself, the jewel is immediately returned, and the Ishmaelite says, "Blessed is the Lord, God of Simeon b. Shaṭaḥ."

21. *Yer. Baba Meẓi'a, loc. cit.*—the story of the money found in the wheat.

22. For a general treatment of *kiddush ha-Shem* and *ḥillul ha-Shem*, see M. Kadushin, *The Theology of Seder Eliahu* (New York, 1932), pp. 64–71, and *RM*, p. 45, n. 1. See also below, p. 231 f.

23. This is not the case in regard to the public reading of the Torah, but here too, as we shall see, there is a corporate act of *kiddush ha-Shem* because of the presence of the *ẓibbur* for the public reading.

24. Albeck, *op. cit.*, Supplements, pp. 502 f., summarizes there the views of both post-talmudic authorities and of modern scholars.

25. *Tosefta Soṭah* VI.3; *Soṭah* 30b (פורס על שמע), a baraita. Cf. also *Mechilta*, ed. Horovitz and Rabin (Frankfurt am Main, 1928), p. 118, and *Mekhilta D'Rabbi Sim'on*, ed. Epstein and Melamed (Jerusalem, 1955), pp. 72 f.

26. L. Ginzberg, *A Commentary on the Palestinian Talmud* (New York, 1941), I, 251 f., and II, 179 and 201 (each individual recited Ḳeri'at Shema'). Albeck, *op. cit.*, *ad Megillah* IV.3, says that the leader recited the first half of a verse and the congregation responded with the second half; but see above, p. 84, as to the obligation upon every individual to recite the Shema' "with his own mouth." L. Finkelstein says that originally the phrase פורס את שמע meant "to promulgate the Shema' "—see his article "The Meaning of the Word פרס," *Jewish Quarterly Review*, N.S., XXXII, No. 4, 387 ff.

27. Ginzberg, *op. cit.*, I, 63.

28. *Ibid.*, I, 70 and n. 75. That is why, he says, they had the custom in Galilee לפרוס על שמע של ערבית בבה״כ קודם תפלת ערבית.

29. See *ibid.*, I, 252, on the words פסוקא and סופר.

30. *RM*, pp. 89–93, especially pp. 92 f.

31. Ginzberg, *op. cit.*, I, 74; II, 277. See also above, p. 91.

32. *Megillah* 23b, and above, p. 132 f. and n. 12 there.

33. *Megillah* 23b—כל דבר שבקדושה לא יהא פחות מעשרה. That דבר in this context means "word" can be seen from Rashi to *ibid.*, 27b, *s.v.* ליכא: שאין אומרים דבר שבקדושה פחות מעשרה. Further, the term שבקדושה must refer in this context to *ḳiddush ha-Shem* because the maxim is derived from "Ye shall not profane My holy Name, but I will be hallowed among the children of Israel" (Lev. 22:32). See also below, n. 35. In another context, דבר שבקדושה is used in connection with the honor due a *kohen*, and there it has a different meaning (see the gloss on the term by R. Asher to *Nedarim* 62a, end).

34. See Rashi on the mishnah in *Megillah* 23b, *s.v.* אין פורסין. When he includes there "the First Berakah before Ḳeri'at Shema'" he does so because of the Ḳedushah in that berakah, as R. Nissim, *ad loc.*, points out. With respect to the meaning of the word פרס itself, Rashi is of two minds, for in *Soṭah* 30b, *s.v.* כסופר, he assigns to it a different meaning, one that R. Nissim (*loc. cit.*) cites in the name of the Ge'onim. The confusion as to the meaning of the word stems of course, from the difficulty of reconciling the mishnah with its interpretation in the Gemara. We may be sure, however, that Rashi would never have stated the halakah regarding Ḳaddish, Baraku, and the Ḳedushah without having a basis for it in tradition.

35. Asheri on the mishnah in *Megillah* 23b: שיאמר הוא דבר שבקדושה הרי הוא מקדש השם בעשרה.

36. *Berakot* 21b.

37. *Masseket Soferim* X.8(7), ed. J. Muller (Leipzig, 1878), p. xviii. See his notes there, p. 150, as to the correct text. The peculiar variant of seven or six men instead of the "ten" has been explained, though, it seems, not explained away; see Tosafot to *Megillah* 23b, *s.v.* ואין, and Asheri, *loc. cit.*

38. According to the Ge'onim, פורסין את שמע refers to the berakot of the Shema', the mishnah laying down the halakah that a person may recite these berakot in behalf of others only when there are "not less than ten" (see R. Nissim, *loc. cit.*). Once more, the halakah is indubitably rooted in tradition, despite the meaning assigned to פרס.

39. Baer, *Seder 'Abodat Yisra'el* (Roedelheim, 1868), p. 76, and the notes. The sources are discussed by Finkelstein ("The Meaning of the Word פרס," p. 394, n. 23). He shows there that the two tannaitic sources, *Berakot* VII.3 and *Sifre Deut.*

306, ed. Friedmann (Vienna, 1864), 132b, take for granted that Baraku and its response are to be recited both before Ḳeri'at Shema' and before the berakah on the reading of the Torah. It seems to us that *Sifre Deut.* 306, also takes for granted that Baraku and the response of the Ḳaddish constitute *ḳiddush ha-Shem.* (On the Zimmun, which, requiring three men and not ten, is not an act of *ḳiddush ha-Shem*, see below, p. 160.) After applying the first part of Deut. 32:3 to Baraku and the second part of that verse to its response, and thus similarly to the response of the Ḳaddish, which is here broken into two parts, the passage tells of *nissim* (miracles) performed by God "in order to sanctify His great Name in the world" and, moreover, applies to these *nissim* Deut. 32:3, the very verse which the rabbis apply in the same passage to Baraku and the response of the Ḳaddish. This would indicate that not only were these corporate acts taken for granted in tannaitic times, but that they were regarded from the very beginning as *ḳiddush ha-Shem.* Notice also above, p. 135, that in those acts of *ḳiddush ha-Shem* in which the Gentiles "acknowledge" the God of the Jews, the formula attributed to them reflects the berakah formula.

40. Ginzberg, *op. cit.*, I, 174 f.

41. Above, p. 70. Ginzberg, *loc. cit.*, cites this example as well as Birkat ha-Zimmun.

42. R. Jose does not make of Birkat ha-Zimmun an exception; see below, pp. 161 f.

43. "Blessed is the Name of His glorious Kingship forever," the response after the first verse of the Shema', although both a berakah and a response and in that respect like the response in Baraku, is otherwise not at all similar to the latter. The response after the Shema' emphasizes the concept of God's kingship (see above, p. 81); it is a berakah reflecting a specific experience, that of accepting the kingship of God. Unlike the response in Baraku, it does not complete an act of *ḳiddush ha-Shem.* That is why it is said by the individual when he recites the Shema' in private.

44. Below, p. 232. R. Joseph Karo seems to have overlooked completely the response to Baraku. In the בית יוסף to *Ṭur 'Oraḥ Ḥayyim*, par. 69, he says that Baraku is a call to say a berakah, and hence that the Yoẓer must be recited, for otherwise a person will appear to be a כופר, a denier of God, since the call to say a berakah was issued and he did not respond to the call. See the דרישה ופרישה, *ad loc.* Elbogen, and others, too, take Baraku to be simply a call to prayer (see J. Elbogen, תולדות התפלה והעבודה בישראל [Tel Aviv and Berlin, 1924], p. 17).

45. Elbogen, *op. cit.*, pp. 107 f., for the details.

46. *Megillah* IV.1–2. See the Mishnah here for the occasions, at that period, when more than the minimum number of men could be called up.

47. Elbogen, *op. cit.*, p. 115. See also L. Zunz, הדרשות בישראל (Hebrew translation, Jerusalem, 1947), pp. 193 f.

48. *Megillah* IV.1, and see Elbogen, *loc. cit.*, for the sources for these berakot.

49. Elbogen, *loc. cit.*

50. *Soṭah* 39b. The rabbis emphasize the importance of responding with "Amen" to a berakah, and some even say, "Greater is he who responds with 'Amen' than he who recites the berakah" (*Berakot* 53b). The one who responds participates, as it were, in the saying of the berakah.

51. *Soṭah* 39a.

52. *Berakot* 8a.

53. See Maimonides, *Mishneh Torah*, Hilkot *Sefer Torah* X.1 for a summary of the twenty things, any one of which disqualifies a scroll for public reading.

54. *RM*, pp. 178 f.

55. See the discussion of this tradition and others in Elbogen, *op. cit.*, p. 108, and see Ginzberg, *op. cit.*, III, 145, n. 168.

56. For the text and rabbinic sources of these berakot, see Baer, *op. cit.*, p. 123, and the notes there and on p. 124; and see also above, p. 114.

57. Above, pp. 89 ff., and mark how this berakah differs.

58. See the discussion of this idea above, p. 90 f.

59. The wording of this second berakah is apparently of later origin: see Elbogen, *op. cit.*, p. 115.

60. Baer, *loc. cit.*

61. Above, n. 39, and the reference there to Finkelstein's illuminating note.

62. Rabbenu Nissim, to *Megillah* 23b, explicitly declares that it is not *dabar shebi-ḳedushah*. The Me'iri, *ad loc.*, does regard it as such, but only because of Baraku: שהרי צריך לומר ברכו.

63. A statement recited before the public reading of the Torah indicates that Baraku and its response are to be taken as constituting an act of worship in itself. The statement reads, "Ascribe, all of you, greatness unto our God, and render honor to the Torah" (Baer, *op. cit.*, p. 123 and the notes there; Singer, *The Daily Prayer Book* (London, 1890), p. 67). "Ascribe, all of you, greatness unto our God" relates to the interpretation of Deut. 32:3 in *Sifre Deut.* par. 306, ed. Friedmann, p. 132b, in which the first part of that verse, rendered as "when I proclaim the Name of the Lord," is applied to the leader saying Baraku, and the second part, "ascribe ye greatness unto our God," to the response by the congregation in the synagogue. The statement before the reading of the Torah is directed to the congregation—"all of you"—and the congregation is thus instructed to do two things: to respond to Baraku and to "render honor to the Torah" as it is being read. Our text of the statement is found in *Seder R. Amram*, ed. A. L. Frumkin (Jerusalem, 1912), I, 154a, and in *Maḥzor Vitry*, ed. S. Hurwitz (Nuremburg, 1923), p. 72, but the statement has a somewhat different form in *Masseket Soferim*, XIV.11. Linked with the public reading of the Torah is the public reading of the lection from the Prophets, the *Hafṭarah*, with its own berakot (see Elbogen, *op. cit.*, p. 117), and hence *Megillah* IV.3 names the *Hafṭarah*, too, as requiring the presence of "not less than ten."

64. D. de S. Pool, *The Kaddish* (2d ed.; New York, 1929), pp. 8 f.

65. Baer, *op. cit.*, pp. 129 f., the text and the notes.

66. *Malkut* is kingship, not kingdom, as in the response to the Shema' (see above, p. 81). If so, then it is not a matter of the establishment of His kingdom but of the recognition of His kingship. As to וימליך, notice "you have made Him King" (דאמליכתיה), *ibid.*, and the reference there.

67. The same verse is used as a proof-text in a passage of the Mekilta, telling that God will punish the wicked nations, and hence make Himself known to them (see *Mekilta*, ed. J. Z. Lauterbach [Philadelphia, 1933] I, 192 f.).

68. After Ps. 113:2. The term לעלם ולעלמי עלמיא is an emphatic term, used in the Aramaic for the Hebrew לעולם ועד. Similar terms are employed in Targum Jonathan and Targum Yerushalmi for לעולם ועד—see the material given by

Finkelstein, "The Meaning of the Word פרס" (XXXIII, No. 1), pp. 36 f., and Kimḥi on Isa. 6:3.

69. See the geonic references to the Ḳaddish as sanctifying God in J. Mann, "Changes in the Divine Service," *Hebrew Union College Annual*, IV, 267, n. 49.

70. See Tosafot to *Berakot* 3a, *s.v.* ועונין, end.

71. See *Masseket Soferim* X.8(7), ed. Muller, p. xviii, and see the notes there, pp. 150, 152.

72. See the reference in n. 34, above.

73. See the authorities quoted by C. L. Ehrenreich in his notes to his edition of *Sefer Abudraham* (Cluj [Klausenberg], 1927), p. 243.

74. There grew up various forms of the Ḳaddish, and that is true of all of them. These later forms add various Aramaic prayers after the original paragraph of the Ḳaddish. On the forms of the Ḳaddish, see Pool, *op. cit.*, pp. 79 ff.

75. The phrase used in the Mishnah is: עוברין לפני התיבה. On that expression, see Elbogen, *op. cit.*, p. 25.

76. *Rosh ha-Shanah* 34b, and Lieberman, *Tosefeth Rishonim* (Jerusalem, 1937), I, 217.

77. See Maimonides, *Mishneh Torah*, Hilkot *Tefillah*, IX. 3, and cf. *ibid.*, VIII.9 and the sources in the commentaries there.

78. In Palestine the Tefillah was recited aloud by the *individuals* at the synagogue service (see Ginzberg, *op. cit.*, III, 16 f., 20 f., and see also *ibid.*, II, 277, n. 2).

79. *Rosh ha-Shanah*, IV.5.

80. For this name see Elbogen, *op. cit.*, pp. 49 f.

81. Baer, *op. cit.*, p. 236, and Elbogen, *op. cit.*, pp. 52 f.

82. Baer, *op. cit.*, p. 89; Elbogen, *loc. cit.*, for this and other forms of the declaration.

83. *Masseket Soferim* XVI.12, ed. Muller, p. xxxi.

84. For the texts, see Baer, *op. cit.*, pp. 89 f., 218, 236 f., and his notes.

85. Elbogen, *op. cit.*, pp. 51–54.

86. *RM*, pp. 59 ff.

87. A. Bertholet, "*Das Buch Hesekiel*," in *Kurzer Hand-Kommentar zum Alten Testament*, IV, 18, who says that Isa. 6:3 had an influence on Ezek. 3:12, and notice there Luzzatto's suggestion as to the original reading.

88. *RM*, p. 253, n. 131. For *ha-Kabod* as used interchangeably with *Shekinah*, see *ibid.*, p. 74 and n. 36 there. On the concept of *gilluy Shekinah*, see *ibid.*, pp. 228 ff. Targum Jonathan on Ezek. 3:12, instead of the construct, has *Yeḳara'*, the Aramaic for *ha-Kabod*, and so also on *ibid.*, 1:28, 10:4, etc. On the term, see *RM*, pp. 332 f.

89. Mark how in this midrashic comment the rabbinic '*olam* for "world" takes the place of the biblical "the whole earth." On '*olam* as "world", see *RM*, pp. 293 f.

90. This accords with a tannaitic tradition. R. 'Aḳiba says the *ḥayyot* do not see *ha-Kabod* and R. Simeon adds that the angels, too, do not—*Sifra* on Lev. 1:1, ed. Weiss (Vienna, 1862), p. 4a (*Numbers R.* XIV, end), and see *RM*, p. 235, n. 60. Again, according to *Exod. R.* XXIII, end, He is not revealed to the *ḥayyot*, despite their carrying the Throne, and it is the *ḥayyot* who, when the time has come for them to say *shirah* (the song to God), say that they do not know in which place He is, but that in every place where He may be, "Blessed . . . from His place." See

below, p. 148, on the ministering angels. *Pirke de R. Eliezer*, IV, end, obviously builds on this earlier tradition, and not very successfully. After saying that the *ḥayyot* proclaim, "Blessed," etc., it adds that Israel "respond[s] and say[s], 'Hear, O Israel. . . .' " Does Israel respond to the angels? See the comment here by R. David Luria, p. 11b, n. 60. This Midrash cannot be dated earlier than the eighth century (see Zunz, *op. cit.*, p. 140).

91. It is hardly conceivable that the two verses would have been brought together without a connecting idea. That idea, as we have seen in the preceding note, is tannaitic, and *Exod. R.* XXIII, end, we think, presupposes the Ḳedushah. A halakah with regard to the connecting idea, *'Ofannim*, is given in *Yer. Berakot* V.3, 9c, and has as an authority R. Joshua b. Levi (see below, n. 93).

92. Above, n. 90, on the failure of the attempt to integrate "Hear, O Israel" with the praises of the angels.

93. In *Yer. Berakot* V.3, 9c, R. 'Abun states that, since the Trisagion (קדושתא) had already been recited by the *ẓibbur* (in the case of the leader who became mute at *'Ofannim*), for the new leader to continue with *'Ofannim* is like having him start with a berakah (כמי שהוא תחלת ברכה). That statement means, it seems to us, that R. 'Abun, and R. Joshua b. Levi whom he quotes, regard "Blessed be," etc. (Ezek. 3:12), as a berakah, for the words ממקום שפסק must refer to *'Ofannim*. Those words are so taken at one point by the Lebush, *'Oraḥ Ḥayyim*, 62. The codists take *'Ofannim* itself to refer to the Ḳedushah of the Yoẓer.

94. This is not true of the Ḳedushah having for its introduction the כתר formula, a formula still retained in the Ḳedushah of the Musaf of the Sephardic rite. That introductory formula, however, changes the entire character of the Ḳedushah. "The conception conveyed by it is the mystical idea that God receives his 'crown' from Israel as from the heavenly host, when they adore him by means of the Trisagion" (Ginzberg, *Geonica* [New York, 1909], I, 132). The mystics referred to here are the *yorede merkabah* (see the reference in *ibid.*, n. 1), and that mystical school was not representative of the rabbinic tradition. The concept of *gilluy Shekinah* has nothing to do with *merkabah* mysticism (*RM*, pp. 260 f.). For the versions of the כתר formula, see A. L. Gordon, *'Oẓar Ha-Tefillot*, I, pp. 728 f. The כתר formula was employed in Babylon in every 'Amidah-Ḳedushah, Ginzberg points out, and "when the other countries yielded to the influence of the Babylonian schools and introduced the קדושת מוסף, they took over the formula כתר with it" (see his *Geonica*, II, 48–49).

95. *Berakot* 21b, and *Dikduke Soferim*, *ad loc.* Without doubt, קדוש is the correct reading but the word probably refers to the Ḳedushah; see, for example, in *Masseket Soferim*, *loc. cit.*

96. See Ginzberg, *Commentary*, III, 438. But see above, n. 93.

97. According to Ginzberg (*Geonica*, I, 130 ff. and II, 48 f.), the Ḳedushah was put into the 'Amidah by the Babylonian mystics, and was accepted in Palestine only under duress. But this influence of Babylon, and of the mystics as well, must be dated as in the geonic period. We deal with the question of the influence of Babylon on the 'Amidah below, pp. 150 f. Finkelstein develops the theory that the Ḳedushah was added to the 'Amidah in Palestine in the second century during the Hadrianic persecutions, and that the Shema' was by then already part of the 'Amidah; see his article referred to above, p. 263, n. 21.

98. Elbogen, *op. cit.*, pp. 18 f. He takes the Ḳedushah here, therefore, to be a late insertion.

99. Above, p. 94.

100. On the *shirah* of the angels being the Ḳedushah, see above, n. 90, and the following note.

101. *Ḥagigah* 14a; *Ḥullin* 91b (where *shirah* is equated to the Ḳedushah), and the commentaries there; *Bereshit R.* LXXVIII.1, ed. Theodor and Albeck (Berlin, 1927), pp. 916 f., and see the references and notes there.

102. Above, p. 94.

103. *Tosefta Berakot* I.9, ed. S. Lieberman, pp. 3 f., and Lieberman, *Tosefta Ki-Fshuṭah* (New York, 1955), I, 11, especially his quotations from the ראבי"ה and his comment on them. See also Ginzberg, *Geonica*, I, 129.

104. See the section on "Rabbinic Dogma" in *RM*, pp. 340 ff.

105. Divergencies and contradictions are inherent in Haggadah because a characteristic of haggadic interpretation is the multiple interpretation of biblical texts (*RM*, pp. 104–107). They are a feature, too, of the category of significance, a category which permits a value concept—in this case, the concept of *ḳiddush ha-Shem*—to have concretizations akin to poetry, a kind of "valuational poetry" (*ibid.*, pp. 112 f., and *OT*, pp. 213–217). On "indeterminacy of belief," see *RM*, pp. 131 ff.

106. This is Ginzberg's opinion and also that of Finkelstein, *op. cit.* Ginzberg, however, maintains that the Ḳedushah in the 'Amidah is "specifically Babylonian" (Ginzberg, *loc. cit.*).

107. Above, n. 90.

108. *Ibid.*

109. *Ḥullin* 91b, a baraita. (For the range of the opinions, see above, p. 148.)

110. *Ibid.* See the following note.

111. *Ibid.*, and *Sifre* on Deut., par. 306, end, ed. Friedmann, p. 132b (*Yalḳuṭ Shime'oni*, par. 542). The Sifre here states that the ministering angels mention God's Name only after Israel has mentioned it in the Shema', and this seems to be an earlier version. *Ḥullin* 91b apparently has expanded on it. See also the version in *Bereshit R.* LXV, ed. Theodor and Albeck, pp. 738 f., and the other versions given in the notes there.

112. *Ḥullin* 91b. Interpretations by R. 'Abin, an Amora of the fourth century who spent part of his life in Babylon, reflect a change in attitude, although Israel is still favored by God as against the angels. Whereas the angels are given one *ḳedushah*, he says, Israel is given two *ḳedushot*, but only because they are exposed to the rule of the evil *yeẓer*. Again, he says, the angels in saying "Holy" three times in the Trisagion make three "crowns" for God, but He gives two of them to Israel. This interpretation has an affinity, certainly, with the כתר introduction (cf. above, n. 94), and yet here Israel is the recipient of the "crowns" made by the angels. Both these interpretations are in *Leviticus R.* XXIV.8, ed. Margulies, pp. 562 f.

113. Above, p. 145 f.

114. The longer forms of the reference to the *ḥayyot* more nearly resemble the one in the Yoẓer and hence are the earlier forms. See also Elbogen, *op. cit.*, p. 53.

115. Above, n. 93. Long before the time of R. 'Abin, the *ẓibbur* recited the verses aloud.

116. Above, p. 145.

117. See Ginzberg, *Geonica*, II, 48 and the sources given there, and 52.

118. On the berakah of the Ḳedushat ha-Shem and also on the changes in it resulting from the insertion of the Ḳedushah, see above, pp. 99 f.

119. Lieberman, *Tos. Kif.*, I, 34, *s.v.* אבא, who concludes that where there was wine (Palestine), a berakah was recited by the leader and that the people did not recite the evening service at all. Where there was no wine (Babylon), this berakah also constituted the Ḳiddush ha-Yom, and he suggests that this may have been its original function, too, where there was wine. See also Ginzberg (*Commentary*, III, 170), who holds it likely that because the people came on Friday evening to hear a scholar lecture, the Friday evening service was instituted before the evening service on weekdays, but that at first the Friday evening service consisted only of a Berakah מעין שבע; cf. *ibid.*, pp. 172 f.

120. Ginzberg, *Geonica*, II, 48 f. and 52.

121. Ginzberg, *ibid.*, and I, 132 f. For the כתר formula and *merkabah* mysticism, see above, n. 94.

122. Ginzberg, *Geonica*, I, 133.

123. "Many of the Geonim, as well as most of the old authorities down to and including Maimonides" held that the Ḳedushah in the Yoẓer, too, is *dabar shebi-ḳedushah*, and Saadia and others of the Geonim therefore formulated abridged versions of the Yoẓer for the individual's worship, versions which omitted the Ḳedushah (see Ginzberg, *Geonica*, p. 130 and the notes there). On Saadia's version, see above, p. 95, and n. 214; and see אוצר הגאונים, ed. B. Lewis (Haifa, 1928), I, Part I, 52 f., for other versions. Rashi was among those who regarded the Ḳedushah in the Yoẓer as an intrinsically corporate act (see above, p. 137 and n. 34 there). Asheri, however, holds the Ḳedushah in the Yoẓer to be part of the narrative (*ad Berakot* 21b and *Megillah* 23b) and so do the pupils of R. Jonah and others; hence the "general practice" is, according to Karo, also for the individual to say this Ḳedushah. See *Ṭur 'Oraḥ Ḥayyim*, par. 59, and *Bet Joseph*, *ad loc.* The Tosefta implies Asheri's view (see above, p. 147).

124. *Leviticus R.* XXIII.4, ed. Margulies, pp. 530 f.

125. *Ibid.* The passage interprets the verse, "as a lily among thorns" (Song of Sol. 2:2), the leader being the "lily" and the others in such a *ẓibbur* being the "thorns."

126. See *Tosefot Yom Ṭob*, *ad loc.*, on תנחומי אבלים, and see also Lieberman, *Tos. Kif.*, I, 49 and *Yer. Pesaḥim* VIII.8, 36b, cited by him there.

127. See the explanations of these terms in Albeck's commentary to the Mishnah, *ad loc.* Birkat Ḥatanim is also said, on occasion, during the seven days of the celebration (Maimonides, Hilkot *Berakot* II.9–10, and the sources in the *Kesef Mishneh* there).

128. Lieberman, *op. cit.*, pp. 49 f. and p. 50, beginning ומסתבר.

129. *Ibid.*, p. 50 and n. 62.

130. *Ibid.*, p. 50. *Ketubbot* 8b gives the texts of four berakot as constituting the series in Birkat 'Abelim, whereas *Tos. Berakot* III.23 gives three as the number. Lieberman suggests that Birkat 'Abelim may once have included a berakah relating to the mourners (the Second Berakah) similar in content to the Fourth Berakah in the Babli.

131. Lieberman, *op. cit.*, pp. 50–53. There were evidently also special forms of Birkat ha-Mazon for *Ḥatanim* (*ibid.*, p. 50, n. 60).

132. *Ibid.*, p. 52.

133. *Ibid.*

134. *Ibid.*, p. 51 and n. 67. In Birkat 'Abelim, one of the versions had as its closing formula מעורר ברחמים יצורים (a phrase referring to the resurrection of the dead) (*ibid.*).

135. *Kohelet R.* VII.7. Here among the deeds of lovingkindness performed by God—הקב"ה גומל חסדים—are Birkat Ḥatanim (Adam and Eve) and Birkat 'Abelim (Jacob). Cf. *Bereshit R.* VIII.13, ed. Theodor, p. 67. On Birkat Ḥatanim as *gemilut ḥasadim*, see *Pirḳe de R. Eliezer*, Chap. XII, end, and on Birkat 'Abelim as *gemilut ḥasadim*, see *ibid.*, Chap. XVII, end, and Luria, *ad loc.*

136. Above, p. 21.

137. *Leviticus R.* XXIII.4, ed. Margulies, pp. 530 f.

138. See, for example, *'Abot* IV.18; *Mo'ed Kaṭan* 21b (within the thirty days); *ibid.*, 28b (the comforting by the four elders); *Yer. 'Abodah Zarah* I.3, 39c (mourners of the Gentiles are to be comforted as well as those of Israel).

139. *Ketubbot* 8b.

140. The peculiarity of this berakah and the one following in Birkat 'Abelim has been noticed by W. Jawitz, מקור הברכות (Berlin, 1910), p. 15. He makes no attempt to account for it, however.

141. *Ketubbot, loc. cit.*

142. *Ibid.*, and Rashi there, *s.v.* האל הגדול.

143. Above, p. 102. On the room for differences of opinion with respect to details of this dogma, see *RM*, p. 362.

144. See discussion above, pp. 113 f.

145. On the fourth berakah of the Babli (*Ketubbot* 8b), see above, n. 130.

146. On such use of the first person plural and its implications, see above, pp. 108 ff.

147. With regard to the groom—*Berakot* 6b (R. Huna'), and with regard to the bride—*Ketubbot* 16b–17a. In Maimonides, Hilkot *'Ebel* XIV.1, gladdening the bride and the groom is among the things designated as *gemilut ḥasadim.*

148. Above, p. 152.

149. *Pirḳe de R. Eliezer*, Chap. XII, end. On the *ḥazzan* or *ḥazan*, see *OT*, p. 283, n. 291.

150. *Ketubbot* 8a; Singer, *op. cit.*, p. 299.

151. *Ketubbot* 17a.

152. Lieberman, *op. cit.*, p. 50 and n. 60.

153. On the wine here being optional, see Maimonides, Hilkot *'Ishut* X.3–4, and the *Maggid Mishneh, ad loc.*

154. *Ketubbot* 7b–8a. Singer, *loc. cit.*

155. See Ginzberg, *Commentary*, III, pp. 228 f. He quotes there a Palestinian morning berakah which begins with "Blessed art Thou, O Lord our God, King of the world, Who hast created [בראת] Adam [אדם הראשון] in his form and in his image [בדמותו ובצלמו]," and he takes בדמותו ובצלמו to refer to man's own form and image as being different from those of the rest of the creatures—an interpretation for which he adduces proof from rabbinic and medieval sources. He also calls attention to the close similarity between this Palestinian berakah and the Third Berakah of our Birkat Ḥatanim. See also the following note.

156. Rashi, to *Ketubbot*, *loc. cit.*, interprets "Who hast formed man" to refer to the groom, and והתקין לו ממנו בנין עדי עד to refer to the bride. These phrases, accordingly, relate at once both to the marriage of Adam and Eve, and to the present marriage, the occasion for the berakot. Such usage is not uncommon in rabbinic literature, and it reflects the idea of corporate personality (*RM*, p. 218 and the references there in n. 70).

157. Above, p. 153.

158. N. 155 above.

159. Above, p. 153.

160. Rashi, *loc. cit.*

161. Above, n. 156, and the reference there to the idea of corporate personality.

162. Above, p. 155, and the reference in n. 144 there.

163. The remaining three berakot given in *Ketubbot* 8a are also to be accounted for. The Second Berakah, as its very wording indicates, is an alternative to the Third. According to R. Ḥananel (cited by Tosafot, *ibid.*, *s.v.* שהכל), the Second Berakah was sometimes not said at all, as reported in the Gemara (*loc. cit.*). Rashi accounts for the Sixth Berakah, and for its having both an opening and a closing formula, by pointing to its usage, for it is the only berakah said on most of the days when no new guest is present. He takes the First Berakah to refer to the assembled folk, a gathering engaged in an act of *gemilut ḥasadim*, and he associates the berakah with the haggadah which tells of the marriage of Adam and of God's performance of such an act of *gemilut ḥasadim* on that occasion.

164. Above, p. 112 f, where the moral connotation of the concept of man is discussed.

165. Above, n. 135.

166. When the act is neither a corporate act of worship nor an act of martyrdom, ethical concepts are concretized in an act of *ḳiddush ha-Shem*. See above, pp. 133 f., where we discuss such an aspect. On the interweaving of other concepts with that of *ḳiddush ha-Shem*, see the examples in *Sifre Deut.*, par. 306, ed. Friedmann, p. 132b (the concept of *nes*) and *TE*, pp. 67 ff.

167. *Berakot* VII.1.

168. Zimmun itself refers to the manner in which Birkat ha-Mazon is said on these occasions, one of the men reciting it and the rest responding, "Amen" (Lieberman, *Tos. Kif.*, I, 100, and references there).

169. *Berakot* 49b–50a (Mishnah and Gemara); and see Maimonides, Hilkot *Berakot* V.2.

170. *Berakot* 46b and Tosafot, *s.v.* להיכן.

171. *Tos. Berakot* VI.1, ed. Lieberman, p. 32, and the sources referred to there. See also Lieberman, *Tos. Kif.*, I, *loc. cit.*

172. *Berakot* 46a, and see Maimonides, *loc. cit.* Notice, too, the expression by R. Jose in *Berakot* VII.3—הן מברכין. Cf., also, Ginzberg, *Commentary*, I, pp. 174 f.

173. Above, p. 138.

174. In *Sifre Deut.*, par. 306, ed. Friedmann, p. 132b, Deut. 32:3 is applied both to Baraku and to Zimmun. If that verse, which is to be rendered in this connection, "When I proclaim the Name of the Lord, ascribe ye greatness to our God," is to relate not only to Baraku but also to Zimmun, then the call in Zimmun, too, must proclaim "the Name of the Lord." R. 'Aḳiba in *Berakot* VII.3 holds that when ten

or more are present, the call in Zimmun is the same as in Baraku, according to the authorities cited in הערות, *ad loc.*, ed. Herzog (Jerusalem, 1945), p. 28a. See also Albeck in his *Commentary to Zera'im*, pp. 336 f. Another verse, Ps. 34:4 is also applied to Birkat ha-Zimmun. See the baraita in *Berakot* 48b (Rabbi), and cf. *ibid.*, 45a, where both verses are given. On Zimmun as also referring to Birkat ha-Zimmun, see Rashi on the mishnah, *ibid.*, *s.v.* שלשה שאכלו, and on the Gemara, *ibid.*, *s.v.* מה״מ.

175. Above, pp. 138 f.

176. *Berakot* VII.3, and Maimonides, *loc. cit.*, V.4.

177. On *'Elohenu*, our God, as a term for God, see *RM*, p. 196, and the following discussion there.

178. *Megillah* 23b; *Berakot* 45b: כיון דבעי לאדכורי שם שמים. *Derek ereẓ* is a decided factor in other acts of worship as well. For example, in the Tefillah, a person must not make petition for "his needs" in the first three berakot, but these berakot must be of praise only, and the reason for that is *derek ereẓ* (*Berakot* 34a). On this phase of *derek ereẓ*, that of good manners, see above, p. 41 f., p. 47.

179. Listed in *Megillah* IV.3 among the matters requiring "not less than ten" are "the standing up and sitting down" of the group returning from a burial, and the valuation of immovable property dedicated to the Sanctuary, and these are not acts of worship at all.

180. *Berakot* 50a—R. Joseph.

181. According to Epstein, the words אחד עשרה ואחד עשר רבוא in *Berakot* VII.3 were added later, and R. Joseph's statement originally was similar in style to the one by R. Joḥanan in the Yerushalmi (see the next note): מבוא לנוסח המשנה, pp. 430 f. Albeck, *loc. cit.*, holds, on the contrary, that these words represent an ancient halakah, and that the mishnah, therefore, contains three opinions: that of the *Ḥakamim*, that of R. Jose, and that of R. 'Aḳiba. See also above, n. 174.

182. *Yer. Berakot* VII.3, 11c—R. Joḥanan.

183. *Berakot* VII.3.

184. *Yer. Berakot, loc. cit.* The question is asked here of how the rabbis interpret Ps. 68:27, the verse used by R. Jose in *Berakot* VII.3 as support for his view, and two answers are given—one anonymous and one by R. Ḥanina b. 'Abbahu. The anonymous answer is that the word "assemblies," in the plural, in that verse does not refer, as R. Jose would have it, to the sizes (plural) of the assemblies, but that it is to be understood in a distributive sense, each assembly (singular) being an entity in itself: a *ẓibbur*. R. Ḥanina says that the *ketib* is במקהלת (singular) and therefore the word has reference to an assembly (a *ẓibbur*). In our present text, incidentally, there is no *ketib* for that word. Between this statement and the one in which the view of the *Ḥakamim* is distinguished from that of R. Jose is another passage. That passage deals with different verses as interpreted by different authorities, the interpretations teaching that *'edah*, a congregation, consists of ten, and that the phrase "children of Israel" refers to ten. They are the same verses as are used in the Babli (see above, p. 137, and the notes there) in order to elucidate the concept of *ḳiddush ha-Shem*. Here, however, there is no reference to that concept, and the passage is placed here in order to emphasize that ten are an *'edah*, a *ẓibbur*. The passage is used in *Yer. Megillah* IV.4, 75b, apparently with reference to *kiddush ha-Shem*, though the corresponding section in the Babli is more pointed, and once more in *Yer. Sanhedrin* I.6, 19c, where it is connected with the mishnah being interpreted.

185. On the importance of "Amen", see above, n. 50.

186. Above, n. 168.

187. Above, p. 143, n. 77; also the berakot of the Shema'.

Notes to Chapter VII

1. Ps. 63:3. The Jewish Publication Society version renders it "so have I looked for Thee."

2. *Ibid.*, 17:15, J.P.S. version. בהקיץ, however, may mean "in the waking state."

3. *Ibid.*, 42:3. The Massoretic reading is difficult and וְאֵרָאֶה here is supported by rabbinic interpretations of the very similar phrase in Exod. 23:17; see M. Kadushin, *The Rabbinic Mind* (New York, 1952), p. 240. (To be referred to hereafter as *RM.*) See also the *Commentary on Psalms*, H. P. Chajes (Kiev, 1908), p. 94.

4. See the lengthy discussion of this concept in *RM*, pp. 228 ff.

5. Above, p. 272, n. 190, and the references there.

6. *Yoma* 9b–10a; *ibid.*, 21b (baraita).

7. *RM*, p. 253, n. 131, and Ginzberg, *A Commentary on the Palestinian Talmud* (New York, 1941), III, 395–7.

8. We have discussed details of this controversy in *RM*, pp. 245–49.

9. Above, p. 127, and n. 176 there.

10. The *Ḥakamim* of the Mishnah reject that assumption (see above, p. 129).

11. Above, Chap. V, sec. D.

12. *RM*, p. 238, and see the entire discussion there.

13. See the discussion referred to in the preceding note.

14. Above, Chap. V, secs. C.–D.

15. *Berakot* IV.5, and *ibid.*, 30a: the baraita on "directing the heart" toward the Land of Israel, Jerusalem, and so on. See the Pupils of R. Jonah, *ad loc.*

16. See *Berakot* IV.6, and *Tos. Berakot* III.14–16, ed. S. Lieberman (New York, 1955), pp. 15 f., and see also the discussion of the various sources by Lieberman, *Tosefta Ki-Fshuṭah* (New York, 1955), I, 43 f. The matters involved there are discussed below, p. 192.

17. *Berakot* 34a, bottom—a baraita. On the difference in the practices of Palestine and Babylon, see Ginzberg, *op. cit.*, I, 181 f.

18. "We acknowledge Thee" is a phrase linked in rabbinic literature with the acceptance of God's kingship (see above, p. 90, and on the phrase itself, p. 260, n. 178). A late midrash finds support in Gen. 24:28 for the bowing at these two berakot; see Ginzberg, *loc. cit.*, and see also the Pupils of R. Jonah, *ad loc.*

19. *Berakot* 34a–b. "The greater he is, the more he must humble and lower himself": Rashi, *ad loc.*, *s.v.* כהן גדול.

20. *Yoma* 53b. To your left, "which is the right of the Holy One Blessed be He" (Raba'). See *Ṭur 'Oraḥ Ḥayyim*, par. 123.

21. *Sanhedrin* 22a.

22. Rashi to *Yoma* 53b, *s.v.* לשמאל.

23. *Yer. Berakot* IX.1, 13a.

24. *Tos. Berakot* III.6, ed. Lieberman, p. 12, and see his *Tos. Kif.* I, 30, and the sources there.

25. For the sources and references, see *RM*, p. 208, n. 21, and *ibid.*, p. 209, n. 24. "Blessed art Thou, O Lord" is itself taken from Ps. 119:12

26. *RM*, pp. 226 f. The name *Shekinah* is sometimes used in contexts of God's nearness only, and sometimes in contexts of *gilluy Shekinah*. See *ibid.*, pp. 253 f., and n. 131 on p. 253.

27. F. von Hügel, *The Mystical Element in Religion* (2d ed.; New York, 1923), II, 283 f. Although describing a type of mysticism which is certainly not normal mysticism, Baron von Hügel emphatically denies that there can be "a specifically distinct, self-sufficing, purely mystical mode of apprehending Reality." See the discussion in *OT*, pp. 237 ff.

28. Above, pp. 67 f.

29. For a more extensive treatment of this topic, in which a number of other concepts are given as well, see "Organismic Development" in *RM*, pp. 288 ff.

30. Above, pp. 78 ff.

31. Above, pp. 82 f.

32. Above, p. 80, where a similar interpretation of Lev. 18:2 is also quoted, but here God reminds them that they had accepted His kingship at Sinai.

33. The first verse in the Shema' is interpreted as a call by God and a response to Him by Israel—see above, p. 86.

34. Above, p. 87.

35. On other examples of similar differences between rabbinic and biblical usage of the same conceptual terms, see above, pp. 27 f.

36. Above, p. 63, and the references there.

37. Above, p. 120.

38. On this entire matter, see above, pp. 107 ff.

39. There are several illustrative examples in the discussion cited in the preceding note. An entire list of such examples is furnished by the berakot on awakening and arising in the morning, and given in *Berakot* 60b. On opening his eyes, a person is to say, "Blessed . . . Who openest the eyes of the blind"; on sitting up, "Blessed . . . Who loosest them that are bound"; on dressing, "Who clothest the naked"; and so on. In most of these berakot, the awareness of the self is conceptualized through the concept of man, and in several, through the concept of Israel. When, however, an individual does not perform one of these acts—e.g., if he has to remain in bed and cannot get dressed—he is not to say the berakah referring to the act. See Tosafot to *Berakot* 60b, *s.v.* כי פרים, and Maimonides, Hilkot *Tefillah*, VII.7–8, which are based on *Megillah* 24b. Retention of self-identity does not permit saying a berakah which cannot refer to the individual qua individual.

40. Above, p. 107.

41. On the topic of this paragraph, see above, pp. 113–115.

42. Above, p. 158 f.

43. *Derek ereẓ* is a factor in several acts of worship; see above, p. 160 and n. 178 there.

Humility is expressed in the obeisances during the Tefillah (above, p. 165 f. and n. 19 there).

44. Above, Chap. VI, sec. E., "Berakot as *Gemilut Ḥasadim.*"

45. On these emphatic trends, see above, Chap. II, sec. C., "The Role of Emphasis."

46. See the preceding note.

47. We called attention to that especially when we discussed the berakah on bread, the First Berakah of the Birkat ha-Mazon, and a number of the berakot in the Tefillah. See also p. 285, n. 39.

48. Yehezkel Kaufmann, *Toledot ha-'Emunah ha-Yisre'elit* (Tel Aviv, 1947), III, 71.

49. *Ibid.*, p. 125.

50. *Ibid.*, p. 193.

51. *Ibid.*, p. 282. On Jeremiah, and his particular teaching, see *ibid.*, pp. 443 f.

52. *Ibid.*, pp. 71 f.

53. *Ibid.*, pp. 116 f.

54. *Ibid.*, p. 194.

55. *Ibid.*, pp. 444 f. Kaufmann calls attention to the cultic aspect of the covenant, which made the breaking of the covenant all the more sinful in the eyes of Jeremiah (Jer. 34:15, 18); and to Jeremiah's telling the people to pray (*ibid.*, 29:7, 12).

56. For this paragraph, see Kaufmann, *op. cit.*, I, pp. 603 ff. For a comprehensive treatment, see *ibid.*, pp. 396–416.

57. A criticism leveled against Kaufmann is that he argues, as in this case, from "negative evidence." That kind of criticism harbors an underlying scientific fallacy, as Kroeber indicates. "It cannot be too much emphasized that for probability findings to be worth anything they must be in terms of the total situation. . . . Negative evidence is particularly likely to be overlooked, both by the biased and by the inexperienced. We are so constituted, as primates, that occurrences impress us more than absences. The business of science is to train us in being critical enough to see both positive and negative evidence" (A. L. Kroeber, *Anthropology* [New York, 1948], p. 552).

58. For this paragraph, see Kaufmann, *op. cit.*, III, pp. 79–81, 445, 77.

59. The biblical phrase דרך כל הארץ (Gen. 19:31; I Kings 2:2) is hardly to be taken as the biblical antecedent of the rabbinic concept, despite the similarity of the terms. At most, the biblical phrase points to what we have called the first phase of *derek ereẓ*, the phase referring to phenomena or modes of behavior common to all of mankind, and that is the only phase in which *derek ereẓ* is not a subconcept of Torah (see above, pp. 51 f.). On instances where the rabbinic term has wider and sometimes even different connotations than a similar term or phrase in the Bible, see *RM*, pp. 290–96. Notice there, too, how the rabbinic concept of *ger* has its antecedents in the ideas of the prophets.

60. *OT*, pp. 142 f.

61. *Ibid.*, pp. 109–10, and n. 72.

62. In that respect, the berakot and the other acts of worship have some kinship with the Haggadah, for the Haggadah, too, helps to keep the value concepts vivid, as we have indicated in *RM*, p. 84. The acts of worship, however, are living experience, and so are more effective than Haggadah which is, after all, not experience.

63. *RM*, pp. 315 f.

64. *Ibid.* A striking statement is the passage in *Lev. R.* XXII.8, telling that the sacrifices were given Israel in order to wean them away from idolatry. See *ibid.*, ed. Margulies, pp. 517 f., and the note there. As he indicates, this view has much in common with that of Maimonides, *Guide for the Perplexed*, III, Chaps. 32 and 46. Abarbanel (*Commentary to the Pentateuch*, Introd. to Leviticus), in support of Maimonides' view, points especially to this passage in *Lev. R.*, and he also quotes other rabbinic passages which say that God desires study of Torah rather than sacrifices.

65. M. Kadushin, *The Theology of Seder Eliahu* (New York, 1952), pp. 129 f.

66. *Ibid.*

67. Nonsacrificial worship, in its various forms, was developed after the period of the prophets. From the prophets' attitude toward prayer and fasting as means of supplication, no sound conclusion can be drawn as to what their attitude might have been toward the various forms of nonsacrificial worship. To be sure, the prophets negate prayer and fast-days in the same way as they negate the sacrifices (see Kaufmann, *op. cit.*, III, p. 72; and see also *ibid.*, IV, pp. 141 f., 145 f., and especially n. 129). But prayer, though obviously a religious act and one that is found even among primitive peoples, is not *'abodah*, or worship in the rabbinic sense, and neither is fasting. Prayer and fasting are forms of supplication, cries for help, and they are not inherently interrelated with the ethical sphere.

68. The difference between descriptive or analytic terms and organismic value concepts is discussed in *OT*, pp. 250 f. See also *RM*, p. 8.

69. Evelyn Underhill, *Mysticism* (Meridian ed., New York, 1957), p. 81.

70. *Ibid.*, pp. 127 ff., 168 ff.

71. *Ibid.*, p. 170.

72. *Ibid.*, p. 304.

73. *Ibid.*, p. 170.

74. *Ibid.*, p. 417, quoting Delacroix.

75. *Ibid.*, p. 304.

76. *Ibid.*, pp. 169, 201.

77. *Ibid.*, pp. 399, 416. In another work, Miss Underhill describes the ideal of monasticism as being not only "separation from the world," but as the "total oblation of personality" and as "death to self" (*Worship* [New York, 1957], p. 252).

78. *RM*, p. 81.

79. There are even a few instances of religious experience where the larger self is not called forth at all; see above, p. 107.

80. See the discussion in *RM*, pp. 167 f. A degree of asceticism is advocated by the rabbis as a requisite to the study of Torah, but not out of disdain for the flesh; see *OT*, pp. 53 ff.

81. These theories go back to W. Robertson-Smith's interpretation of "peace-offerings," *shelamim*: see his *The Religion of the Semites* (Meridian ed., New York, 1956), pp. 236 ff., especially pp. 239 f., and see also his summary with regard to "sacramental communion," *ibid.*, pp. 439 f.

82. Kaufmann, *op. cit.*, I, 563 ff.

83. *Ibid.*

84. F. M. Cornford, *From Religion to Philosophy* (New York, 1957), p. 112, and see the entire discussion there; cf. Underhill, *Mysticism*, p. 24, n. 1.

85. The idea of communion with God, as expressed in the term *deveḳut*, is a basic idea in Kabbalah and Ḥasidism. "In general Hebrew usage, *Devekuth* only means attachment or devoutness, but, since the thirteenth century, it has been used by the mystics in the sense of close and most intimate communion with God. Whereas in Catholic mysticism, 'Communion' was not the last step on the mystical way . . . in Kabbalism it is the last grade of ascent to God. It is not union, because union with God is denied to man even in that mystical upsurge of the soul, according to Kabbalistic theology. But it comes as near to union as a mystical interpretation of Judaism would allow. . . ." G. G. Scholem, "*Devekuth*, or Communion with God," *Review of Religion*, XIV, No. 2 (January, 1950), 115. See also Scholem's treatment of the idea (*ibid.*, pp.134–39), and in *Major Trends in Jewish Mysticism* (Jerusalem, 1941), p. 121, and *Reshit ha-Kabbalah* (Jerusalem and Tel Aviv, 1948), pp. 114 f. and 142 f. Cf. I. Tishby's view regarding *deveḳut* and *unio mystica* in *Mishnat ha-Zohar*, II (Jerusalem, 1961), 289, n. 69. Tishby also points out that *deveḳut* is definitely a nonrabbinic idea, and he quotes *Ketubbot* 111b and *Soṭah* 14a to prove that the rabbis deny the very possibility of any such phenomenon (*op. cit.*, p. 284 f.).

86. On the communicable and noncommunicable factors in the acceptance of *malkut Shamayim*, see above, p. 169.

87. Underhill, *Mysticism*, p. 99.

88. *Ibid.*, p. 100.

89. *Ibid.*, pp. 28, 101.

90. In *Ta'anit* 11a–b (Malter, ed. minor, pp. 77 f.; ed. major, p. 40), R. Eleazar is quoted as saying, "One should always regard oneself as if the Holy One were within him, for it is said, 'The Holy One in the midst of thee' [Hosea 11:9]." This statement does not teach that God is immanent in man. In the first place, the idea is qualified by the important word כאלו—"as if" or "as though." Notice how this word makes of the idea which it qualifies merely a figure of speech (above, p. 166; and see also p. 240, n. 29). Second, the statement is incidental to the point made in the passage, and this point is simply that man must not afflict himself (see Malter, ed. minor, p. 78, n. 185). On *Shekinah* as not standing for immanence, see *RM*, pp. 255 ff. and 221 f.

91. Underhill, *Mysticism*, p. 414.

92. W. F. Albright, *From the Stone Age to Christianity* (Baltimore, 1940), p. 167.

93. On the difference between philosophic interpretation and rabbinic interpretation, see *RM*, pp. 98–107.

94. Albright, *op. cit.*, p. 137, giving a somewhat different interpretation. There is no evidence, it seems to us, that the text contains an idea which is "close to monotheism." On the contrary, the phrase, "Honor [the] god in his way" implies that the god is to be honored in accordance with his particular mode of worship. This idea is in alignment, it seems to us, with the quotation in H. Frankfort, *Ancient Egyptian Religion* (2d ed.; New York, 1961), p. 24: "And so the gods entered into their bodies of every kind of wood, of every kind of stone, of every kind of clay, of every kind of thing which grows upon him (Ptah), in which they have taken form." Frankfort's view, incidentally, has some points in common with our organismic view. He speaks of "a multiplicity of approaches" and of "a multiplicity of

answers" (pp. 18 f.) and also of "several separate avenues of approach" (pp. 91 f., 121 f.). We have indicated, similarly, that the same situation may be interpreted at one time by one value concept and at another time by a different one. The question is whether the Egyptian "approaches" and "answers" are true concepts; that is, whether they are values crystallized in abstract, general terms.

95. W. Warde Fowler, *The Religious Experience of the Roman People* (London, 1911), p. 238. Fowler believes that "a man or men inspired by a new national feeling" were those who "took advantage of the uncompleted Etruscan temple . . . to settle there a new Jupiter, better and greater than any other, to whom his people would be for ever grateful, and in whom they would for ever put their trust" (*ibid.*, p. 239). Similarly, there were a number of Junos, each Juno—meaning, each local image of Juno—being designated in a special manner (*ibid.*, p. 318 and p. 332, n. 17).

96. Albright, *op. cit.*, p. 161.

97. *Ibid.*

98. *Ibid.*, p. 164 f. At the other extreme is the view that regards a particular statue not merely as a manifestation of the deity but as the deity itself. A scene on a lekythos, or oil jar, "represents Cassandra flying from Ajax and taking refuge at the xoanon [statue of the goddess] of Athene," and a detail in that scene shows that Athene, "statue though she be, is apparently about to move to the rescue" and "has sent as her advance guard her sacred animal, a great snake" (Jane Harrison, *Prolegomena to the Study of Greek Religion* [4th ed.; New York, 1957], p. 305).

99. Albright, *op. cit.*, p. 167.

100. *'Abodah Zarah* 54b: the mishnah and the baraita, where the correct reading in both, changed by the censor, is עבודה זרה. See also *Rosh ha-Shanah* 31a.

101. In the tractate *'Abodah Zarah.*

102. Above, p. 79. The first verse of the Shema' is associated with the martyrdom of R. 'Aḳiba precisely because it negates emperor-worship. "Iron combs were applied to prevent R. 'Aḳiba from his recitation." See *RM*, p. 131, note, which refers to an article by Lieberman. In *Giṭṭin* 57b, the same verse is quoted by one of the martyr-brothers as a negation of idolatry. On the versions of the legend, see Gerson D. Cohen, מעשה חנה ושבעת בניה בספרות העברית, offprint from ספר היובל לכבוד מרדכי מנחם קפלן (New York, 1953). He demonstrates that the questions asked by the "king" and the answers given by the brothers, which are to be found only in the rabbinic versions, reflect Roman procedures and martyrs' responses in rabbinic times.

103. Maimonides, *Mishneh Torah*, Hilkot *Ḳeri'at Shema'* I.2, ed. Hyamson (New York, 1949), p. 94a.

104. See the *Kesef Mishneh* and the other commentaries, *ad loc.*

105. See the discussion above, p. 79.

106. A striking instance is to be found in the long statement by R. Isaiah di Trani the Younger, quoted in שלטי הגבורים to Alfasi, *'Abodah Zarah* 17b. The study of philosophy may lead to heresy, he states there, and he declares that the main aim of the Torah is to teach fear of God and proper conduct. Thus, Moses commanded us he continues, "Hear, O Israel, the Lord our God, the Lord is One." Moses did not say that we are to arrive at knowledge of God through philosophy, "but to believe concerning the Unity in accordance with tradition [אלא להאמין היחוד ע״פ שמועה וע״פ קבלה]." (R. Isaiah relates שמועה, tradition, to שמע.) Opposed as he was to philosophy,

R. Isaiah nevertheless interprets the Shema' to refer to the unity of God. On the other hand, he obviously also understands it "in accordance with tradition," and this can only mean as an acknowledgment of God's kingship. (This point is entirely missed by modern writers referring to R. Isaiah's statement, for they "correct" the text and assume that להאמין היחוד ought to read להאמין ביחוד. See now the text in מעט דבש, הוצאת ד. ששון [Oxford, 1928], p. 47, a book called to my attention by Dr. Saul Lieberman.)

107. Above, p. 90.

108. So Singer, *Prayer Book* (London, 1890), p. 40; others have similar renderings. See also I. Abrahams, *A Companion to the Authorized Daily Prayer Book* (2d ed.; London, 1922), p. xlix.

109. On auxiliary ideas, see *RM*, pp. 52 ff., 220 ff.

110. *Ibid.*, pp. 221 f.

111. Above, pp. 79 and 83.

112. Above, p. 81.

113. Above, p. 83.

114. P. 82 f. and n. 125 there.

115. Above, p. 79 and cf. Ginzberg, *Commentary*, I, 228 (the remark in parentheses).

116. *Tos. Berakot* III.4, ed. Lieberman, p. 12: המתפלל צריך שיכוין את לבו. The parallel in *Berakot* 31a adds לשמים, but this word is not found in the MSS and in the quotations by medieval authorities; see Lieberman, *Tos. Kif.*, I, 28, bottom.

117. *Berakot* 30b—R. Eleazar. A related statement by the same teacher is in *Yer. Berakot* II.4, 5a.

118. *'Erubin* 65a—Rab. R. Ḥanina did not say the Tefillah on a day when he was upset (*ibid.*).

119. *Berakot* 30b.

120. Maimonides, Hilkot *Tefillah*, IV.15 (X.1), and see the *Kesef Mishneh*, *ad loc.*, and his reference to R. Asher.

121. Above, p. 83.

122. *Berakot* 34b, a baraita. "In one" is taken to refer to the First Berakah, 'Abot.

123. *Berakot* III.1.

124. Ginzberg, *Commentary*, II, 34 f. (where he cites *Deut. R.* IX.1), and see also *ibid.*, pp. 54 f.

125. *Berakot* II.4 and Rashi to *ibid.*, 16a, *s.v.* מה שאינן. As to the rule with respect to Ḳeri'at Shema' in this mishnah, see Bertinoro, *ad loc.* On the characterization of the Tefillah as *raḥame*, see above, p. 106.

126. Above, p. 119.

127. Above. See also *Berakot* 29b and Rashi, *ibid.*, *s.v.* מי.

128. *Yer. Berakot* V.1, 9a: שהיה לבי מתכוין בתפילה; *Tos.*, *ibid.*, III.20, ed. Lieberman, p. 17, and the parallels and sources given there; and see also *Tos. Kif.*, I, 46 f.

129. *Berakot* 24b. This does not apply to a person in a congregation, for he might disturb others.

130. *Berakot* VI.1.

131. *Ibid.*, 40a.

132. *Berakot* VI.1. R. Judah does not state here his opinion regarding the berakah on fruits of the earth in general (see Lieberman, *Tos. Kif.*, I, 59).

133. *Tos. Berakot* IV.4, ed. Lieberman, p. 19, and *Tos. Kif.*, *loc. cit.*, *s.v.* ועל ירקות and *s.v.* פרי. See also *ibid.*, *s.v.* אדמה. Lieberman suggests that R. Judah may be disagreeing in this baraita with the statement on שהכל in *Berakot* VI.2; in that case, the latter would refer only to the fruit of trees and the fruits of the earth mentioned in that mishnah and not to "everything," wine and bread included, as the Babli (*Berakot* 12a) assumes, for R. Judah's berakah reads, "Who, by His word, causest the earth to produce."

134. אוצר הגאונים *Berakot*, Part II, p. 75. Nevertheless, as the Gaon goes on to say, a berakah is valid if at least the close refers to the occasion, and he cites *Berakot* 12a, where not only berakot on liquids are mentioned, but also the First Berakah of the Shema'.

135. *Yebamot* 52b; cf. *Baba Batra'* 53b, 54a.

136. *Tos. Ḳiddushin* I.3; cf. *Ḳiddushin* 2b. (Cohabitation was one of the three forms of *ḳiddushin* or betrothal [*Ḳiddushin* I.1; *'Eduyyot* IV.7], but was discouraged by the rabbis.)

137. *Yebamot* 102b, 106a; *Ketubbot* 74a; *Tos. Yebamot* XII.13. This and the two preceding examples are cited by Michael Higger, *Intention in Talmudic Law* (doctoral dissertation) (New York, 1927), pp. 29 ff.

138. *Giṭṭin* III.1; IV.2. Tosafot, *ibid.*, 22b, *s.v.* והאי לאו, indicates how in some particulars divorce and *ḥaliẓah* differ with respect to *kawwanah*.

139. For example, *Nedarim* III.7–9; VIII.6.

140. Higger, *op. cit.*, pp. 19–21.

141. See Rashi *ad Zebuḥim* 41b, *s.v.* כגון שנתן; *ad Menaḥot* 2b, *s.v.* אבל מחשבה. With regard to *piggul* (a sacrifice to be rejected because of a wrong intention in the mind of the officiating priest), see Tosafot *ad Baba Meẓi'a* 43b, *s.v.* החושב, and the references there.

142. An instance of *maḥashabah* is the declaration of the intention to misappropriate a trust (see Tosafot, *Baba Meẓi'a*, and Rashi, *ad loc.* See also *Tosefot Yom Ṭob* to *Baba Meẓi'a* III.12, *s.v.* החושב.

143. *Berakot* V.1: כדי שיכונו את לבם למקום. The mishnah in the Gemara has לאביהם שבשמים. The reference to God, למקום, is not found in the mishnah of the Yerushalmi as given in the printed editions, but the Cambridge MS (ed. Lowe) does have it. See R. Jonah who, in his commentary on Alfasi *ad loc.*, points out that this passage does not refer to *kawwanah* in the saying of the Tefillah.

144. Above, p. 165.

145. As can be seen, too, from the discussion by Lieberman, *Tos. Kif.*, I, 43, *s.v.* סומה, and from the sources quoted there.

146. Above, pp. 165 f.

147. *Tos. Berakot* III.14, ed. Lieberman, p. 15, and the parallels there.

148. כל זמן שהיו ישראל מסתכלים כלפי מעלה ומשעבדין את לבם לאביהם שבשמים.

149. On other tannaitic interpretations of the same passages, see the discussion in *RM*, p. 347 n. 32.

150. Bertinoro on *Rosh ha-Shanah* III.8. See also Edeles' remarks, *ad loc.*

151. *Yebamot* 105b, and see Lieberman, *Tos. Kif.*, *lot. cit.*

152. Witness the term שעבוד מלכיות, "subjection to the empires"—*Berakot* 12b; *ibid.*, 34b, and elsewhere.

153. *Mechilta*, ed. Horovitz and Rabin (Frankfurt am Main, 1928), p. 176, and the parallels and variants referred to in the notes there and in the note on line 12, p. 173.

154. See also translation and discussion of this mishnah in Judah Goldin, *The Living Talmud* (New York, 1957), pp. 30 f.

155. *Tos. Rosh ha-Shanah* III (II).6, ed. Zuckermandel and Lieberman (Jerusalem, 1937), p. 212.

156. אין הכל הולך אלא אחר כוונת הלב.

157. *Tos. Berakot* III.4, ed. Lieberman, p. 12, and the sources there, and see *Tos. Kif.*, I, 29, top. See also above, p. 188.

158. *Menaḥot* XIII.11, and *ibid.*, 110a, where the baraita clearly indicates that the statement refers to having the proper intention; cf. Rashi, *s.v.* לבעל הדין. Cf. also *Zebaḥim* IV.6, ed. Albeck (Jerusalem and Tel Aviv, 1956), p. 22, and the notes there and on p. 355.

159. *Berakot* 5b.

160. *Ibid.*, 17a, and see Rashi, *ad loc.*

161. Above, p. 190.

162. Above, p. 86.

163. Above, p. 69.

164. Above, p. 187.

165. Above, p. 187.

166. *Yer. Berakot* II.4, 5a.

167. *Ibid.*, according to the reading in a Genizah MS (see Ginzberg, *Commentary*, I, 346).

168. *Ibid.*

169. *Ibid.*, II.1, 4a bottom, and Ginzberg, *op. cit.*, I, 227 f.

170. There are several statements on *kawwanah* in the Yerushalmi which only appear to be negative but which are not so in fact. R. Jose's statement in *Yer. Shabbat* I.5, 3a (*ibid.*, *Berakot* I.5, 3b) is not to be taken as though Ḳeri'at Shema' does not require *kawwanah* at all for, as the sequel shows, the first three verses do require *kawwanah* (see Ginzberg, *op. cit.*, I, 125, 128). Similar "negative" statements in *Yer. Berakot* II.5, 5a bottom on *kawwanah* in Ḳeri'at Shema' and the saying of the Tefillah relate to *Parah* VII.9, the question being whether *kawwanah* in these acts of worship constitutes, technically, "diversion of attention"; see Ginzberg, *op. cit.*, I, 356–358.

171. *Berakot* 13a; *Pesaḥim* 114b; cf. *'Erubin* 95b: מצות צריכות כוונה.

172. *Rosh ha-Shanah* 28b; *Pesaḥim*, *loc. cit.*: מצות אין צריכות כוונה.

173. See *Rosh ha-Shanah* 28b.

174. *Ibid.*

175. See *Maggid Mishneh* to Maimonides, Hilkot *Shofar*, II.4, *s.v.* המתעסק, where he distinguishes between *mit'assek* (to do something without practical purpose) according to the proponents of the positive principle and *mit'assek* according to the proponents of the negative principle.

176. *Berakot* 13a (*Rosh ha-Shanah* 28b), and above, p. 83 and n. 127 there.

177. According to an interpretation of the Pupils of R. Jonah to *Berakot* 12a, *s.v.* אמנם, the proponents of the negative principle hold that in the case of deeds as, for example, the lifting of the *lulab*, the deed serves in place of *kawwanah*, but that when the miẓwah consists solely of an oral act, *kawwanah* is required. R. Joel Sirkis rightly points out in a marginal note, however, that the reading of the Shema' is an oral act and yet that it does not require *kawwanah* according to the proponents of the negative principle. A. J. Heschel, in *God in Search of Man* (Philadelphia, 1956), pp. 317 f., n. 3, refers to the interpretation of the Pupils of R. Jonah just cited. In his view, the issue between the proponents of the two opposing principles is "whether all religious acts should be regarded as analogous to the sacrifice or as analogous to the Deed of Divorce." In the case of sacrifices, "no intention is considered as if there were proper intention," whereas in the case of a Deed of Divorce, "absence of intention invalidates the act." See also the discussion on *kawwanah*, *ibid.*, pp. 314 ff.

178. *Pesaḥim* 114b.

179. Post-talmudic authorities, as well, are divided on the question as to whether miẓwot require *kawwanah*. Alfasi, Asheri (see Asheri to *Rosh ha-Shanah* 28b), and Maimonides in his *Commentary to the Mishnah*, as well as in the *Mishneh Torah* (see *Tosefot Yom Ṭob* to *Sukkah* III.14, *s.v.* מסני), are proponents of the positive principle, but there are other authorities (cited by the *Maggid Mishneh*, *loc. cit.*) who are proponents of the negative principle. Tosafot to *Berakot* 12a, *s.v.* לא, not only emphatically asserts that miẓwot do not require *kawwanah*, but also applies that principle to a person who was passing behind a synagogue and heard the Tefillah and did not have *kawwanah*, an instance *not* given in *Rosh ha-Shanah* III.7, and to which mishnah this statement in Tosafot obviously refers. There was a feeling, too, among some medieval authorities that genuine *kawwanah* was hardly, or rarely, possible in their day. See Tosafot to *Berakot* 17b, *s.v.* רב ששא, and *Ṭur 'Oraḥ Ḥayyim*, par. 101; and see also the commentaries on Maimonides, Hilkot *Ḳeri'at Shema'* IV.7. The *Migdal 'Oz* there calls attention to the contradiction in the stricture by R. Abraham b. David.

180. N. H. Ṭur-Sinai, ספר איוב (Tel Aviv, 1954), p. 119; also Duhm, *Die Psalmen*, *Kurzer Hand-Commentar zum A.T.* (Leipzig and Tübingen, 1899), p. 202. Cf. *Targum Jonathan* on Ps. 78:8.

181. Ṭur-Sinai, *loc. cit.*

182. In an essay entitled "Kawwana," H. G. Enelow (*Selected Works* [privately printed, 1935], IV, 256 f.), takes other biblical verses as well to be the "foreshadowing" of *kawwanah*. He also discusses in this essay the various ways in which the term was used by medieval Jewish philosophers and "the kabbalistic construction of kawwana."

183. Above, pp. 168–170.

Notes to Chapter VIII

1. M. Kadushin, *Organic Thinking* (New York, 1938), pp. 95 f. (this book will be referred to hereafter as *OT*).

2. M. Kadushin, *The Rabbinic Mind* (New York, 1952), pp. 124 f. (this book will be referred to hereafter as *RM*). On the hermeneutic rules, see *ibid.*, pp. 91, 123.

3. *Ibid.*, p. 126, and the references there.

4. Above, p. 36.

5. S. Schechter, *Studies in Judaism: First Series* (Philadelphia, 1919), p. 112. Naḥmanides' statement is found at the beginning of his commentary on Maimonides' *Sefer ha-Miẓwot.* See also Simon Greenberg, *The Multiplication of the Mitzvot, Mordecai M. Kaplan Jubilee Volume* (New York, 1953), p. 386 and n. 32 there. On the number 613, see Ginzberg's note, *ibid.*, p. 388, and the reference in the following note there.

6. S. Schechter, *Some Aspects of Rabbinic Theology* (New York, 1910), p. 141. See also his remarks on the homiletical character of R. Simla'i's statement, *ibid.*, pp. 138 f.

7. *Ibid.*, pp. 141 f.

8. *'Erubin* 54b. See Rashi, *ad loc.*

9. *Sifra* on Lev. 25:1, ed. Weiss (Vienna, 1862), p. 105a. At the beginning of his introduction to *Zera'im*, in his commentary on the Mishnah, Maimonides quotes this and the preceding statement as showing that the "explanations," namely, the details of a miẓwah, were given to Moses orally by God. He illustrates with an example of the miẓwah of the *sukkah* (the building and dwelling in a booth as ordained in Lev. 23:42).

10. *RM*, pp. 353 ff.

11. On the term "Midrash," see Bacher, ערכי מדרש (Tel Aviv, 1923), *s.v.* מדרש. See also *Ḳiddushin* 49b.

12. *Sifra* on Lev. 26:14, ed. Weiss, 11b. See also other such passages in *RM*, pp. 354 f.

13. כל מלי דרבנן אסמכינהו על לאו דלא תסור: *Berakot* 19b. See also I. H. Weiss, דור דור ודורשיו (4th ed.; Wilna, 1904), II, 49 f.

14. *Midrash Tannaim*, ed. Hoffmann (Berlin, 1909), p. 103, and the references there.

15. See, e.g., *Num. R.* XIV.4.

16. *Beẓah* 3b; cf. *Shabbat* 34a. See Ginzberg, *A Commentary on The Palestinian Talmud* (New York, 1941), I, 150 f.

17. Ginzberg's view (*loc. cit.*) is somewhat different.

18. *Yebamot* 20a. Similarly, in the case in *Ḥullin* 106a.

19. *Yer. Yebamot* II.4, 3d.

20. See G. Alon, מחקרים (Tel Aviv, 1958), II, 113. We are indebted to Alon for several references used in this discussion.

21. See also Greenberg's discussion on *miẓwot de-rabbanan—op. cit.*, pp. 386 ff.

22. See *Soṭah* 44b, and Rashi, *ad loc.*, who explains the term to refer to a transgression of "the words of the *Soferim.*" Cf. *Menaḥot* 36a.

23. *Pesiḳta Rabbati*, ed. Friedmann (Vienna, 1880), p. 7b, and the parallels referred to there.

24. *Yer. Sukkah* III.4, 53d, על מצות הדלקת נר חנכה. See below, n. 27. We have discussed the shift from the second to the third person in the Birkat ha-Miẓwot elsewhere (*RM*, pp. 266 ff.).

25. *Yer. Sukkah, loc. cit.*

26. Cf. Babli *Sukkah* 46a. The words מצות לולב and מצות זקנים there refer to the endings of berakot, and hence not as Rashi interprets them (see שירי קרבן to *Yer. Sukkah, loc. cit.*).

27. *Num. R.* XIV.4; *Pesikta Rabbati*, ed. Friedmann, p. 9a–b. The authorities are changed around in this version but the text in the Yerushalmi seems to be correct; see R. Samuel Strashun's note to *Num. R.*, *loc. cit.* The norm has been established that in the berakot rabbinical ordinances, too, are to be characterized as mizwot of God; see Maimonides, Hilkot *Berakot* XI.3, and the *Kesef Mishneh*, *ad loc.* But the rule is established on the basis of the discussion in the Babli, and that discussion is rather puzzling. In the Babli (*Shabbat* 23a; *Sukkah* 46a), the berakah on the light of Ḥanukkah ends with וצונו להדליק נר של חנוכה. According to that ending, kindling the light of Ḥanukkah is a mizwah of God, even though this is not emphasized as strongly as in Rab's berakah. But the Babli continues by asking, "And where has He commanded us?" Two answers are given, one referring to Deut. 11:17 and the other to Deut. 32:7. The question and the answers by only associating the rabbinical ordinance with mizwot qualify the berakah itself; indeed, on that basis, we should have expected the ending in the berakah to refer to *mizwat Zekenim*, and not to the specific manner of kindling the light of Ḥanukkah.

28. Sifra, ed. Weiss, 23b; *Shebuot* III.6; *ibid.*, 21b. "On which he stands sworn from Mount Sinai" (*ibid.*, 22b; *Makkot* 22a).

29. Mekilta on Exod. 21:6, ed. Horovitz and Rabin (Frankfurt am Main, 1928), p. 253.

30. L. Ginzberg, *Legends of the Jews* (Philadelphia, 1911), III, 97 and IV, 39, n. 215.

31. *Shebuot* 39a. This section of the baraita is a distinct entity in itself, being another interpretation of Deut. 29:14. Cf. *Tanḥuma*, *Nizzabim*, par. 3. Other passages to the same effect *Sifre* on Deut. 11:22, ed. Friedmann, p. 84b; *Tanḥuma*, ed. Buber, II, p. 58b, and the parallels there. ("Even what a faithful pupil will ask his master").

32. *RM*, pp. 341 ff.

33. *Ibid.*, p. 353, and the notes there.

34. Above, p. 170.

35. Greenberg, *op. cit.*, pp. 381–84, and the references cited there. As Greenberg indicates, it is not always easy to determine the meaning of the biblical term, since it may refer either to commands of God or of man.

36. The conceptual term is mizwot, the plural; mizwah (singular) usually refers to one of the mizwot. There are instances, however, where mizwah evidently possesses another connotation, but we shall not engage in an analysis of those instances now.

37. Above, Chaps. III–IV.

38. For example, *Lev. R.*, V.4 ed. Margulies (Jerusalem, 1958), p. 111, and the parallels referred to in the notes there. Men and women are described, in Aramaic, as lovers of mizweta'; see S. Lieberman, *Greek in Jewish Palestine* (New York, 1942), pp. 71 f. and the notes.

39. *Lev. R.* XXXIV.4, ed. Margulies, pp. 779 f. See also *Deut. R.*, ed. Lieberman, p. 36 and n. 10, and the references there.

40. *Yer. Pe'ah* I,15b. See G. Alon, תולדות היהודים (Tel Aviv, 1953), I, 333, and see also, for a discussion of this law, above, p. 24. The Aramaic plural similarly may connote charity; see, for example, *Lev. R.* XXXIV.14, ed. Margulies, p. 806. Add to the sources in Alon, *loc. cit.*, n. 68: *Mekilta*, ed. Horovitz and Rabin, p. 78, and see the notes there.

41. *Tos. Pe'ah* IV.19, ed. Lieberman, p. 60. Lieberman, *Tos. Kif.*, I, 191, calls attention to Maimonides' statement (Hilkot *Mattenot 'Aniyyim* X.1) on the need for being

more careful with regard to "the miẓwah of *ẓedaḳah* than with regard to all the [other] positive miẓwot."

42. *Seder 'Olam*, Chap. V, and *Sanhedrin* 56a (baraita). These and other references are cited in Ginzberg, *Legends*, V, 92, n. 55, where there is a discussion of the subject. See also *ibid.*, I, 71. *Dinim*, here and elsewhere, are the laws according to which the courts render their decisions (Ginzberg, *Commentary*, IV, 62).

43. Above, pp. 42 ff.

44. Above, p. 56.

45. *Seder Eliahu*, ed. Friedmann (Vienna, 1900), p. 74, and see above, p. 43, where other formulations of universal ethics are also given.

46. The passage enumerates the wicked men who, because they engaged in these things, "were uprooted from the world."

47. See *Tanḥuma*, *Teẓe*, par. 2, ed. Buber (Wilna, 1885), V, 17a–b, and *OT*, pp. 111–12.

48. *Makkot* III.15.

49. *Baba' Meẓi'a* IV.3 ff., and the Babli, *ibid.*, 49b–58b, *passim.*

50. *Sifra* on Lev. 25:17, ed. Weiss, p. 107d; *Baba' Meẓi'a* 58b.

51. *Ibid.*

52. *Baba' Meẓi'a* IV.10. See above, p. 48.

53. *Baba' Meẓi'a* 58b. See the other examples at pp. 58b–59b; (also above, p. 60).

54. *Ibid.*

55. *Ibid.*

56. *Ibid.*

57. See, for example, the excellent discussion in M. Lazarus, *The Ethics of Judaism* (Philadelphia, 1901), II, 151–75.

58. *Ibid.*, pp. 167 f.

59. *Ibid.*, pp. 151 f., 155, note. He cites Lev. 25:14, 17; Exod. 22:20; Lev. 19:33; and Deut. 23:16–17.

60. On this point, see also the discussion on other rabbinic concepts above, p. 168. For a more extensive treatment, see *RM*, pp. 288 ff.

61. *Baba' Meẓi'a* 59a, for the latter example. *'Ona'ah*, *gezel*, *ẓedaḳah*, etc., are concepts that are concretized in acts or situations.

62. Above, p. 56.

63. In accordance with the quotation in *Yer. Berakot* V.3, 9c. As has been pointed out, the rendering of *Targum Jonathan* with respect to the halakah itself agrees with the view of the Rabbanan. See *Ḥullin* 68b, and the Sifra on the verse, ed. Weiss, p. 99b.

64. *OT*, pp. 192–96, and *RM*, pp. 110 f.

65. Above, p. 85.

66. Above, p. 128—the decision of R. Joḥanan.

67. See the quotations given by Albeck, *Commentary on Ḳodashim* (Jerusalem and Tel Aviv, 1956), p. 403.

68. For examples, see above, p. 80.

69. *Yer. Berakot* V.3, 9c; *ibid.*, *Megillah* IV.10, 75c, and cf. Babli *Berakot* 33b. We have rendered according to *Yer. Megillah* IV.10, 75c. The text in the Babli is מפני שעושה מדותיו של הקב״ה רחמים ואינן אלא גזירות, and the reading in *Yer. Berakot* seems to have been affected by that text.

70. *Berakot* III.1 (*Megillah* IV.9), and Rashi on the mishnah.

71. See Rashi, *loc. cit.*, and Maimonides, Hilkot *Tefillah* IX.7.

72. See the sources referred to in n. 69 above. Modern writers have assumed that R. Jose b. Bun's comment is of one piece with the rule in the Mishnah. See, for example, Schechter, *Some Aspects of Rabbinic Theology*, p. 10, n. 1, who also cites other scholars. It is true that the rule in the Mishnah is directed against several sectarian practices and doctrines, one of which we have discussed in an earlier work (*RM*, pp. 344 f.). But R. Jose b. Bun was among the last of the great Palestinian Amoraim (Z. Frankel, *Mebo ha-Yerushalmi*, [Breslau, 1870], p. 102a). His warning, if it was such, was certainly not directed against a sect which persisted, after all those hundreds of years, in praying in the synagogue. Actually, however, his statement was not directed against a sect at all, but consists of an objection to a *rabbinic* interpretation which differs from his, and his view therefore represents merely a personal predilection. It no more reflects a sectarian controversy than do the other amoraic interpretations of the rule in the Mishnah.

73. *Sifra*, *Ḳedoshim*, end, ed. Weiss, 93d.

74. Acceptance of *malkut Shamayim* is associated with *gezerot* in the passages cited above, p. 80. But there acceptance of God's kingship precedes acceptance of the decrees.

75. Above, pp. 43 f., and the discussion there.

76. See Rashi to *Yoma* 67b, *s.v.* השטן and תלמוד לומר.

77. See *Pesiḳta de R. Kahana* (Lyck, 1868), ed. Buber, pp. 40a–b, and the parallels there. The interpretation is based on *ḥuḳḳat*, a word taken to refer to *gezerah* (see the plural *ḥuḳḳotai* as used in the Sifra passage just discussed, and cited above, p. 44). The rabbis feel that there are reasons for the *ḥuḳḳim*, and that they will be revealed *le-'atid la-bo*, though not in this world, and that these טעמי תורה were revealed to Moses by God (see *Pesiḳta de R. Kahana*, ed. Buber, 39a–b, and the notes and parallels there).

78. See also Rab's statement in *Niddah* 35b.

79. גדול (ה)מצווה ועושה ממי שאינו מצווה ועושה; the references are given in the notes following.

80. *Ḳiddushin* 31a; *'Abodah Zarah* 23b–24a.

81. *Ḳiddushin* 31a.

82. Above, p. 207.

83. *Baba' Ḳamma'* 38a; *'Abodah Zarah* 2b–3a.

84. On the ethical concepts involved in the seven miẓwot, see above, p. 206.

85. It occurs once more in *Ḳiddushin*, *loc. cit.* (*Baba' Ḳamma'* 87a), where it is quoted with approval by R. Joseph (see Heinemann's discussion, טעמי המצוות, I [3d ed.; Jerusalem, 1954], 23 f.). Heinemann (*ibid.*, p. 24) points out that there are rabbinic statements which praise those who are not "commanded."

86. *Yer. Pe'ah* I.1, 15c; *ibid.*, *Ḳiddushin*, I.7, 61b. Dama's devotion to his parents, his probity, and even his character as a pagan (idol-worshipper) come out more clearly here.

87. מצות לאו ליהנות ניתנו: *Rosh ha-Shanah* 28a; *'Erubin* 31a; *Ḥullin* 89a.

88. Rashi to *Rosh ha-Shanah* 28a, *s.v.* לא ליהנות.

89. See R. Nissim to *Nedarim* 15b, *s.v.* והא מן: מכל אבל הנאה חשוב המצות קיום שאין מקום אי מתהני גופיה בהדי דמקיים מצוה הנאה מקרי. See also the next note.

90. *Rosh ha-Shanah, loc. cit.* Notice there also that only where enjoyment is forbidden because of a vow is the use of the fountain prohibited in the summer, and so similarly in the related case.

91. *Nedarim* 16b.

92. The application is not made specifically, to be sure. According to R. Joseph, the making of an *'erub* is permitted only for a *debar miẓwah*, and going to a house of mourning and going to a wedding feast (*'Erubin* V.1) are taken by R. Joseph to be examples of his principle (*'Erubin* 82a). In a "defense" of R. Joseph in *ibid.*, 31a, the point is made that "all" hold both Raba's principle and R. Joseph's principle. In that case, Raba's principle thus applies to the going to a house of mourning and going to a wedding feast, acts of *gemilut ḥasadim*.

93. On these acts as *gemilut ḥasadim*, see above, p. 281, n. 147.

94. Lazarus, *op. cit.*, I, pp. 283 f.

95. A midrash beginning with a phrase reminiscent of Raba's principle—לא נתנו המצוות אלא לצרוף את הבירייות בהם—is nevertheless not germane to our thesis. It teaches that all the miẓwot are only a means. This midrash is found in *Bereshit R.* XLIV.1, ed. Theodor, p. 424, and has many parallels and versions (see the references and notes there). The meaning of the midrash hinges on the word לצרוף. Margulies has demonstrated that the word means "to test"—see his edition of *Lev. R.*, p. 277, n. 2. The parallel there (*Lev. R.* XII.3) also supplies the last part of the midrash. The passage, then, teaches that the miẓwot were given in order to test men for it makes no difference to God whether an animal be slaughtered at the throat or at the neck, and (*Lev. R.*) that when men meet the tests they are given reward. An unusual idea is thus contained in this midrash; in a related context above (p. 209), for example, it is taught that God has compassion on animals, is concerned for them. Furthermore, the phrase, "the miẓwot were given," refers, as in Raba's principle, to all miẓwot, and hence also to ethical matters, and both the Bible and the rabbis emphasize that these are indeed of concern to God. Medieval philosophers differ as to the meaning of לצרוף in this midrash. According to Heinemann, Maimonides interprets the phrase to mean that the miẓwot, when we obey them, prepare us for the world to come (*op. cit.*, I, 155, n. 124). Naḥmanides takes the word, apparently, to mean "to purify the soul" by teaching ethical modes or qualities; see his *Commentary on the Pentateuch*, Deut. 22:6.

96. *Yoma* VIII.6: וכל ספק נפשות דוחה את השבת. See also *Tos. Shabbat* XV (XVI). 16, ed. Zuckermandel and Lieberman, p. 134.

97. See *Yoma* 82a, and Maimonides, Hilkot *Shabbat* II.1.

98. In connection with this rule, Maimonides declares that the laws of the Torah are *raḥamim*, *ḥesed* (lovingkindness), and peace in the world (*op. cit.*, II.3).

99. *Nazir* VII.1. If there is no one else to attend to it.

100. *Berakot* 19b and Tosafot, *ad loc.*, and compare the parallels. See also *Sifre* on Num. 6:6–7, ed. Horovitz, p. 33 and n. 15 there.

101. *Berakot* 19b–20a, and *Megillah* 3b. In *Berakot* 20a, *s.v.* שב ואל תעשה, Rashi argues that whereas the case concerning the paschal lamb represents an instance of

superseding because of *kebod ha-beriyyot*, this is not true in the case of the high priest and the Nazarite. But see Tosafot, *ibid.*, on the same catchword.

102. *Ketubbot* 17a (*Megillah* 3b, 29a). A funeral escort in general, not a *met mizwah*; see Tosafot, *ibid.*, *s.v.* להוצאת. See also above, p. 29.

103. Above, pp. 176 f.

104. *Kelim* I.6–9. Cf. *Sifre Zuṭṭa*, ed. Horovitz, p. 228, and see the notes there. Although the versions differ, in both the number is actually eleven and not ten. See Albeck's discussion in his edition of *Ṭoharot*, pp. 508 f.; as he says, "ten" need not be taken literally.

105. *Sifre Zuṭṭa*, *loc. cit.* (*Num. R.* VII.8; *Yalkuṭ Shime'oni*, Naso', par. 698).

106. *Mekilta*, ed. J. Z. Lauterbach (Philadelphia, 1933), I, 6; and see *RM*, p. 250.

107. Maimonides declares that the Temple and Jerusalem are permanently holy because of the *Shekinah* (Hilkot *Bet ha-Beḥirah* VI.16).

108. *Zebaḥim* V.1–5.

109. *Ibid.*, V.3, 5. In the Second Temple, the "enclosures" referred to the area within the Gates of Nicanor; see *Tos. Kelim, Baba' Ḳamma'* I.9, 12; *Zebaḥim* 116b. The word "curtains" refers to an analogous area in the period of the Tabernacle in the wilderness.

110. *Zebaḥim* V.6–8.

111. *Ibid.*, בכל העיר. A degree of levitical impurity is permitted in the city, and from that point of view only the *ḳodshe ḳodashim* are to be eaten in "a holy place." See *ibid.*, 55a.

112. *Zebaḥim* V.8. In the *Sifre* on Num. 18:20, ed. Horovitz, p. 142 (bottom), the first-born of the clean cattle is counted among the offerings which may be eaten by the priests outside the Temple and Jerusalem, the category we are about to take up. Lieberman explains this on the ground that the actual *mattanah* (see the next note) takes place wherever the animal is turned over to the priest, so that if the animal develops a blemish, the priest may eat it anywhere; if it is without a blemish and hence to be offered by the priest in the Temple, the animal thus offered is the priest's animal, since the *mattanah* had already taken place (see *Tos. Kif.*, II, 812, beginning אבל). But the criterion we speak of is reflected also in other examples. While the tithe of cattle may be eaten by any person, there are the portions of the thank offering, for example, that must be given the priests, yet both the tithe of cattle and the thank offering are *ḳodashim ḳallim* (*Zebaḥim* V.6, 8). Each of the first two grades has gradations of its own (*ibid.*, X.2–6; and cf. *ibid.*, I.2).

113. "Twenty-four *mattenot kehunah* [were given] to Aaron and his sons" by God (*Tos. Ḥallah* II.7 f., ed. Lieberman, p. 281 f., and the parallels there).

114. *Zebaḥim* V.1 f, 6 f.

115. *Tos. Ḥallah*, II.7, 9. For the term *ḳodshe ha-gebul*, see the reference in the next note.

116. See *Sifre* on Numbers, *pisḳa'* 107, ed. Horovitz, pp. 134 (bottom)–136. Cf. *Tos. Ḥallah* II.10, ed. Lieberman, p. 282.

117. *Ibid.* See Lieberman, *Tos. Kif.*, II, 813, *s.v.* לחייב. The manner in which he quotes the passage in the Sifre enables the seriatim order and the hierarchical gradation to stand out.

118. Sifre on Numbers, *loc. cit.*

119. *Terumot* III.6, 7, and *Ma'aser Sheni* V.11. But compare *Sifre* Deut., *piska'* 303, ed. Friedmann, p. 128b.

120. See *Rosh ha-Shanah* 12b. During the seventh year, of course, the land was fallow.

121. *Ma'aser Sheni* V.10; *Sifre* Deut., *loc. cit*; *Sifra* on Lev. 27:30, ed. Weiss, p. 115a.

122. See the first two references in the preceding note.

123. *Ma'aser Sheni* V.3 (*Pe'ah* VII.6; *'Eduyyot* IV.5), and *Ḳiddushin* 54b. On נטע רבעי and כרם רבעי, see *Tosefot Yom Ṭob* to *Pe'ah* VII.6, *s.v.* כרם, and see Albeck's note in his edition of *Zera'im*, p. 404.

124. See Maimonides, Hilkot *Ma'aser* I.2, and the discussion there in the *Kesef Mishneh*. See also *Yebamot* 74a.

125. *Zebaḥim* IV.6: לשם חשם. (See also *ibid.*, 46b; Sifra, ed. Weiss, p. 7c.)

126. *Ibid.* See also *ibid.*, 2b.

127. See Lieberman, *Tos. Kif.*, I, 479, n. 72, who cites *Ḥallah* II.3, Yer. *Ma'aser Sheni* V.7, 56c, and *ibid.*, *Ḥallah*, Chap. I, end, 58a.

128. Maimonides, Hilkot *Terumot*, IV.16, and the *Kesef Mishneh*, *ad loc.*, and see Lieberman, *Tos. Kif.*, II, 755, who cites these and other references in *ibid.*, n. 40.

129. The term *maḥashabah* is used with reference to sacrifices in *Zebaḥim* IV.6, but in the parallel, *Tos. ibid.*, V.13, verb forms of *kawwanah* are employed as well. See also *Menaḥot* XIII.11, and *ibid.*, 110a. *Maḥashabah* is used with reference to *terumah* in *Giṭṭin* 31a, and see also Maimonides, *loc. cit.*

130. This holds true of the manner whereby all the things in the hierarchy become *ḳedushot*. According to R. Jose, if a man sets apart *terumah*, the first tithe, and *ma'aser sheni*, the acts make the portions holy even if they have not been designated by name, although, as Lieberman points out, he is required to make these designations afterward (see *Tos. Ma'aser Sheni* IV.14, ed. Lieberman, p. 267, and *Tos. Kif.*, II, 775).

131. Above, p. 191. On the uttering of an intention in a context other than that of *ḳedushah*, see n. 142 on p. 291.

132. *Ma'aser Sheni* IV.7.

133. *RM*, p. 181.

134. *Rosh ha-Shanah* II.7 and III.1.

135. *Ibid.*, II.8–9.

136. *Yer. Rosh ha-Shanah* I.3, 57b.

137. *Mekilta*, ed. Lauterbach, III, p. 203.

138. See Albeck's discussion of this *bet din* in his edition of *Mo'ed*, pp. 305 f., and see also n. 2 there.

139. *Rosh ha-Shanah* 24a.

140. This is the way the rabbis interpret the verse, as we can see from the examples about to be given.

141. *Mechilta de-Rabbi Simon b. Jochai*, ed. Hoffmann, p. 107, and the parallels in the notes. Cf. *Mekhilta D'Rabbi Sim'on b. Jochai*, ed. Epstein-Melamed, pp. 148 f., and the notes. "To make it holy" means to make the entire day holy, and the day begins on Sabbath Eve. See Rashi to the parallel in *Pesaḥim* 106a.

142. *Mekhilta D'Rabbi Sim'on, loc. cit.*

143. *Ibid.*

144. *Mechilta*, ed. Horovitz and Rabin, p. 30 (*Pesaḥ*); Sifre, ed. Horovitz, p. 194 (*Pesaḥ*); Sifra, ed. Weiss, p. 102b (*Sukkot*).

145. *Rosh ha-Shanah* 32a, where this rule is applied to that day.

146. *RM*, p. 181.

147. *RM*, pp. 171 ff.

148. *Ibid.*, pp. 171, 178 (bottom), 180 f. On *tefillin* as higher in the hierarchy than *mezuzot*, see *Menaḥot* 32a (baraita) and Rashi, *ad loc.* On *sefarim*, see *RM*, p. 172, n. 24.

149. See Maimonides, Hilkot *Sefer-Torah*, X.1.

150. Maimonides, Hilkot *Tefillin*, Chaps. I–III.

151. Above, p. 219.

152. Maimonides, *loc. cit.*, I.15, and the *Kesef Mishneh* there. See also Lieberman, *Tos. Kif.*, I, 47 f.

153. On that dogma, see *RM*, pp. 348 f.

154. *Ibid.*, p. 350.

155. *Megillah* III.1, 3, and *ibid.*, 26a.

156. In *RM*, pp. 178 f., we discussed also the matter of the holiness transmitted by a *Sefer Torah* to its accessories, and concluded that such transmission does not imply the notion that a holy object possesses theurgical efficacy. In all these instances, *ḳedushah* has no other effect but that of transmitting itself; it is not regarded as having any physical effect, nor as a spiritual agency which, if properly applied, can affect the welfare of the individual or the community.

157. *Soṭah* 39a (*Num. R.* XI.4)—the berakah of the priests before they bless the people.

158. Above, pp. 217 f.

159. *Yebamot* XI.2.

160. ולא הוא לוי הוא ישראל: Yer. *Nazir* VII.1, end. On the ranking of the groups, see *Horayot* III.8; cf. *Yebamot* II.4.

161. Alon, מחקרים בתולדות ישראל, I, 148–76, especially pp. 158 ff.

162. *Ibid.*, p. 174.

163. *Ibid.* Both "the contrary tradition" and the tradition with which it is in conflict have their roots in the Bible (*ibid.*, p. 175).

164. *Seder Eliahu*, ed. Friedmann, p. 72; cited by Alon, *loc. cit.*

165. Alon, *op. cit.*, p. 176. He points out (*ibid.*, p. 161, n. 61) that those who organized themselves into groups whose purpose it was to observe the laws of levitical purity did so because they were thus able to help each other observe those laws. Their purpose was not to acquire additional *ḳedushah* for themselves through laws not incumbent on everyone, for they taught that such laws, and others not generally observed at the time, were nevertheless laws intended for all Israel.

166. *Ibid.*, p. 176, and nn. 114 and 115.

167. *Ḥagigah* II.5; just as the priest does before eating *terumah* (*ibid.*).

168. The stressing of a concept is apparent in most of the other hierarchies as well: In the case of the holy areas, the concept stressed is *gilluy Shekinah*; in the case of sacrifices and tithes, it is *kehunah*; in the case of holy objects, it is Torah. The holy

days involve a large number of concepts, and the problem of accounting for the hierarchy is too complicated to be taken up here.

169. It was this organismic quality of the value complex that sectarian thought apparently lacked. The Sadducees maintained that *ḳedushah* was limited to the priests, while the Essenes insisted on the application of the laws of levitical purity to all Israel and at all times. See Alon's remarks, *op. cit.*, p. 176.

170. *Horayot* III.8. This statement, be it noted, comes at the end of a mishnah ranking the various groups in the people.

171. *Ḳinyan Torah* (*'Abot* VI.5). See *OT*, pp. 49 f. and the notes there. On "thirty" and on "twenty-four," see *Maḥzor Vitry*, pp. 558 f.

172. See *OT*, p. 42.

173. In the discussion of these phases, soon to follow, we have drawn upon the material in Schechter, *Aspects*, pp. 199 ff., although our discussion also contains rabbinic material not given there. In the analysis we depart from Schechter in a number of respects. We ought to add that Schechter's analysis is the first modern treatment of *ḳedushah*, and that it is most suggestive.

174. *Sifra* to Lev. 20:7, ed. Weiss, 91d. See Schechter, *Aspects*, p. 208, n. 2.

175. *Num. R.* XVII.7. See the longer quotation in Schechter, *loc. cit.*

176. *Mekilta*, ed. Lauterbach, III, p. 157.

177. *Lev. R.* XXIV.8, ed. Margulies, pp. 562 f.

178. Margulies, *ibid.*, n. 7, and mark the reading in the conclusion of the parallel cited there, referring to the *ḳedushot*: והלואי יהיו כופין אותן.

179. *Tanḥuma*, ed. Buber, III, p. 37b. Cf. also *Pesiḳta' de R. Kahana'*, ed. Buber, p. 16a.

180. *Tanḥuma*, ed. Buber, III, p. 37a; Schechter, *Aspects*, p. 200.

181. *Mekilta*, ed. Lauterbach, III, 157.

182. Above, p. 203.

183. Schechter, *Aspects*, p. 201.

184. *Ibid.*, p. 200 and the note there. Source is *Sifra*, ed. Weiss, 86c.

185. *Ibid.*, p. 201, and the note. Sources are *Mekilta*, ed. Horovitz and Rabin, p. 127; *Shabbat* 133b.

186. *Sifre* on Deut. 11:22, ed. Friedmann, p. 85a. "Called"—since biblical verses speak of Him as merciful and gracious (Exod. 34:6), and as righteous and loving (Ps. 145:17).

187. *Seder Eliahu*, ed. Friedmann, p. 65.

188. See Schechter, *Aspects*, p. 202, and the reference to *Gen. R.* LVIII.9.

189. See also Schechter, *Aspects*, pp. 203 f.

190. Above, p. 99.

191. For example, *Kelim* I.1–4, and *ibid.*, I.5.

192. *RM*, pp. 180 f.: מעלין בקדש ולא מורידין.

193. *Pesaḥim* I.6 (*'Eduyyot* II.1) and *ibid.*, 14a. The rabbis were reluctant to add to the sphere of *ṭum'ah*: *Beẓah* 7a ('Abaye) and Rashi, *ad loc.*

194. Maimonides, Hilkot *Ṭum'at 'Okelin* XVI.8 and the commentaries and the sources and references there. Maimonides states this again in the *Moreh Nebukim*, Part III, Chap. XLII.

195. *Sifra* on Lev. 16:16, ed. Weiss, p. 81c.

196. Tosafot to the parallel in *Shebu'ot* 7b, *s.v.* יש: דלאו טומאה ממש נינהו אלא בלשון טומאה נכתבו.

197. Above, p. 25. Malbim to Sifra, *loc. cit.*, attempts to work out categories of another kind, but in doing so he is obliged to put the cardinal sins and defiling the Temple into one category.

198. *Lev. R.* XXIV.4, ed. Margulies, p. 556. See the notes.

199. *Sifra* on Lev. 19:2, ed. Weiss, p. 86c: פרושים היו.

200. Cf. *Lev. R.* XXIV.6, ed. Margulies, pp. 559 f., and the parallel in the notes. See also Rashi on Lev. 19:2.

201. *Sifra* on Lev. 18:30, ed. Weiss, p. 86d, and the references there.

202. Schechter, *Aspects*, p. 206.

203. *Mekilta*, ed. Friedmann, 63a; (ed. Horovitz and Rabin, p. 209).

204. *Sifra*, 93b. Cf. *Num. R.* IX.7.

205. Schechter, *op. cit.*, p. 206 and the discussion following there.

206. *Sifra* on Lev. 11:43, and R. Abraham b. David of Posquière's first explanation. But notice that he gives a second, made by others, in which it is obvious that they take the Sifra statement to refer altogether to nonhierarchical *ṭum'ah*; and notice, too, how Schechter (*Aspects*, p. 207, n. 2) on the basis of this second explanation even suggests an emendation.

207. *Pesaḥim* 104a; *'Abodah Zarah* 50a, and Rashi and Tosafot, *ad loc.* In the version in *Koheleth R.* IX.9, R. Menaḥem is called נחום איש קדש קדשים.

208. *Makkot* III.15. See above, p. 207.

209. *Yebamot* 20a. (Cf. Sifre, ed. Friedmann, p. 95a): קדש עצמך במותר לך.

210. *Shebu'ot* 18b. For his sexual precaution R. Judah the Prince was called "the holy" (*Shabbat* 118b). See L. Epstein, *Sex Laws and Customs in Judaism* (New York, 1948), p. 147.

211. *Ta'anit* 11a, ed. Malter, p. 77 (ed. minor), and the sources referred to there.

212. Above, pp. 132 f.

213. Above, pp. 133 f.

214. Above, pp. 135 f.

215. See the discussions on the Ḳaddish (above, pp. 141 f.) and the Ḳedushah (pp. 142 ff.).

216. See Maimonides, Hilkot *'Abot ha-Tum'ot* VI.1, and the *Kesef Mishneh* there.

217. *Ibid.*, VI.2, and the sources in the commentaries.

218. *Ibid.*, VI.6, and the sources in the *Kesef Mishnah, ad loc.*

219. The acknowledgment by the individual Gentile was only a partial acknowledgment since it did not commit him.

220. *RM*, p. 289.

221. Holtz, "Kiddush Hashem and Hillul Hashem," *Judaism*, X, No. 4 (1961), 360 ff.

222. Above, p. 203.

223. Above, p. 186.

224. Above, pp. 197 f.

225. Above, p. 202 f. and p. 295, n. 27; Baer, סדר עבודת ישראל (Roedelheim, 1868), p. 439, and the notes and references there; Singer, *Daily Prayer Book* (London, 1890), p. 274. For the character of the objects employed in such acts, see the discussion in *RM*, pp. 170 ff.

226. For example, when putting on the *ṭallit* (*Berakot* 60b). See the following note.

227. For example, on the washing of the hands (*ibid.*), and on the taking of the *lulab* (*Sukkah* 46a). For the differences implied in these two usages, see *Pesaḥim* 7a–b, and the commentaries there, and see Lieberman, *Tos. Kif.*, I, 115 f., and his reference to the long discussion by Ibn Plat found in the *Sefer ha-Pardes*, ed. H. L. Ehrenreich (Budapest, 1924), pp. 195 ff.

228. כל המצוות מברך עליהן עובר לעשייתן—*Pesaḥim* 7b (and parallels). The exception is immersion (*ibid.*, and see Tosafot, *ibid.*, *s.v.* על הטבילה). For other occasions when the berakah is said after the act, and the reasons given therefor, see Lieberman, *op. cit.*, p. 113, *s.v.* המכסה, and pp. 116 f. R. 'Amram Gaon, quoted by R. Jonah to *Berakot* 60b, teaches that the rule in *Pesaḥim* 7b refers specifically to the Birkat ha-Miẓwot but not necessarily to other berakot. See also the discussion in *Sefer Abudraham*, ed. H. L. Ehrenreich (Cluj-Klausenburg, 1935), pp. 68 f.

229. We noticed above (p. 65) that there must be no interruption between the recitation of the berakah on bread and the eating of the first morsel. The rule that there must be no interruption between the berakah and the act to which the berakah refers holds with respect to all berakot. See Maimonides, Hilkot *Berakot* I.8 and the *Kesef Mishneh*, *ad loc.*

230. Above, pp. 108 ff.

231. *Mechilta*, ed. Horovitz and Rabin, p. 127, and the parallels there.

232. For the term *hiddur miẓwah*, see the halakah in *Baba Ḳamma'* 9b.

233. Above, p. 223, and the reference to Schechter in the note.

234. Above.

235. Maimonides, *Sefer ha-Miẓwot*, שורש רביעי, although his interpretation as a whole is not the same as ours.

236. שכל המצות טעונות ברכה (*Yer. Berakot* VI.1, 10a).

237. *Tos. Berakot* VI (VII).9, ed. Lieberman, p. 36— העושה כל המצות מברך עליהן.

238. Above, pp. 205 ff.

239. Lieberman, *Tos. Kif.*, I, 112, *s.v.* העושה.

240. *Ibid.*

241. See the *responsum* by Ibn Plat in S. Asaf, ספרן של ראשונים (Jerusalem, 1935), p. 200 ff. See also Lieberman, *loc. cit.*, n. 39, who refers to Asaf and others, and see also *RM*, p. 174, n. 31.

242. *Roḳeah*, 366 (cited by Lieberman, *loc. cit.*, text) lays down the rule that all the miẓwot to which non-Jews are also expected to conform—miẓwot having to do with charity, respect for the aged, and the like—do not require a berakah. But he does not take into account, as does Ibn Plat, the many other miẓwot which do not require a berakah.

243. Above, pp. 215 f.

244. Maimonides, Hilkot *Berakot*, XI.2.

245. *Kesef Mishneh* to *ibid.* Maimonides regards these two categories as basic general categories (see above, p. 250, n. 95, and the stricture there).

246. The law is in Deut. 22:8, and it adds the explanation, "that thou bring not blood upon thy house, if any man fall from thence." See *Sifre* Deut. to this verse, ed. Friedmann, p. 116a.

247. *Sefer Abudraham*, ed. Ehrenreich, p. 81, and the references given by Ehrenreich in n. 198 there. See also *Siddur R. Saadia*, p. 101.

248. See the explanation given by Ibn Plat, *loc. cit.*

Index